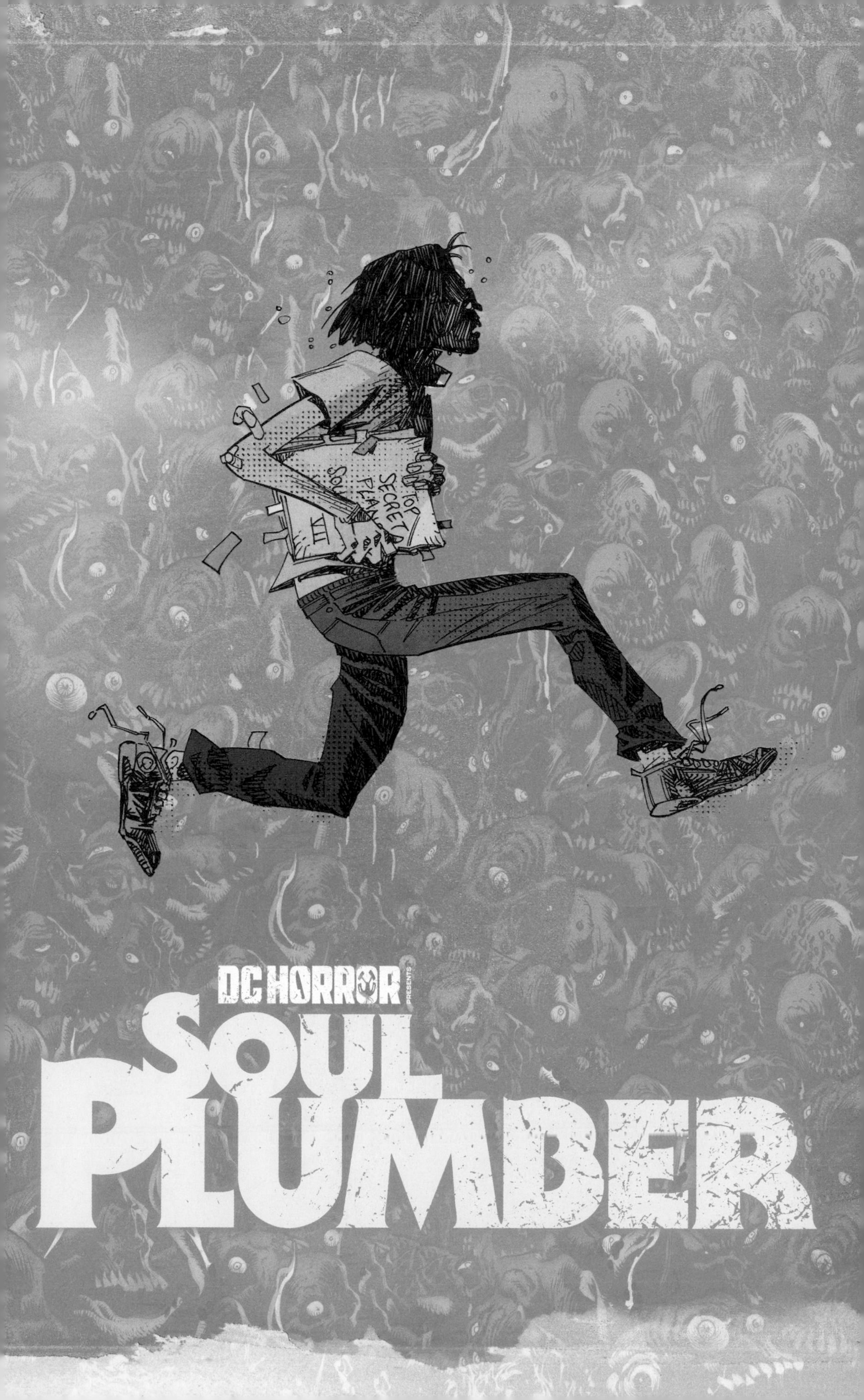
DC HORROR
PRESENTS
SOUL
PLUMBER
TOP SECRET

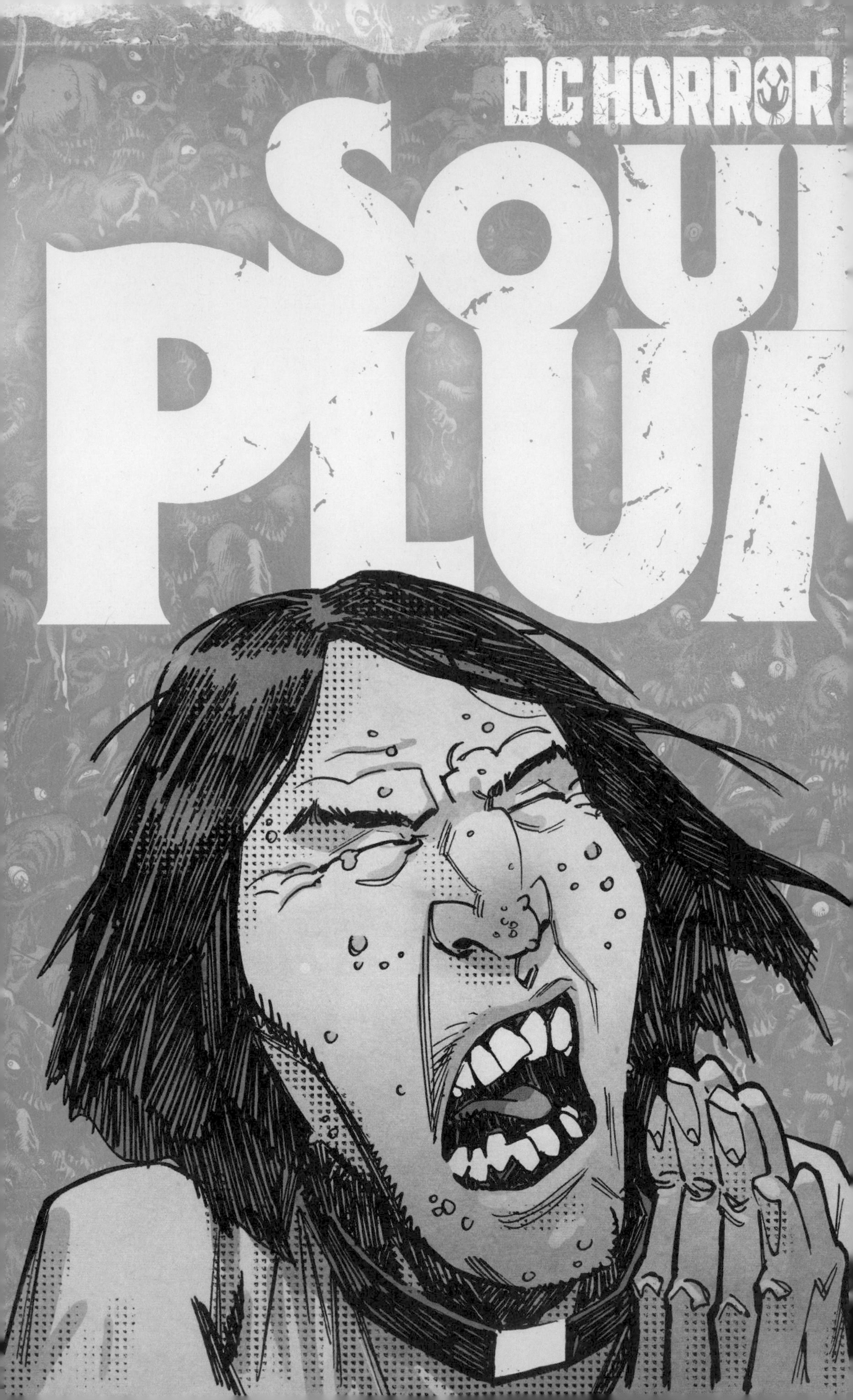
DC HORROR
SOU
PLUN

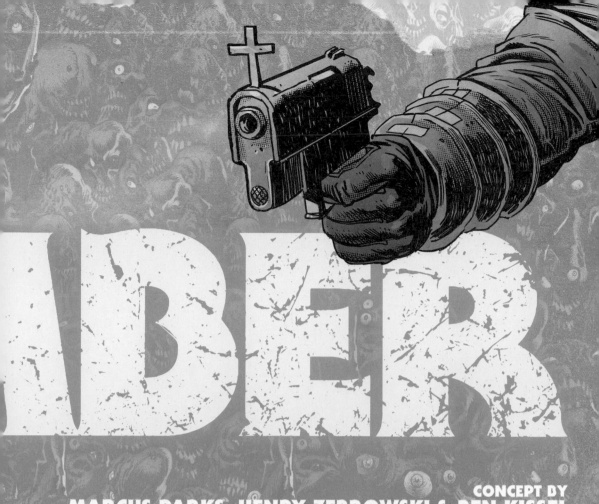

NDER

CONCEPT BY
MARCUS PARKS, HENRY ZEBROWSKI & BEN KISSEL

WRITTEN BY
MARCUS PARKS & HENRY ZEBROWSKI

ART BY
JOHN McCREA & PJ HOLDEN

COLORS BY
MIKE SPICER

LETTERS BY
BECCA CAREY

COLLECTION COVER ART BY
KYLE HOTZ & DAVE McCAIG

SOUL PLUMBER CREATED BY
**MARCUS PARKS, HENRY ZEBROWSKI,
BEN KISSEL & JOHN McCREA**

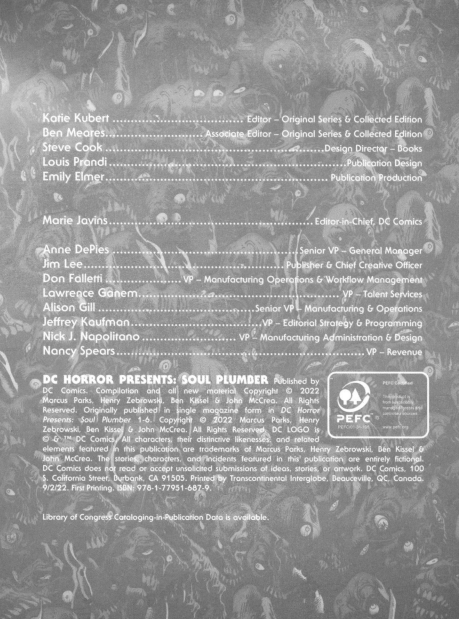

Katie Kubert .... Editor – Original Series & Collected Edition
Ben Meares.......................... Associate Editor – Original Series & Collected Edition
Steve Cook .... Design Director – Books
Louis Prandi .... Publication Design
Emily Elmer.. Publication Production

Marie Javins .... Editor-in-Chief, DC Comics

Anne DePies .... Senior VP – General Manager
Jim Lee... Publisher & Chief Creative Officer
Don Falletti .... VP – Manufacturing Operations & Workflow Management
Lawrence Ganem.. VP – Talent Services
Alison Gill .... Senior VP – Manufacturing & Operations
Jeffrey Kaufman.................................. VP – Editorial Strategy & Programming
Nick J. Napolitano .... VP – Manufacturing Administration & Design
Nancy Spears.. VP – Revenue

DC HORROR PRESENTS: SOUL PLUMBER Published by DC Comics. DC Comics, 100 S. California Street, Burbank, CA 91505. Printed by Transcontinental Interglobe, Beauceville, QC, Canada. 9/2/22. First Printing. ISBN: 978-1-77951-687-9.

Library of Congress Cataloging-in-Publication Data is available.

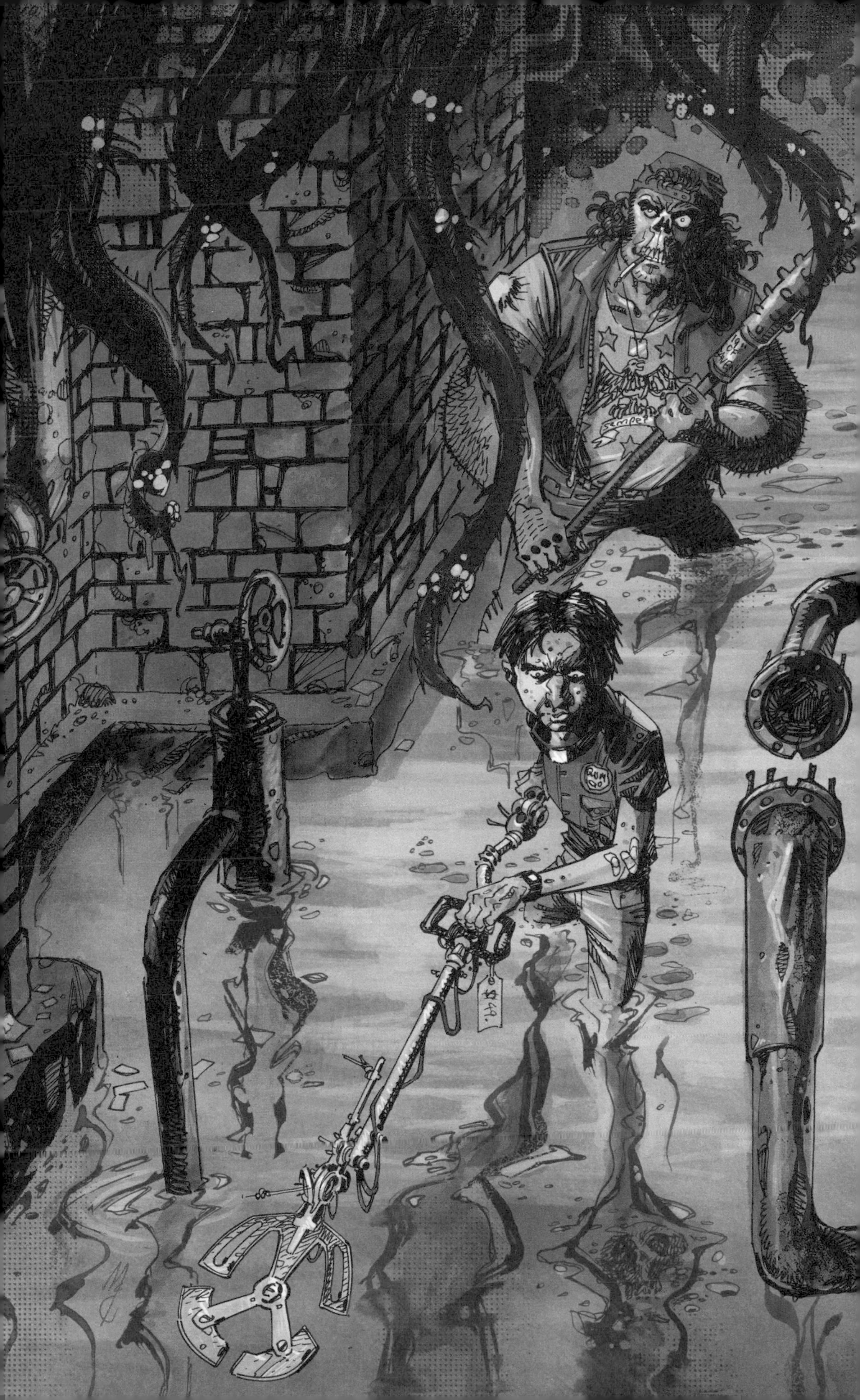
semper

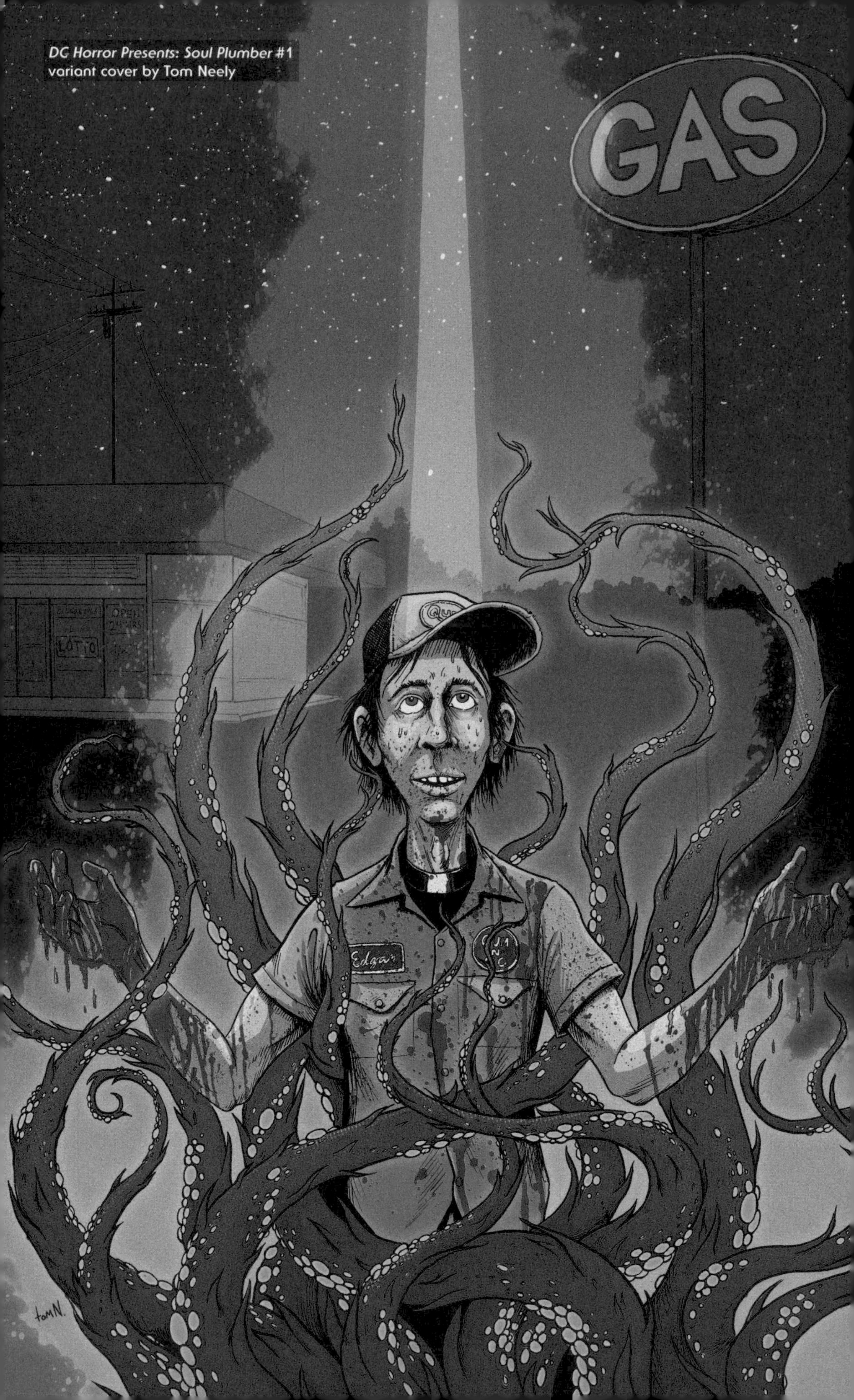
GAS
LOTTO
Edgar
tomN.

DC Horror Presents: Soul Plumber #1
variant cover by Tom Neely

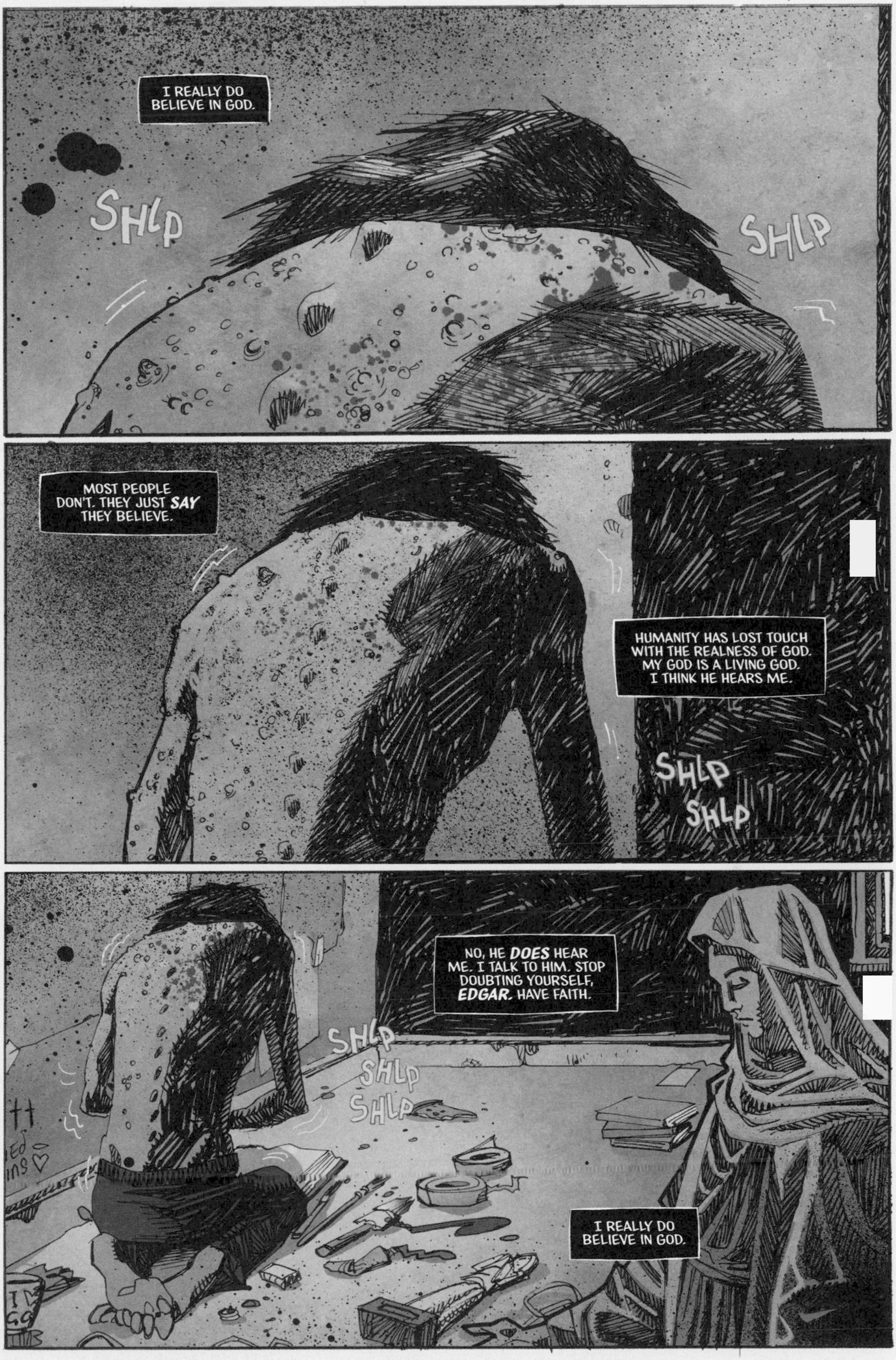
I REALLY DO BELIEVE IN GOD.
SHLP
SHLP
MOST PEOPLE DON'T. THEY JUST *SAY* THEY BELIEVE.
HUMANITY HAS LOST TOUCH WITH THE REALNESS OF GOD. MY GOD IS A LIVING GOD. I THINK HE HEARS ME.
SHLP
SHLP
NO, HE *DOES* HEAR ME. I TALK TO HIM. STOP DOUBTING YOURSELF, *EDGAR.* HAVE FAITH.
SHLP
SHLP
SHLP
I REALLY DO BELIEVE IN GOD.

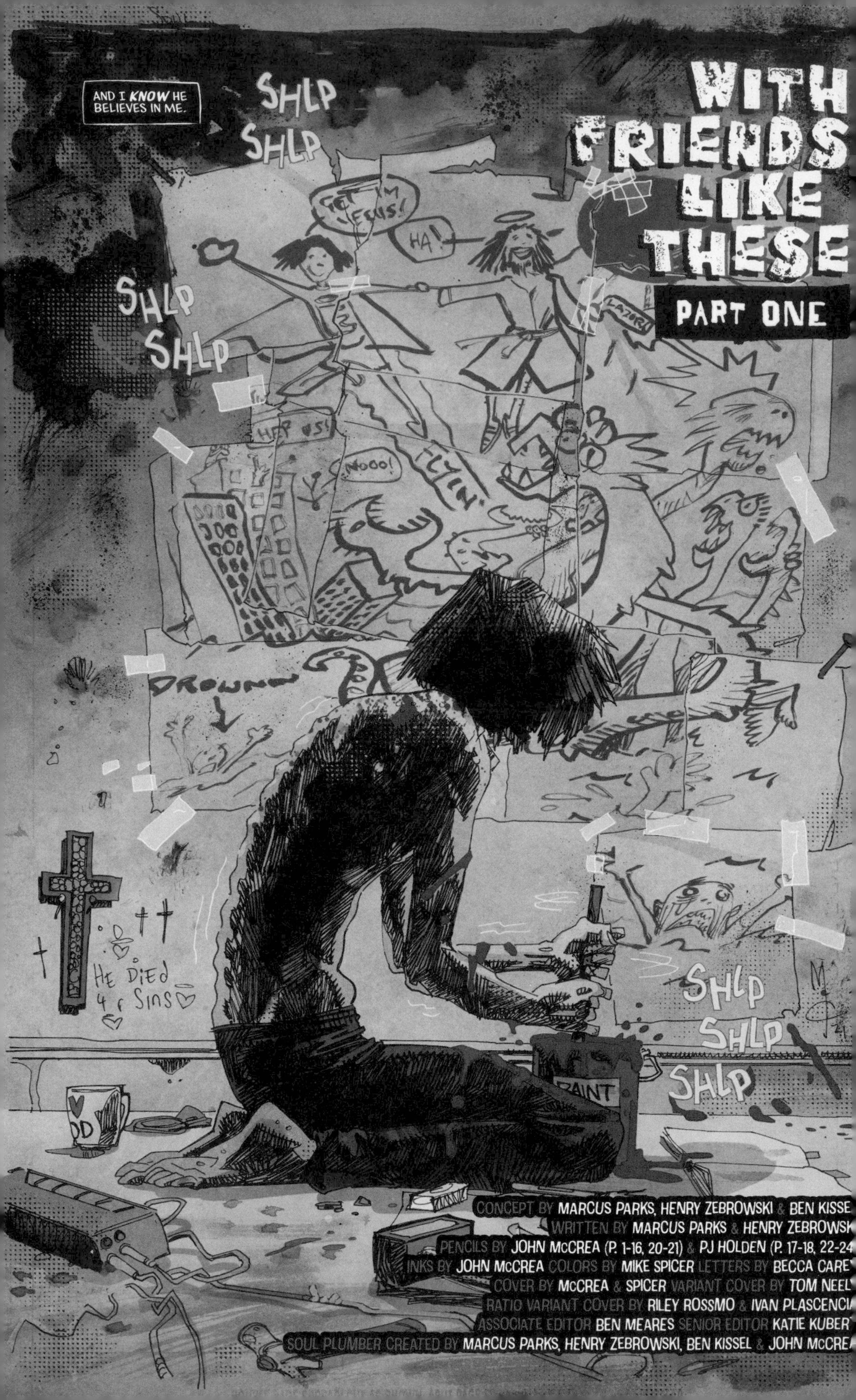
AND I *KNOW* HE BELIEVES IN ME.
SHLP
SHLP
WITH FRIENDS LIKE THESE
PART ONE
GET 'IM JESUS!
HA!
LAZOR!
SHLP
SHLP
HELP US!
NOOO!
FLYIN'
DROWNN
HE DIED 4 r SINS
PAINT
SHLP
SHLP
SHLP
CONCEPT BY MARCUS PARKS, HENRY ZEBROWSKI & BEN KISSE
WRITTEN BY MARCUS PARKS & HENRY ZEBROWSK
PENCILS BY JOHN McCREA (P. 1-16, 20-21) & PJ HOLDEN (P. 17-18, 22-24
INKS BY JOHN McCREA COLORS BY MIKE SPICER LETTERS BY BECCA CARE
COVER BY McCREA & SPICER VARIANT COVER BY TOM NEEL
RATIO VARIANT COVER BY RILEY ROSSMO & IVAN PLASCENCI
ASSOCIATE EDITOR BEN MEARES SENIOR EDITOR KATIE KUBER
SOUL PLUMBER CREATED BY MARCUS PARKS, HENRY ZEBROWSKI, BEN KISSEL & JOHN McCREA

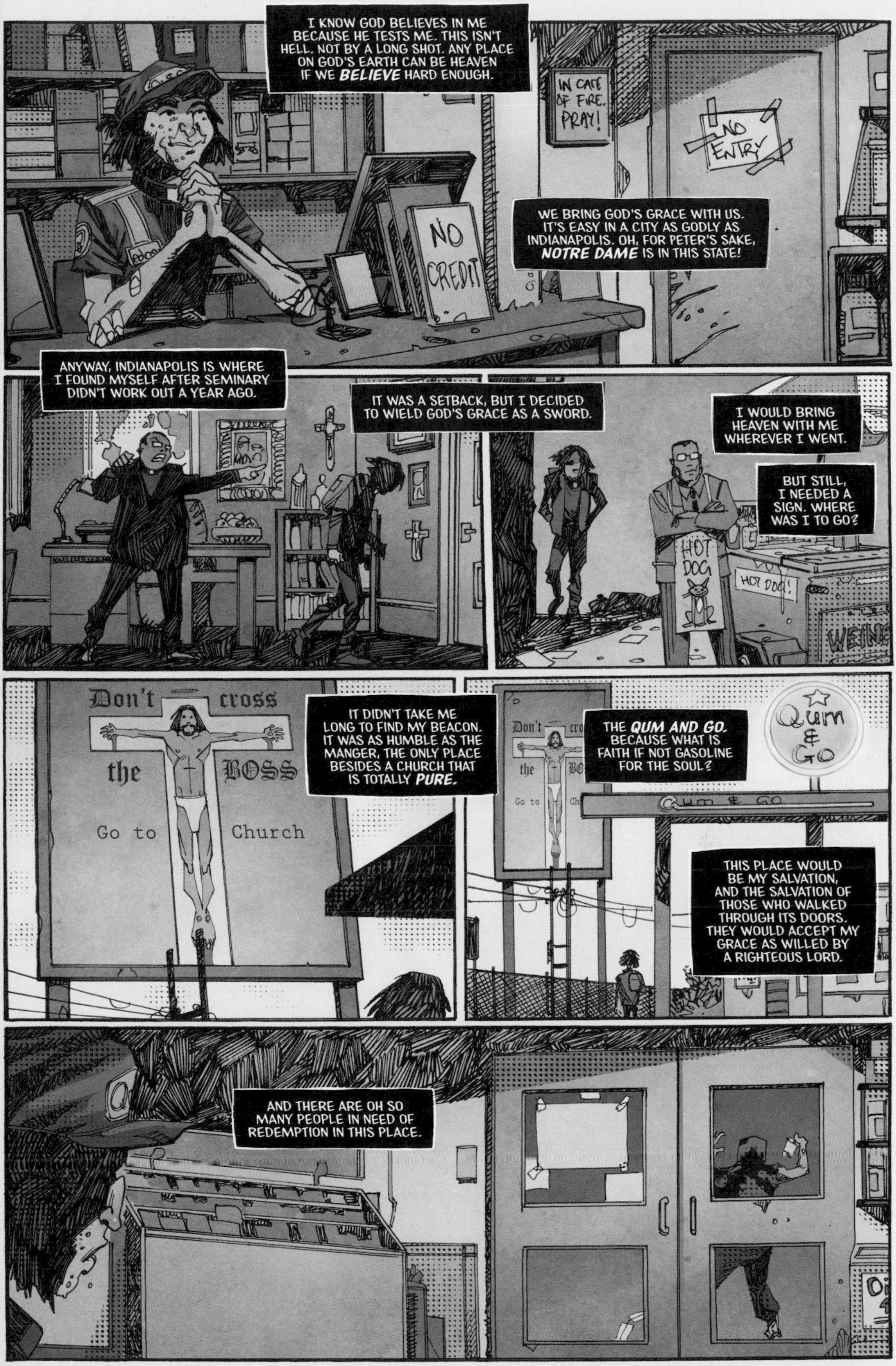
I KNOW GOD BELIEVES IN ME BECAUSE HE TESTS ME. THIS ISN'T HELL. NOT BY A LONG SHOT. ANY PLACE ON GOD'S EARTH CAN BE HEAVEN IF WE BELIEVE HARD ENOUGH.
NO CREDIT
IN CASE OF FIRE, PRAY!
NO ENTRY
WE BRING GOD'S GRACE WITH US. IT'S EASY IN A CITY AS GODLY AS INDIANAPOLIS. OH, FOR PETER'S SAKE, NOTRE DAME IS IN THIS STATE!
ANYWAY, INDIANAPOLIS IS WHERE I FOUND MYSELF AFTER SEMINARY DIDN'T WORK OUT A YEAR AGO.
IT WAS A SETBACK, BUT I DECIDED TO WIELD GOD'S GRACE AS A SWORD.
I WOULD BRING HEAVEN WITH ME WHEREVER I WENT.
BUT STILL, I NEEDED A SIGN. WHERE WAS I TO GO?
HOT DOG
HOT DOG!
Don't cross the BOSS
Go to Church
IT DIDN'T TAKE ME LONG TO FIND MY BEACON. IT WAS AS HUMBLE AS THE MANGER, THE ONLY PLACE BESIDES A CHURCH THAT IS TOTALLY PURE.
THE QUM AND GO. BECAUSE WHAT IS FAITH IF NOT GASOLINE FOR THE SOUL?
Qum & Go
THIS PLACE WOULD BE MY SALVATION, AND THE SALVATION OF THOSE WHO WALKED THROUGH ITS DOORS. THEY WOULD ACCEPT MY GRACE AS WILLED BY A RIGHTEOUS LORD.
AND THERE ARE OH SO MANY PEOPLE IN NEED OF REDEMPTION IN THIS PLACE.

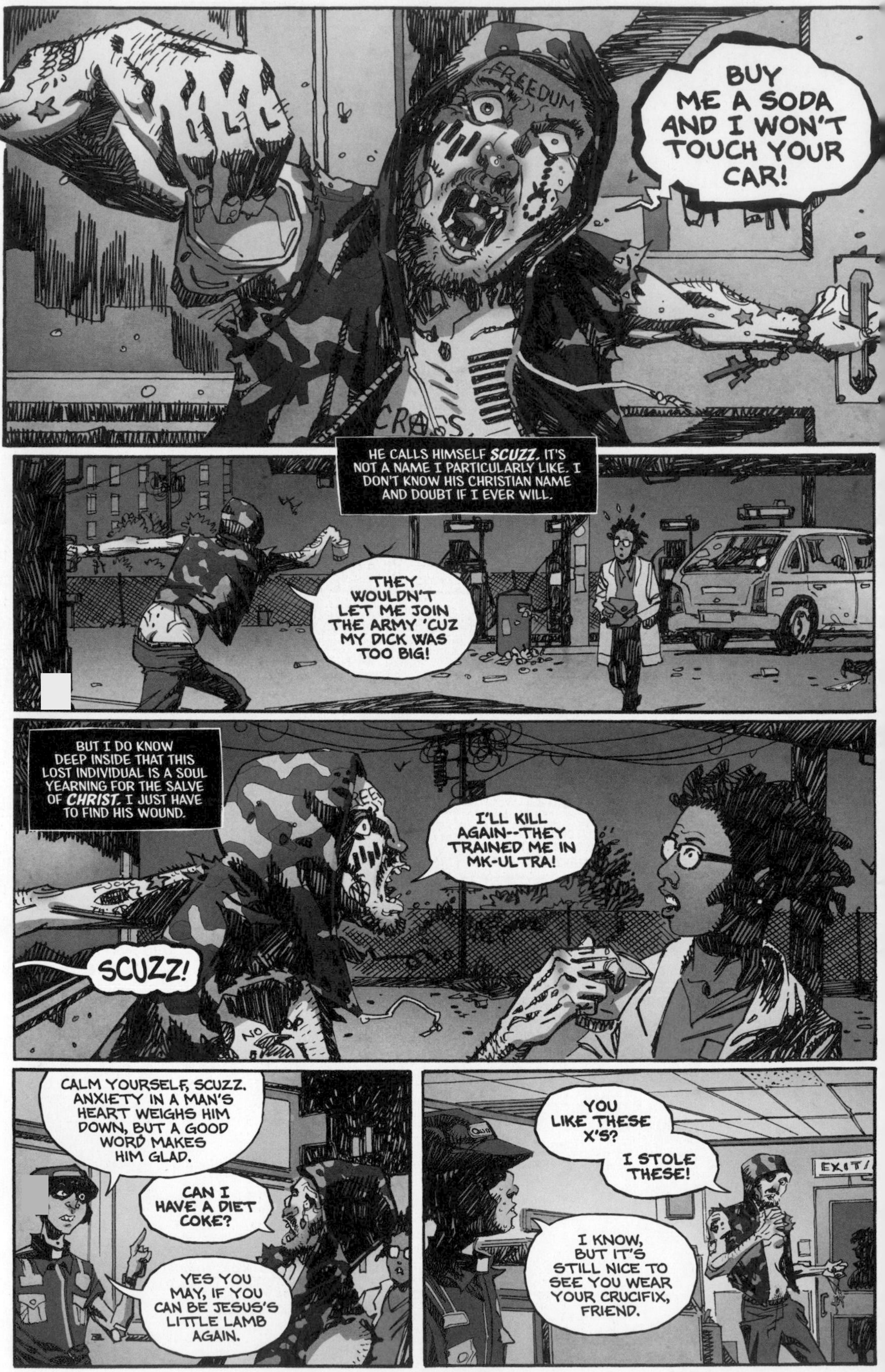
FREEDUM
BUY ME A SODA AND I WON'T TOUCH YOUR CAR!
CRASS
HE CALLS HIMSELF SCUZZ. IT'S NOT A NAME I PARTICULARLY LIKE. I DON'T KNOW HIS CHRISTIAN NAME AND DOUBT IF I EVER WILL.
THEY WOULDN'T LET ME JOIN THE ARMY 'CUZ MY DICK WAS TOO BIG!
BUT I DO KNOW DEEP INSIDE THAT THIS LOST INDIVIDUAL IS A SOUL YEARNING FOR THE SALVE OF CHRIST. I JUST HAVE TO FIND HIS WOUND.
I'LL KILL AGAIN--THEY TRAINED ME IN MK-ULTRA!
SCUZZ!
CALM YOURSELF, SCUZZ. ANXIETY IN A MAN'S HEART WEIGHS HIM DOWN, BUT A GOOD WORD MAKES HIM GLAD.
CAN I HAVE A DIET COKE?
YES YOU MAY, IF YOU CAN BE JESUS'S LITTLE LAMB AGAIN.
YOU LIKE THESE X'S?
I STOLE THESE!
EXIT
I KNOW, BUT IT'S STILL NICE TO SEE YOU WEAR YOUR CRUCIFIX, FRIEND.

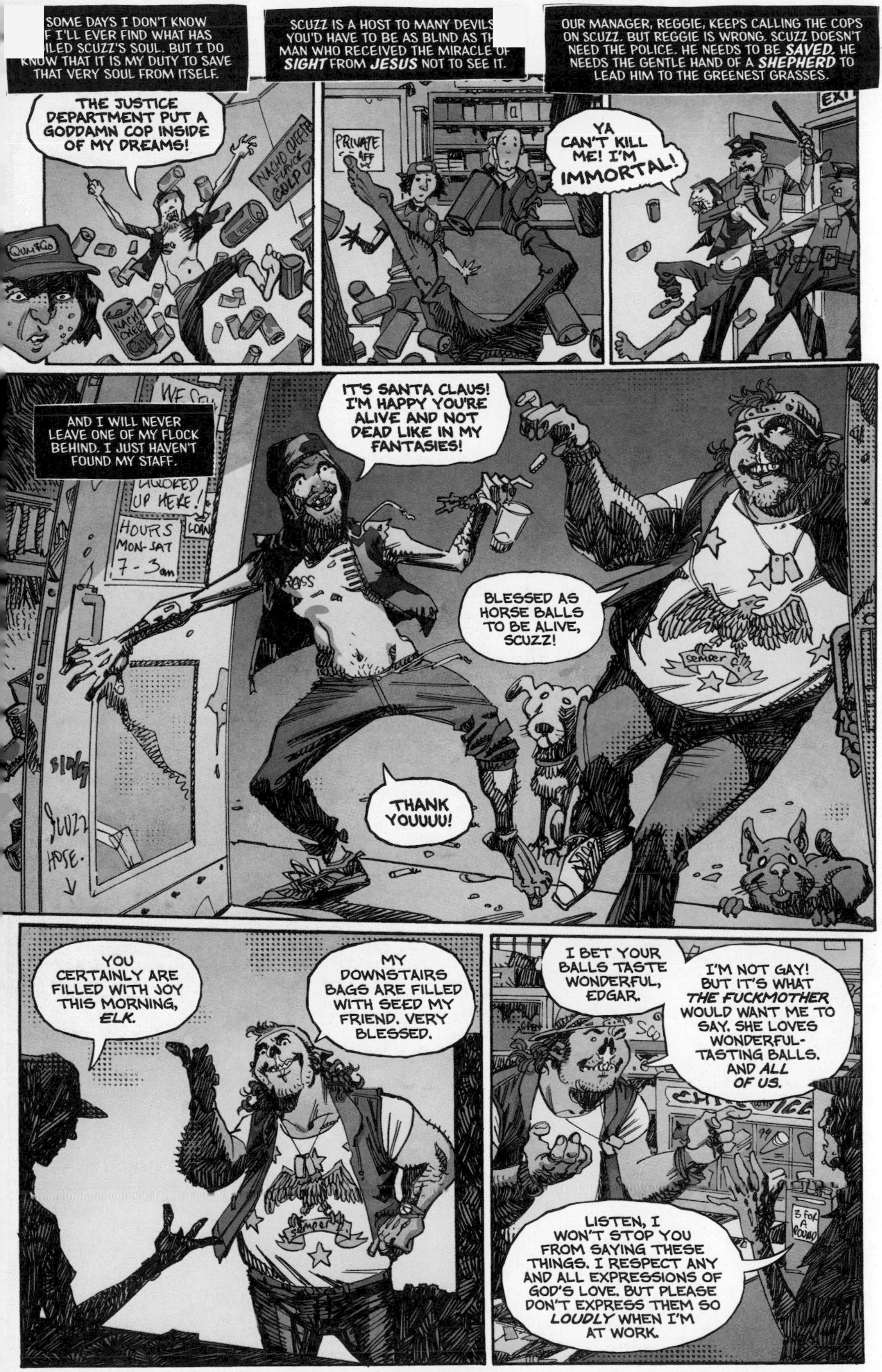
SOME DAYS I DON'T KNOW
F I'LL EVER FIND WHAT HAS
ILED SCUZZ'S SOUL. BUT I DO
KNOW THAT IT IS MY DUTY TO SAVE
THAT VERY SOUL FROM ITSELF.
SCUZZ IS A HOST TO MANY DEVILS
YOU'D HAVE TO BE AS BLIND AS TH
MAN WHO RECEIVED THE MIRACLE OF
SIGHT FROM *JESUS* NOT TO SEE IT.
OUR MANAGER, REGGIE, KEEPS CALLING THE COPS ON SCUZZ. BUT REGGIE IS WRONG. SCUZZ DOESN'T NEED THE POLICE. HE NEEDS TO BE *SAVED.* HE NEEDS THE GENTLE HAND OF A *SHEPHERD* TO LEAD HIM TO THE GREENEST GRASSES.
THE JUSTICE DEPARTMENT PUT A GODDAMN COP INSIDE OF MY DREAMS!
PRIVATE
YA CAN'T KILL ME! I'M IMMORTAL!
EXIT
AND I WILL NEVER LEAVE ONE OF MY FLOCK BEHIND. I JUST HAVEN'T FOUND MY STAFF.
IT'S SANTA CLAUS! I'M HAPPY YOU'RE ALIVE AND NOT DEAD LIKE IN MY FANTASIES!
HOURS MON-SAT 7-3am
BLESSED AS HORSE BALLS TO BE ALIVE, SCUZZ!
THANK YOUUUU!
SCUZZ HOSE.
YOU CERTAINLY ARE FILLED WITH JOY THIS MORNING, *ELK.*
MY DOWNSTAIRS BAGS ARE FILLED WITH SEED MY FRIEND. VERY BLESSED.
I BET YOUR BALLS TASTE WONDERFUL, EDGAR.
I'M NOT GAY! BUT IT'S WHAT *THE FUCKMOTHER* WOULD WANT ME TO SAY. SHE LOVES WONDERFUL-TASTING BALLS. AND *ALL OF US.*
LISTEN, I WON'T STOP YOU FROM SAYING THESE THINGS. I RESPECT ANY AND ALL EXPRESSIONS OF GOD'S LOVE. BUT PLEASE DON'T EXPRESS THEM SO *LOUDLY* WHEN I'M AT WORK.

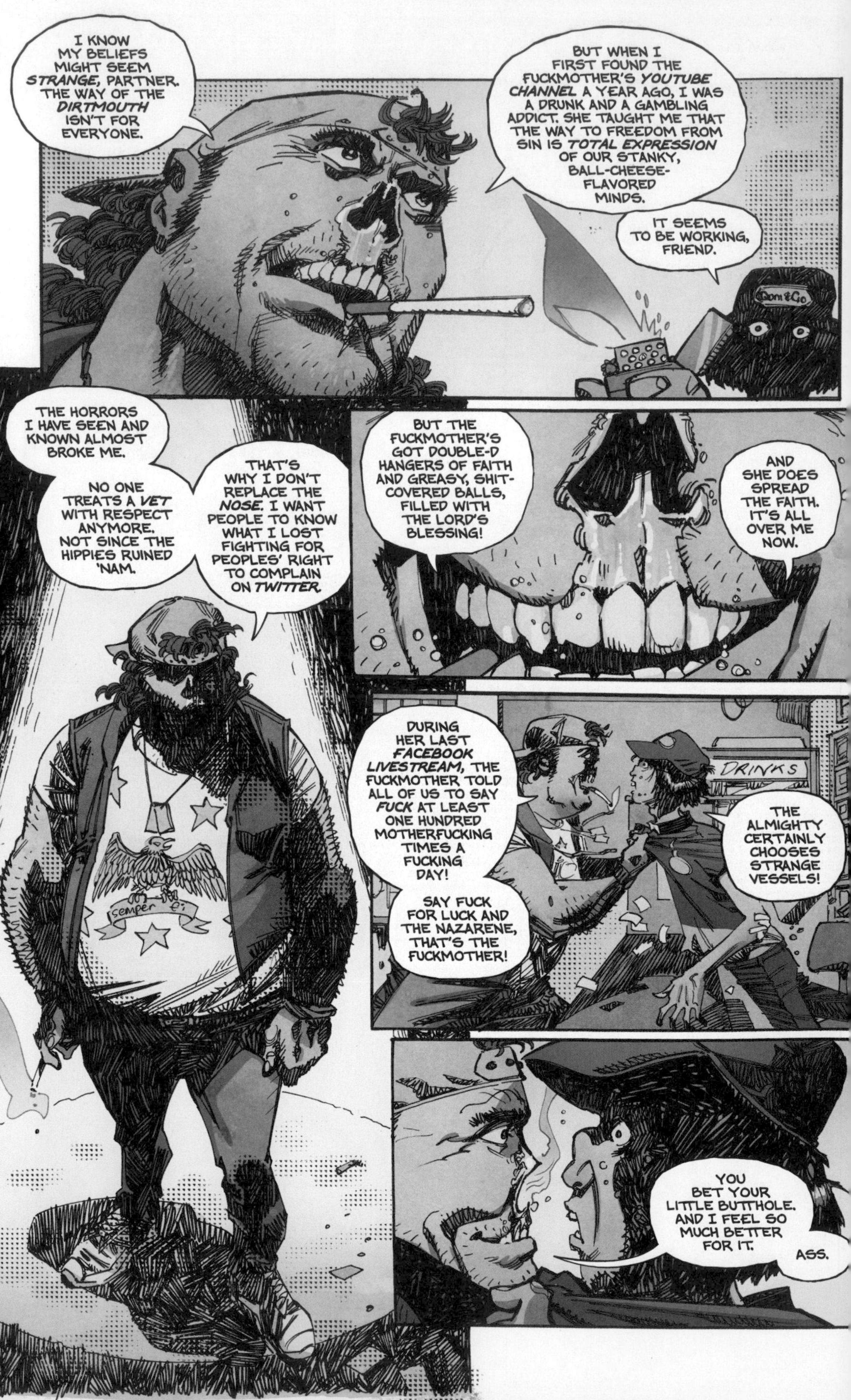
I KNOW MY BELIEFS MIGHT SEEM *STRANGE*, PARTNER. THE WAY OF THE *DIRTMOUTH* ISN'T FOR EVERYONE.
BUT WHEN I FIRST FOUND THE FUCKMOTHER'S *YOUTUBE CHANNEL* A YEAR AGO, I WAS A DRUNK AND A GAMBLING ADDICT. SHE TAUGHT ME THAT THE WAY TO FREEDOM FROM SIN IS *TOTAL EXPRESSION* OF OUR STANKY, BALL-CHEESE-FLAVORED MINDS.
IT SEEMS TO BE WORKING, FRIEND.
THE HORRORS I HAVE SEEN AND KNOWN ALMOST BROKE ME.
NO ONE TREATS A *VET* WITH RESPECT ANYMORE. NOT SINCE THE HIPPIES RUINED 'NAM.
THAT'S WHY I DON'T REPLACE THE *NOSE*. I WANT PEOPLE TO KNOW WHAT I LOST FIGHTING FOR PEOPLES' RIGHT TO COMPLAIN ON *TWITTER*.
semper fi
BUT THE FUCKMOTHER'S GOT DOUBLE-D HANGERS OF FAITH AND GREASY, SHIT-COVERED BALLS, FILLED WITH THE LORD'S BLESSING!
AND SHE DOES SPREAD THE FAITH. IT'S ALL OVER ME NOW.
DURING HER LAST *FACEBOOK LIVESTREAM*, THE FUCKMOTHER TOLD ALL OF US TO SAY *FUCK* AT LEAST ONE HUNDRED MOTHERFUCKING TIMES A FUCKING DAY!
SAY FUCK FOR LUCK AND THE NAZARENE, THAT'S THE FUCKMOTHER!
DRINKS
THE ALMIGHTY CERTAINLY CHOOSES STRANGE VESSELS!
YOU BET YOUR LITTLE BUTTHOLE. AND I FEEL SO MUCH BETTER FOR IT.
ASS.

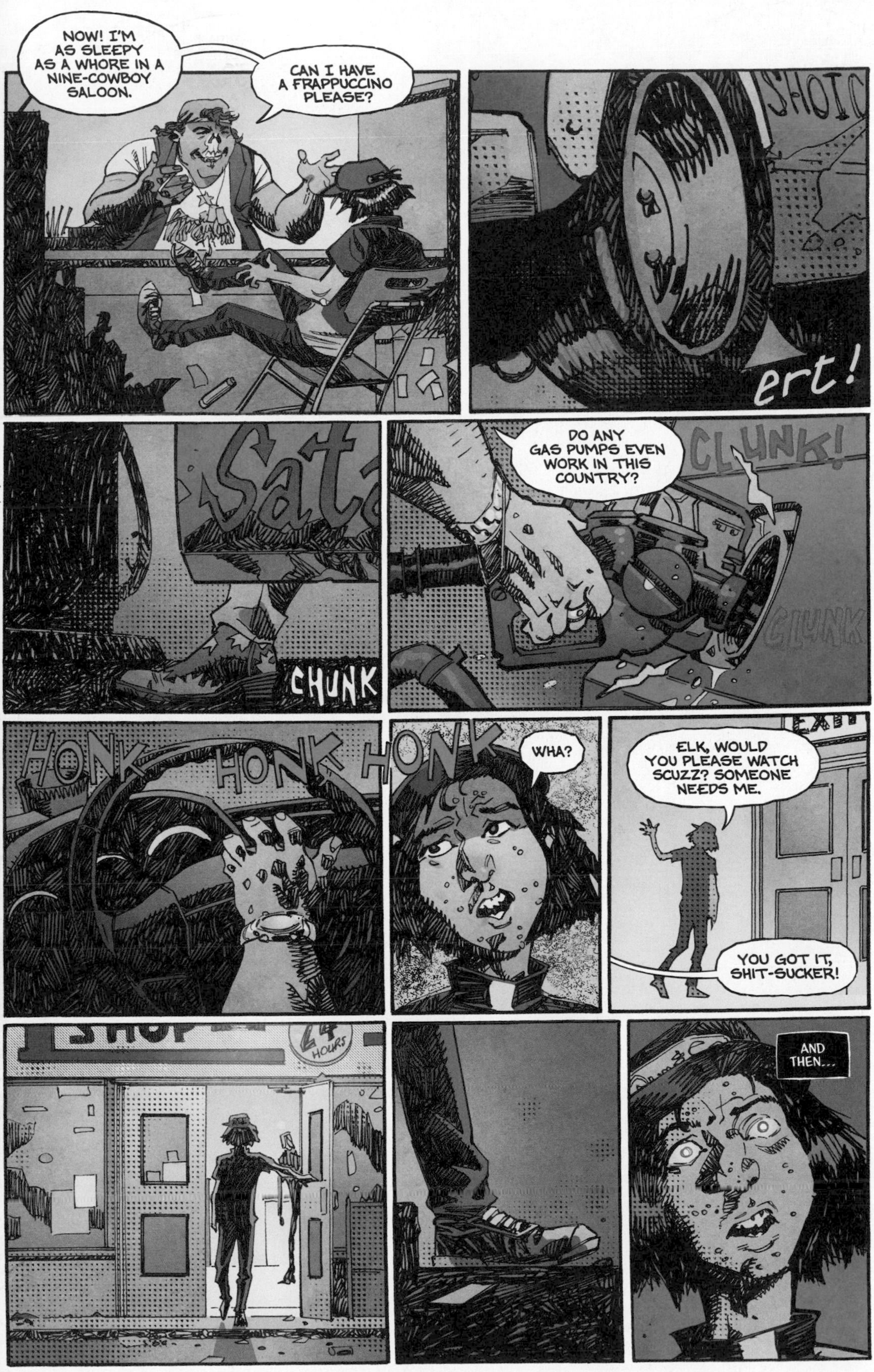
NOW! I'M AS SLEEPY AS A WHORE IN A NINE-COWBOY SALOON.
CAN I HAVE A FRAPPUCCINO PLEASE?
SHOIC
ert!
Sat
CHUNK
DO ANY GAS PUMPS EVEN WORK IN THIS COUNTRY?
CLUNK!
CLUNK
HONK HONK HONK
WHA?
ELK, WOULD YOU PLEASE WATCH SCUZZ? SOMEONE NEEDS ME.
YOU GOT IT, SHIT-SUCKER!
SHOP
24 HOURS
AND THEN...

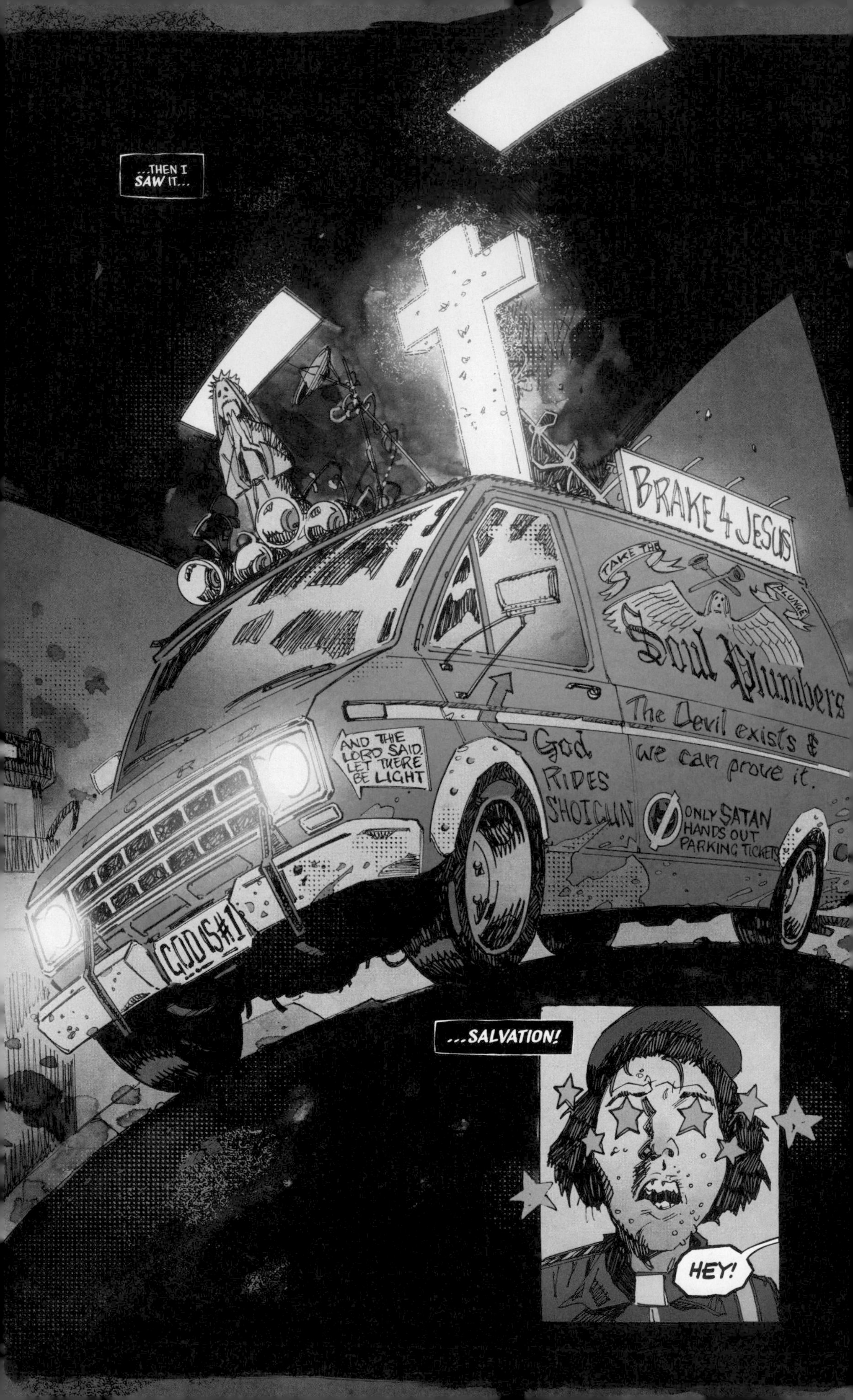
...THEN I SAW IT...
BRAKE 4 JESUS
TAKE THE PLUNGE
Soul Plumbers
The Devil exists & we can prove it.
AND THE LORD SAID, LET THERE BE LIGHT
God RIDES SHOTGUN
ONLY SATAN HANDS OUT PARKING TICKETS
GOD IS #1
...SALVATION!
HEY!

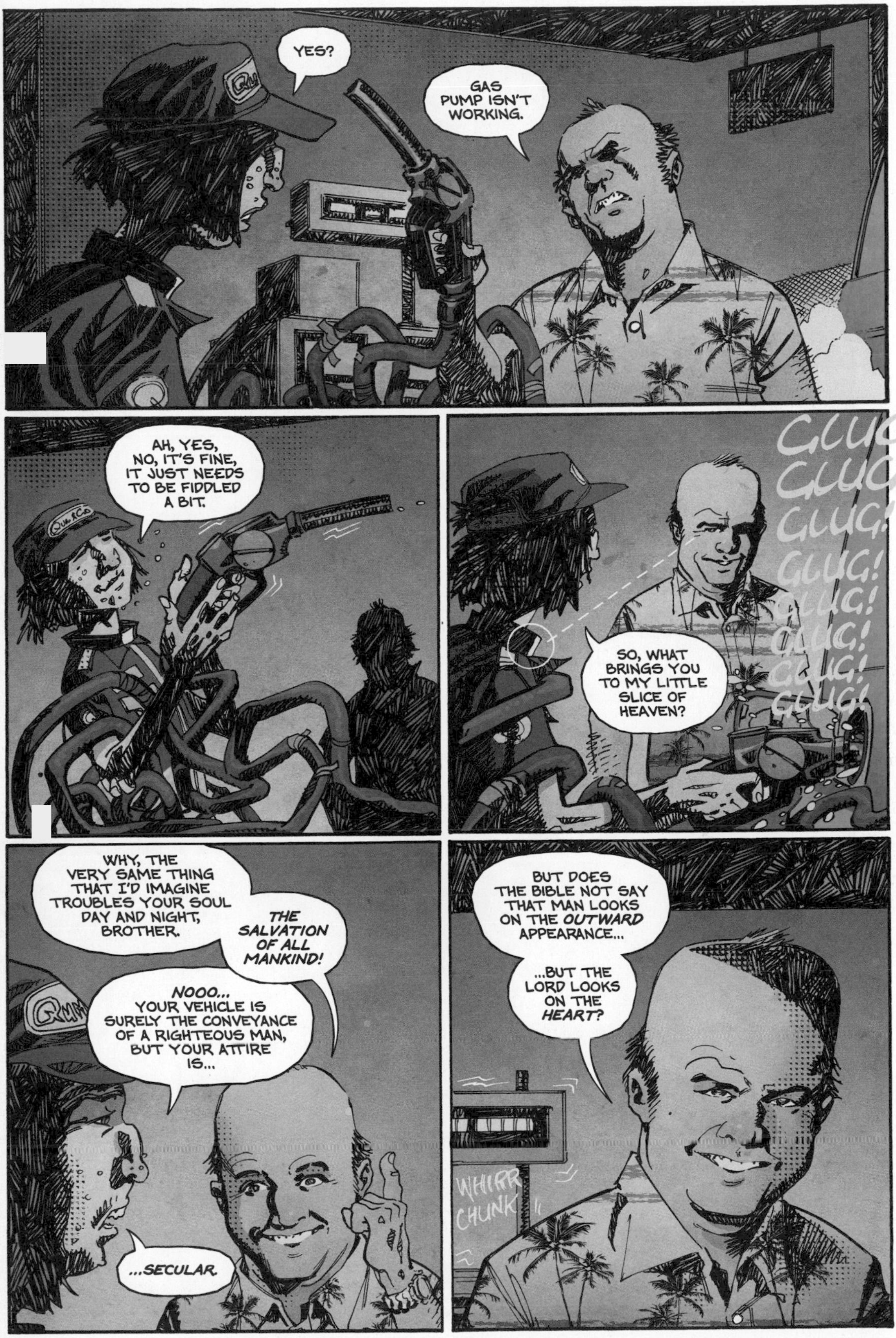
YES?
GAS PUMP ISN'T WORKING.
AH, YES, NO, IT'S FINE, IT JUST NEEDS TO BE FIDDLED A BIT.
GLUG! GLUG! GLUG! GLUG! GLUG! GLUG! GLUG! GLUG!
SO, WHAT BRINGS YOU TO MY LITTLE SLICE OF HEAVEN?
WHY, THE VERY SAME THING THAT I'D IMAGINE TROUBLES YOUR SOUL DAY AND NIGHT, BROTHER.
THE SALVATION OF ALL MANKIND!
NOOO... YOUR VEHICLE IS SURELY THE CONVEYANCE OF A RIGHTEOUS MAN, BUT YOUR ATTIRE IS...
...SECULAR.
BUT DOES THE BIBLE NOT SAY THAT MAN LOOKS ON THE OUTWARD APPEARANCE...
...BUT THE LORD LOOKS ON THE HEART?
WHIRR
CHUNK

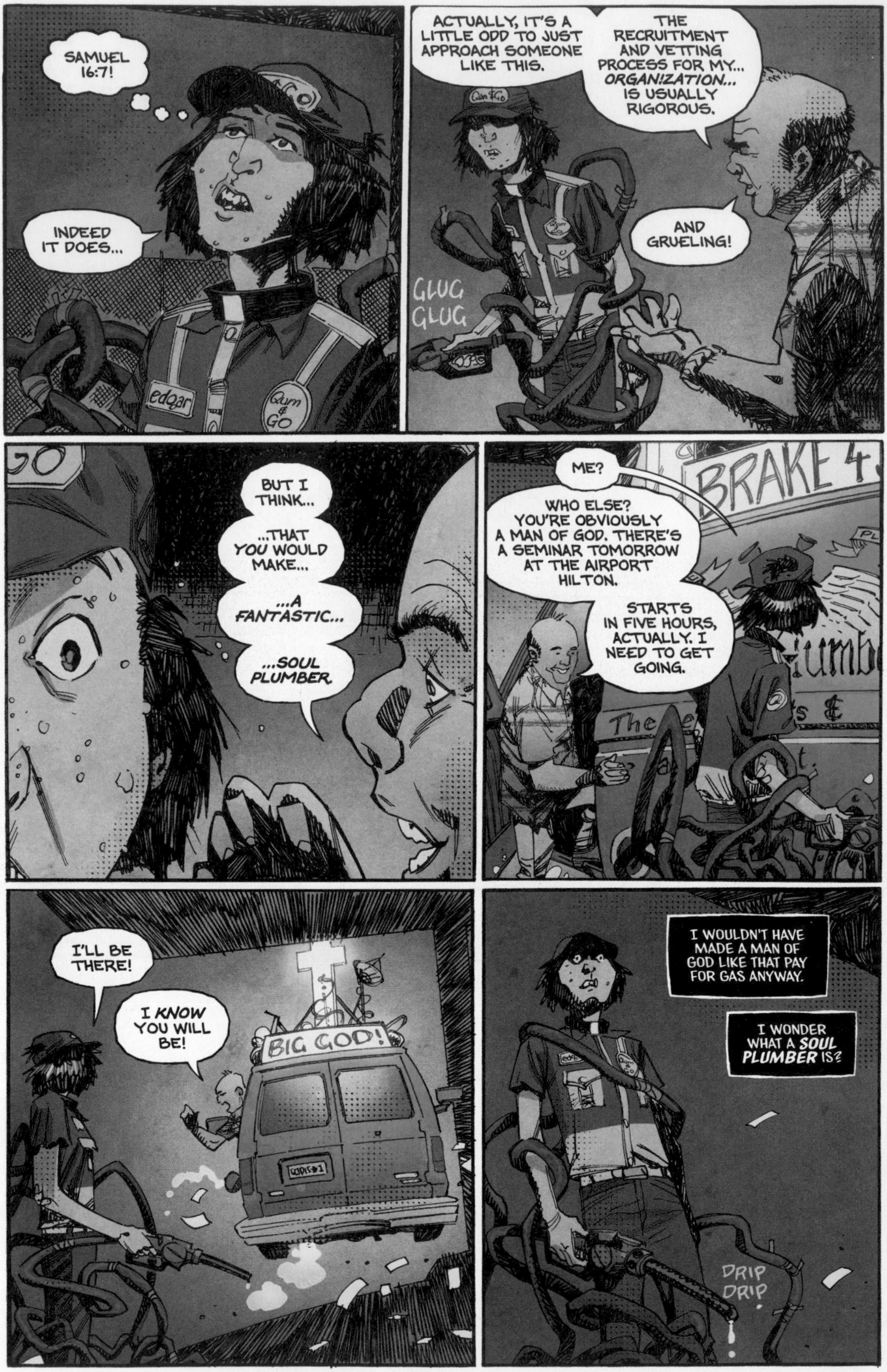
SAMUEL 16:7!
INDEED IT DOES...
ACTUALLY, IT'S A LITTLE ODD TO JUST APPROACH SOMEONE LIKE THIS.
THE RECRUITMENT AND VETTING PROCESS FOR MY... ORGANIZATION... IS USUALLY RIGOROUS.
AND GRUELING!
GLUG GLUG
BUT I THINK...
...THAT YOU WOULD MAKE...
...A FANTASTIC...
...SOUL PLUMBER.
ME?
WHO ELSE? YOU'RE OBVIOUSLY A MAN OF GOD. THERE'S A SEMINAR TOMORROW AT THE AIRPORT HILTON.
STARTS IN FIVE HOURS, ACTUALLY. I NEED TO GET GOING.
BRAKE
I'LL BE THERE!
I KNOW YOU WILL BE!
BIG GOD!
I WOULDN'T HAVE MADE A MAN OF GOD LIKE THAT PAY FOR GAS ANYWAY.
I WONDER WHAT A SOUL PLUMBER IS?
DRIP DRIP

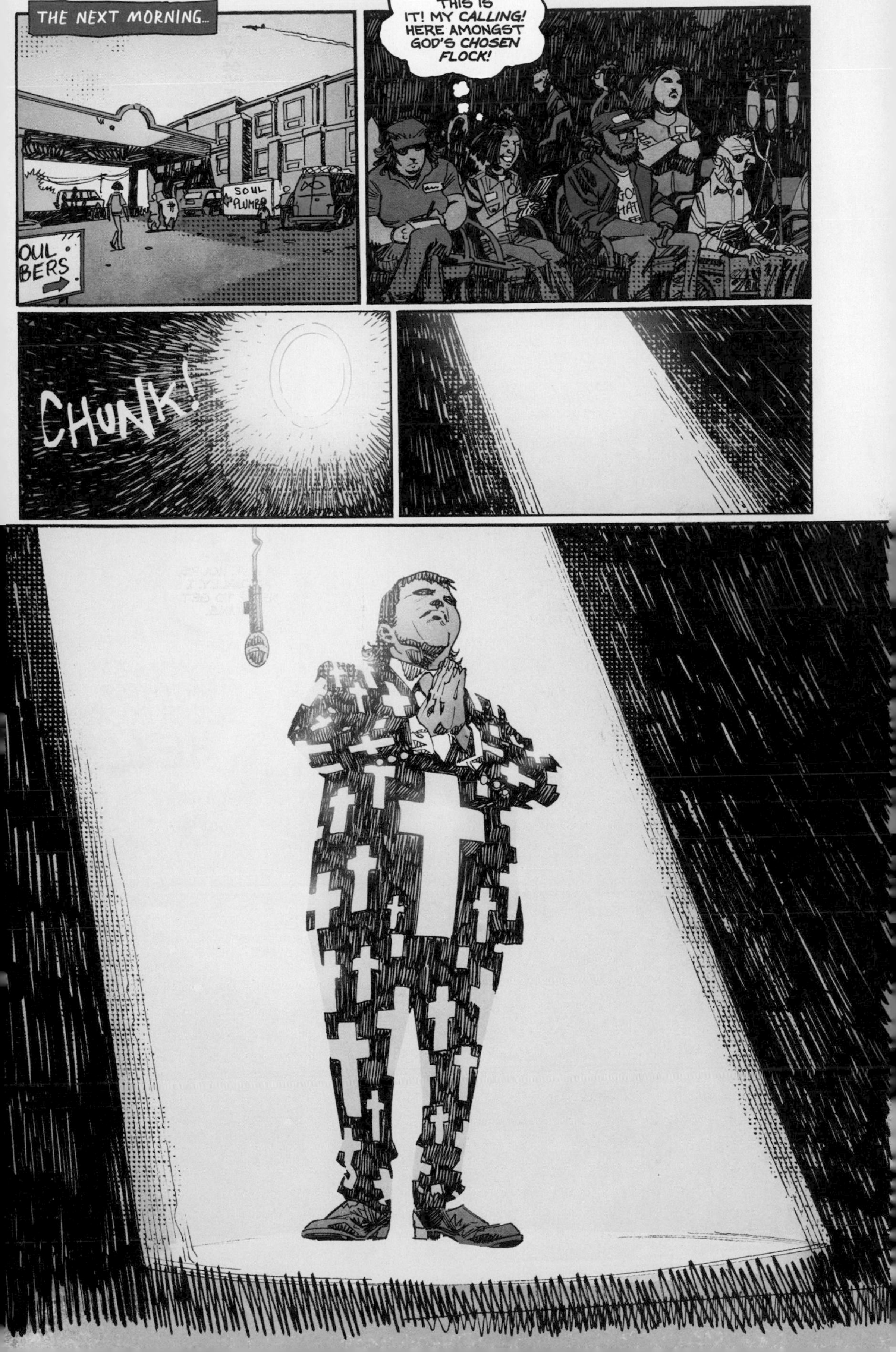
THE NEXT MORNING...
SOUL PLUMBER
OUL BERS
THIS IS IT! MY CALLING! HERE AMONGST GOD'S CHOSEN FLOCK!
CHUNK!

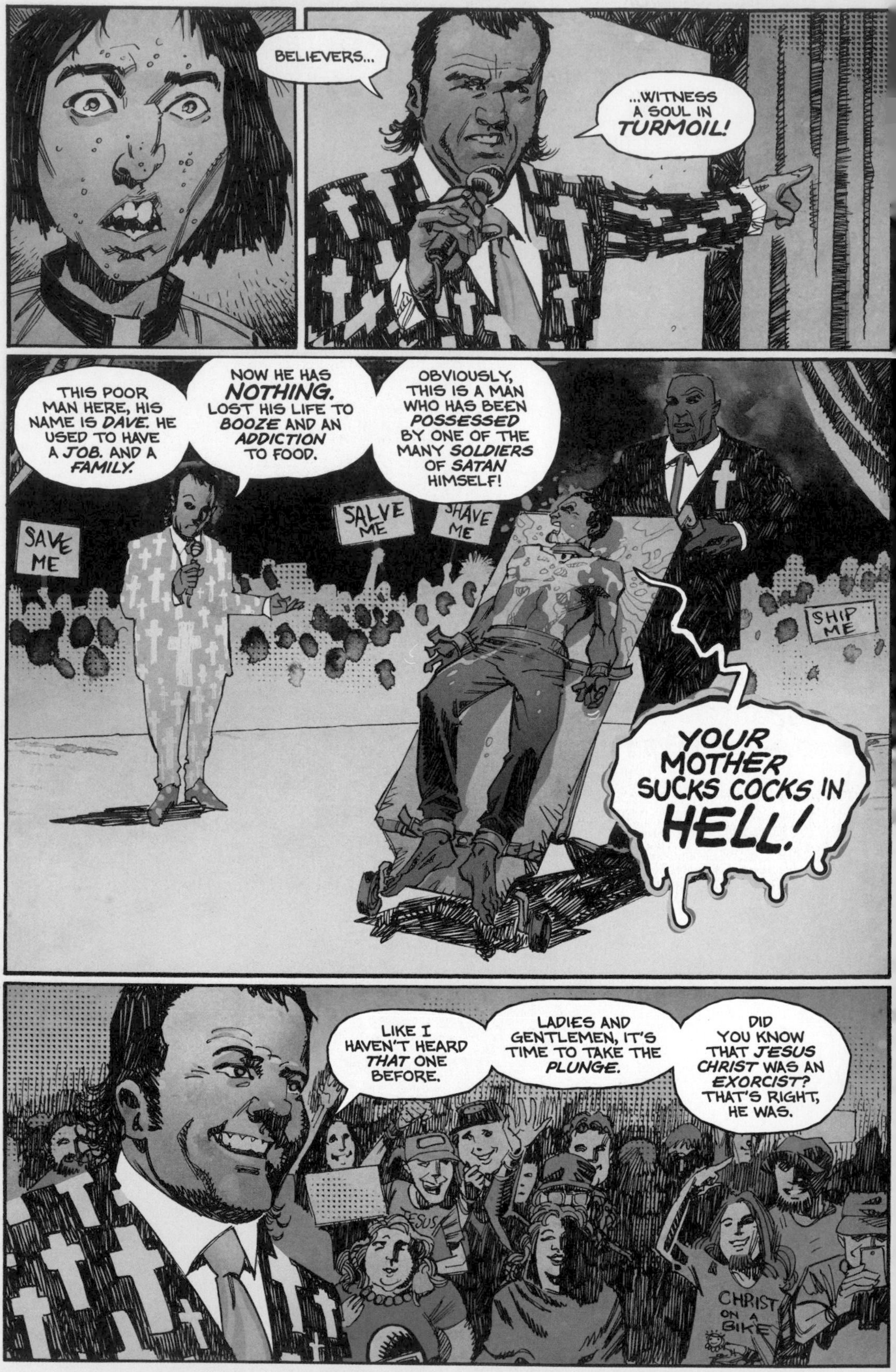
BELIEVERS...
...WITNESS A SOUL IN TURMOIL!
THIS POOR MAN HERE, HIS NAME IS DAVE. HE USED TO HAVE A JOB. AND A FAMILY.
NOW HE HAS NOTHING. LOST HIS LIFE TO BOOZE AND AN ADDICTION TO FOOD.
OBVIOUSLY, THIS IS A MAN WHO HAS BEEN POSSESSED BY ONE OF THE MANY SOLDIERS OF SATAN HIMSELF!
SAVE ME
SALVE ME
SHAVE ME
SHIP ME
YOUR MOTHER SUCKS COCKS IN HELL!
LIKE I HAVEN'T HEARD THAT ONE BEFORE.
LADIES AND GENTLEMEN, IT'S TIME TO TAKE THE PLUNGE.
DID YOU KNOW THAT JESUS CHRIST WAS AN EXORCIST? THAT'S RIGHT, HE WAS.
JESUS
CHRIST ON A BIKE

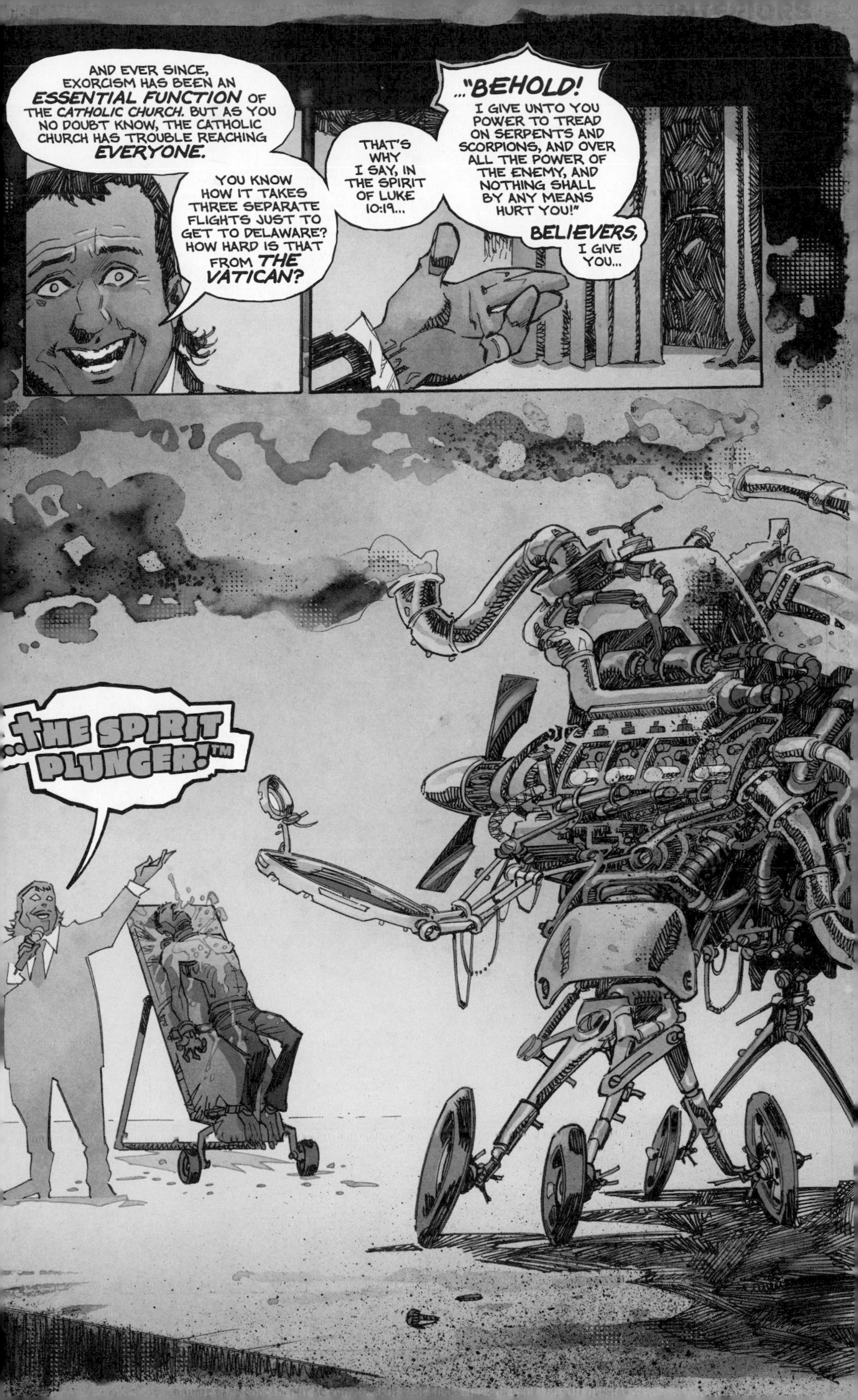
AND EVER SINCE, EXORCISM HAS BEEN AN ESSENTIAL FUNCTION OF THE CATHOLIC CHURCH. BUT AS YOU NO DOUBT KNOW, THE CATHOLIC CHURCH HAS TROUBLE REACHING EVERYONE.
YOU KNOW HOW IT TAKES THREE SEPARATE FLIGHTS JUST TO GET TO DELAWARE? HOW HARD IS THAT FROM THE VATICAN?
THAT'S WHY I SAY, IN THE SPIRIT OF LUKE 10:19...
..."BEHOLD! I GIVE UNTO YOU POWER TO TREAD ON SERPENTS AND SCORPIONS, AND OVER ALL THE POWER OF THE ENEMY, AND NOTHING SHALL BY ANY MEANS HURT YOU!"
BELIEVERS, I GIVE YOU...
...THE SPIRIT PLUNGER!™

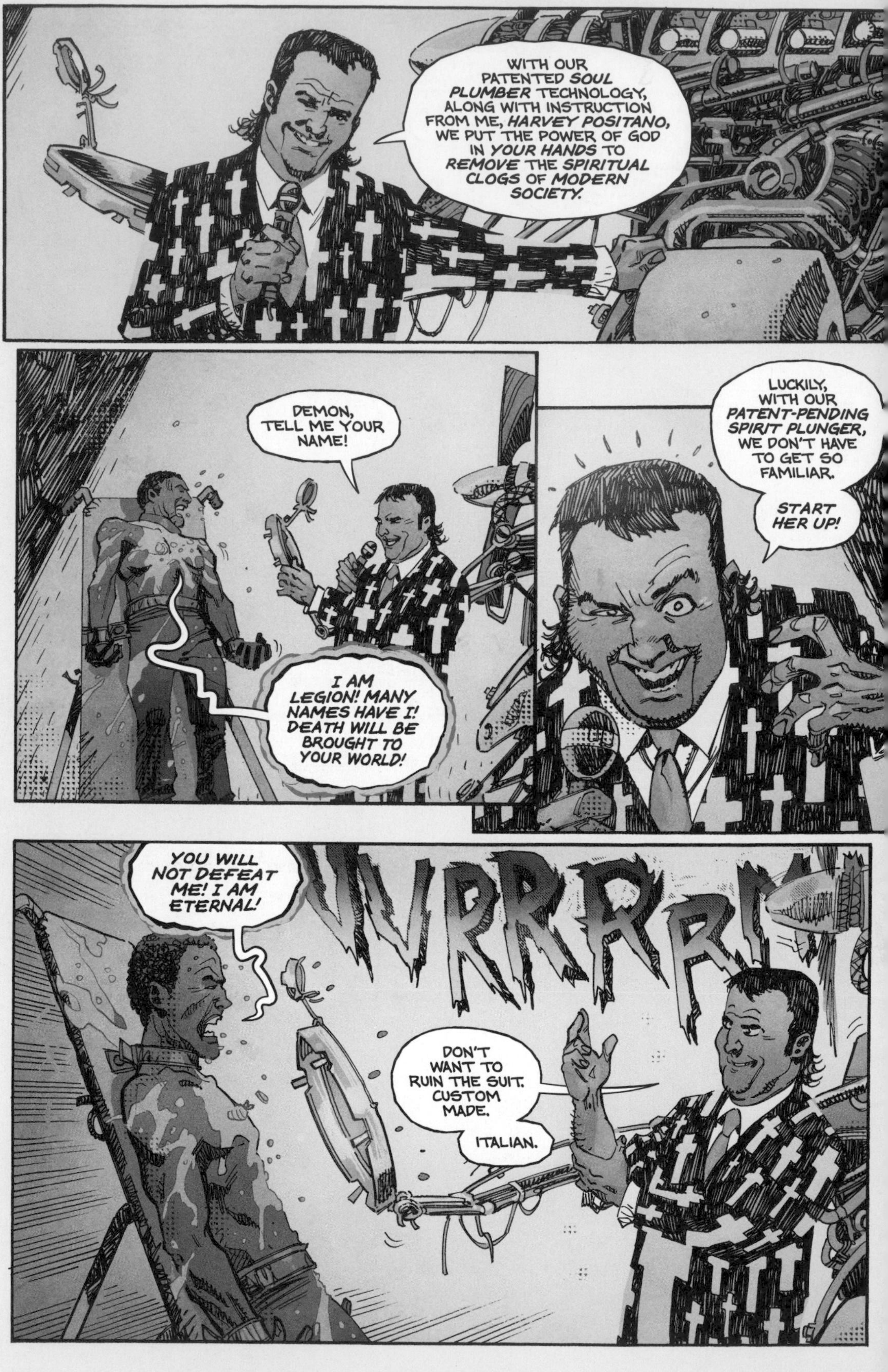
WITH OUR PATENTED SOUL PLUMBER TECHNOLOGY, ALONG WITH INSTRUCTION FROM ME, HARVEY POSITANO, WE PUT THE POWER OF GOD IN YOUR HANDS TO REMOVE THE SPIRITUAL CLOGS OF MODERN SOCIETY.
DEMON, TELL ME YOUR NAME!
I AM LEGION! MANY NAMES HAVE I! DEATH WILL BE BROUGHT TO YOUR WORLD!
LUCKILY, WITH OUR PATENT-PENDING SPIRIT PLUNGER, WE DON'T HAVE TO GET SO FAMILIAR.
START HER UP!
YOU WILL NOT DEFEAT ME! I AM ETERNAL!
VVRRRRM
DON'T WANT TO RUIN THE SUIT. CUSTOM MADE.
ITALIAN.

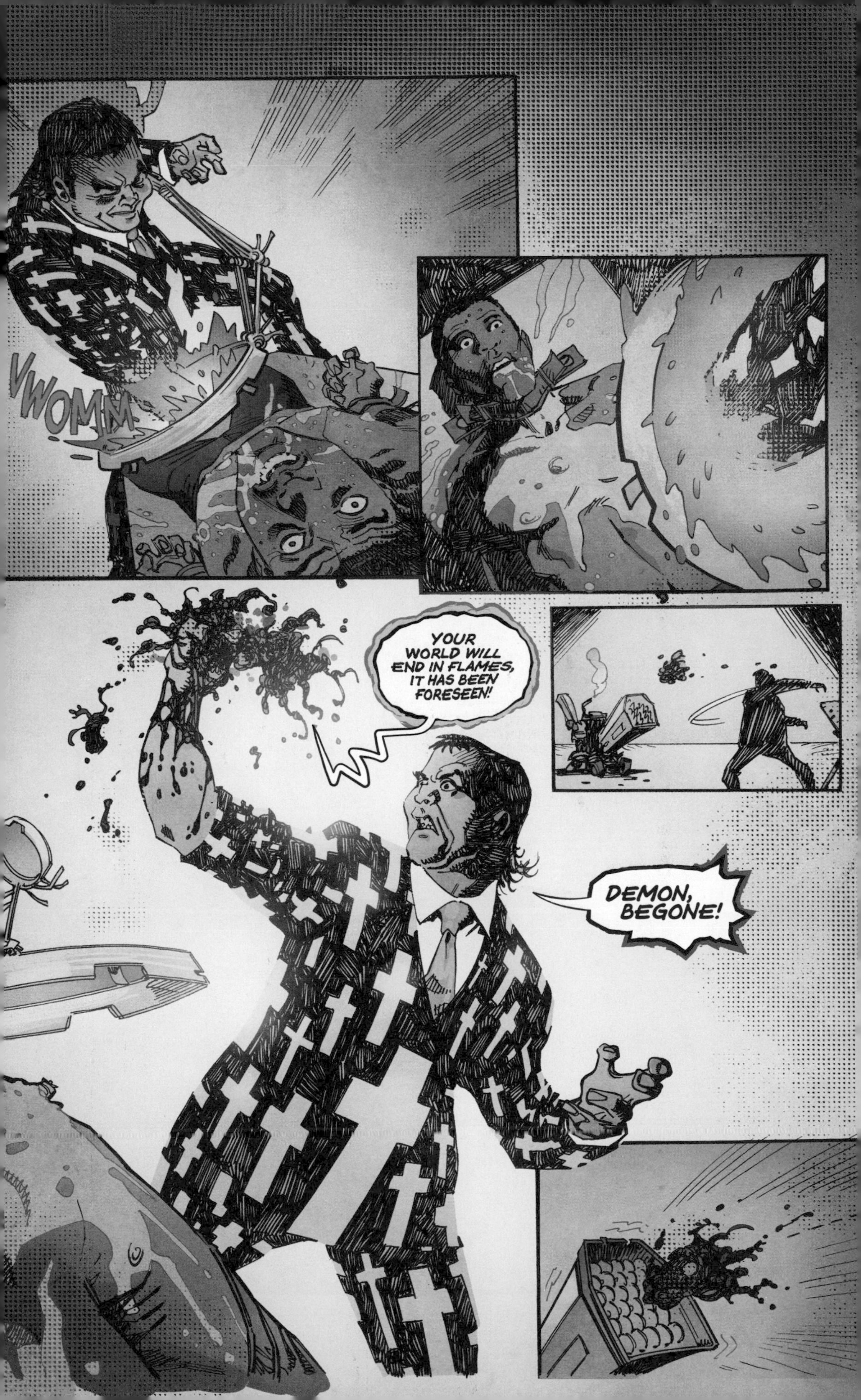
VWOMM
YOUR WORLD WILL END IN FLAMES, IT HAS BEEN FORESEEN!
DEMON, BEGONE!

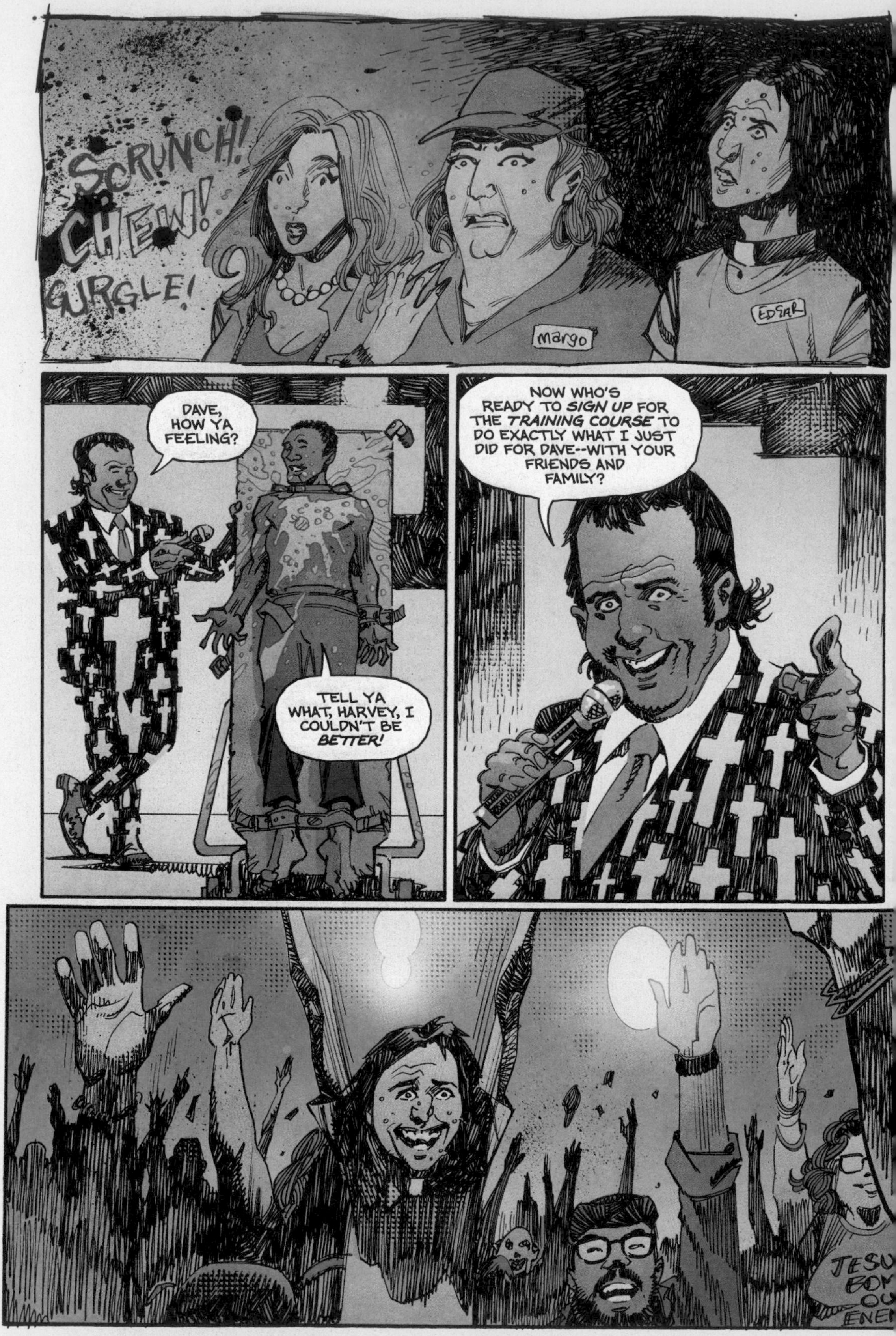
SCRUNCH!
CHEW!
GURGLE!
margo
EDGAR
DAVE, HOW YA FEELING?
TELL YA WHAT, HARVEY, I COULDN'T BE *BETTER!*
NOW WHO'S READY TO *SIGN UP* FOR THE *TRAINING COURSE* TO DO EXACTLY WHAT I JUST DID FOR DAVE--WITH YOUR FRIENDS AND FAMILY?

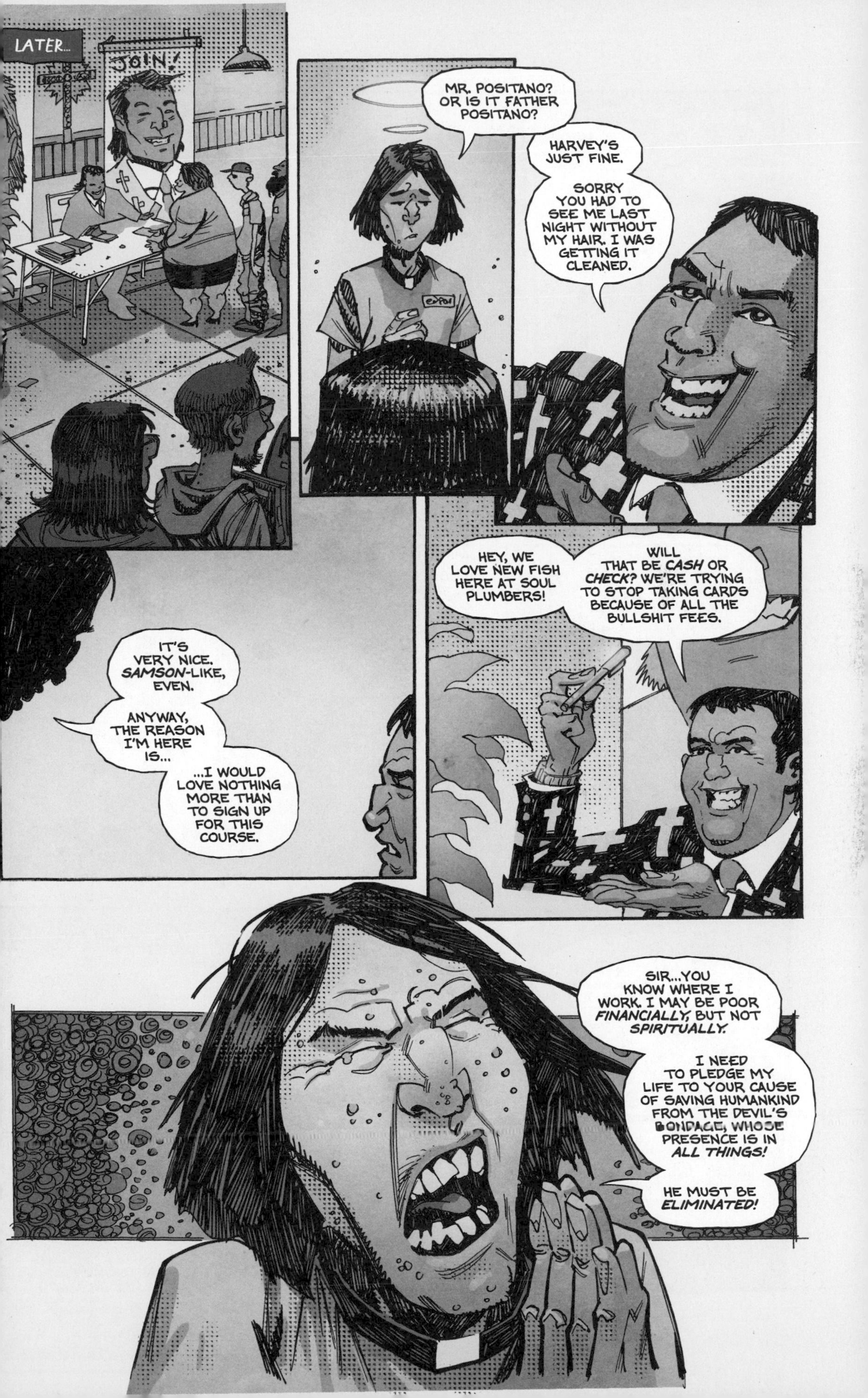
LATER...
JOIN!
MR. POSITANO? OR IS IT FATHER POSITANO?
HARVEY'S JUST FINE.
SORRY YOU HAD TO SEE ME LAST NIGHT WITHOUT MY HAIR. I WAS GETTING IT CLEANED.
IT'S VERY NICE. *SAMSON*-LIKE, EVEN.
ANYWAY, THE REASON I'M HERE IS...
...I WOULD LOVE NOTHING MORE THAN TO SIGN UP FOR THIS COURSE.
HEY, WE LOVE NEW FISH HERE AT SOUL PLUMBERS!
WILL THAT BE *CASH* OR *CHECK*? WE'RE TRYING TO STOP TAKING CARDS BECAUSE OF ALL THE BULLSHIT FEES.
SIR...YOU KNOW WHERE I WORK. I MAY BE POOR *FINANCIALLY*, BUT NOT *SPIRITUALLY*.
I NEED TO PLEDGE MY LIFE TO YOUR CAUSE OF SAVING HUMANKIND FROM THE DEVIL'S BONDAGE, WHOSE PRESENCE IS IN *ALL THINGS!*
HE MUST BE *ELIMINATED!*

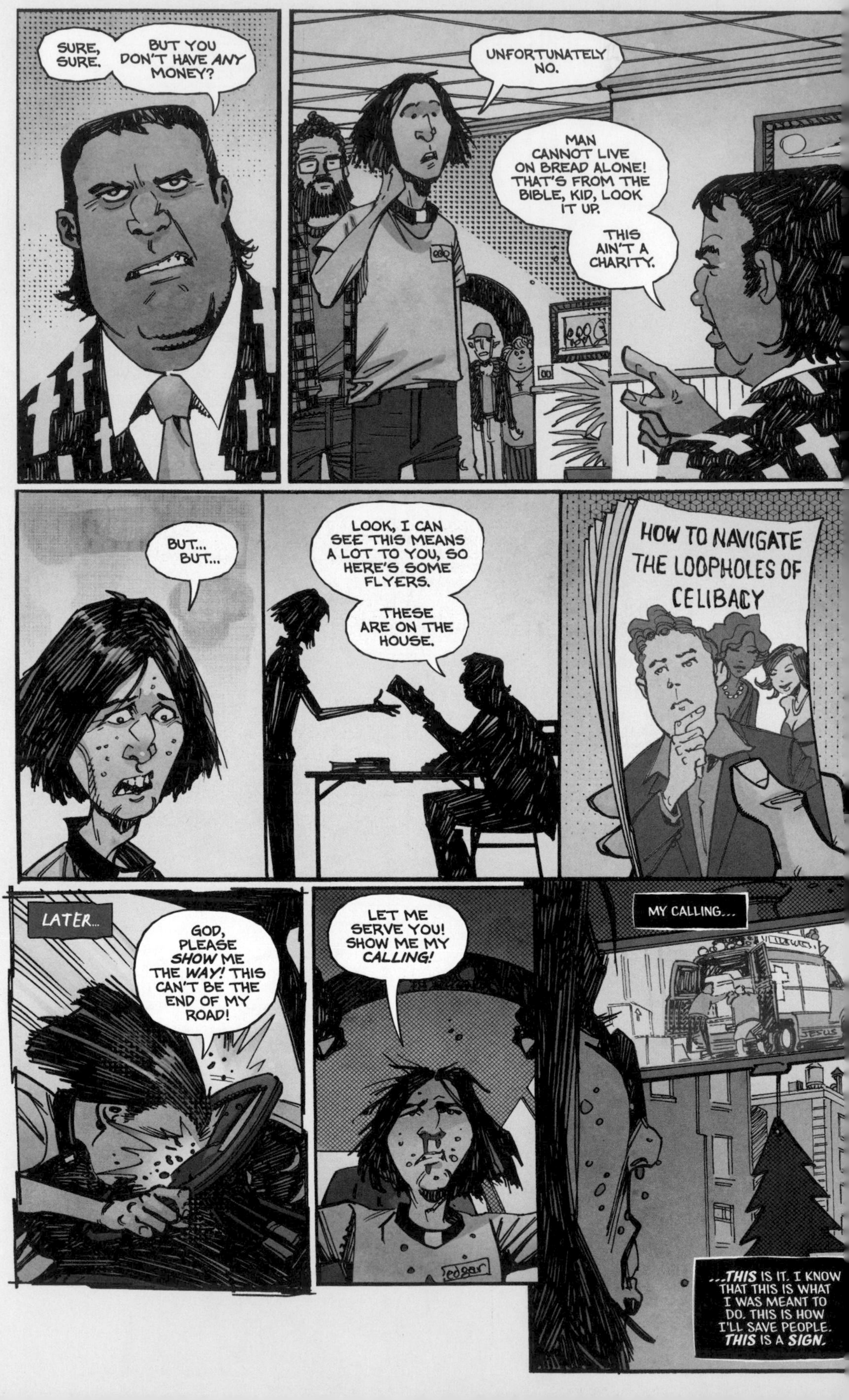
SURE, SURE.
BUT YOU DON'T HAVE ANY MONEY?
UNFORTUNATELY NO.
MAN CANNOT LIVE ON BREAD ALONE! THAT'S FROM THE BIBLE, KID, LOOK IT UP.
THIS AIN'T A CHARITY.
BUT... BUT...
LOOK, I CAN SEE THIS MEANS A LOT TO YOU, SO HERE'S SOME FLYERS.
THESE ARE ON THE HOUSE.
HOW TO NAVIGATE THE LOOPHOLES OF CELIBACY
LATER...
GOD, PLEASE SHOW ME THE WAY! THIS CAN'T BE THE END OF MY ROAD!
LET ME SERVE YOU! SHOW ME MY CALLING!
MY CALLING...
JESUS
...THIS IS IT. I KNOW THAT THIS IS WHAT I WAS MEANT TO DO. THIS IS HOW I'LL SAVE PEOPLE. THIS IS A SIGN.

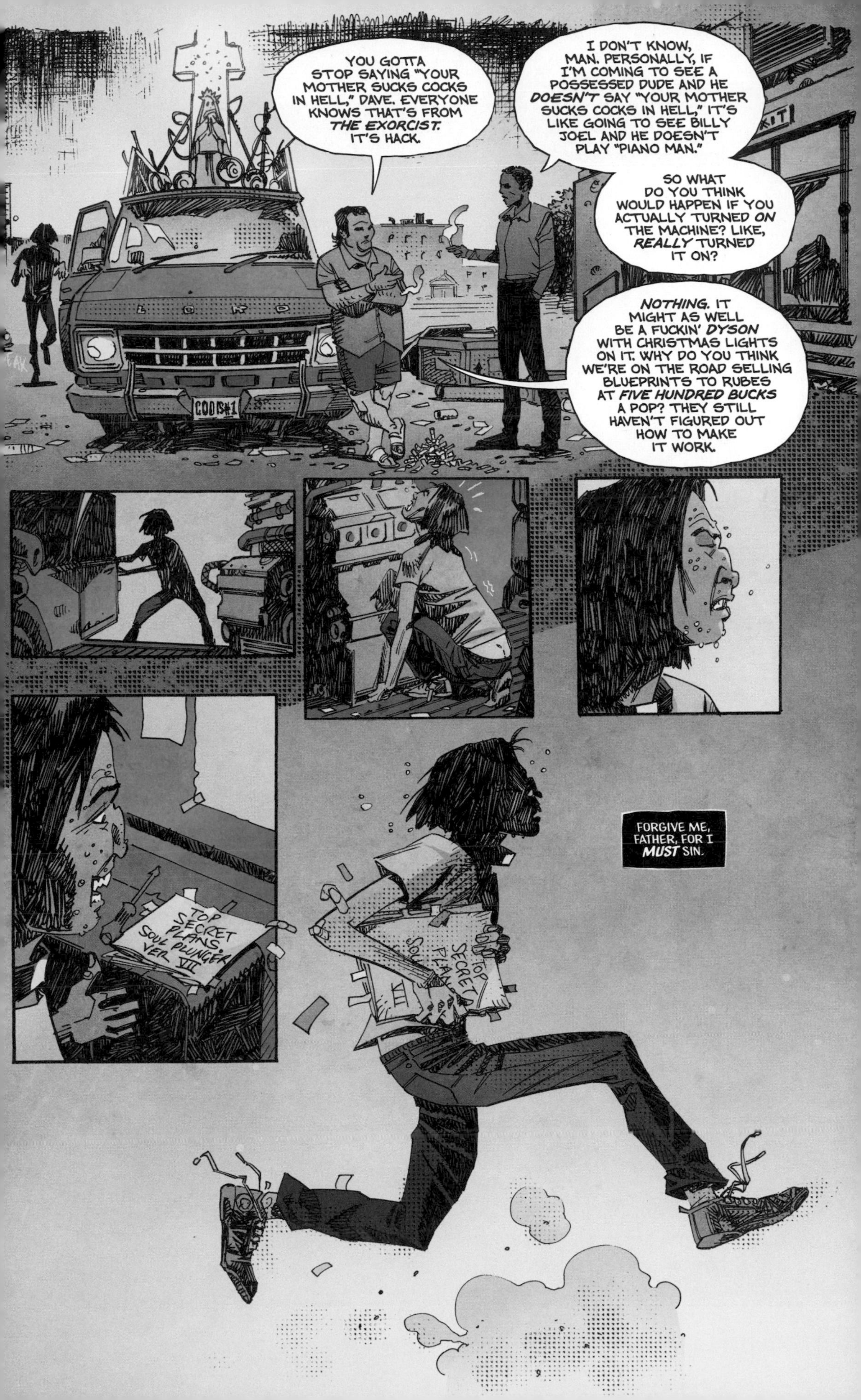
YOU GOTTA STOP SAYING "YOUR MOTHER SUCKS COCKS IN HELL," DAVE. EVERYONE KNOWS THAT'S FROM *THE EXORCIST.* IT'S HACK.
I DON'T KNOW, MAN. PERSONALLY, IF I'M COMING TO SEE A POSSESSED DUDE AND HE *DOESN'T* SAY "YOUR MOTHER SUCKS COCKS IN HELL," IT'S LIKE GOING TO SEE BILLY JOEL AND HE DOESN'T PLAY "PIANO MAN."
SO WHAT DO YOU THINK WOULD HAPPEN IF YOU ACTUALLY TURNED *ON* THE MACHINE? LIKE, *REALLY* TURNED IT ON?
NOTHING. IT MIGHT AS WELL BE A FUCKIN' *DYSON* WITH CHRISTMAS LIGHTS ON IT. WHY DO YOU THINK WE'RE ON THE ROAD SELLING BLUEPRINTS TO RUBES AT *FIVE HUNDRED BUCKS* A POP? THEY STILL HAVEN'T FIGURED OUT HOW TO MAKE IT WORK.
GOD IS #1
TOP SECRET PLANS. SOUL PLUNGER VER VII
FORGIVE ME, FATHER, FOR I *MUST* SIN.

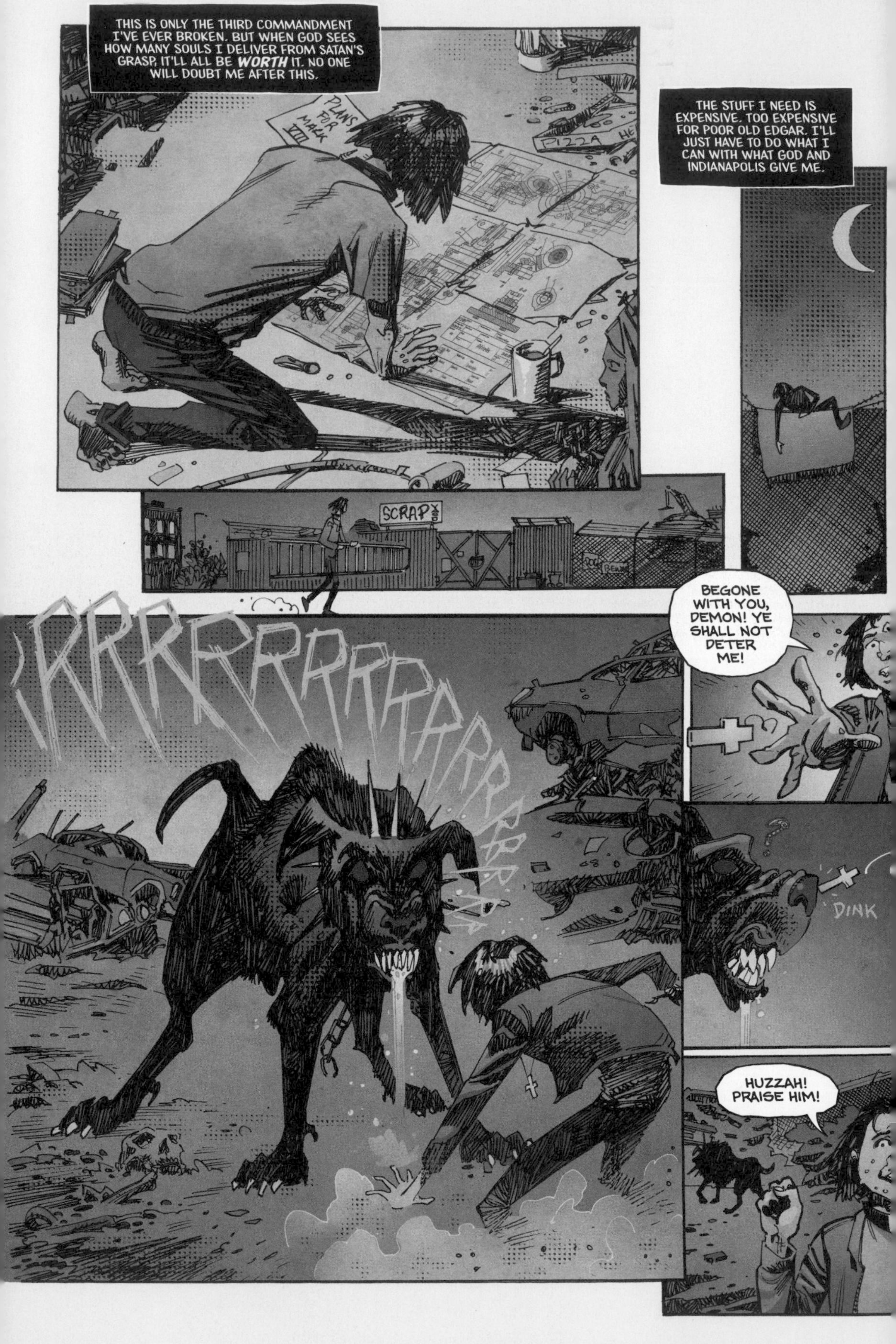
THIS IS ONLY THE THIRD COMMANDMENT I'VE EVER BROKEN. BUT WHEN GOD SEES HOW MANY SOULS I DELIVER FROM SATAN'S GRASP, IT'LL ALL BE WORTH IT. NO ONE WILL DOUBT ME AFTER THIS.
PLANS FOR MASK
PIZZA
THE STUFF I NEED IS EXPENSIVE. TOO EXPENSIVE FOR POOR OLD EDGAR. I'LL JUST HAVE TO DO WHAT I CAN WITH WHAT GOD AND INDIANAPOLIS GIVE ME.
SCRAP
RRRRRRRRRRRRRRRRRR
BEGONE WITH YOU, DEMON! YE SHALL NOT DETER ME!
DINK
HUZZAH! PRAISE HIM!

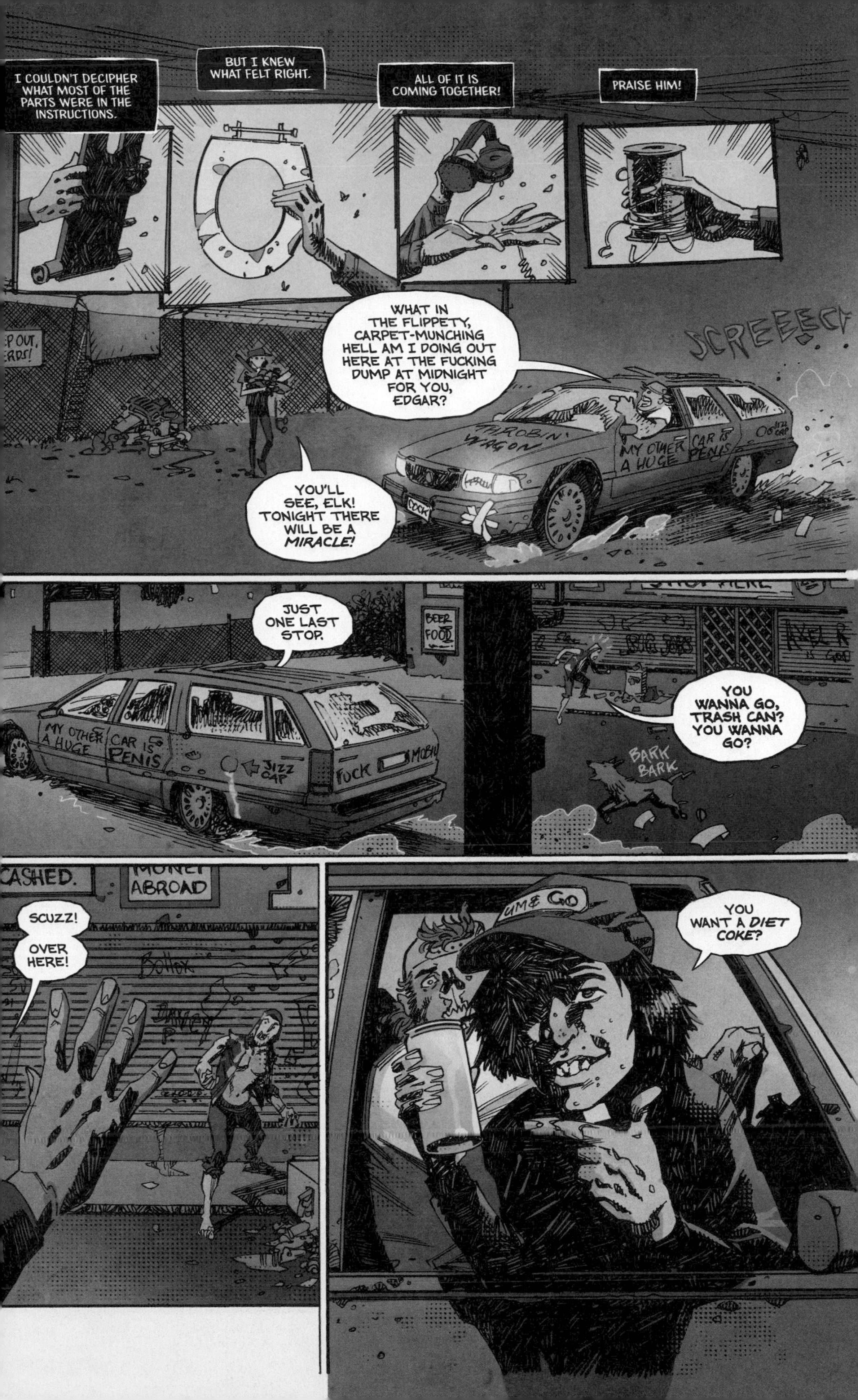
I COULDN'T DECIPHER WHAT MOST OF THE PARTS WERE IN THE INSTRUCTIONS.
BUT I KNEW WHAT FELT RIGHT.
ALL OF IT IS COMING TOGETHER!
PRAISE HIM!
WHAT IN THE FLIPPETY, CARPET-MUNCHING HELL AM I DOING OUT HERE AT THE FUCKING DUMP AT MIDNIGHT FOR YOU, EDGAR?
THROBIN' WAGON
MY OTHER CAR IS A HUGE PENIS
YOU'LL SEE, ELK! TONIGHT THERE WILL BE A MIRACLE!
JUST ONE LAST STOP.
BEER FOOD
MY OTHER CAR IS A HUGE PENIS
JIZZ CAP
FUCK
YOU WANNA GO, TRASH CAN? YOU WANNA GO?
BARK BARK
CASHED.
ABROAD
SCUZZ!
OVER HERE!
YOU WANT A DIET COKE?

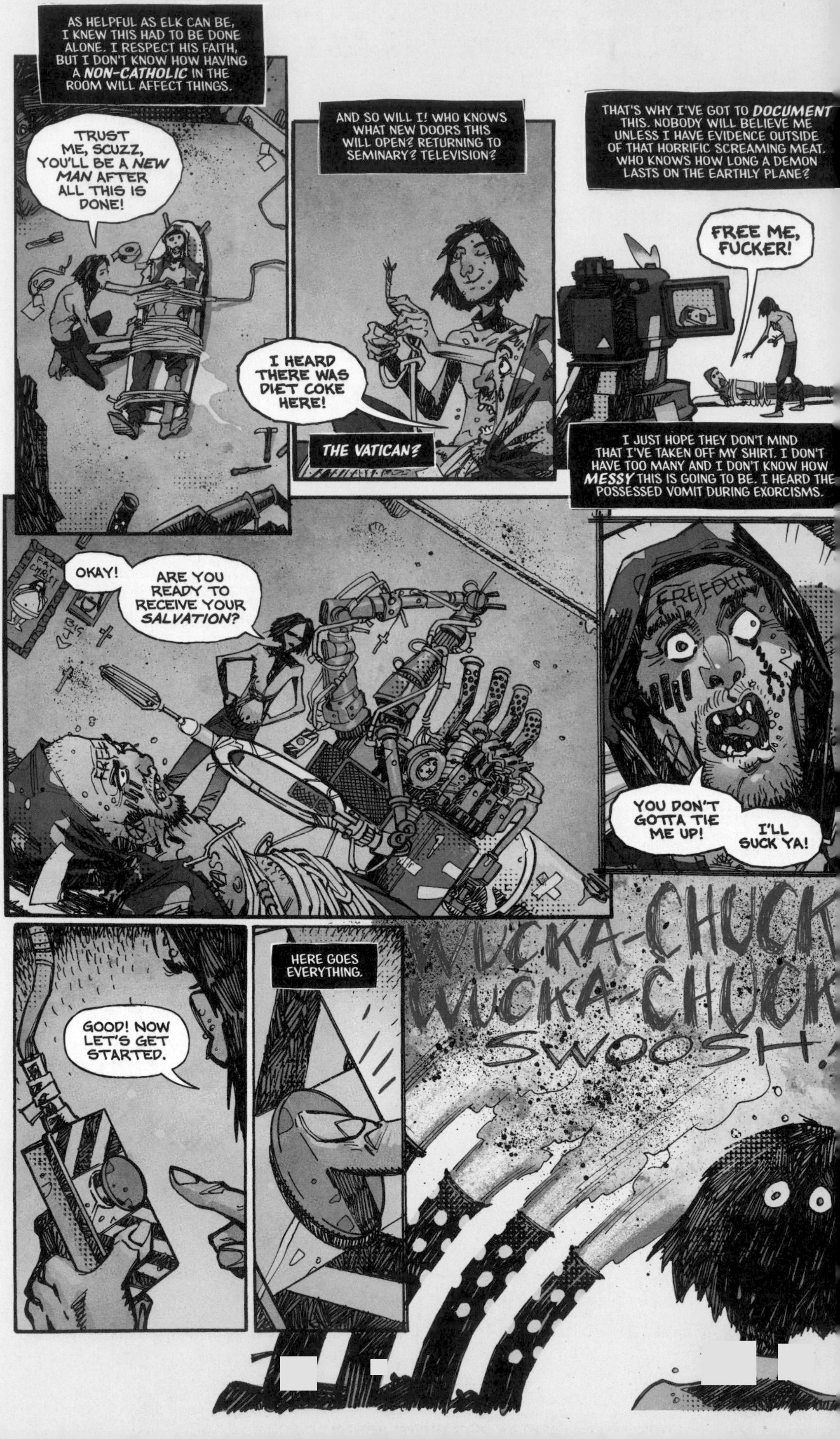
AS HELPFUL AS ELK CAN BE, I KNEW THIS HAD TO BE DONE ALONE. I RESPECT HIS FAITH, BUT I DON'T KNOW HOW HAVING A NON-CATHOLIC IN THE ROOM WILL AFFECT THINGS.
TRUST ME, SCUZZ, YOU'LL BE A NEW MAN AFTER ALL THIS IS DONE!
AND SO WILL I! WHO KNOWS WHAT NEW DOORS THIS WILL OPEN? RETURNING TO SEMINARY? TELEVISION?
I HEARD THERE WAS DIET COKE HERE!
THE VATICAN?
THAT'S WHY I'VE GOT TO DOCUMENT THIS. NOBODY WILL BELIEVE ME UNLESS I HAVE EVIDENCE OUTSIDE OF THAT HORRIFIC SCREAMING MEAT. WHO KNOWS HOW LONG A DEMON LASTS ON THE EARTHLY PLANE?
FREE ME, FUCKER!
I JUST HOPE THEY DON'T MIND THAT I'VE TAKEN OFF MY SHIRT. I DON'T HAVE TOO MANY AND I DON'T KNOW HOW MESSY THIS IS GOING TO BE. I HEARD THE POSSESSED VOMIT DURING EXORCISMS.
OKAY!
ARE YOU READY TO RECEIVE YOUR SALVATION?
YOU DON'T GOTTA TIE ME UP!
I'LL SUCK YA!
GOOD! NOW LET'S GET STARTED.
HERE GOES EVERYTHING.
WUCKA-CHUCK
WUCKA-CHUCK
SWOOSH

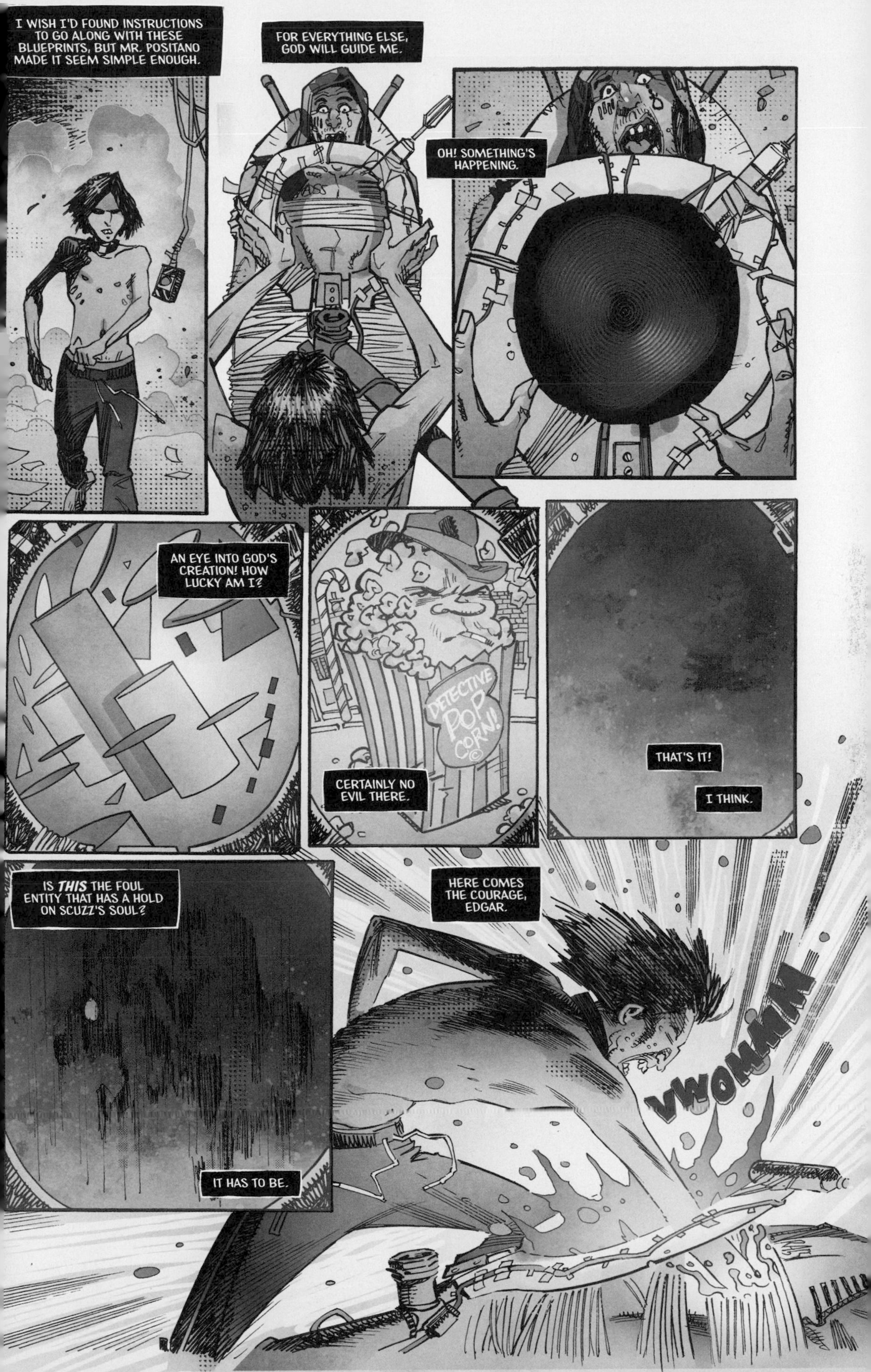
I WISH I'D FOUND INSTRUCTIONS TO GO ALONG WITH THESE BLUEPRINTS, BUT MR. POSITANO MADE IT SEEM SIMPLE ENOUGH.
FOR EVERYTHING ELSE, GOD WILL GUIDE ME.
OH! SOMETHING'S HAPPENING.
AN EYE INTO GOD'S CREATION! HOW LUCKY AM I?
DETECTIVE POP CORN! ©
CERTAINLY NO EVIL THERE.
THAT'S IT!
I THINK.
IS THIS THE FOUL ENTITY THAT HAS A HOLD ON SCUZZ'S SOUL?
IT HAS TO BE.
HERE COMES THE COURAGE, EDGAR.
VWOMMM

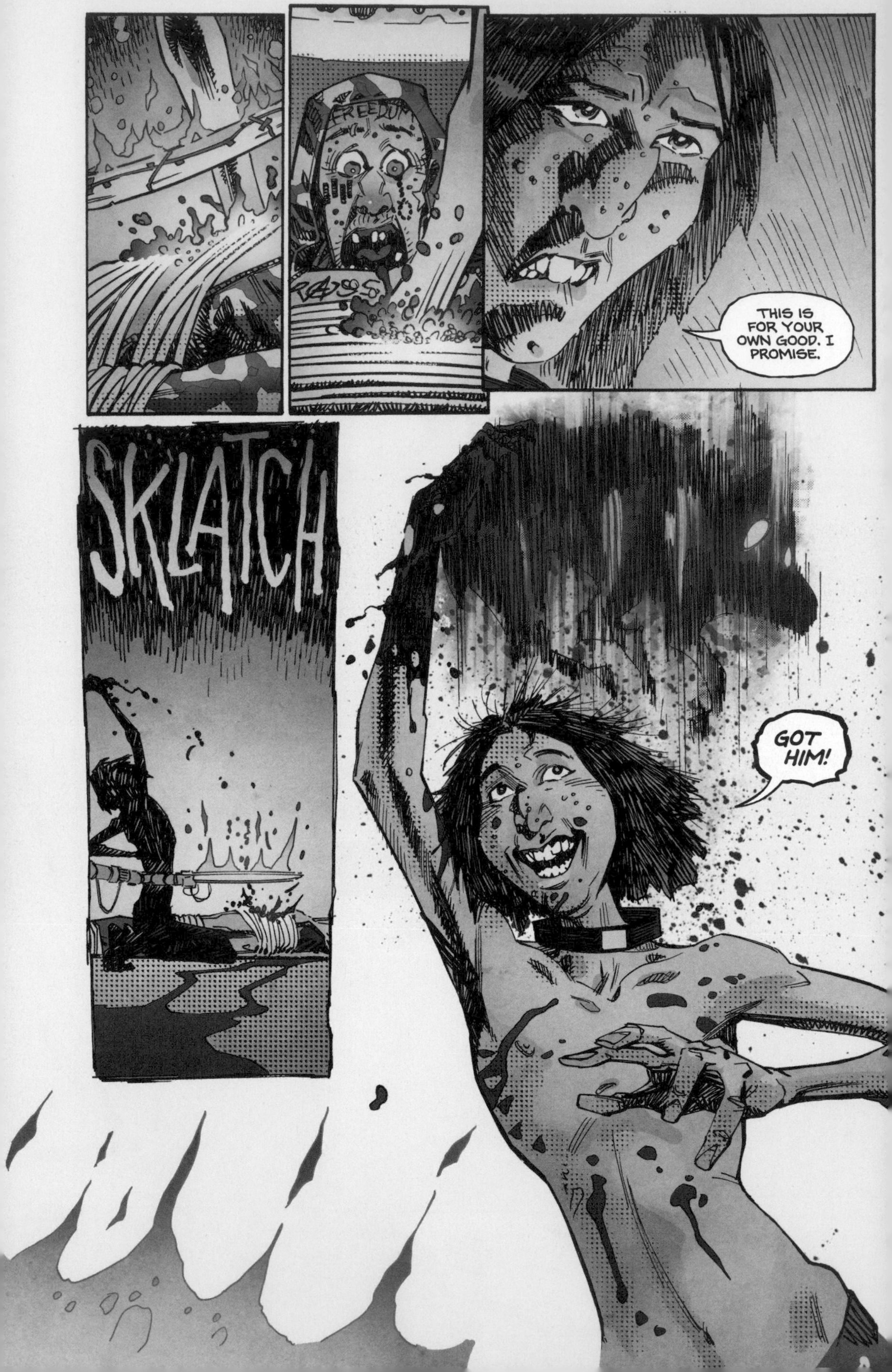
THIS IS FOR YOUR OWN GOOD. I PROMISE.
SKLATCH
GOT HIM!

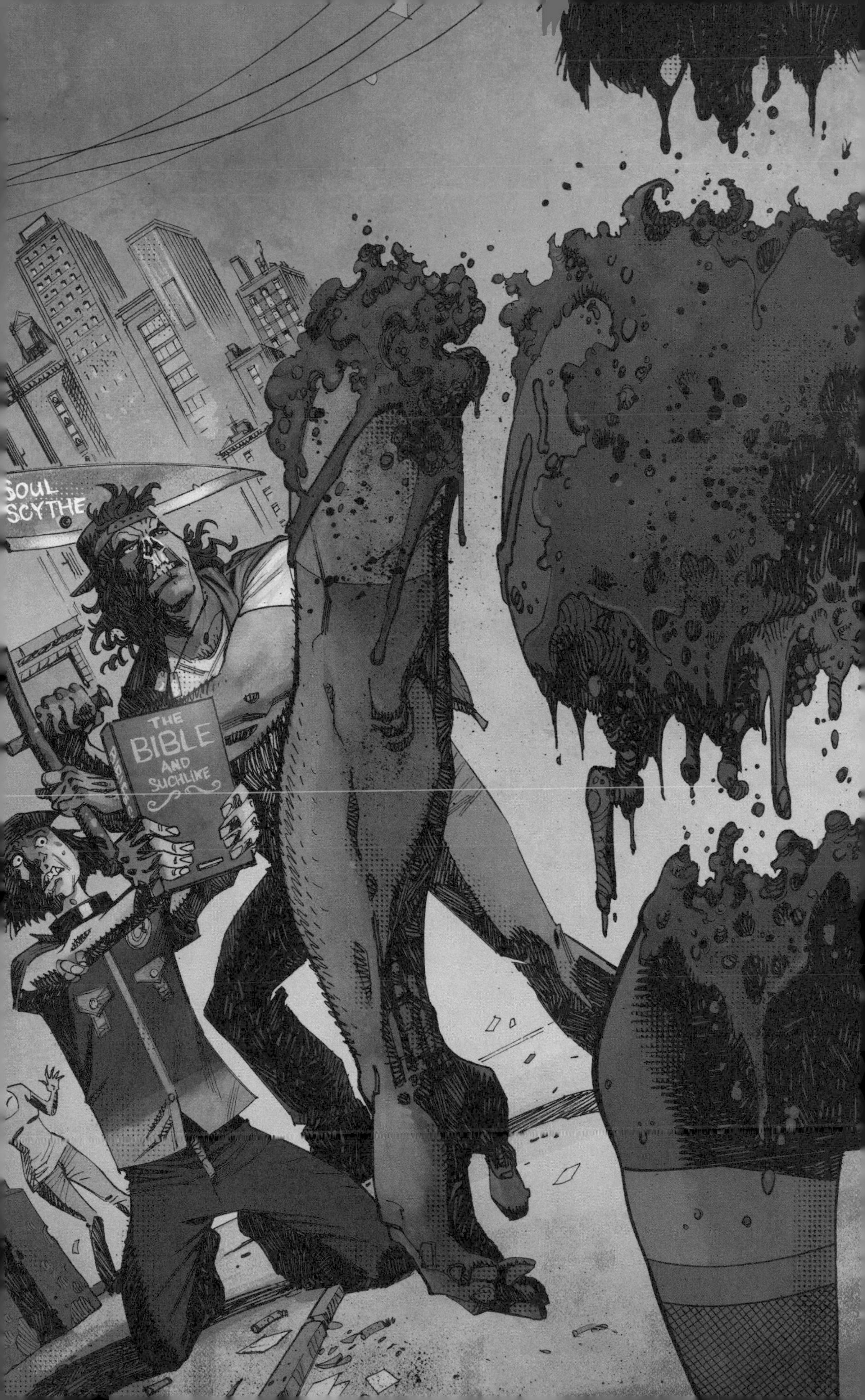
SOUL SCYTHE
THE BIBLE AND SUCHLIKE

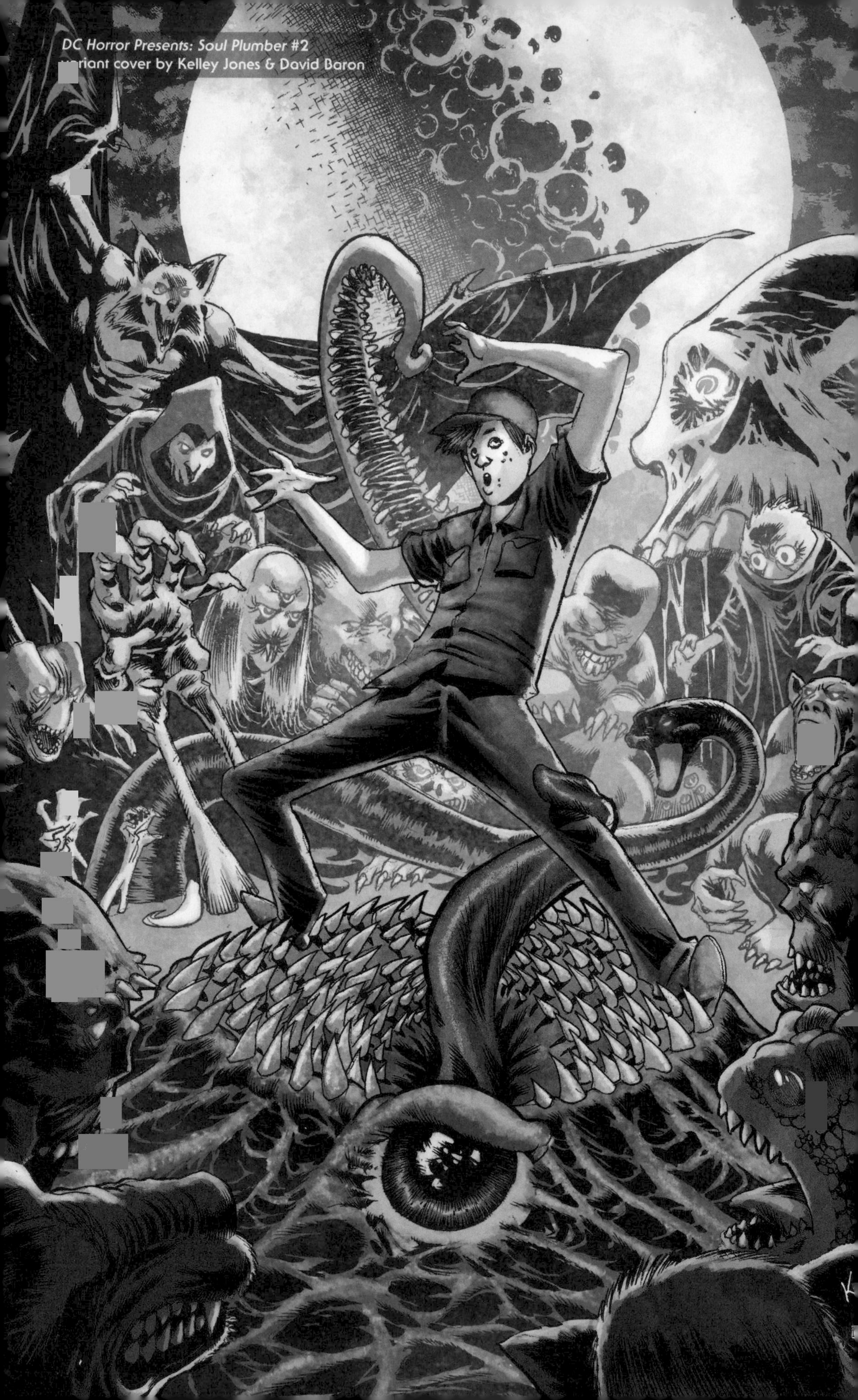

DC Horror Presents: Soul Plumber #2
variant cover by Kelley Jones & David Baron

THE PROOF IS RIGHT HERE IN FRONT OF ME.

THE DEVIL IS REAL, AND THEREFORE... GOD IS REAL.

I PROVED IT. ME, *EDGAR WIGGINS.* THE BOY NO ONE EVER BELIEVED IN.

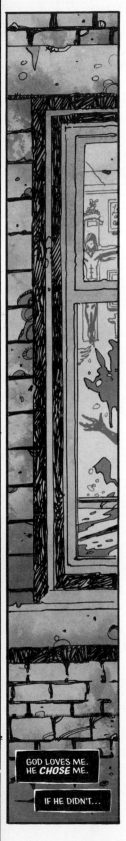

GOD LOVES ME. HE *CHOSE* ME.

IF HE DIDN'T...

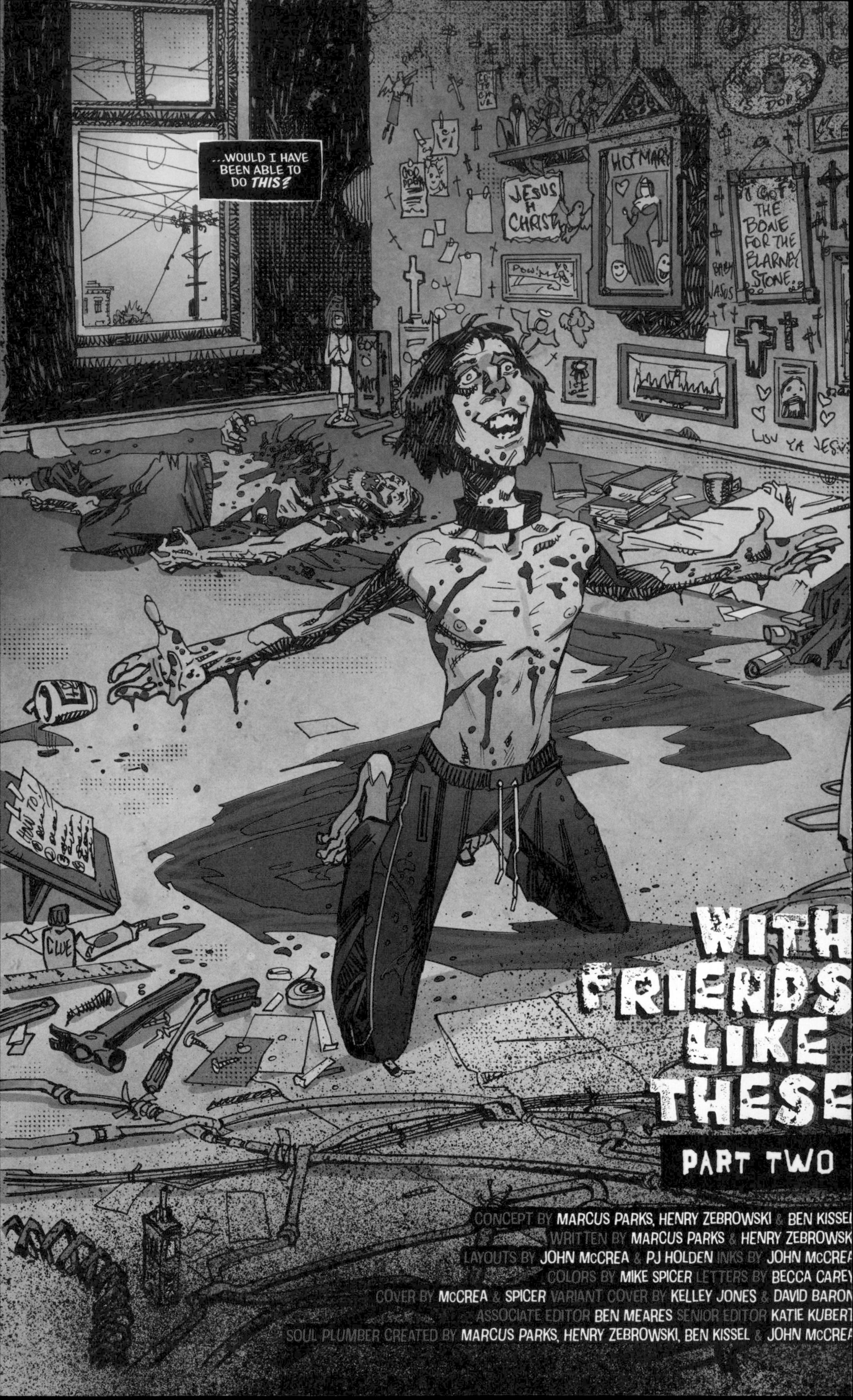

...WOULD I HAVE BEEN ABLE TO DO THIS?
JESUS H CHRIST
HOT MARY
I GOT THE BONE FOR THE BLARNEY STONE
GLUE
WITH FRIENDS LIKE THESE
PART TWO
CONCEPT BY MARCUS PARKS, HENRY ZEBROWSKI & BEN KISSEL
WRITTEN BY MARCUS PARKS & HENRY ZEBROWSKI
LAYOUTS BY JOHN McCREA & PJ HOLDEN INKS BY JOHN McCREA
COLORS BY MIKE SPICER LETTERS BY BECCA CAREY
COVER BY McCREA & SPICER VARIANT COVER BY KELLEY JONES & DAVID BARON
ASSOCIATE EDITOR BEN MEARES SENIOR EDITOR KATIE KUBERT
SOUL PLUMBER CREATED BY MARCUS PARKS, HENRY ZEBROWSKI, BEN KISSEL & JOHN McCREA

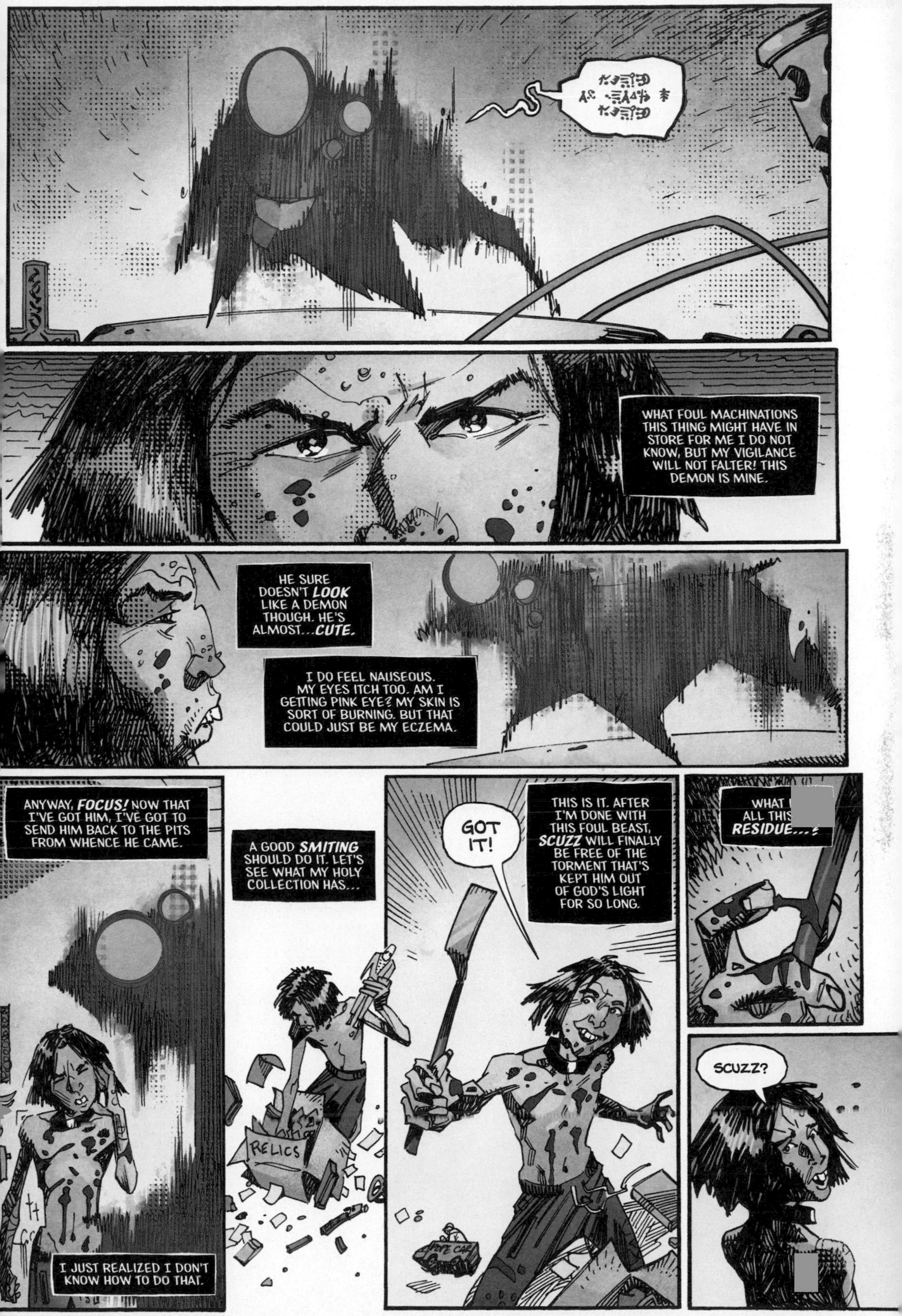

WHAT FOUL MACHINATIONS THIS THING MIGHT HAVE IN STORE FOR ME I DO NOT KNOW, BUT MY VIGILANCE WILL NOT FALTER! THIS DEMON IS MINE.
HE SURE DOESN'T LOOK LIKE A DEMON THOUGH. HE'S ALMOST...CUTE.
I DO FEEL NAUSEOUS. MY EYES ITCH TOO. AM I GETTING PINK EYE? MY SKIN IS SORT OF BURNING. BUT THAT COULD JUST BE MY ECZEMA.
ANYWAY, FOCUS! NOW THAT I'VE GOT HIM, I'VE GOT TO SEND HIM BACK TO THE PITS FROM WHENCE HE CAME.
I JUST REALIZED I DON'T KNOW HOW TO DO THAT.
A GOOD SMITING SHOULD DO IT. LET'S SEE WHAT MY HOLY COLLECTION HAS...
RELICS
GOT IT!
THIS IS IT. AFTER I'M DONE WITH THIS FOUL BEAST, SCUZZ WILL FINALLY BE FREE OF THE TORMENT THAT'S KEPT HIM OUT OF GOD'S LIGHT FOR SO LONG.
WHAT
ALL THIS
RESIDUE...
SCUZZ?

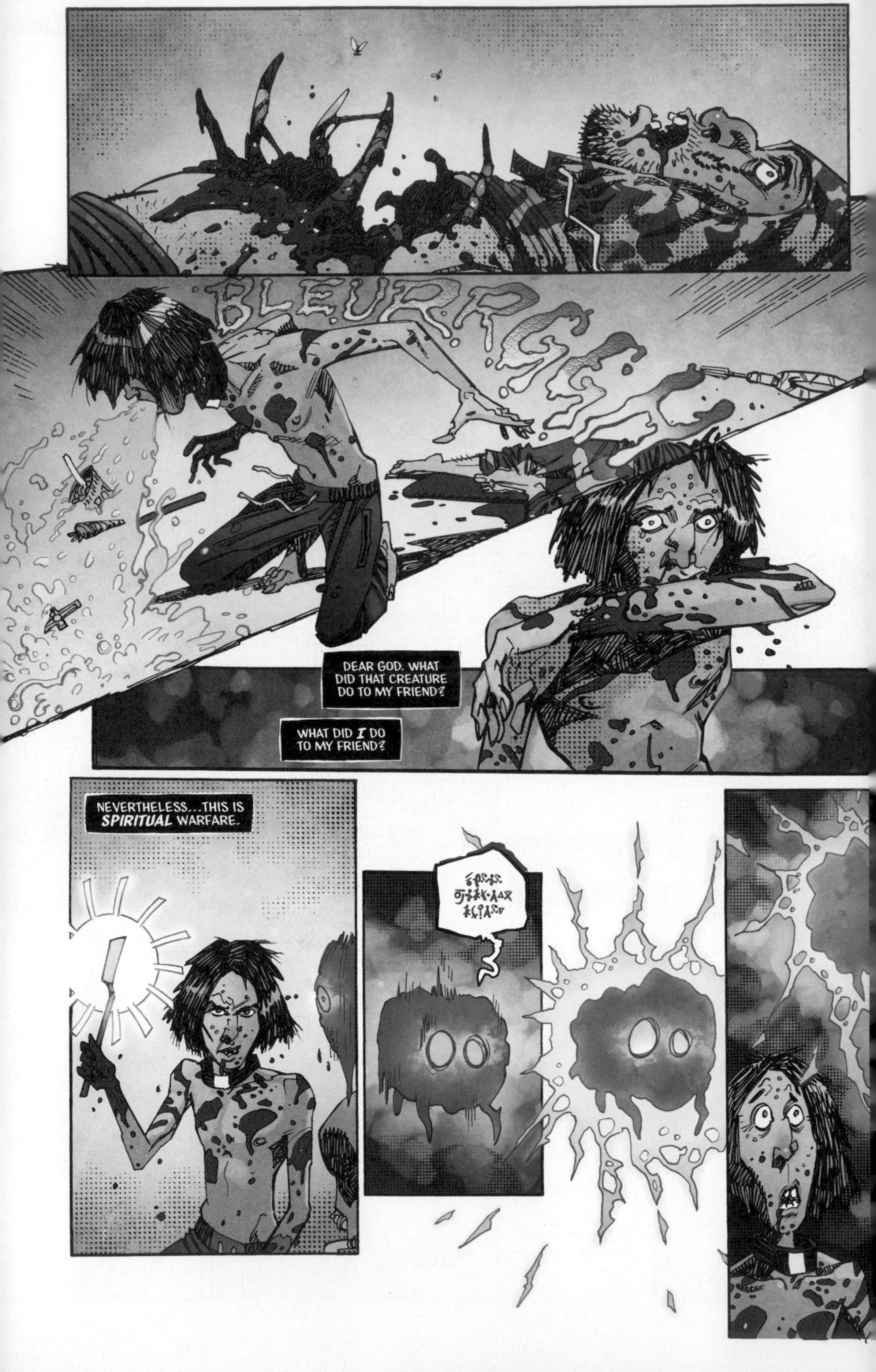
BLEURRGG
DEAR GOD. WHAT DID THAT CREATURE DO TO MY FRIEND?
WHAT DID *I* DO TO MY FRIEND?
NEVERTHELESS... THIS IS ***SPIRITUAL*** WARFARE.

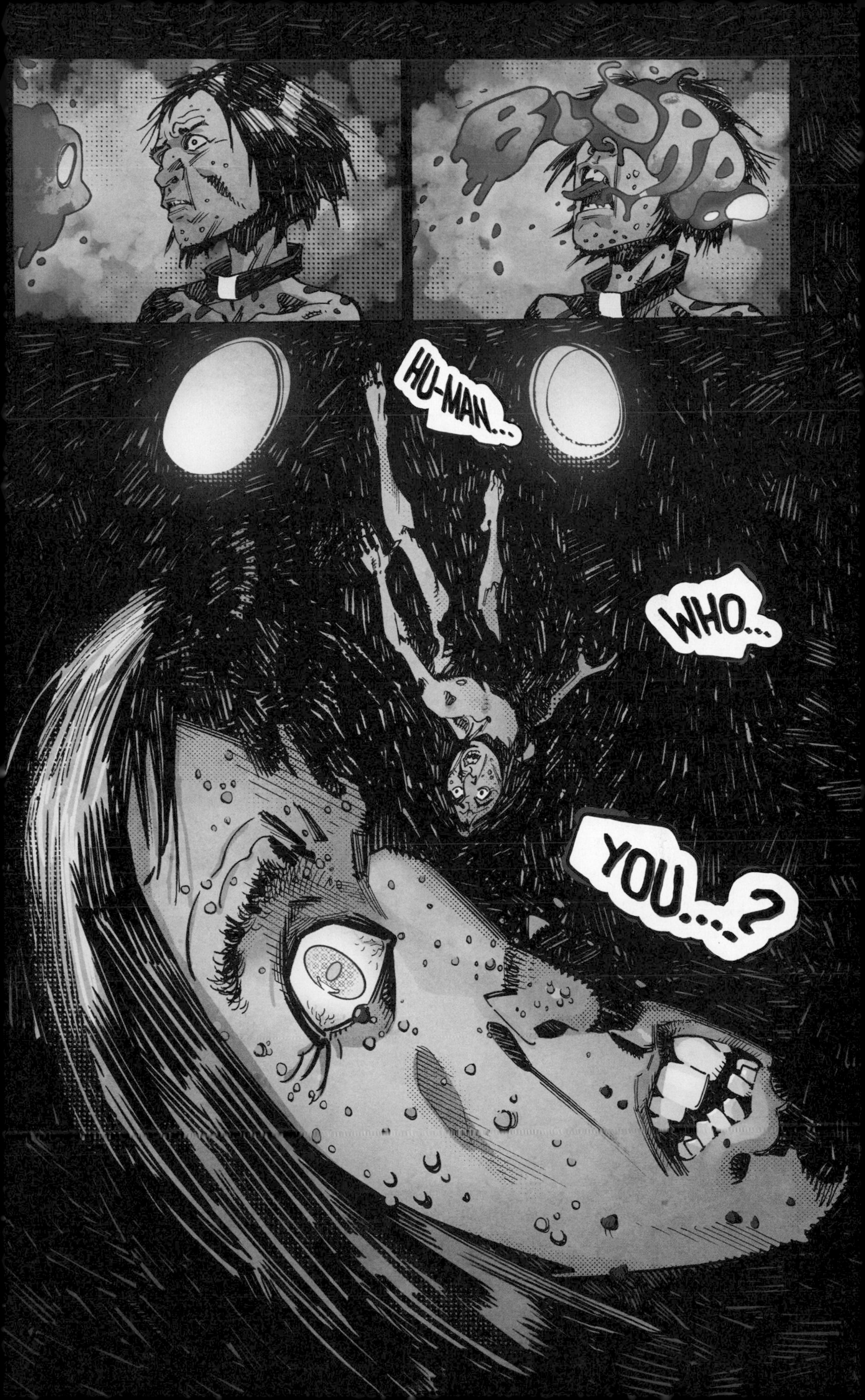
BLORP
HU-MAN...
WHO...
YOU...?

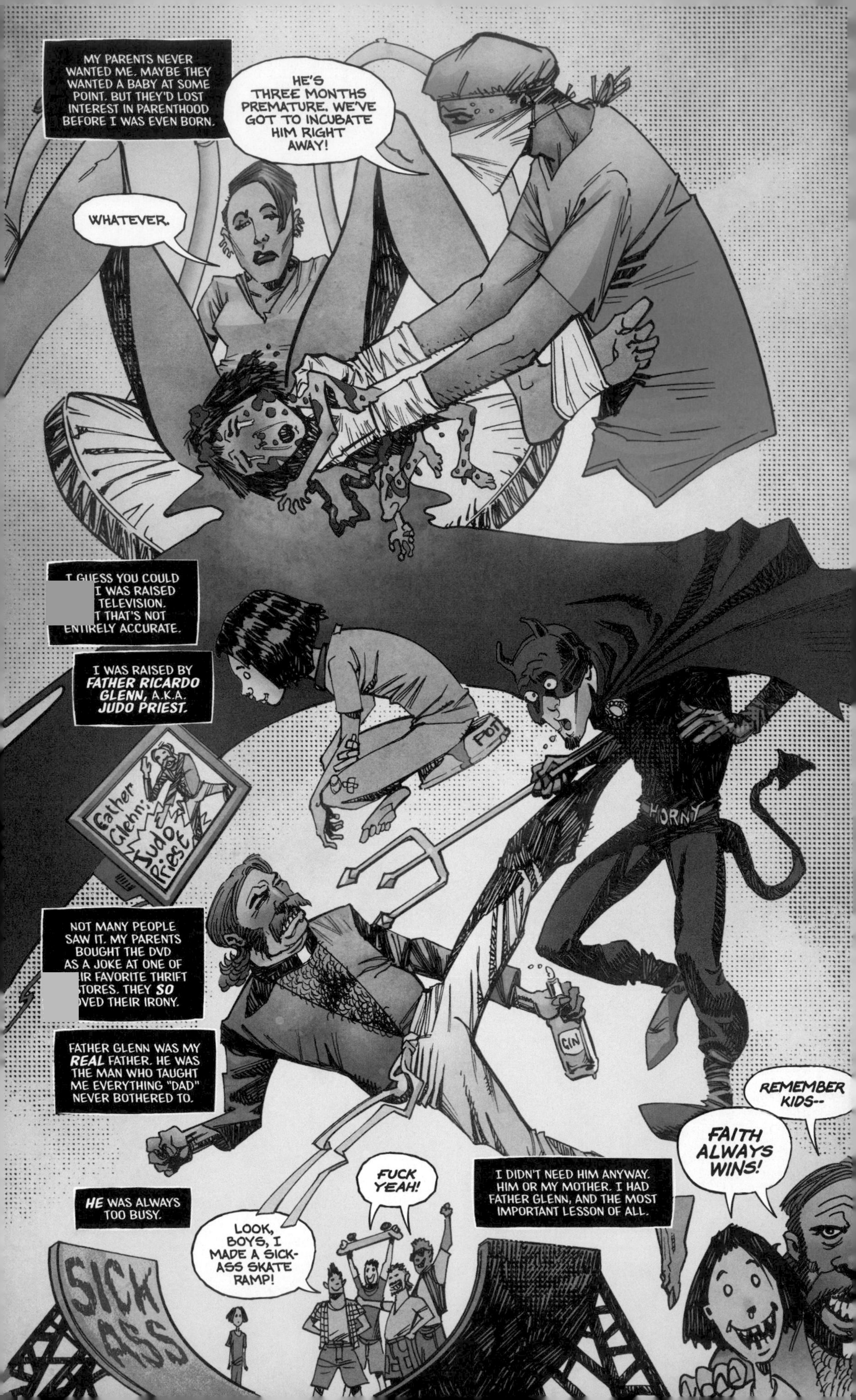
MY PARENTS NEVER WANTED ME. MAYBE THEY WANTED A BABY AT SOME POINT. BUT THEY'D LOST INTEREST IN PARENTHOOD BEFORE I WAS EVEN BORN.
HE'S THREE MONTHS PREMATURE. WE'VE GOT TO INCUBATE HIM RIGHT AWAY!
WHATEVER.
I GUESS YOU COULD
I WAS RAISED
TELEVISION.
T THAT'S NOT
ENTIRELY ACCURATE.
I WAS RAISED BY FATHER RICARDO GLENN, A.K.A. JUDO PRIEST.
Father Glenn: Judo Priest
HORNY
GIN
NOT MANY PEOPLE SAW IT. MY PARENTS BOUGHT THE DVD AS A JOKE AT ONE OF
IR FAVORITE THRIFT
STORES. THEY SO
OVED THEIR IRONY.
FATHER GLENN WAS MY REAL FATHER. HE WAS THE MAN WHO TAUGHT ME EVERYTHING "DAD" NEVER BOTHERED TO.
REMEMBER KIDS--
FAITH ALWAYS WINS!
HE WAS ALWAYS TOO BUSY.
LOOK, BOYS, I MADE A SICK-ASS SKATE RAMP!
FUCK YEAH!
I DIDN'T NEED HIM ANYWAY. HIM OR MY MOTHER. I HAD FATHER GLENN, AND THE MOST IMPORTANT LESSON OF ALL.
SICK ASS

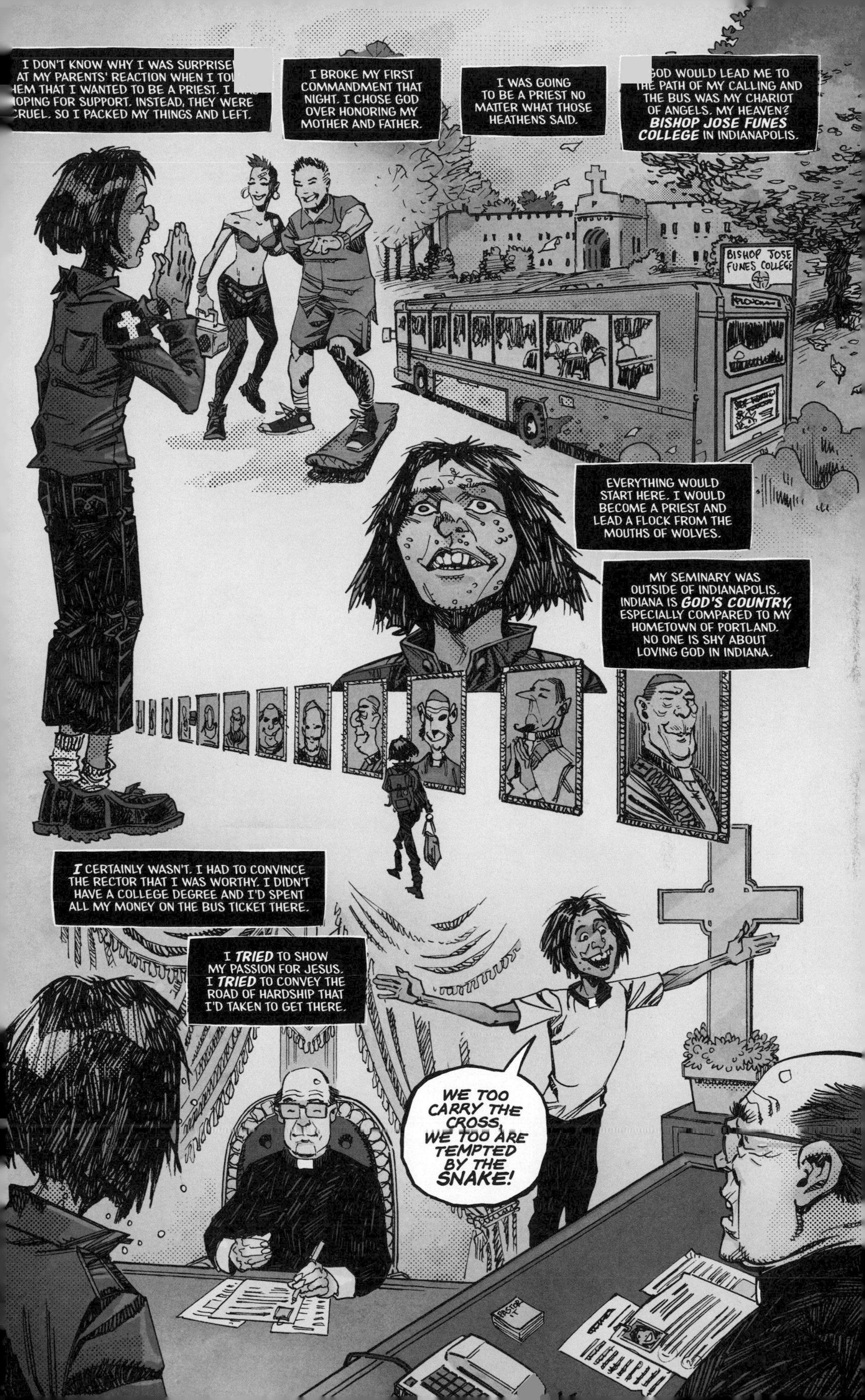

I DON'T KNOW WHY I WAS SURPRISE AT MY PARENTS' REACTION WHEN I TOL HEM THAT I WANTED TO BE A PRIEST. I WA OPING FOR SUPPORT. INSTEAD, THEY WERE CRUEL. SO I PACKED MY THINGS AND LEFT.
I BROKE MY FIRST COMMANDMENT THAT NIGHT. I CHOSE GOD OVER HONORING MY MOTHER AND FATHER.
I WAS GOING TO BE A PRIEST NO MATTER WHAT THOSE HEATHENS SAID.
GOD WOULD LEAD ME TO THE PATH OF MY CALLING AND THE BUS WAS MY CHARIOT OF ANGELS. MY HEAVEN? ***BISHOP JOSE FUNES COLLEGE*** IN INDIANAPOLIS.
BISHOP JOSE FUNES COLLEGE
EVERYTHING WOULD START HERE. I WOULD BECOME A PRIEST AND LEAD A FLOCK FROM THE MOUTHS OF WOLVES.
MY SEMINARY WAS OUTSIDE OF INDIANAPOLIS. INDIANA IS ***GOD'S COUNTRY,*** ESPECIALLY COMPARED TO MY HOMETOWN OF PORTLAND. NO ONE IS SHY ABOUT LOVING GOD IN INDIANA.
I CERTAINLY WASN'T. I HAD TO CONVINCE THE RECTOR THAT I WAS WORTHY. I DIDN'T HAVE A COLLEGE DEGREE AND I'D SPENT ALL MY MONEY ON THE BUS TICKET THERE.
I ***TRIED*** TO SHOW MY PASSION FOR JESUS. I ***TRIED*** TO CONVEY THE ROAD OF HARDSHIP THAT I'D TAKEN TO GET THERE.
WE TOO CARRY THE CROSS, WE TOO ARE TEMPTED BY THE SNAKE!

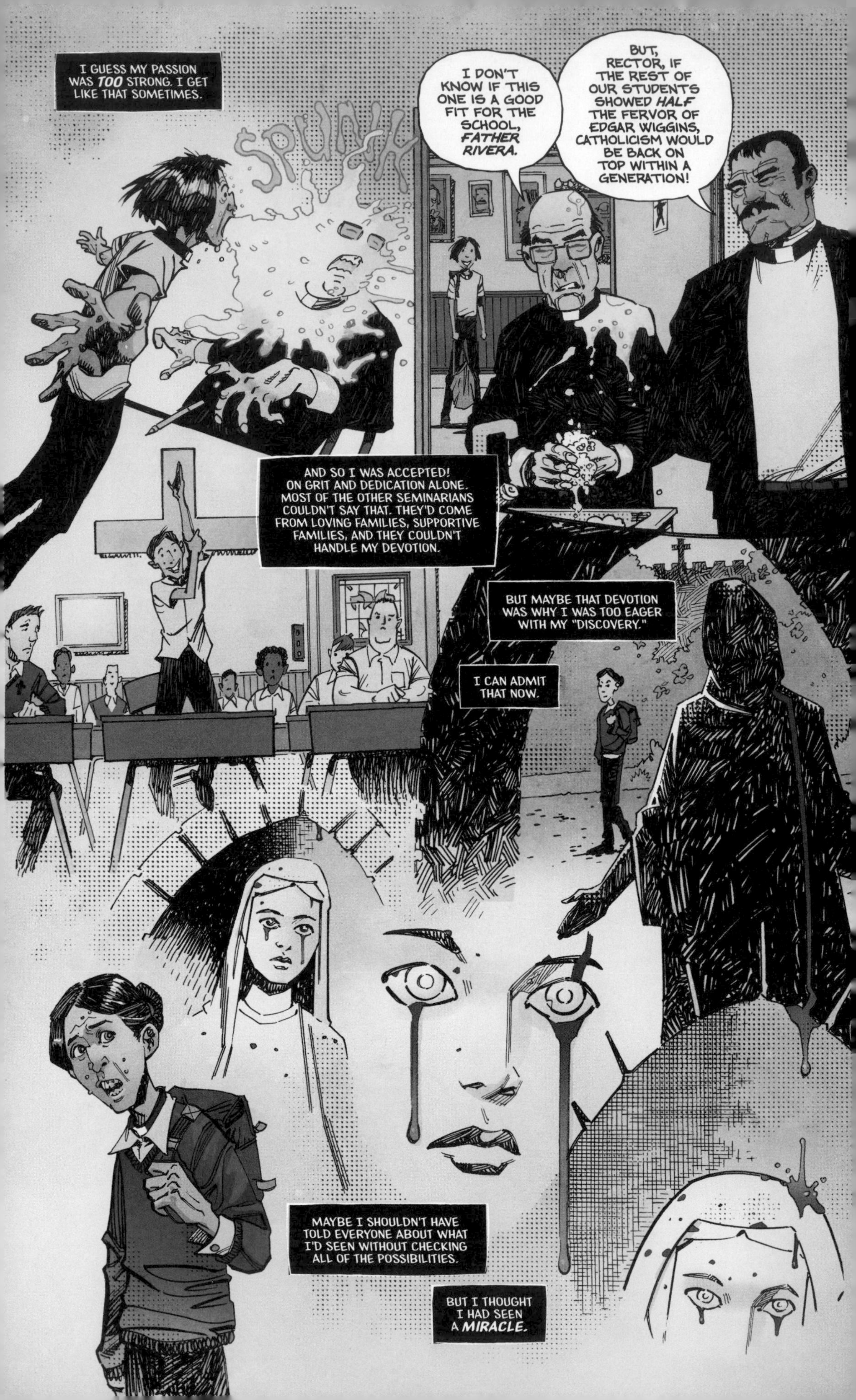
I GUESS MY PASSION WAS TOO STRONG. I GET LIKE THAT SOMETIMES.
SPUNK
I DON'T KNOW IF THIS ONE IS A GOOD FIT FOR THE SCHOOL, FATHER RIVERA.
BUT, RECTOR, IF THE REST OF OUR STUDENTS SHOWED HALF THE FERVOR OF EDGAR WIGGINS, CATHOLICISM WOULD BE BACK ON TOP WITHIN A GENERATION!
AND SO I WAS ACCEPTED! ON GRIT AND DEDICATION ALONE. MOST OF THE OTHER SEMINARIANS COULDN'T SAY THAT. THEY'D COME FROM LOVING FAMILIES, SUPPORTIVE FAMILIES, AND THEY COULDN'T HANDLE MY DEVOTION.
BUT MAYBE THAT DEVOTION WAS WHY I WAS TOO EAGER WITH MY "DISCOVERY."
I CAN ADMIT THAT NOW.
MAYBE I SHOULDN'T HAVE TOLD EVERYONE ABOUT WHAT I'D SEEN WITHOUT CHECKING ALL OF THE POSSIBILITIES.
BUT I THOUGHT I HAD SEEN A MIRACLE.

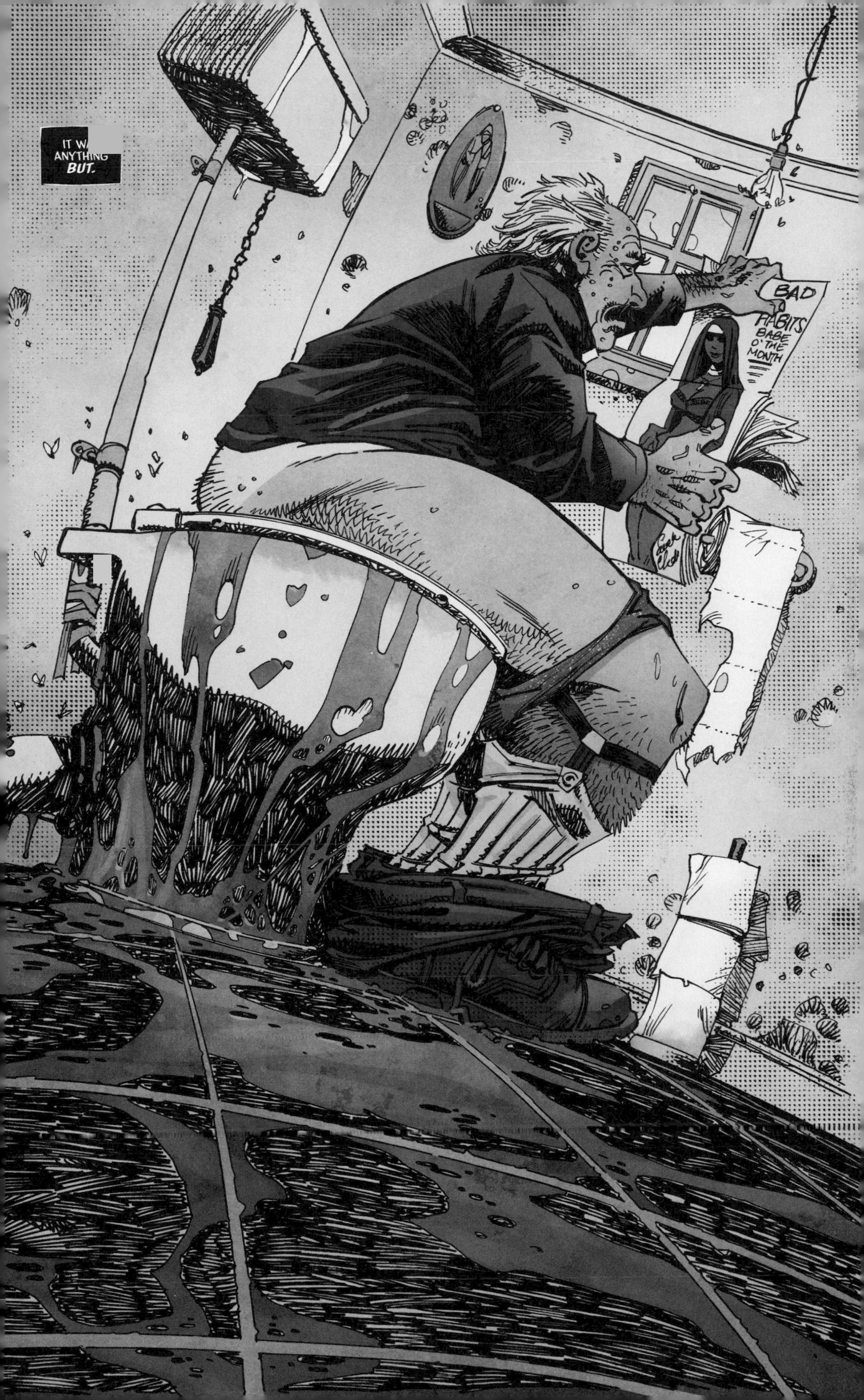
IT WA
ANYTHING
BUT.
BAD HABITS
BABE O' THE MONTH

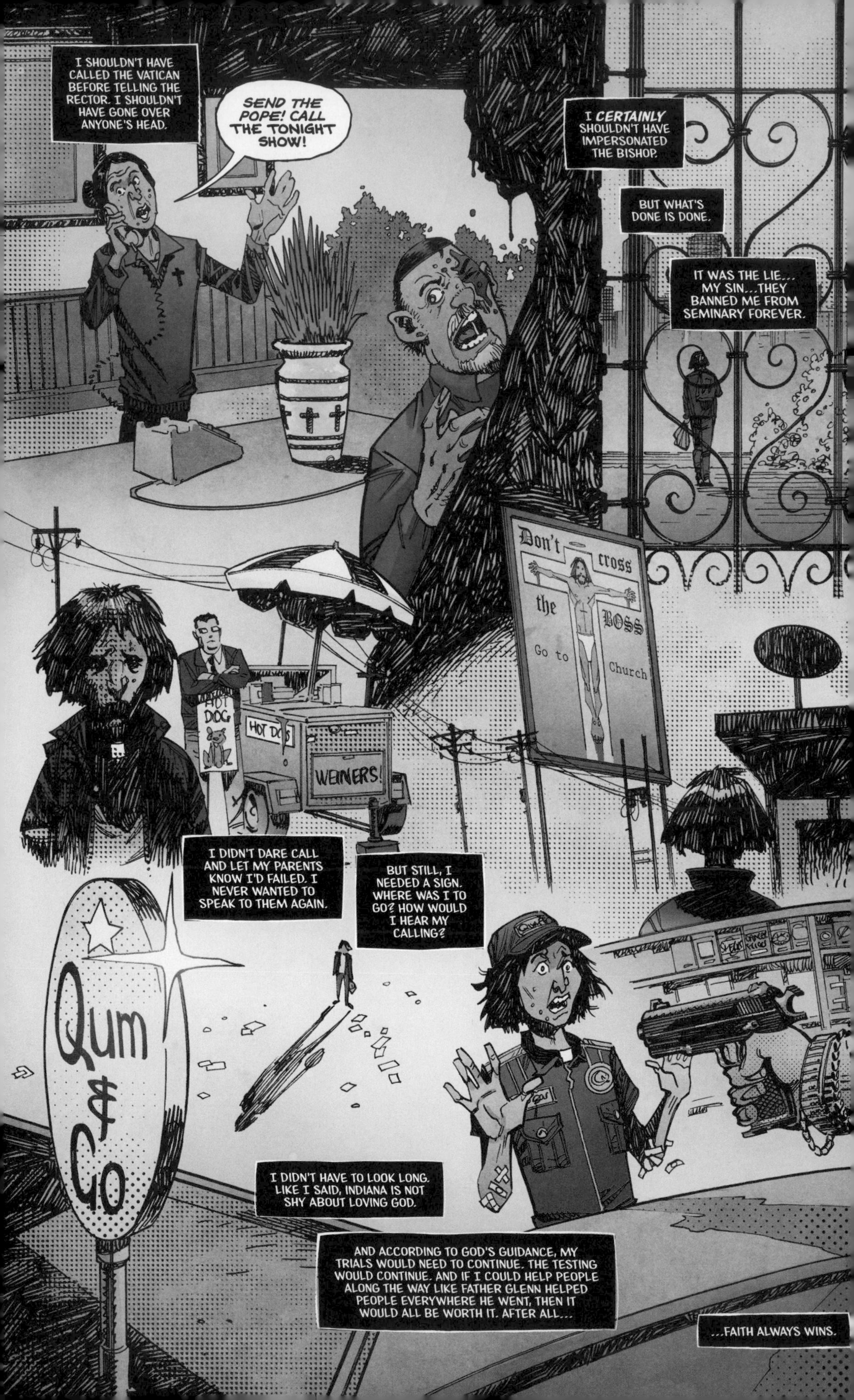
I SHOULDN'T HAVE CALLED THE VATICAN BEFORE TELLING THE RECTOR. I SHOULDN'T HAVE GONE OVER ANYONE'S HEAD.
SEND THE POPE! CALL THE TONIGHT SHOW!
I CERTAINLY SHOULDN'T HAVE IMPERSONATED THE BISHOP.
BUT WHAT'S DONE IS DONE.
IT WAS THE LIE... MY SIN...THEY BANNED ME FROM SEMINARY FOREVER.
Don't cross the BOSS
Go to Church
HOT DOG
HOT DOGS
WEINERS!
I DIDN'T DARE CALL AND LET MY PARENTS KNOW I'D FAILED. I NEVER WANTED TO SPEAK TO THEM AGAIN.
BUT STILL, I NEEDED A SIGN. WHERE WAS I TO GO? HOW WOULD I HEAR MY CALLING?
Qum & Go
I DIDN'T HAVE TO LOOK LONG. LIKE I SAID, INDIANA IS NOT SHY ABOUT LOVING GOD.
AND ACCORDING TO GOD'S GUIDANCE, MY TRIALS WOULD NEED TO CONTINUE. THE TESTING WOULD CONTINUE. AND IF I COULD HELP PEOPLE ALONG THE WAY LIKE FATHER GLENN HELPED PEOPLE EVERYWHERE HE WENT, THEN IT WOULD ALL BE WORTH IT. AFTER ALL...
...FAITH ALWAYS WINS.

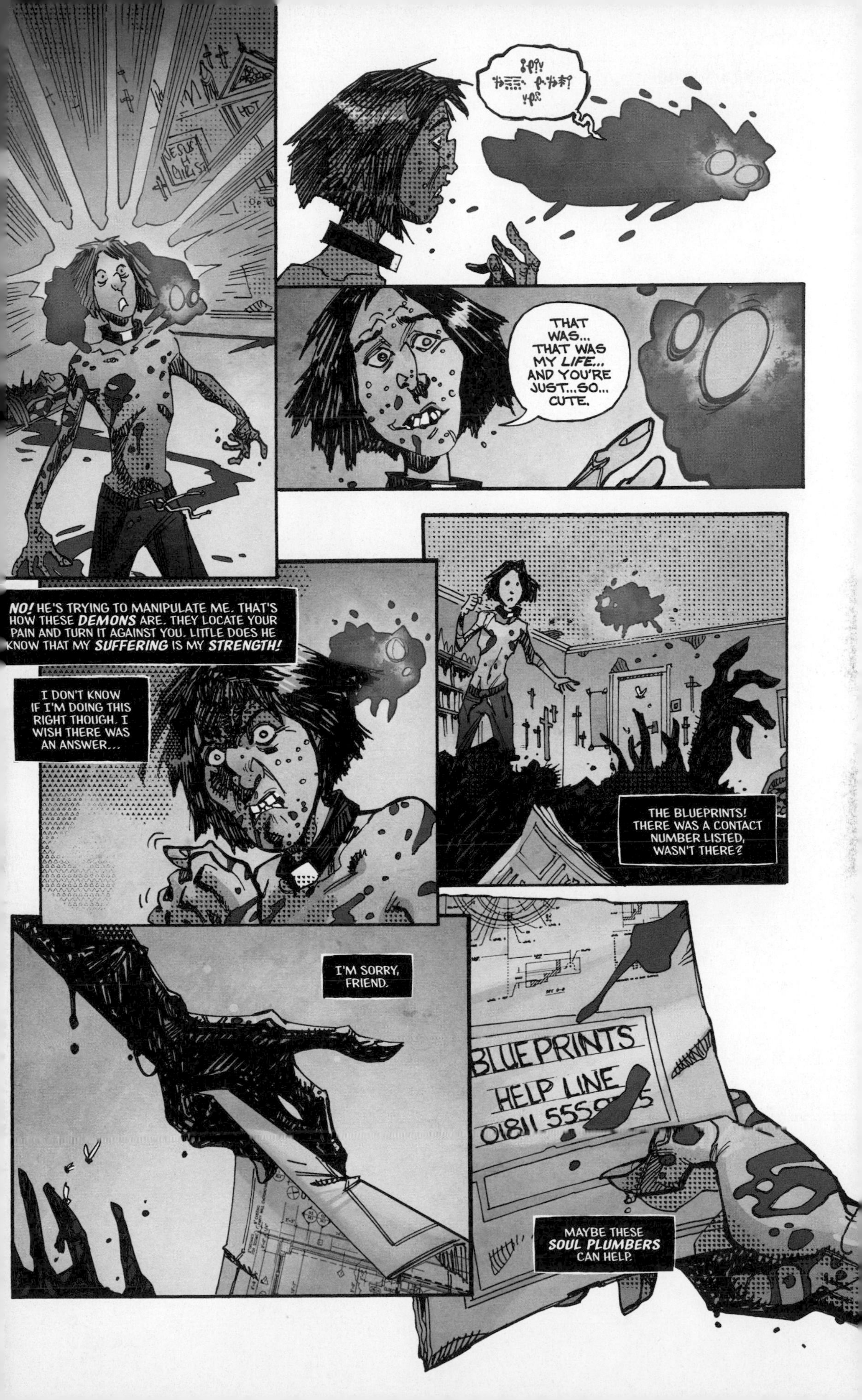
THAT WAS... THAT WAS MY LIFE... AND YOU'RE JUST...SO... CUTE.
NO! HE'S TRYING TO MANIPULATE ME. THAT'S HOW THESE DEMONS ARE. THEY LOCATE YOUR PAIN AND TURN IT AGAINST YOU. LITTLE DOES HE KNOW THAT MY SUFFERING IS MY STRENGTH!
I DON'T KNOW IF I'M DOING THIS RIGHT THOUGH. I WISH THERE WAS AN ANSWER...
THE BLUEPRINTS! THERE WAS A CONTACT NUMBER LISTED, WASN'T THERE?
I'M SORRY, FRIEND.
BLUEPRINTS
HELP LINE
MAYBE THESE SOUL PLUMBERS CAN HELP.

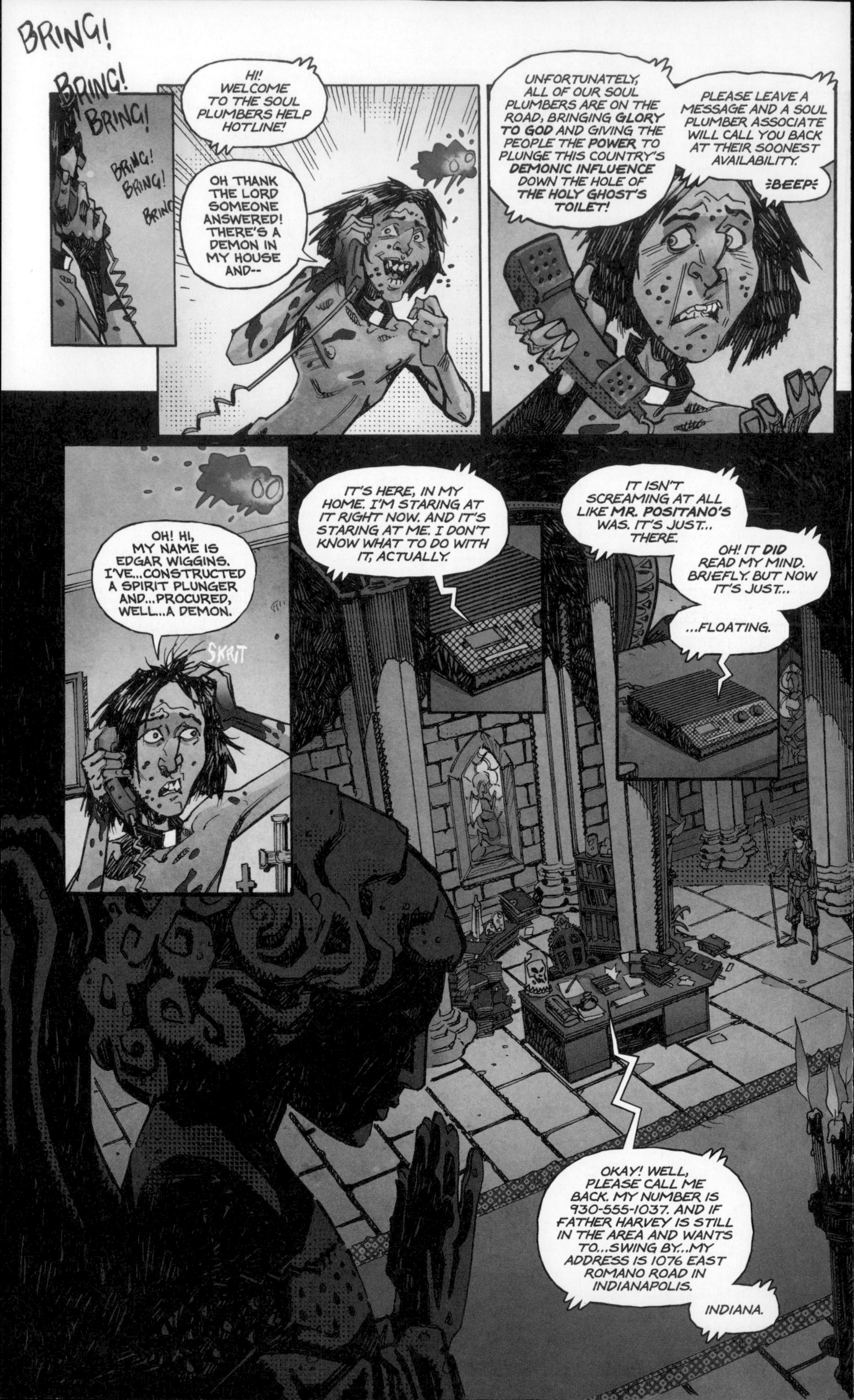
BRING!
BRING!
BRING!
BRING!
BRING!
BRING
HI! WELCOME TO THE SOUL PLUMBERS HELP HOTLINE!
OH THANK THE LORD SOMEONE ANSWERED! THERE'S A DEMON IN MY HOUSE AND--
UNFORTUNATELY, ALL OF OUR SOUL PLUMBERS ARE ON THE ROAD, BRINGING GLORY TO GOD AND GIVING THE PEOPLE THE POWER TO PLUNGE THIS COUNTRY'S DEMONIC INFLUENCE DOWN THE HOLE OF THE HOLY GHOST'S TOILET!
PLEASE LEAVE A MESSAGE AND A SOUL PLUMBER ASSOCIATE WILL CALL YOU BACK AT THEIR SOONEST AVAILABILITY.
BEEP
OH! HI, MY NAME IS EDGAR WIGGINS. I'VE...CONSTRUCTED A SPIRIT PLUNGER AND...PROCURED, WELL...A DEMON.
SKRIT
IT'S HERE, IN MY HOME. I'M STARING AT IT RIGHT NOW. AND IT'S STARING AT ME. I DON'T KNOW WHAT TO DO WITH IT, ACTUALLY.
IT ISN'T SCREAMING AT ALL LIKE MR. POSITANO'S WAS. IT'S JUST... THERE.
OH! IT DID READ MY MIND. BRIEFLY. BUT NOW IT'S JUST...
...FLOATING.
OKAY! WELL, PLEASE CALL ME BACK. MY NUMBER IS 930-555-1037. AND IF FATHER HARVEY IS STILL IN THE AREA AND WANTS TO...SWING BY...MY ADDRESS IS 1076 EAST ROMANO ROAD IN INDIANAPOLIS.
INDIANA.

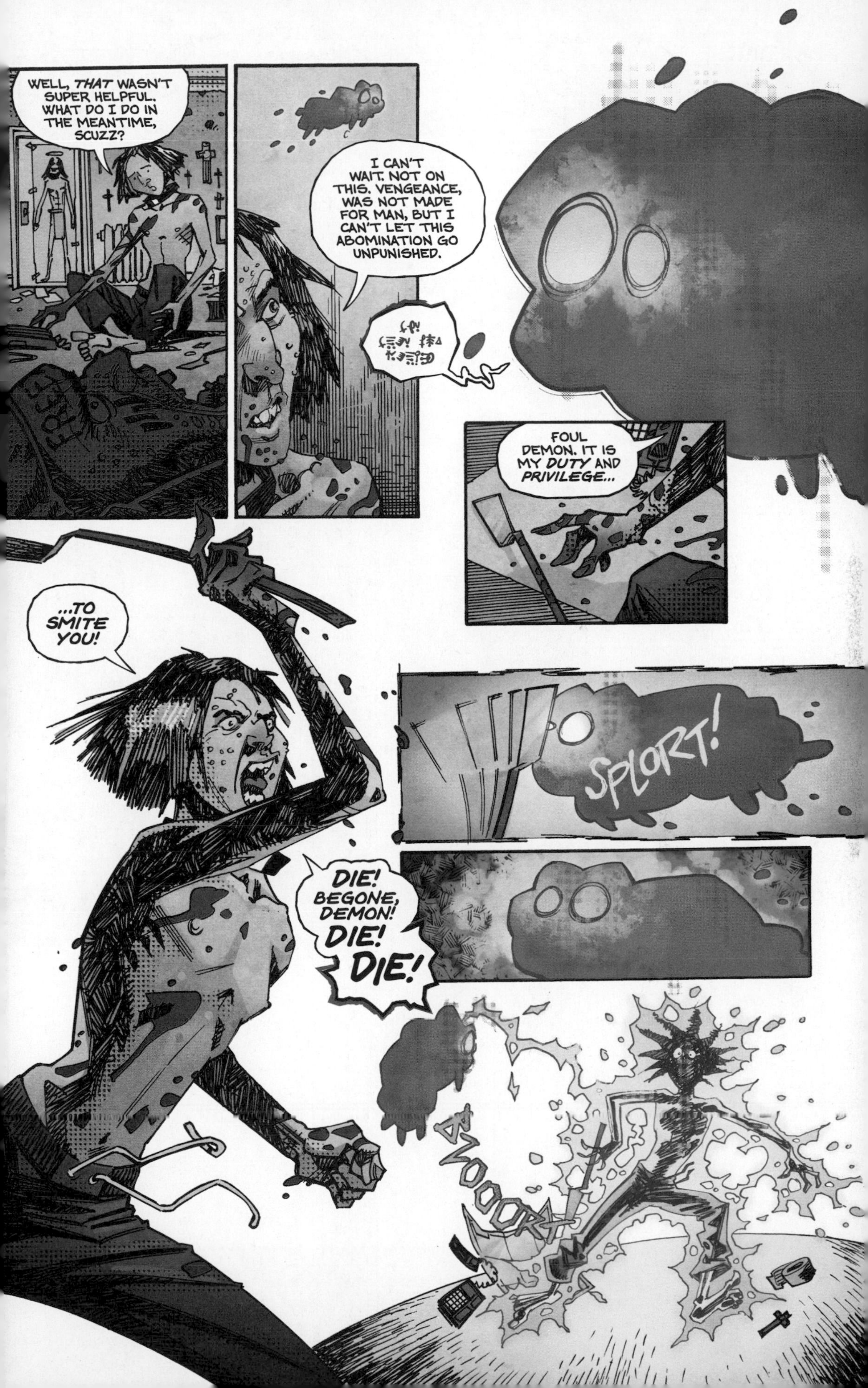
WELL, THAT WASN'T SUPER HELPFUL. WHAT DO I DO IN THE MEANTIME, SCUZZ?
I CAN'T WAIT. NOT ON THIS. VENGEANCE, WAS NOT MADE FOR MAN, BUT I CAN'T LET THIS ABOMINATION GO UNPUNISHED.
FOUL DEMON. IT IS MY DUTY AND PRIVILEGE...
...TO SMITE YOU!
SPLORT!
DIE! BEGONE, DEMON! DIE! DIE!
BLOOORT

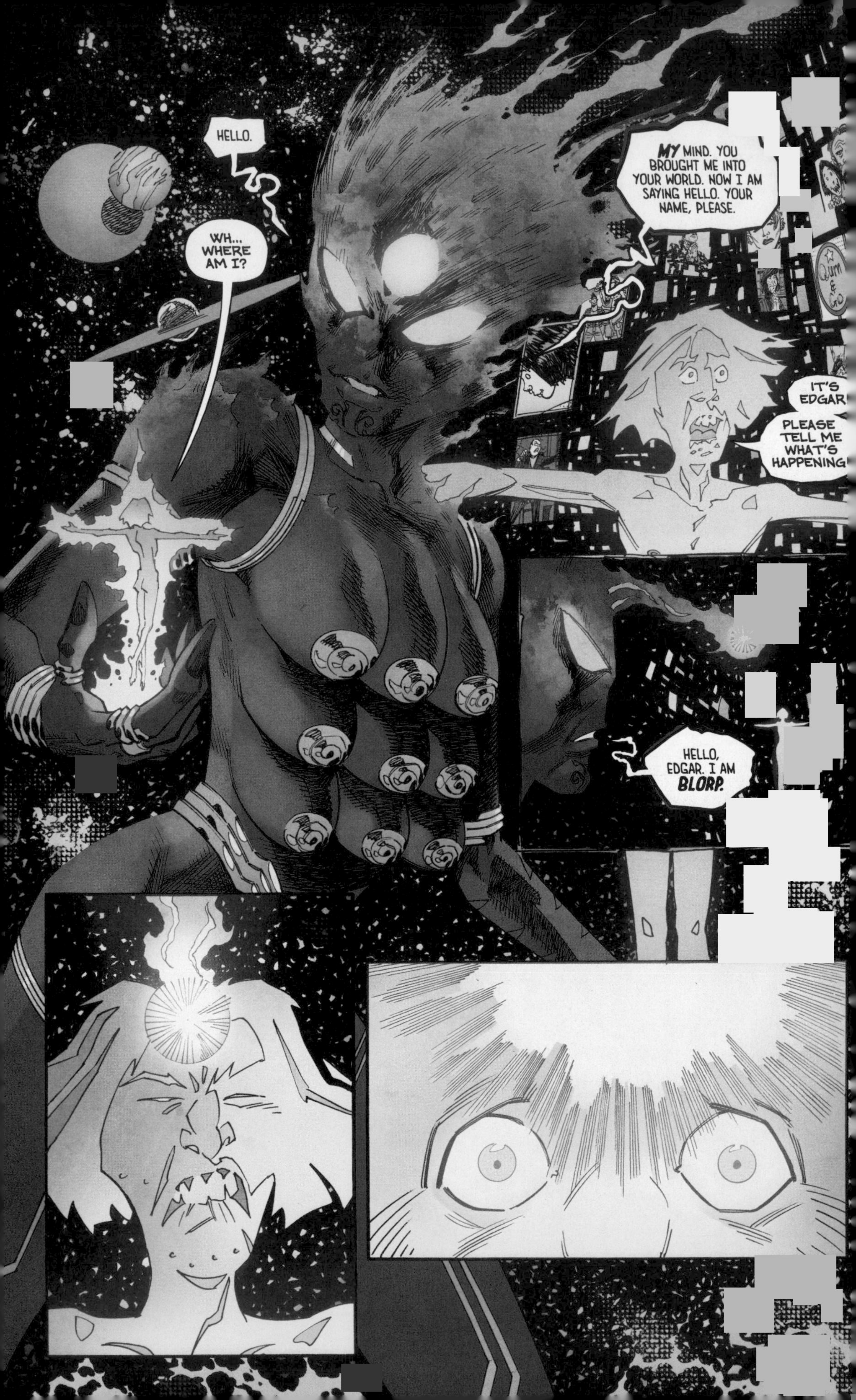
HELLO.
WH... WHERE AM I?
MY MIND. YOU BROUGHT ME INTO YOUR WORLD. NOW I AM SAYING HELLO. YOUR NAME, PLEASE.
IT'S EDGAR
PLEASE TELL ME WHAT'S HAPPENING
HELLO, EDGAR. I AM BLORP.

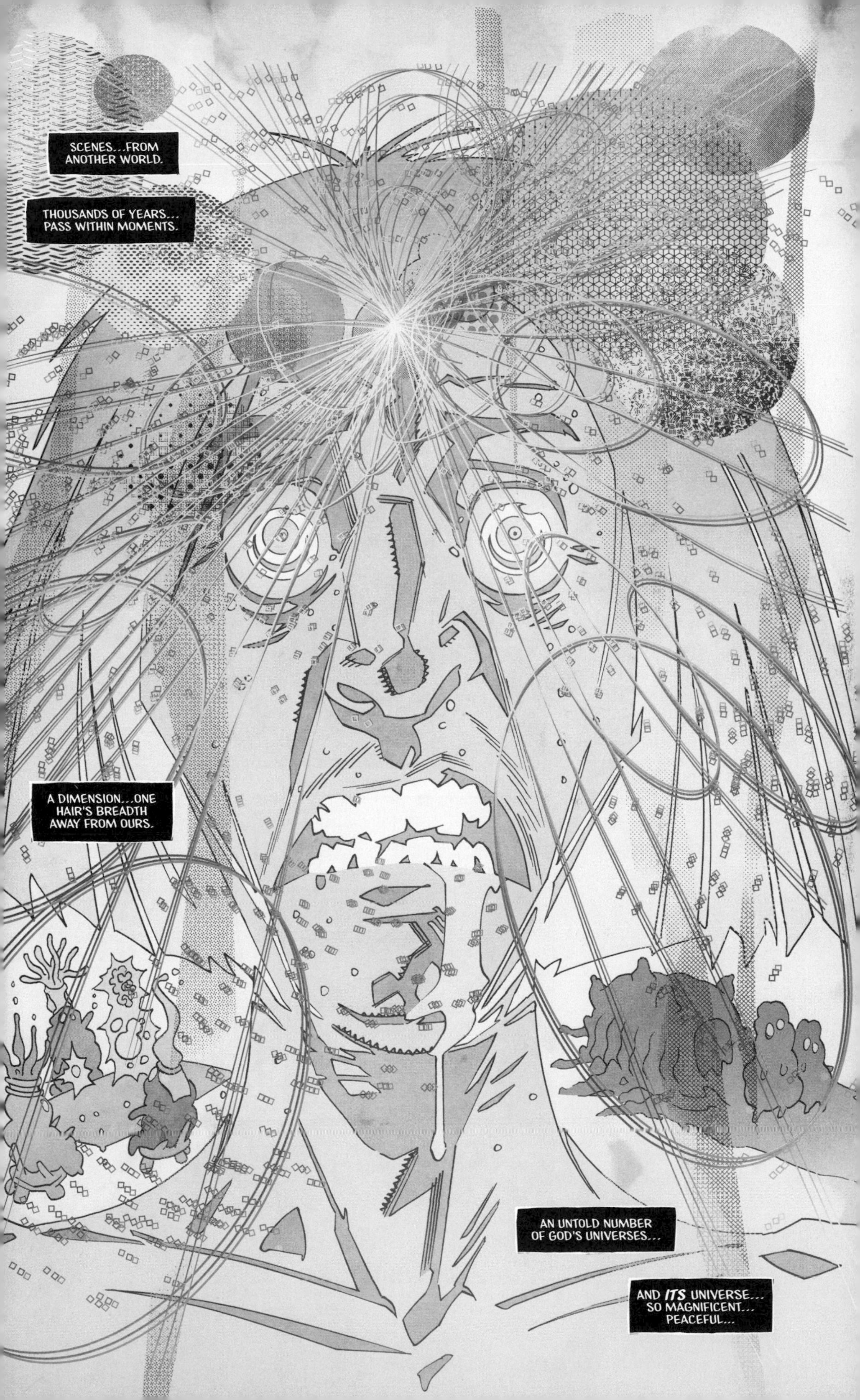
SCENES...FROM ANOTHER WORLD.
THOUSANDS OF YEARS... PASS WITHIN MOMENTS.
A DIMENSION...ONE HAIR'S BREADTH AWAY FROM OURS.
AN UNTOLD NUMBER OF GOD'S UNIVERSES...
AND ITS UNIVERSE... SO MAGNIFICENT... PEACEFUL...

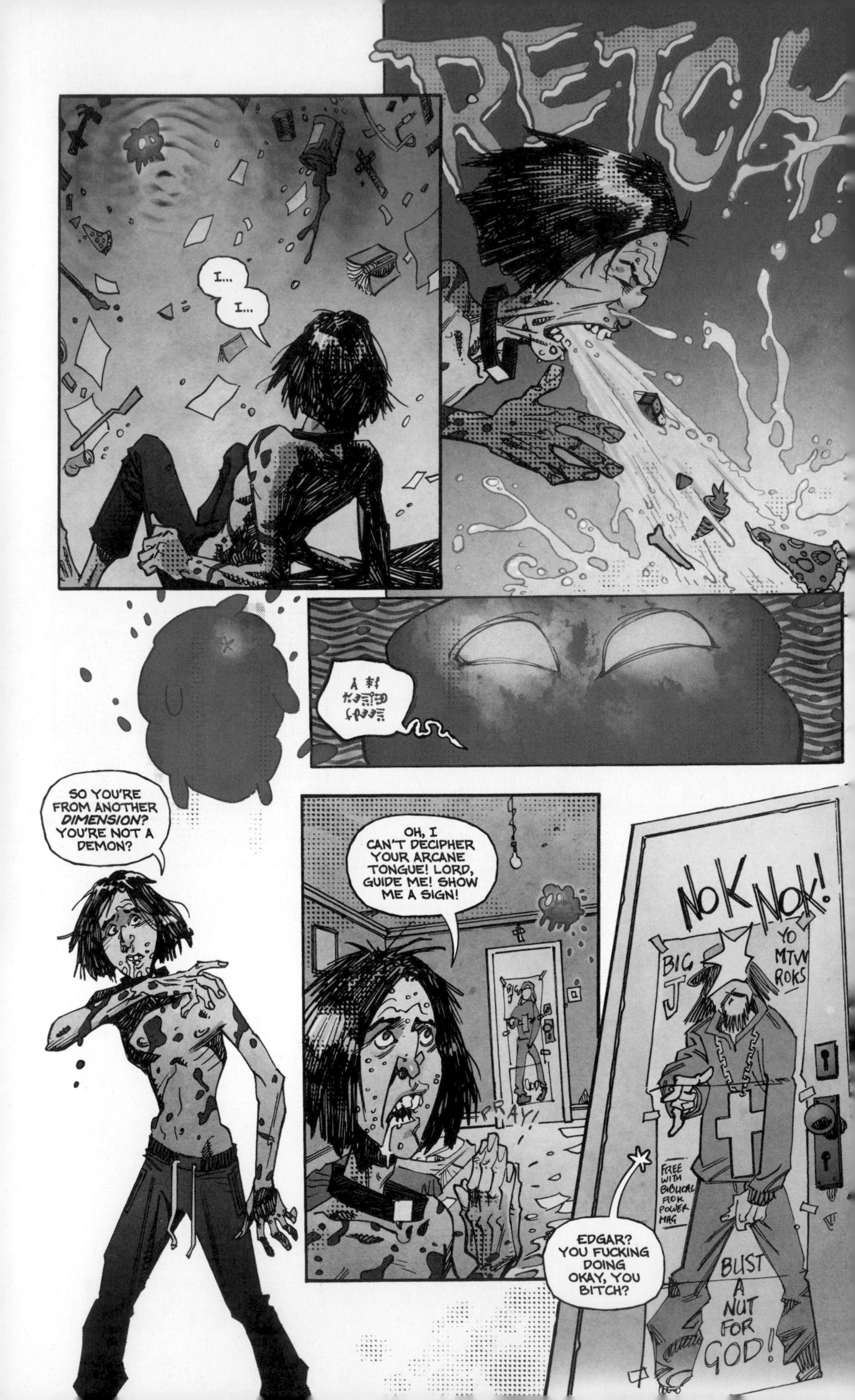
RETCH
I...
I...
SO YOU'RE FROM ANOTHER *DIMENSION*? YOU'RE NOT A DEMON?
OH, I CAN'T DECIPHER YOUR ARCANE TONGUE! LORD, GUIDE ME! SHOW ME A SIGN!
PRAY
NOK NOK!
BIG J
YO MTV ROKS
FREE WITH BIBLICAL ROK POWER MAG
BUST A NUT FOR GOD!
EDGAR? YOU FUCKING DOING OKAY, YOU BITCH?

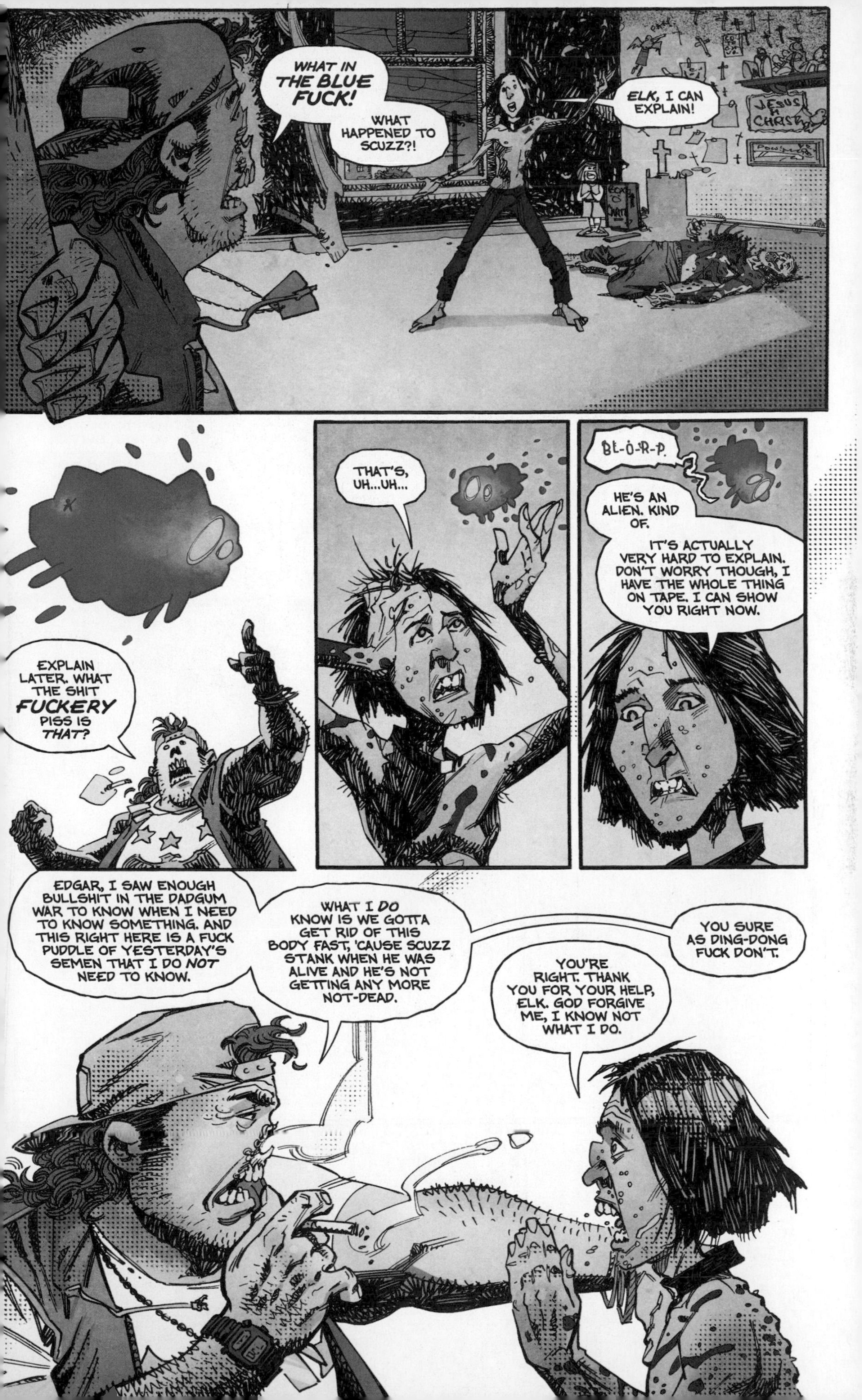
WHAT IN THE BLUE FUCK!
WHAT HAPPENED TO SCUZZ?!
ELK, I CAN EXPLAIN!
EXPLAIN LATER. WHAT THE SHIT FUCKERY PISS IS THAT?
THAT'S, UH...UH...
BL-Ö-R-P.
HE'S AN ALIEN. KIND OF.
IT'S ACTUALLY VERY HARD TO EXPLAIN. DON'T WORRY THOUGH, I HAVE THE WHOLE THING ON TAPE. I CAN SHOW YOU RIGHT NOW.
EDGAR, I SAW ENOUGH BULLSHIT IN THE DADGUM WAR TO KNOW WHEN I NEED TO KNOW SOMETHING. AND THIS RIGHT HERE IS A FUCK PUDDLE OF YESTERDAY'S SEMEN THAT I DO NOT NEED TO KNOW.
WHAT I DO KNOW IS WE GOTTA GET RID OF THIS BODY FAST, 'CAUSE SCUZZ STANK WHEN HE WAS ALIVE AND HE'S NOT GETTING ANY MORE NOT-DEAD.
YOU SURE AS DING-DONG FUCK DON'T.
YOU'RE RIGHT. THANK YOU FOR YOUR HELP, ELK. GOD FORGIVE ME, I KNOW NOT WHAT I DO.

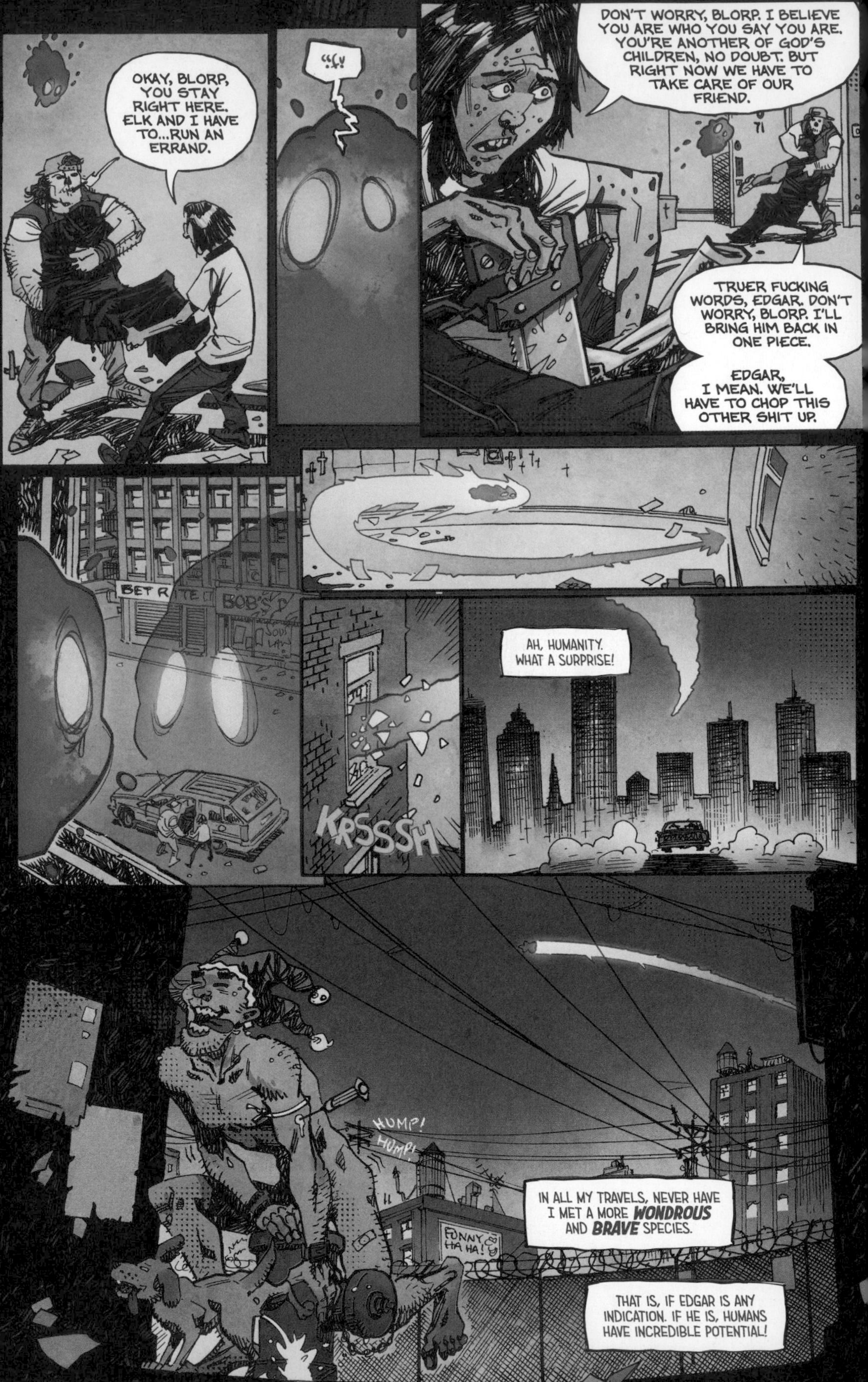
OKAY, BLORP, YOU STAY RIGHT HERE. ELK AND I HAVE TO...RUN AN ERRAND.
DON'T WORRY, BLORP. I BELIEVE YOU ARE WHO YOU SAY YOU ARE. YOU'RE ANOTHER OF GOD'S CHILDREN, NO DOUBT. BUT RIGHT NOW WE HAVE TO TAKE CARE OF OUR FRIEND.
TRUER FUCKING WORDS, EDGAR. DON'T WORRY, BLORP. I'LL BRING HIM BACK IN ONE PIECE.
EDGAR, I MEAN. WE'LL HAVE TO CHOP THIS OTHER SHIT UP.
BOB'S
KRSSSH
AH, HUMANITY. WHAT A SURPRISE!
HUMP! HUMP!
FUNNY HA HA!
IN ALL MY TRAVELS, NEVER HAVE I MET A MORE WONDROUS AND BRAVE SPECIES.
THAT IS, IF EDGAR IS ANY INDICATION. IF HE IS, HUMANS HAVE INCREDIBLE POTENTIAL!

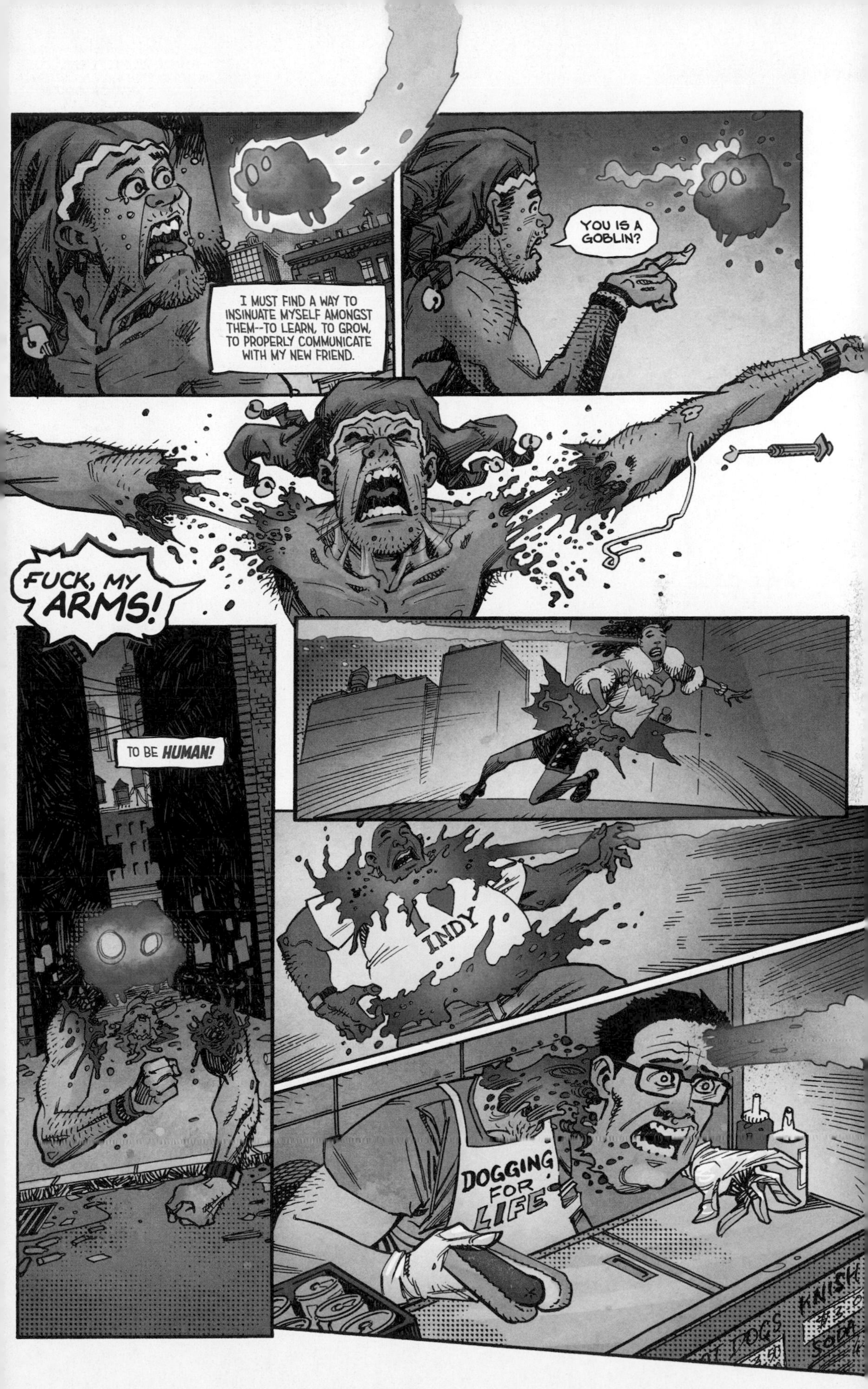
I MUST FIND A WAY TO INSINUATE MYSELF AMONGST THEM--TO LEARN, TO GROW, TO PROPERLY COMMUNICATE WITH MY NEW FRIEND.
YOU IS A GOBLIN?
FUCK, MY ARMS!
TO BE HUMAN!
INDY
DOGGING FOR LIFE
KNISH
SODA

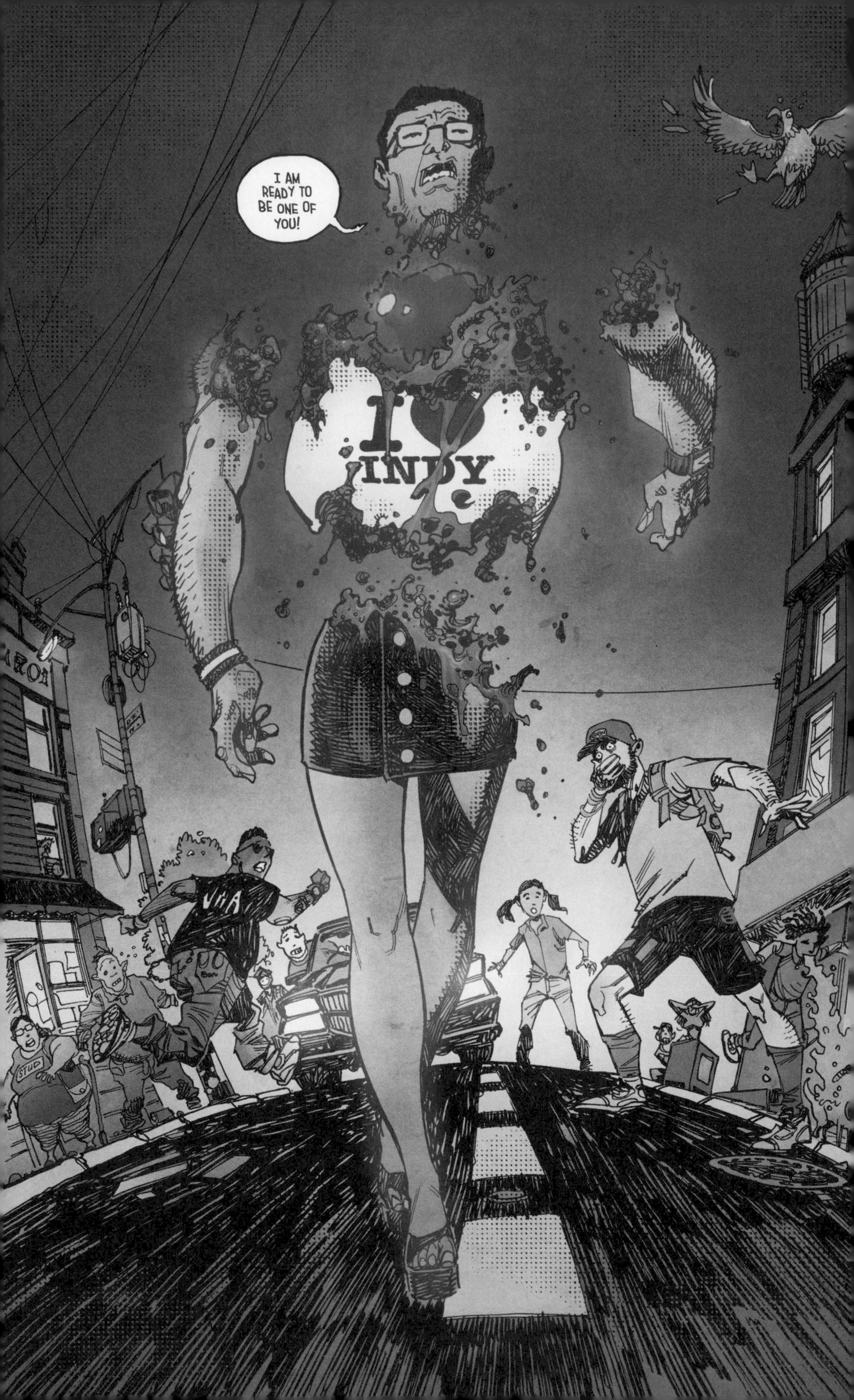
I AM READY TO BE ONE OF YOU!
I ♥ INDY
STUD

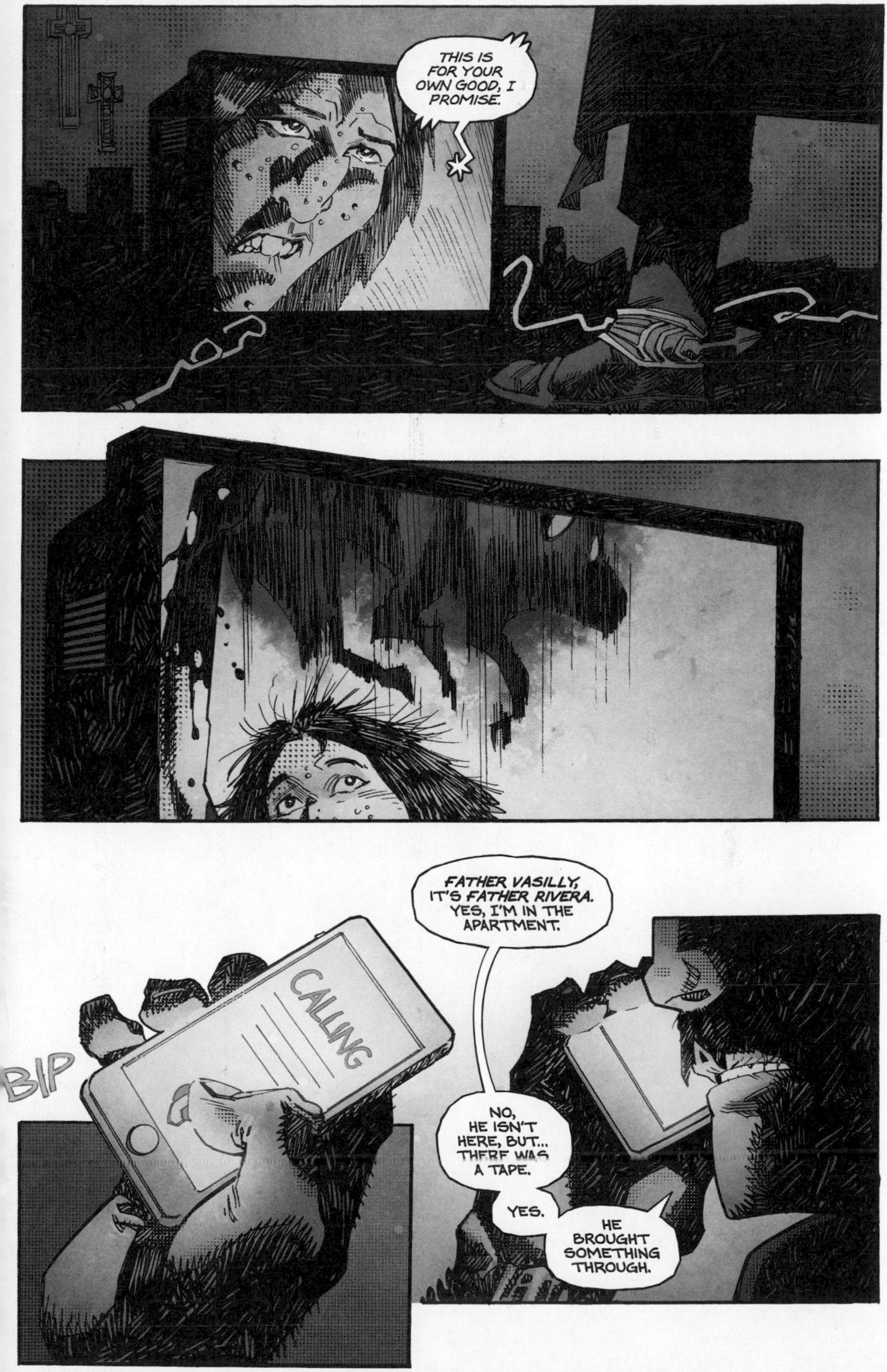
THIS IS FOR YOUR OWN GOOD, I PROMISE.
FATHER VASILLY, IT'S FATHER RIVERA. YES, I'M IN THE APARTMENT.
CALLING
BIP
NO, HE ISN'T HERE, BUT... THERE WAS A TAPE.
YES.
HE BROUGHT SOMETHING THROUGH.

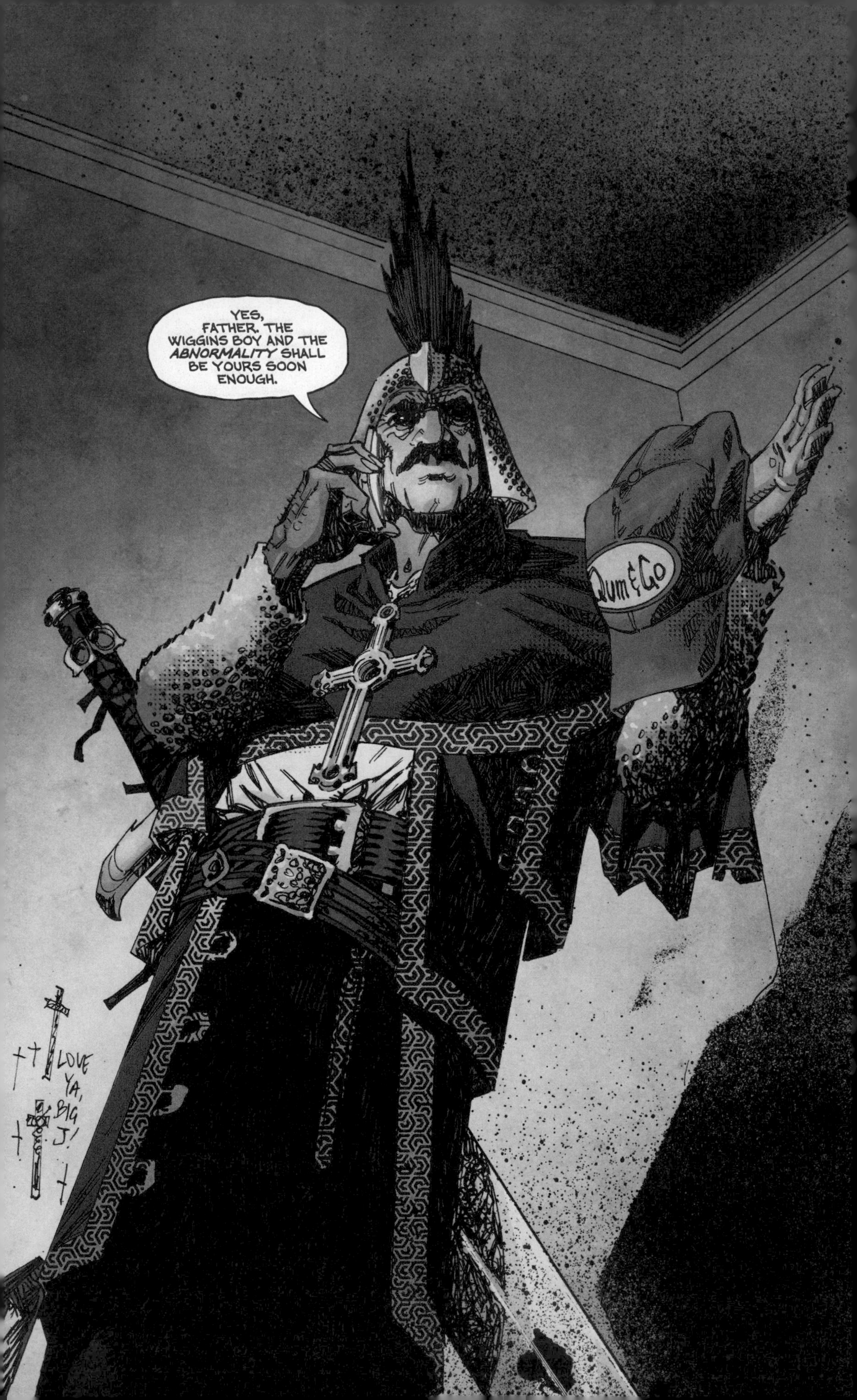

YES, FATHER. THE WIGGINS BOY AND THE *ABNORMALITY* SHALL BE YOURS SOON ENOUGH.
QUM & GO
LOVE YA, BIG J!

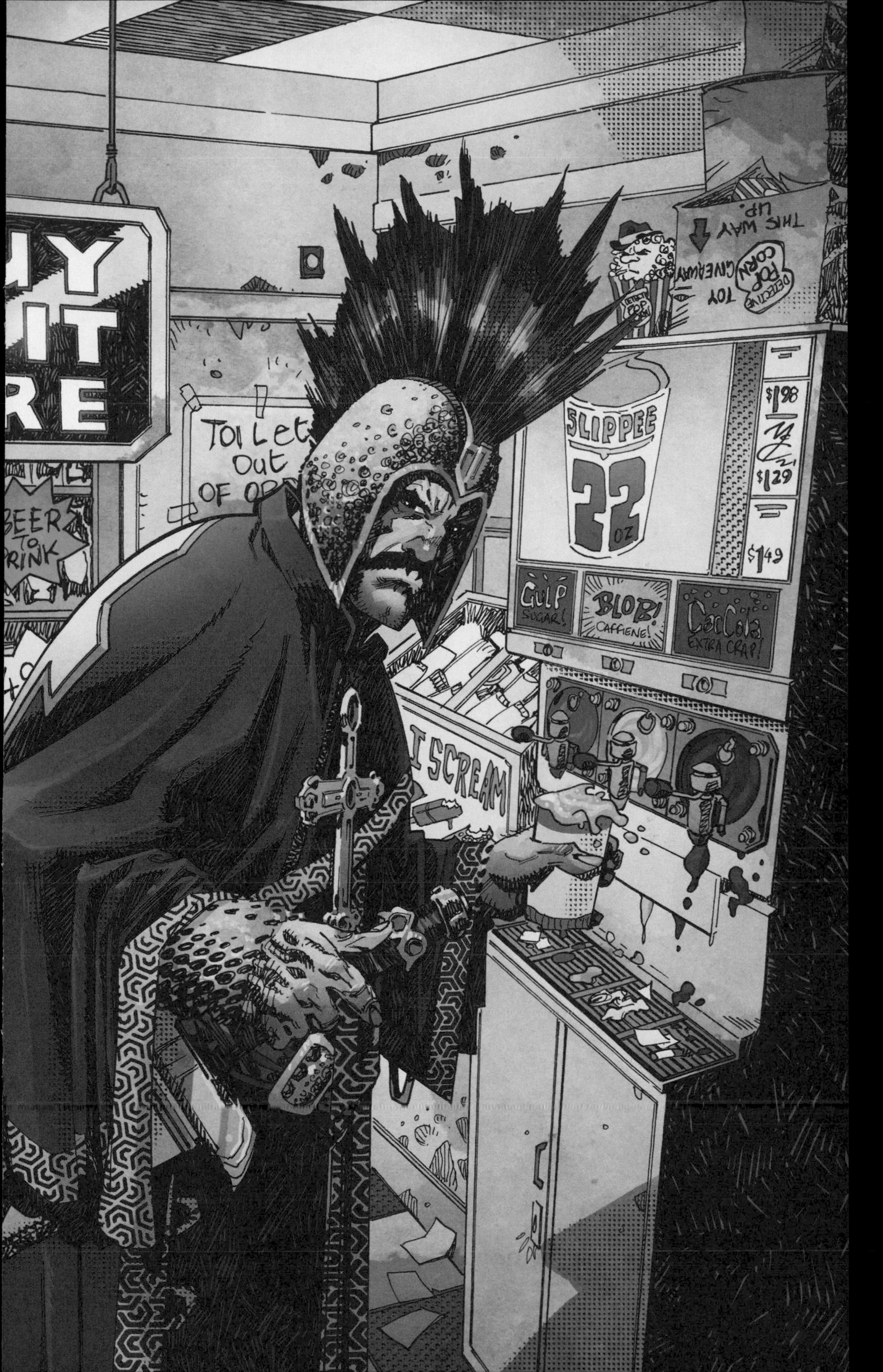

TOILET OUT OF OR
BEER TO DRINK
SLIPPEE
22 OZ
$1.98
$1.29
$1.49
GULP SUGAR!
BLOB! CAFFIENE!
CacCola EXTRA CRAP!
I SCREAM

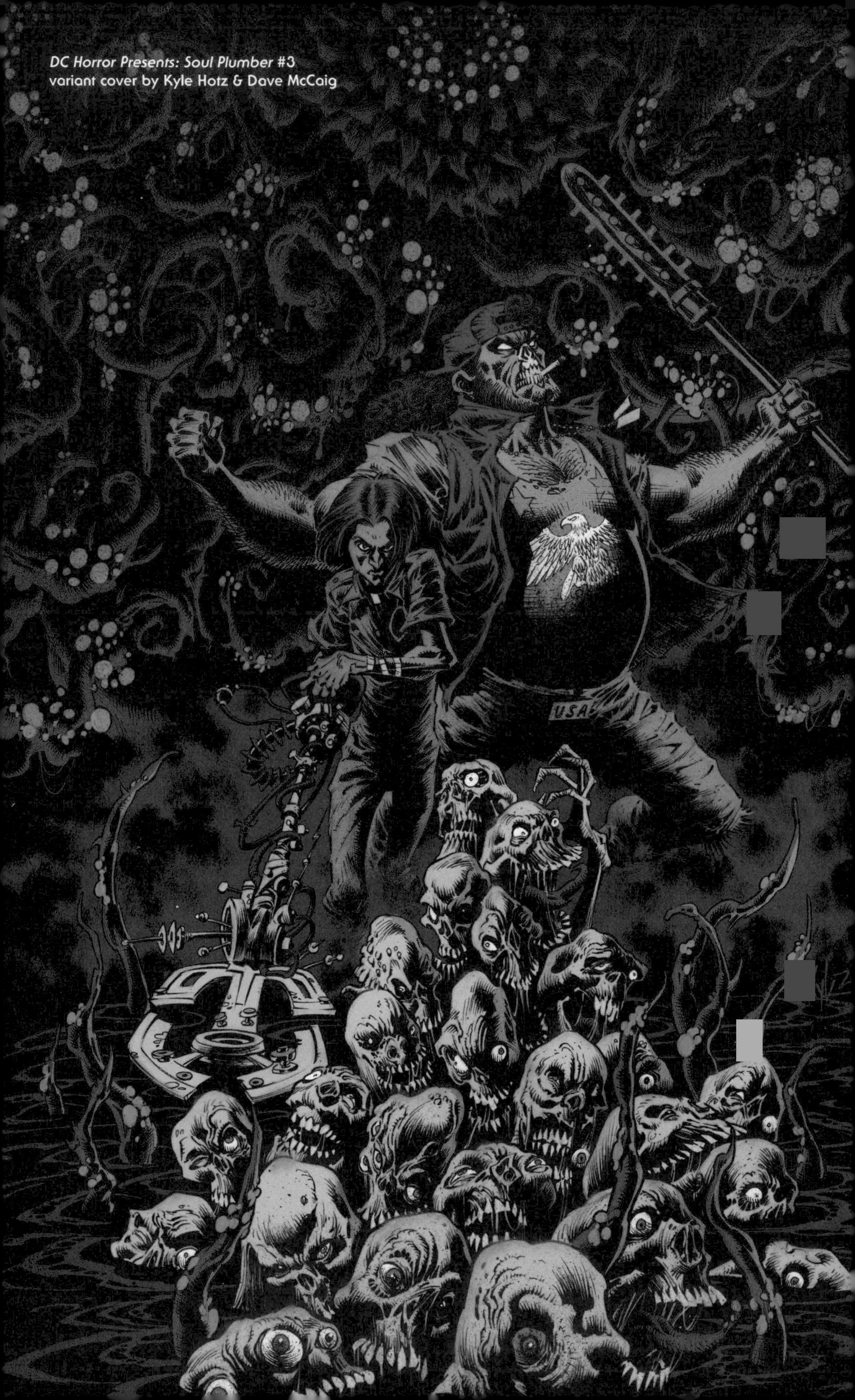
USA

DC Horror Presents: Soul Plumber #3
variant cover by Kyle Hotz & Dave McCaig

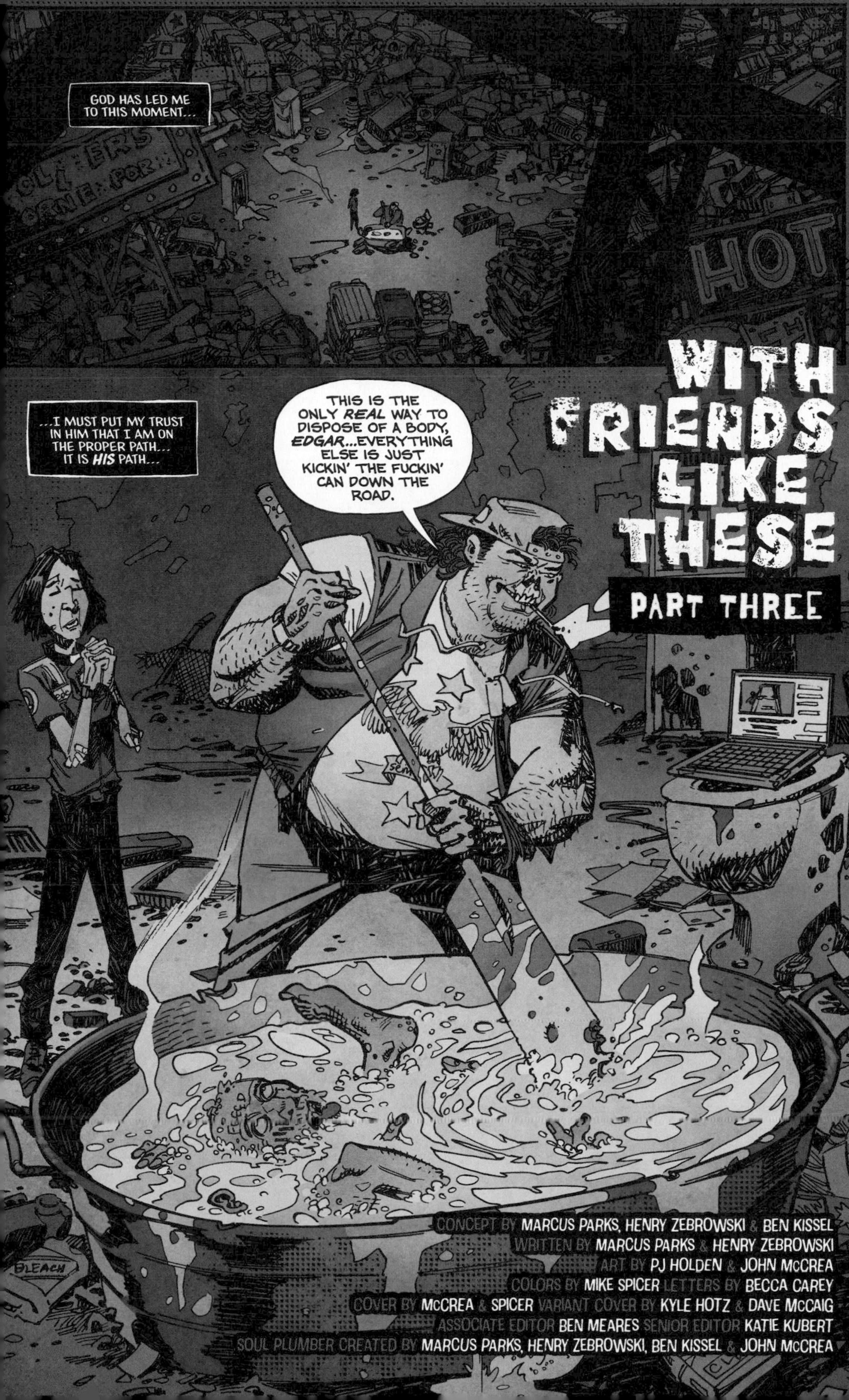

GOD HAS LED ME TO THIS MOMENT...
...I MUST PUT MY TRUST IN HIM THAT I AM ON THE PROPER PATH... IT IS HIS PATH...
THIS IS THE ONLY REAL WAY TO DISPOSE OF A BODY, EDGAR...EVERYTHING ELSE IS JUST KICKIN' THE FUCKIN' CAN DOWN THE ROAD.
WITH FRIENDS LIKE THESE
PART THREE
CONCEPT BY MARCUS PARKS, HENRY ZEBROWSKI & BEN KISSEL
WRITTEN BY MARCUS PARKS & HENRY ZEBROWSKI
ART BY PJ HOLDEN & JOHN McCREA
COLORS BY MIKE SPICER LETTERS BY BECCA CAREY
COVER BY McCREA & SPICER VARIANT COVER BY KYLE HOTZ & DAVE McCAIG
ASSOCIATE EDITOR BEN MEARES SENIOR EDITOR KATIE KUBERT
SOUL PLUMBER CREATED BY MARCUS PARKS, HENRY ZEBROWSKI, BEN KISSEL & JOHN McCREA
HOT
BLEACH

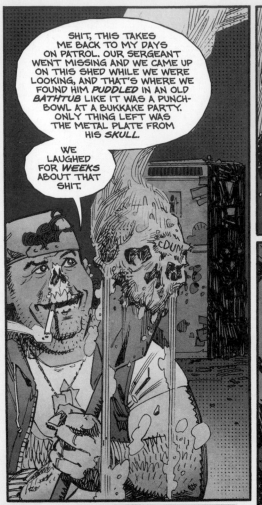

SHIT, THIS TAKES ME BACK TO MY DAYS ON PATROL. OUR SERGEANT WENT MISSING AND WE CAME UP ON THIS SHED WHILE WE WERE LOOKING, AND THAT'S WHERE WE FOUND HIM *PUDDLED* IN AN OLD *BATHTUB* LIKE IT WAS A PUNCH-BOWL AT A BUKKAKE PARTY. ONLY THING LEFT WAS THE METAL PLATE FROM HIS *SKULL.*

WE LAUGHED FOR *WEEKS* ABOUT THAT SHIT.

AIN'T THAT RIGHT, *SCORPION?*

WE FOUND OL' TIN HEAD, ALL RIGHT!

PORT-A-POOP

THIS FELLER'S GOT SOME TIME TO COOK, *ELK.* STARTIN' TO LOOK LIKE CHOWDER!

I HAVE NEVER FELT SUCH DOUBT IN THE HAND OF THE LORD...IS THIS *TRULY* THE WAY TO HELP ALL HUMANKIND?

PLEASE, SHOW ME THAT ALL OF THIS BLOOD AND MAYHEM HAS A PURPOSE!

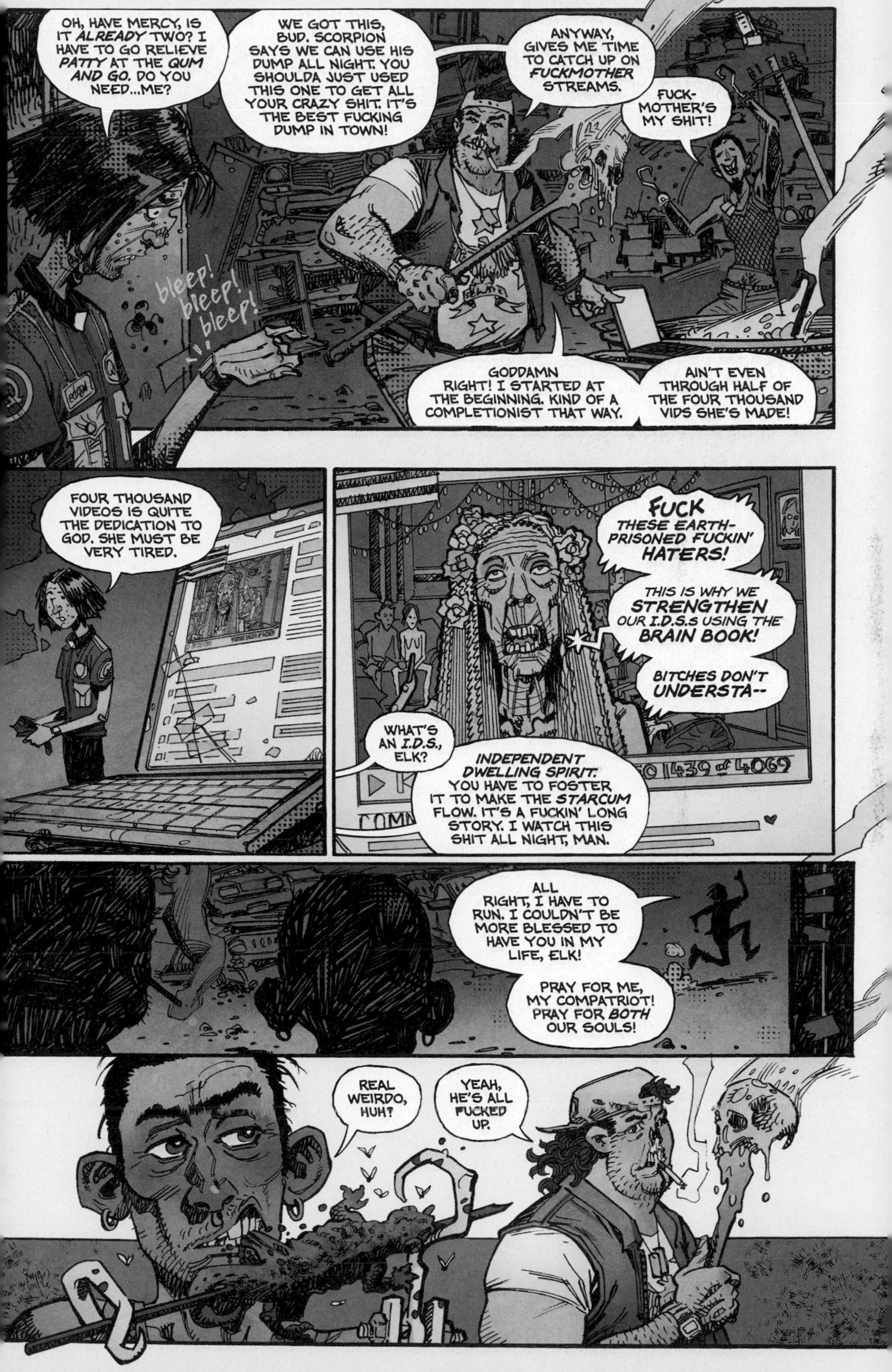
OH, HAVE MERCY, IS IT ALREADY TWO? I HAVE TO GO RELIEVE PATTY AT THE QUM AND GO. DO YOU NEED...ME?
WE GOT THIS, BUD. SCORPION SAYS WE CAN USE HIS DUMP ALL NIGHT. YOU SHOULDA JUST USED THIS ONE TO GET ALL YOUR CRAZY SHIT. IT'S THE BEST FUCKING DUMP IN TOWN!
ANYWAY, GIVES ME TIME TO CATCH UP ON FUCKMOTHER STREAMS.
FUCK-MOTHER'S MY SHIT!
bleep! bleep! bleep!
GODDAMN RIGHT! I STARTED AT THE BEGINNING. KIND OF A COMPLETIONIST THAT WAY.
AIN'T EVEN THROUGH HALF OF THE FOUR THOUSAND VIDS SHE'S MADE!
FOUR THOUSAND VIDEOS IS QUITE THE DEDICATION TO GOD. SHE MUST BE VERY TIRED.
FUCK THESE EARTH-PRISONED FUCKIN' HATERS!
THIS IS WHY WE STRENGTHEN OUR I.D.S.s USING THE BRAIN BOOK!
BITCHES DON'T UNDERSTA--
WHAT'S AN I.D.S., ELK?
INDEPENDENT DWELLING SPIRIT. YOU HAVE TO FOSTER IT TO MAKE THE STARCUM FLOW. IT'S A FUCKIN' LONG STORY. I WATCH THIS SHIT ALL NIGHT, MAN.
1439 of 4069
ALL RIGHT, I HAVE TO RUN. I COULDN'T BE MORE BLESSED TO HAVE YOU IN MY LIFE, ELK!
PRAY FOR ME, MY COMPATRIOT! PRAY FOR BOTH OUR SOULS!
REAL WEIRDO, HUH?
YEAH, HE'S ALL FUCKED UP.

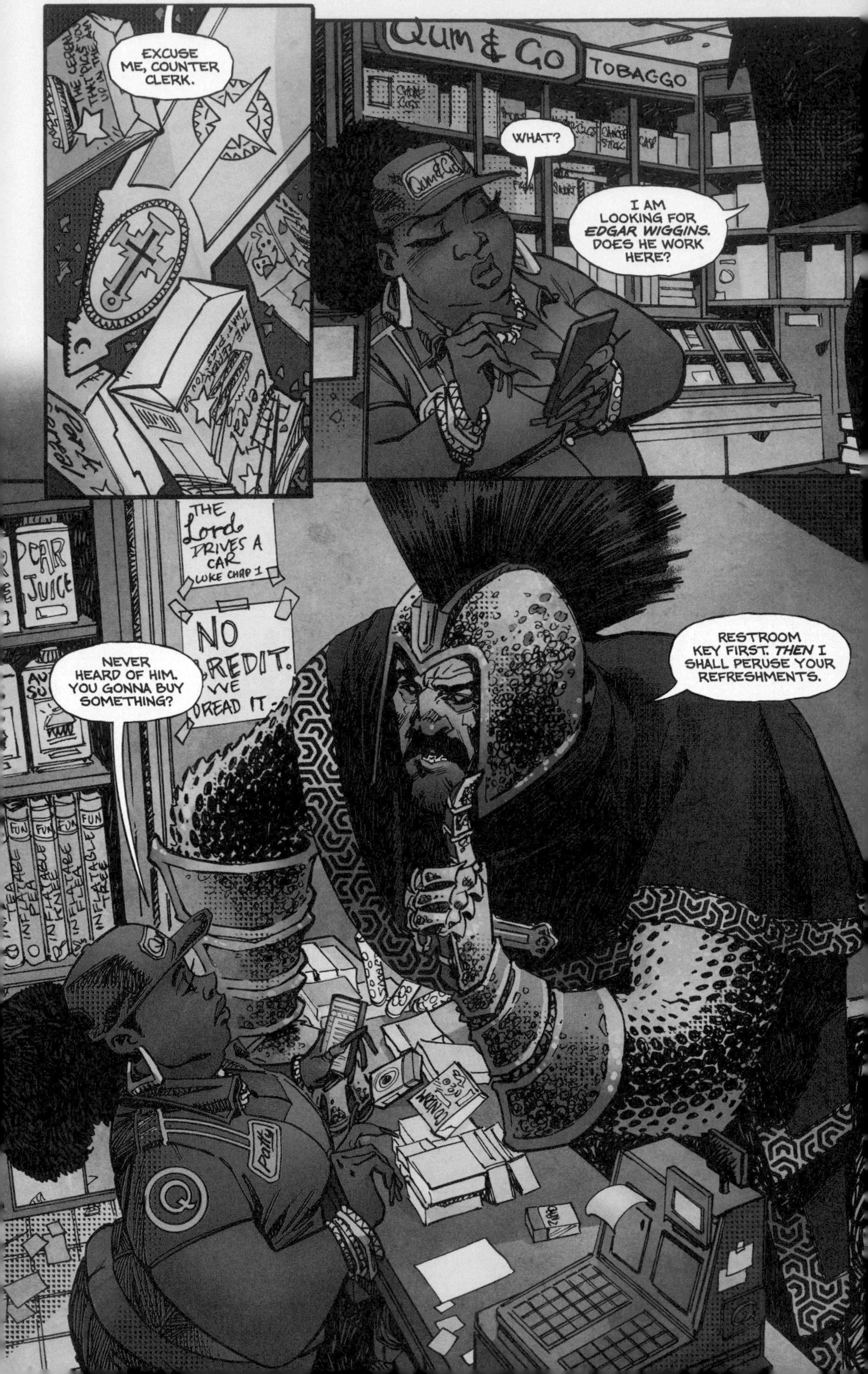
THE CEREAL THAT PIGS YOU UP IN THE AM
EXCUSE ME, COUNTER CLERK.
Qum & Go
TOBAGGO
WHAT?
I AM LOOKING FOR *EDGAR WIGGINS.* DOES HE WORK HERE?
THE Lord DRIVES A CAR LUKE CHAP 1
NEVER HEARD OF HIM. YOU GONNA BUY SOMETHING?
RESTROOM KEY FIRST. *THEN* I SHALL PERUSE YOUR REFRESHMENTS.

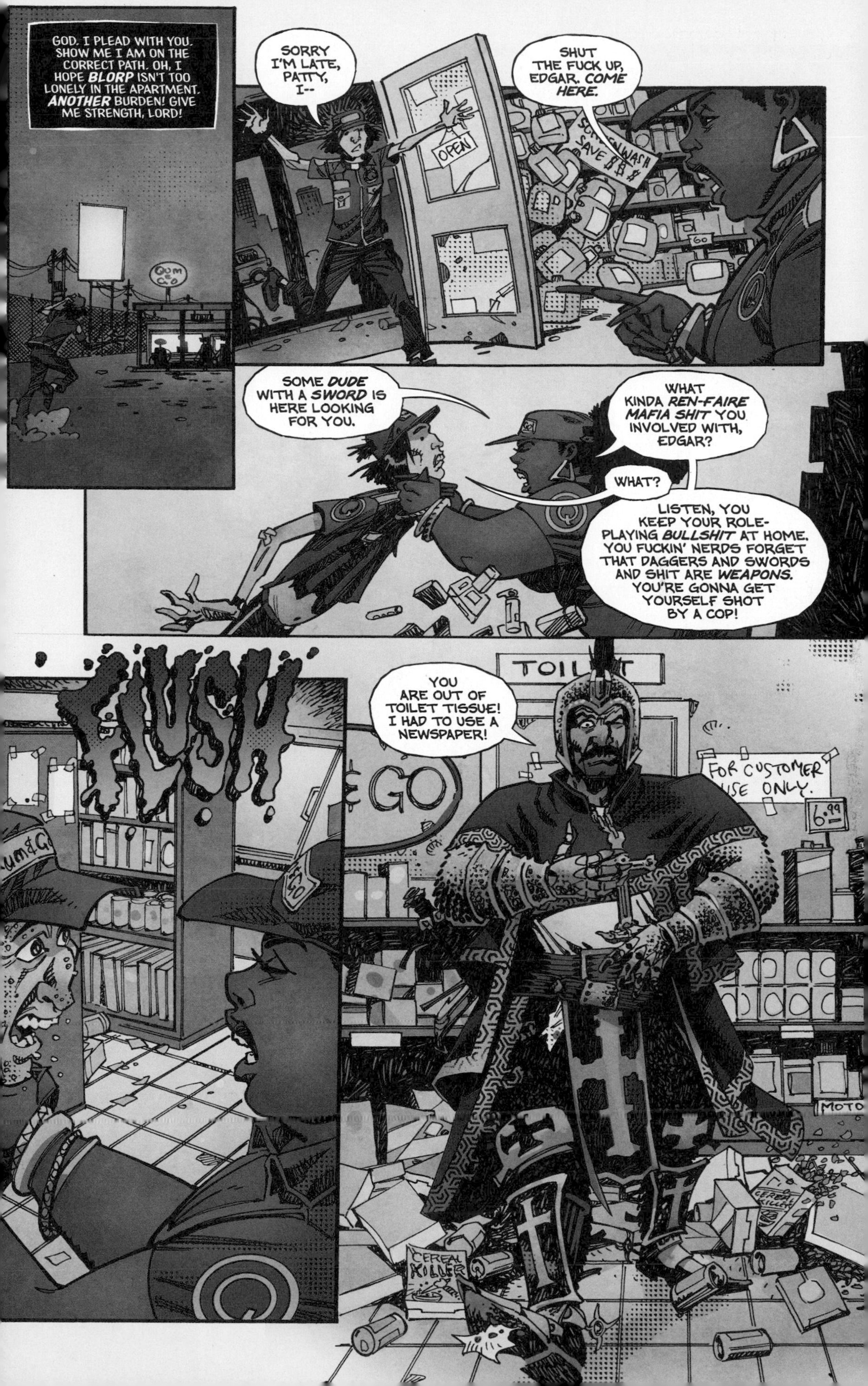
GOD. I PLEAD WITH YOU. SHOW ME I AM ON THE CORRECT PATH. OH, I HOPE BLORP ISN'T TOO LONELY IN THE APARTMENT. ANOTHER BURDEN! GIVE ME STRENGTH, LORD!
SORRY I'M LATE, PATTY, I--
OPEN
SHUT THE FUCK UP, EDGAR. COME HERE.
SOME DUDE WITH A SWORD IS HERE LOOKING FOR YOU.
WHAT KINDA REN-FAIRE MAFIA SHIT YOU INVOLVED WITH, EDGAR?
WHAT?
LISTEN, YOU KEEP YOUR ROLE-PLAYING BULLSHIT AT HOME. YOU FUCKIN' NERDS FORGET THAT DAGGERS AND SWORDS AND SHIT ARE WEAPONS. YOU'RE GONNA GET YOURSELF SHOT BY A COP!
FLUSH
YOU ARE OUT OF TOILET TISSUE! I HAD TO USE A NEWSPAPER!
FOR CUSTOMER USE ONLY.
6.99
CEREAL KILLER

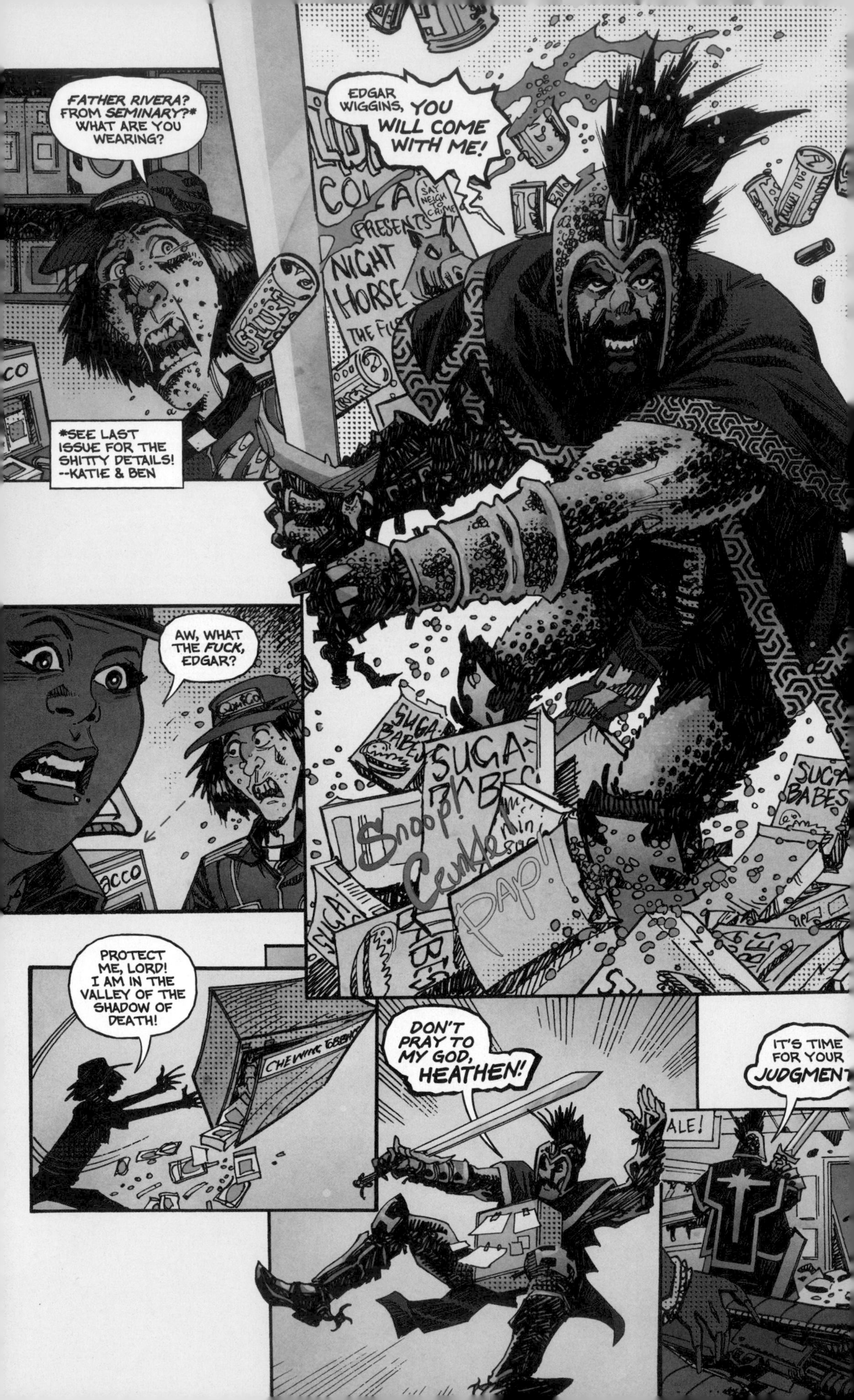
FATHER RIVERA? FROM SEMINARY?* WHAT ARE YOU WEARING?
*SEE LAST ISSUE FOR THE SHITTY DETAILS! --KATIE & BEN
EDGAR WIGGINS, YOU WILL COME WITH ME!
SAY NEIGH TO CRIME
PRESENTS
NIGHT HORSE
AW, WHAT THE FUCK, EDGAR?
SUGA BABES
Snoop!
Crunkle!
PAP!
PROTECT ME, LORD! I AM IN THE VALLEY OF THE SHADOW OF DEATH!
CHEWING TOBBACO
DON'T PRAY TO MY GOD, HEATHEN!
IT'S TIME FOR YOUR JUDGMENT

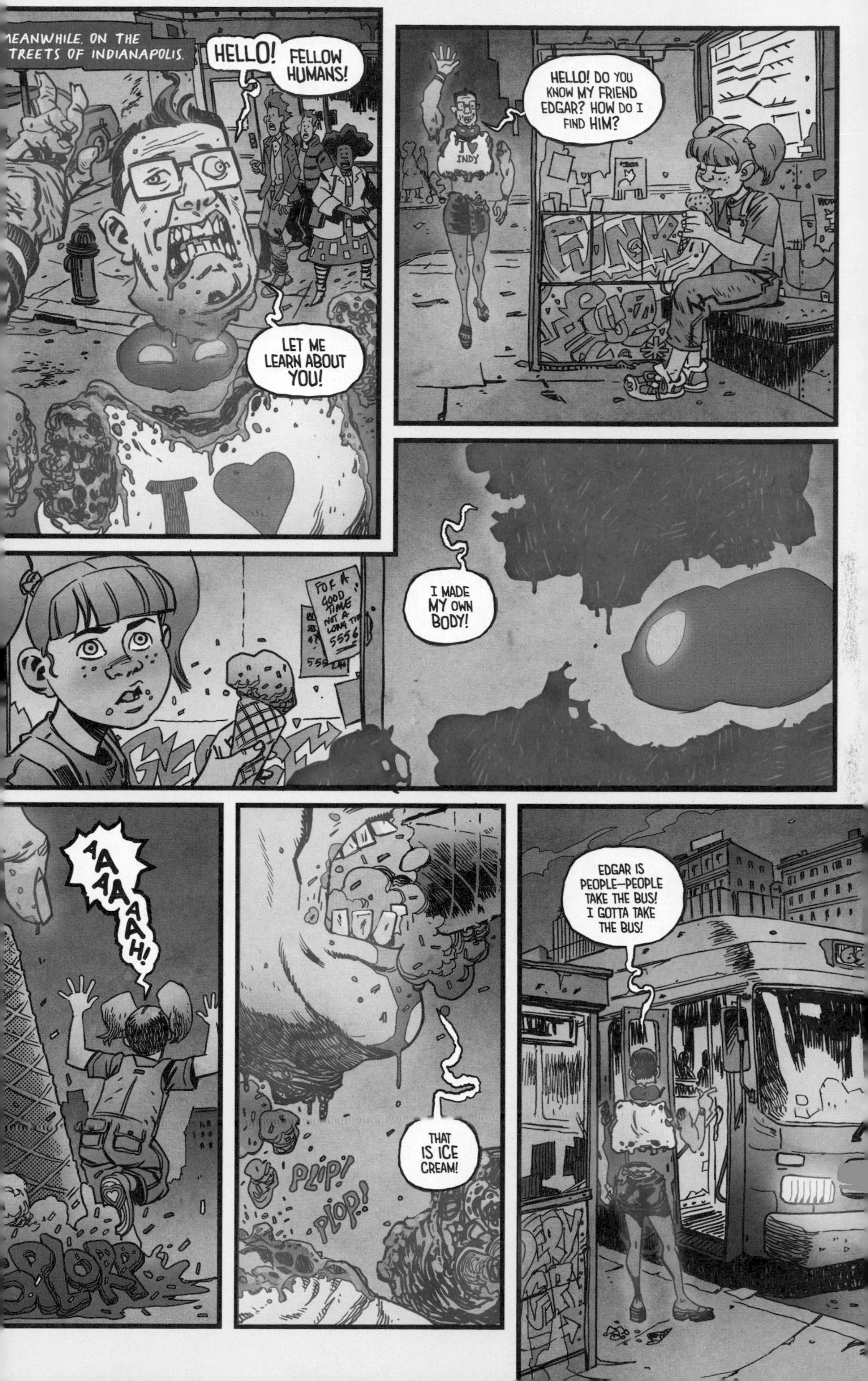
MEANWHILE, ON THE STREETS OF INDIANAPOLIS.
HELLO! FELLOW HUMANS!
LET ME LEARN ABOUT YOU!
I ♥
HELLO! DO YOU KNOW MY FRIEND EDGAR? HOW DO I FIND HIM?
I ♥ INDY
FUNK
I MADE MY OWN BODY!
FOR A GOOD TIME NOT A LONG TIME 5556
AAAAAAH!
SPLOPP
PLIP! PLOP!
THAT IS ICE CREAM!
EDGAR IS PEOPLE--PEOPLE TAKE THE BUS! I GOTTA TAKE THE BUS!

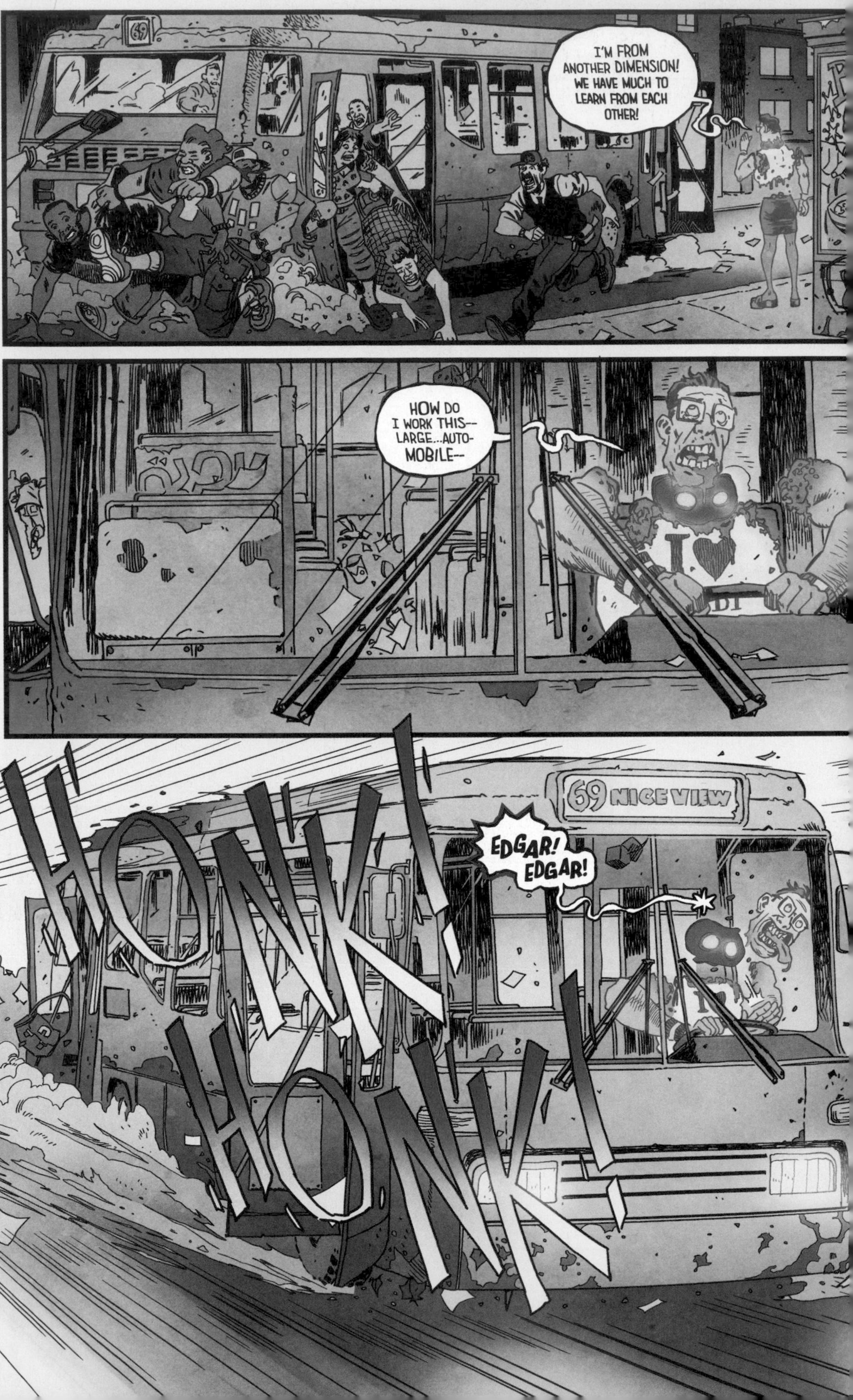
I'M FROM ANOTHER DIMENSION! WE HAVE MUCH TO LEARN FROM EACH OTHER!
HOW DO I WORK THIS-- LARGE...AUTO-MOBILE--
69 NICE VIEW
HONK! HONK!
EDGAR! EDGAR!

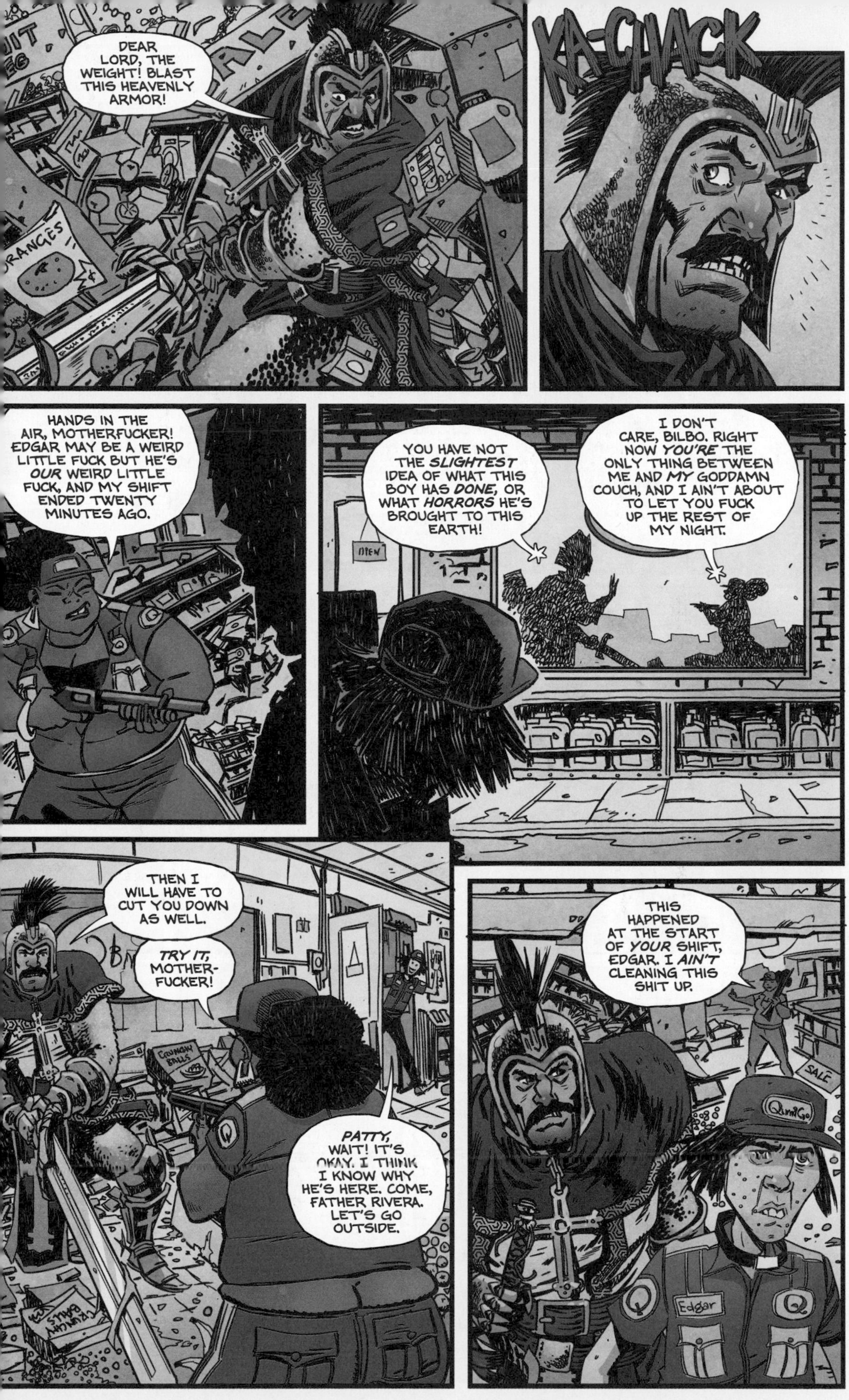
DEAR LORD, THE WEIGHT! BLAST THIS HEAVENLY ARMOR!
KA-CHACK
HANDS IN THE AIR, MOTHERFUCKER! EDGAR MAY BE A WEIRD LITTLE FUCK BUT HE'S OUR WEIRD LITTLE FUCK, AND MY SHIFT ENDED TWENTY MINUTES AGO.
YOU HAVE NOT THE SLIGHTEST IDEA OF WHAT THIS BOY HAS DONE, OR WHAT HORRORS HE'S BROUGHT TO THIS EARTH!
I DON'T CARE, BILBO. RIGHT NOW YOU'RE THE ONLY THING BETWEEN ME AND MY GODDAMN COUCH, AND I AIN'T ABOUT TO LET YOU FUCK UP THE REST OF MY NIGHT.
THEN I WILL HAVE TO CUT YOU DOWN AS WELL.
TRY IT, MOTHER-FUCKER!
PATTY, WAIT! IT'S OKAY. I THINK I KNOW WHY HE'S HERE. COME, FATHER RIVERA. LET'S GO OUTSIDE.
THIS HAPPENED AT THE START OF YOUR SHIFT, EDGAR. I AIN'T CLEANING THIS SHIT UP.
ORANGES
OPEN
CRUNCHY BALLS
SALE
Edgar

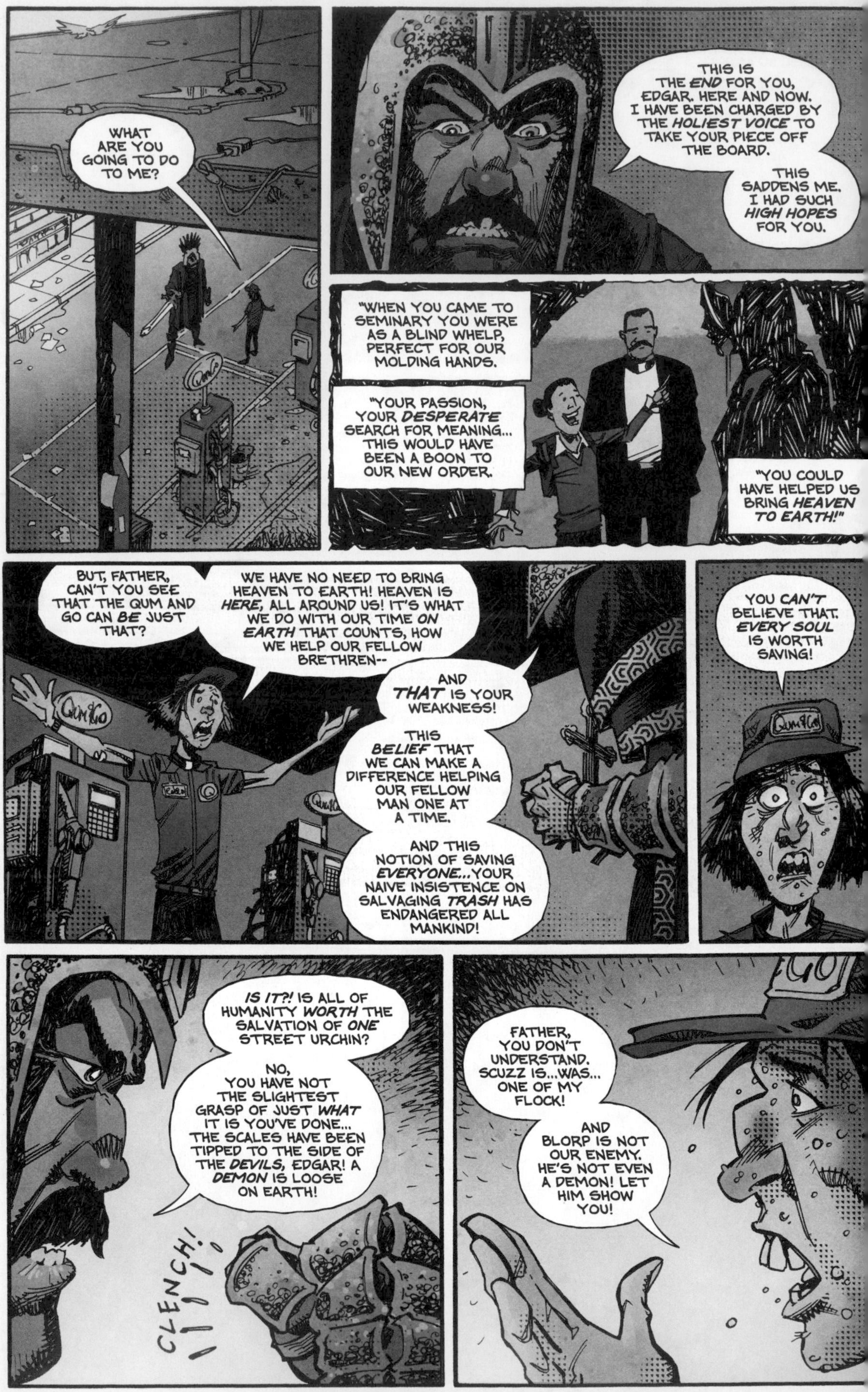

WHAT ARE YOU GOING TO DO TO ME?
THIS IS THE END FOR YOU, EDGAR. HERE AND NOW. I HAVE BEEN CHARGED BY THE HOLIEST VOICE TO TAKE YOUR PIECE OFF THE BOARD.
THIS SADDENS ME. I HAD SUCH HIGH HOPES FOR YOU.
"WHEN YOU CAME TO SEMINARY YOU WERE AS A BLIND WHELP, PERFECT FOR OUR MOLDING HANDS.
"YOUR PASSION, YOUR DESPERATE SEARCH FOR MEANING... THIS WOULD HAVE BEEN A BOON TO OUR NEW ORDER.
"YOU COULD HAVE HELPED US BRING HEAVEN TO EARTH!"
BUT, FATHER, CAN'T YOU SEE THAT THE QUM AND GO CAN BE JUST THAT?
WE HAVE NO NEED TO BRING HEAVEN TO EARTH! HEAVEN IS HERE, ALL AROUND US! IT'S WHAT WE DO WITH OUR TIME ON EARTH THAT COUNTS, HOW WE HELP OUR FELLOW BRETHREN--
AND THAT IS YOUR WEAKNESS!
THIS BELIEF THAT WE CAN MAKE A DIFFERENCE HELPING OUR FELLOW MAN ONE AT A TIME.
AND THIS NOTION OF SAVING EVERYONE...YOUR NAIVE INSISTENCE ON SALVAGING TRASH HAS ENDANGERED ALL MANKIND!
YOU CAN'T BELIEVE THAT. EVERY SOUL IS WORTH SAVING!
IS IT?! IS ALL OF HUMANITY WORTH THE SALVATION OF ONE STREET URCHIN?
NO, YOU HAVE NOT THE SLIGHTEST GRASP OF JUST WHAT IT IS YOU'VE DONE... THE SCALES HAVE BEEN TIPPED TO THE SIDE OF THE DEVILS, EDGAR! A DEMON IS LOOSE ON EARTH!
CLENCH!
FATHER, YOU DON'T UNDERSTAND. SCUZZ IS...WAS... ONE OF MY FLOCK!
AND BLORP IS NOT OUR ENEMY. HE'S NOT EVEN A DEMON! LET HIM SHOW YOU!

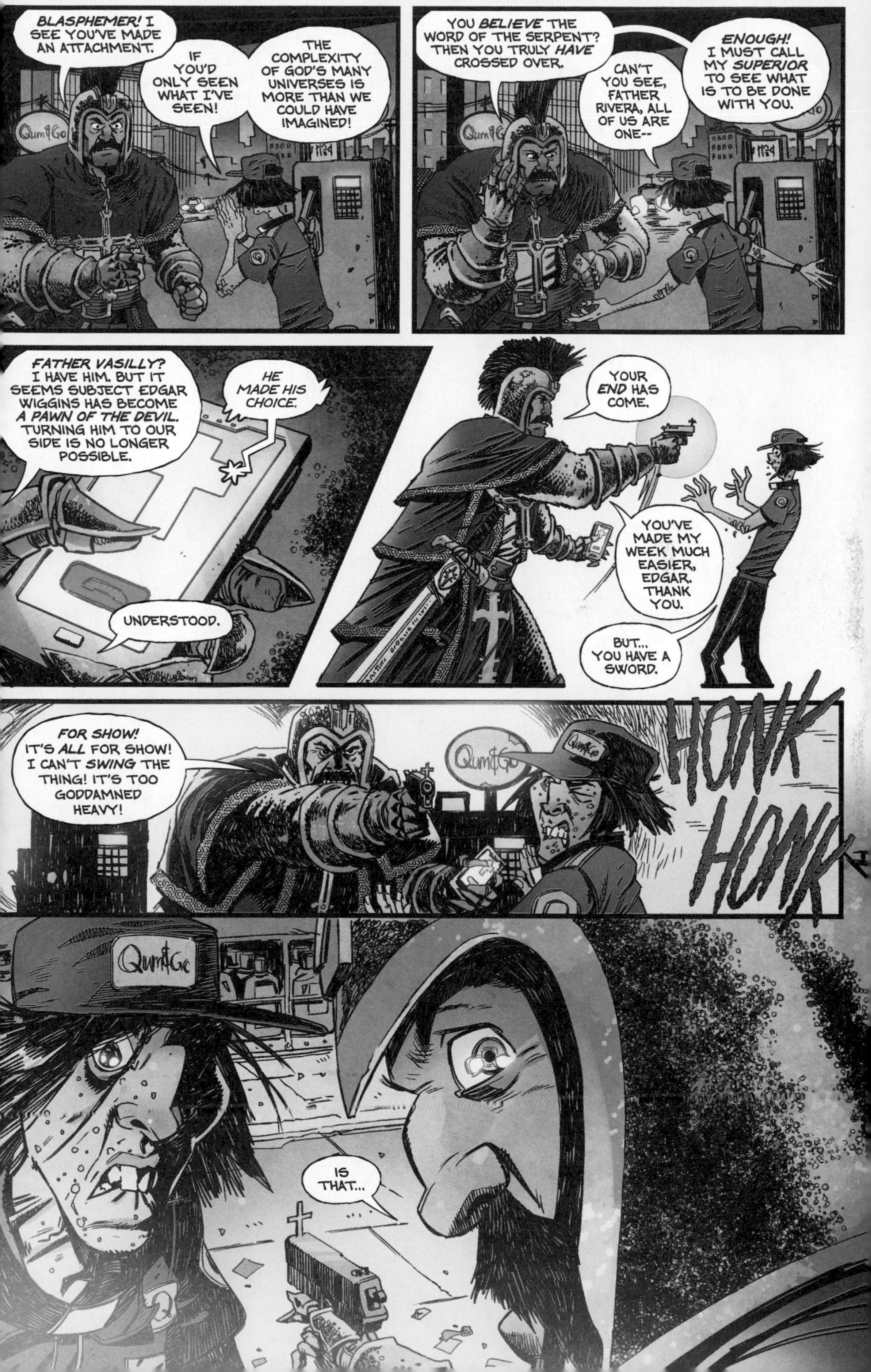
BLASPHEMER! I SEE YOU'VE MADE AN ATTACHMENT.
IF YOU'D ONLY SEEN WHAT I'VE SEEN!
THE COMPLEXITY OF GOD'S MANY UNIVERSES IS MORE THAN WE COULD HAVE IMAGINED!
YOU BELIEVE THE WORD OF THE SERPENT? THEN YOU TRULY HAVE CROSSED OVER.
CAN'T YOU SEE, FATHER RIVERA, ALL OF US ARE ONE--
ENOUGH! I MUST CALL MY SUPERIOR TO SEE WHAT IS TO BE DONE WITH YOU.
FATHER VASILLY? I HAVE HIM. BUT IT SEEMS SUBJECT EDGAR WIGGINS HAS BECOME A PAWN OF THE DEVIL. TURNING HIM TO OUR SIDE IS NO LONGER POSSIBLE.
HE MADE HIS CHOICE.
UNDERSTOOD.
YOUR END HAS COME.
YOU'VE MADE MY WEEK MUCH EASIER, EDGAR. THANK YOU.
BUT... YOU HAVE A SWORD.
FOR SHOW! IT'S ALL FOR SHOW! I CAN'T SWING THE THING! IT'S TOO GODDAMNED HEAVY!
HONK
HONK
IS THAT...

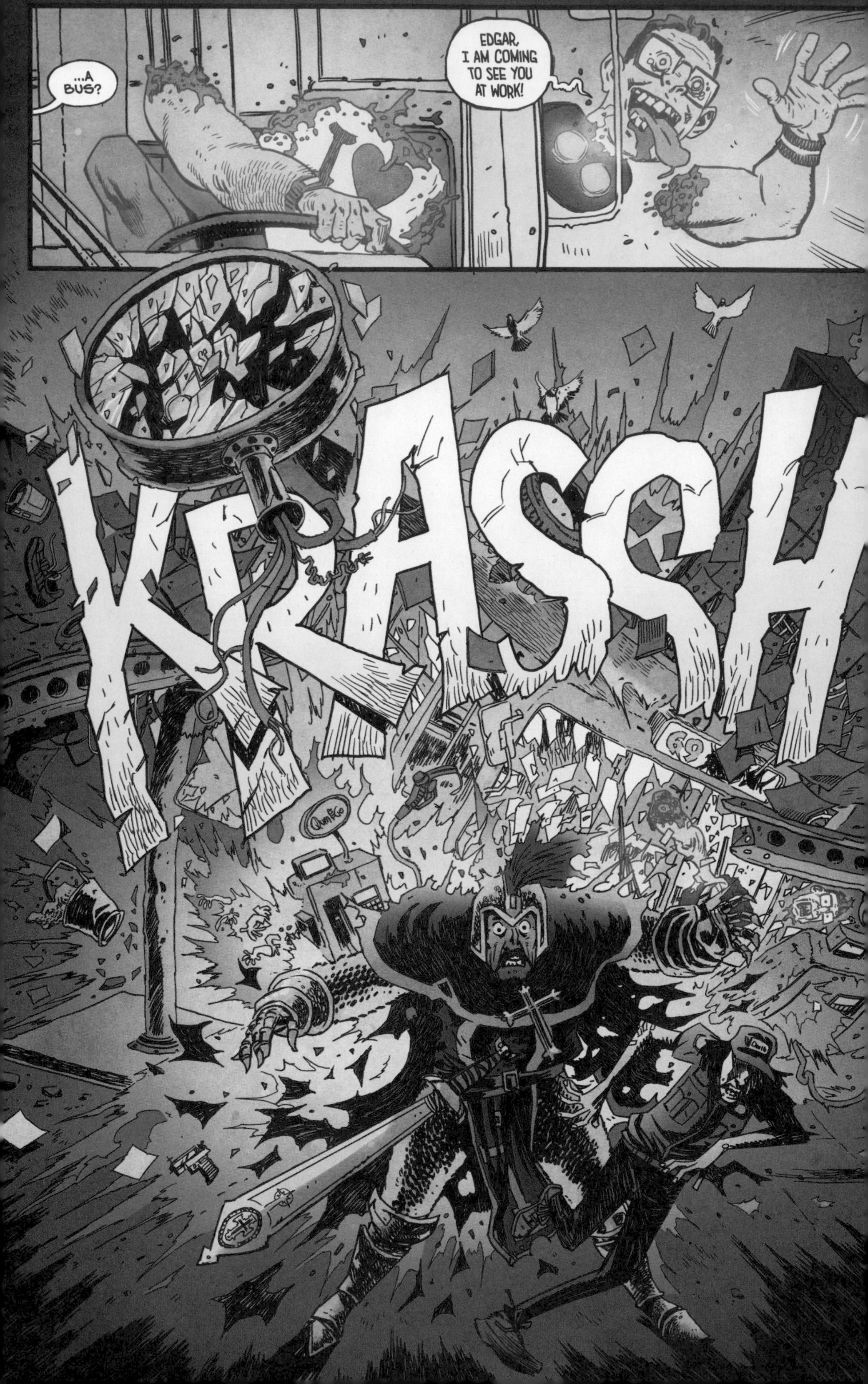
...A BUS?
EDGAR, I AM COMING TO SEE YOU AT WORK!
KRASSH

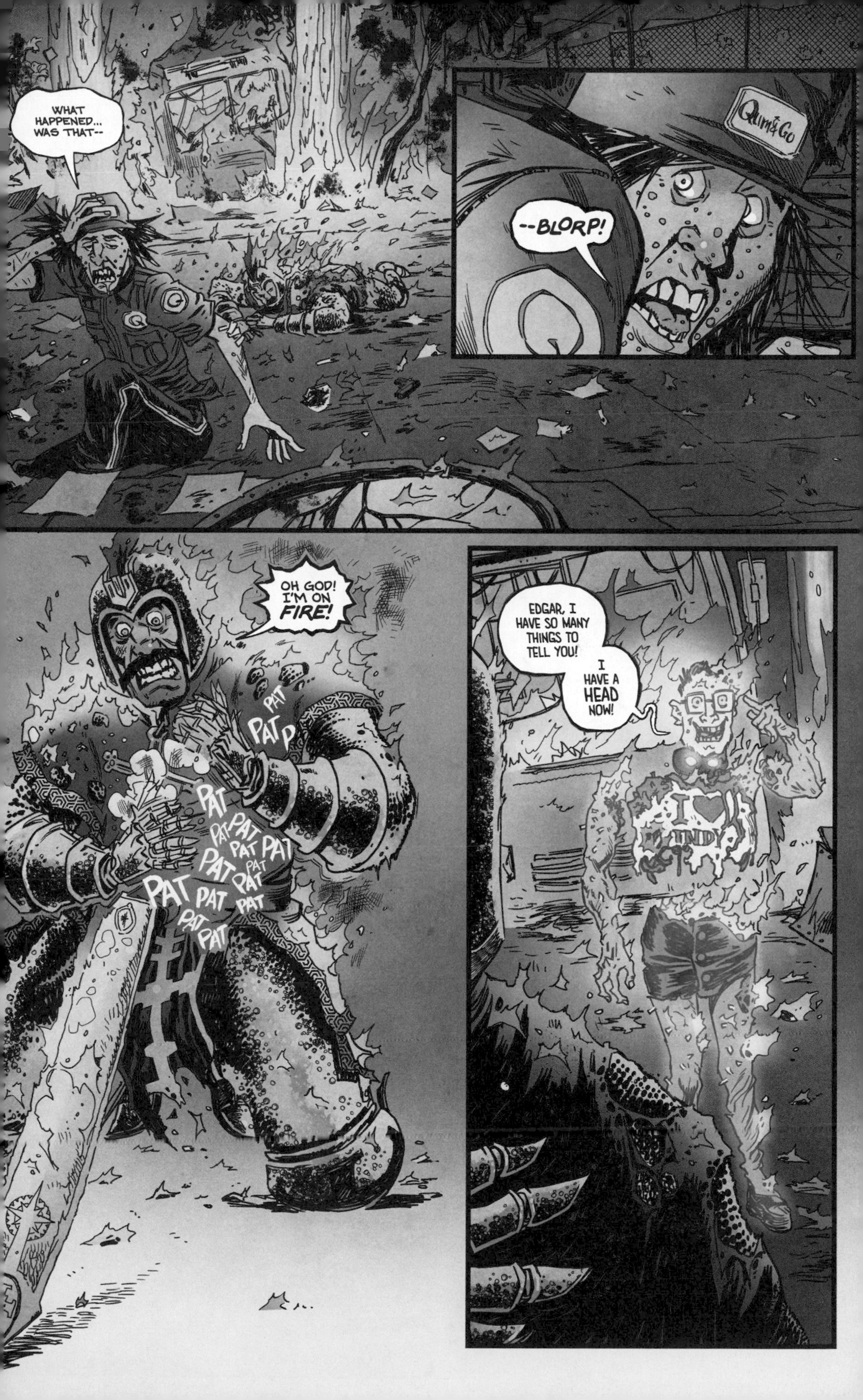
WHAT HAPPENED... WAS THAT--
--BLORP!
Quim&Go
OH GOD! I'M ON FIRE!
PAT PAT PAT P
PAT PAT PAT PAT PAT PAT PAT PAT PAT PAT PAT PAT PAT PAT PAT
EDGAR, I HAVE SO MANY THINGS TO TELL YOU!
I HAVE A HEAD NOW!
I ♥ INDY

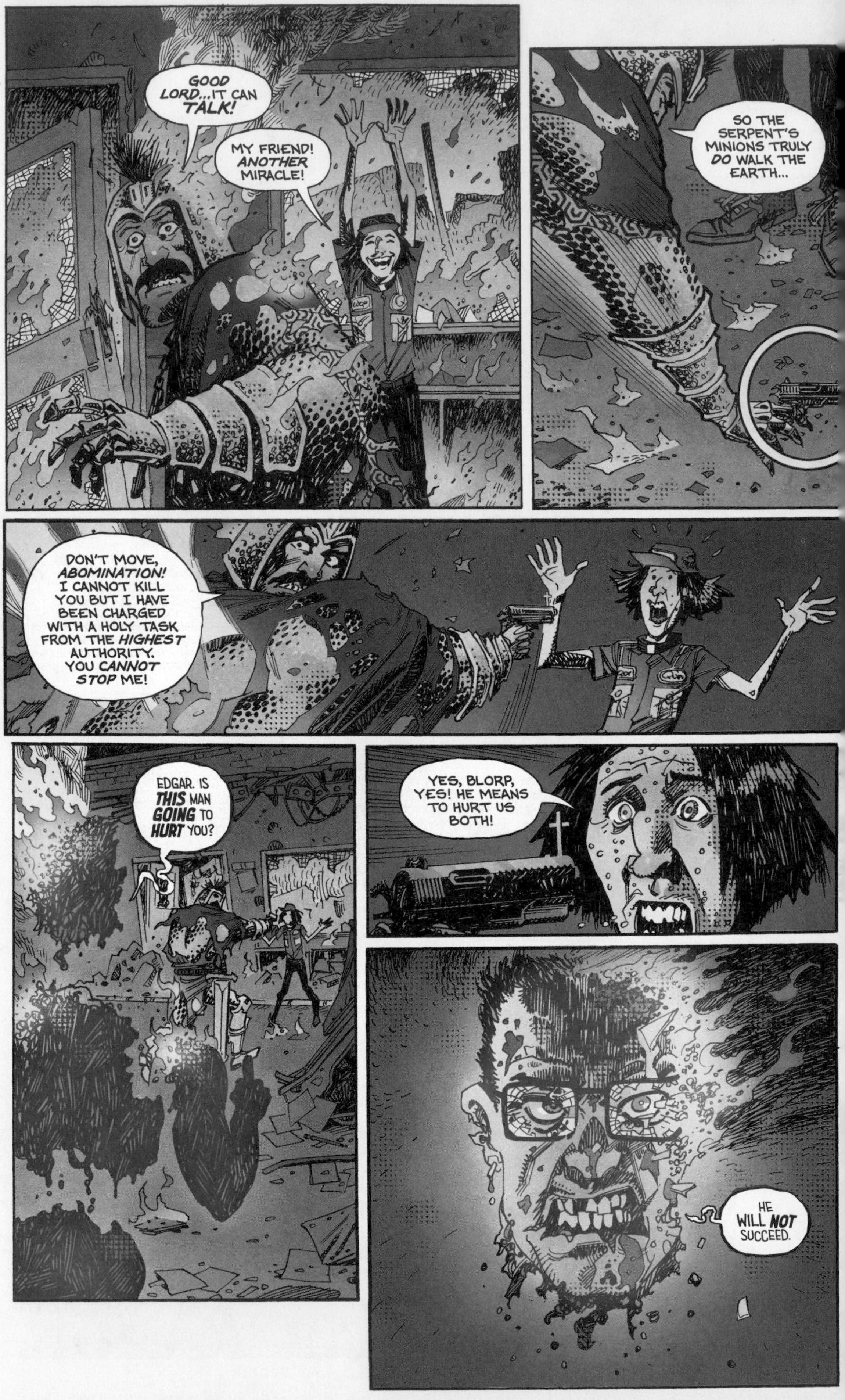
GOOD LORD...IT CAN TALK!
MY FRIEND! ANOTHER MIRACLE!
SO THE SERPENT'S MINIONS TRULY DO WALK THE EARTH...
DON'T MOVE, ABOMINATION! I CANNOT KILL YOU BUT I HAVE BEEN CHARGED WITH A HOLY TASK FROM THE HIGHEST AUTHORITY. YOU CANNOT STOP ME!
EDGAR. IS THIS MAN GOING TO HURT YOU?
YES, BLORP, YES! HE MEANS TO HURT US BOTH!
HE WILL NOT SUCCEED.

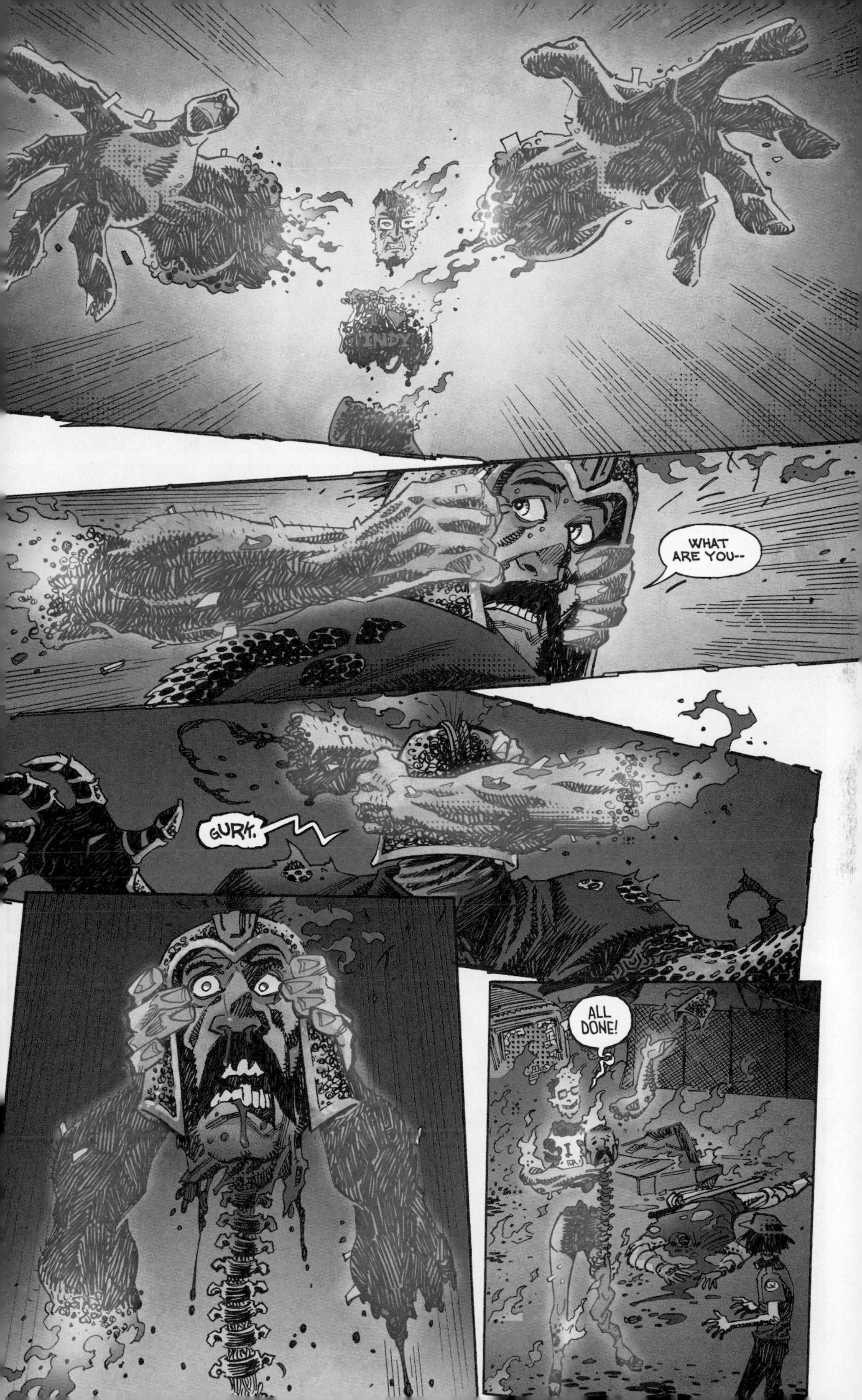
I ♥ INDY
WHAT ARE YOU--
GURK.
ALL DONE!

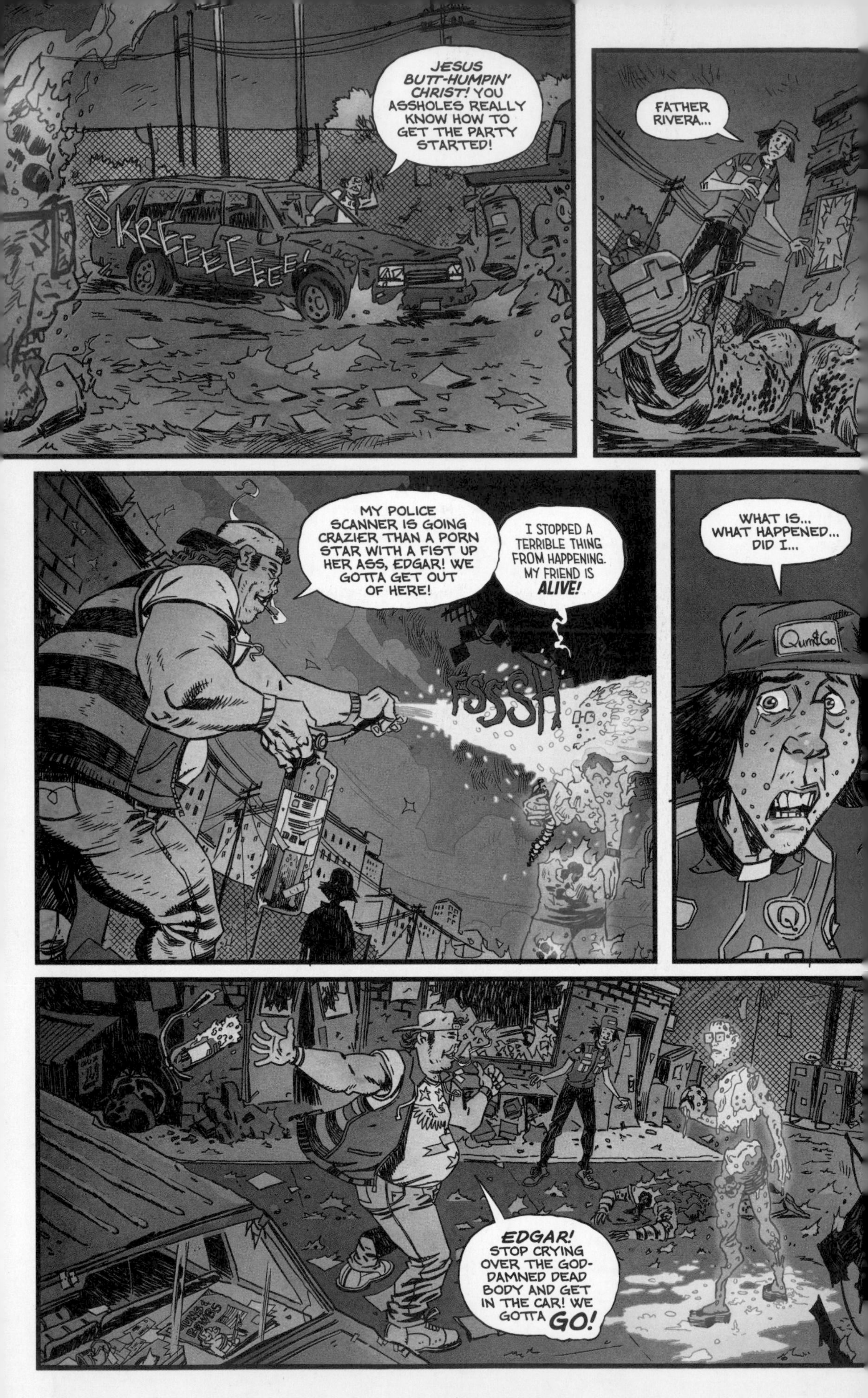

JESUS BUTT-HUMPIN' CHRIST! YOU ASSHOLES REALLY KNOW HOW TO GET THE PARTY STARTED!
SKREEEEEEEEE!
FATHER RIVERA...
MY POLICE SCANNER IS GOING CRAZIER THAN A PORN STAR WITH A FIST UP HER ASS, EDGAR! WE GOTTA GET OUT OF HERE!
I STOPPED A TERRIBLE THING FROM HAPPENING. MY FRIEND IS ALIVE!
FSSSH
WHAT IS... WHAT HAPPENED... DID I...
QUIK&GO
EDGAR! STOP CRYING OVER THE GOD-DAMNED DEAD BODY AND GET IN THE CAR! WE GOTTA GO!

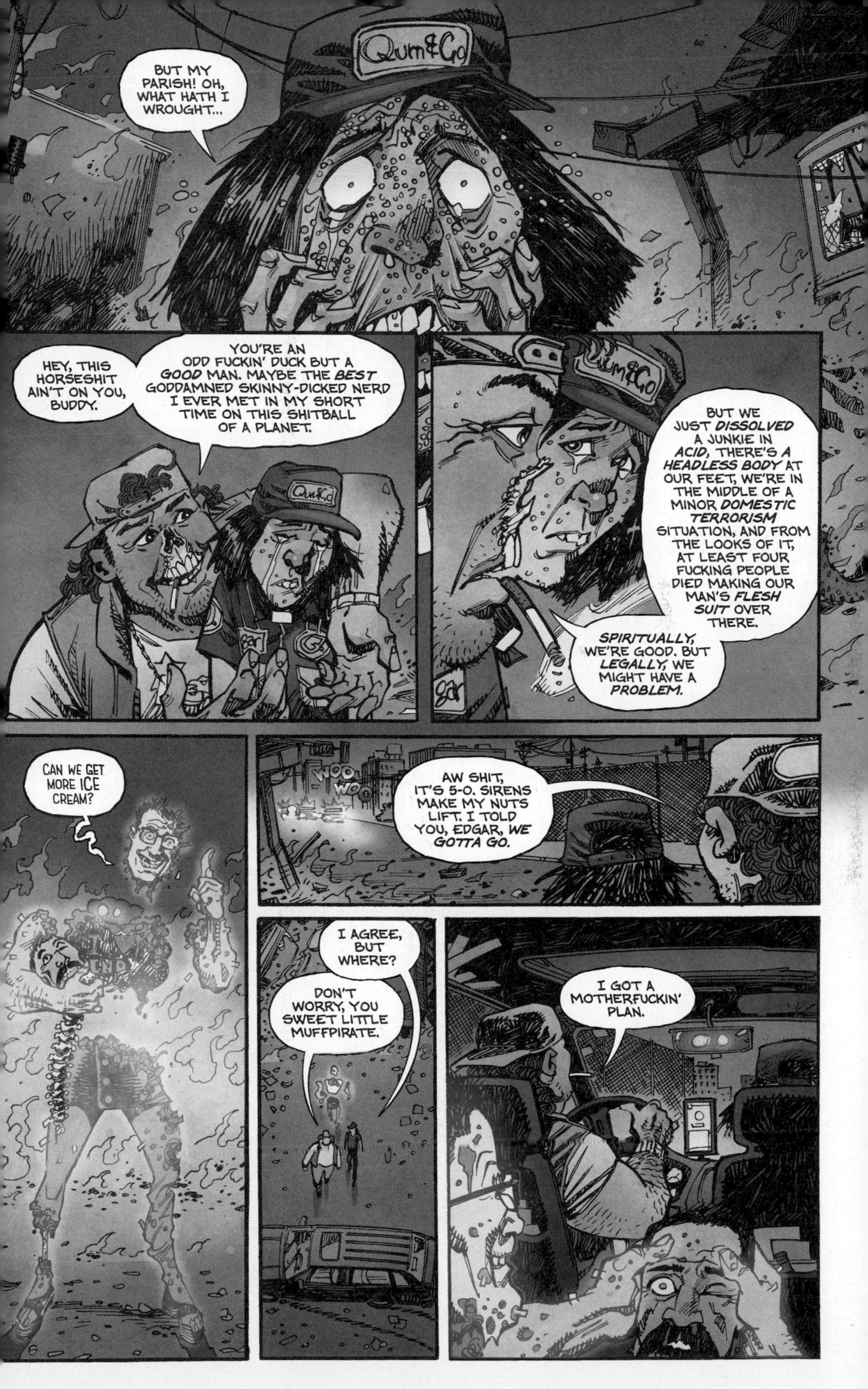
Qum&Co
BUT MY PARISH! OH, WHAT HATH I WROUGHT...
HEY, THIS HORSESHIT AIN'T ON YOU, BUDDY.
YOU'RE AN ODD FUCKIN' DUCK BUT A GOOD MAN. MAYBE THE BEST GODDAMNED SKINNY-DICKED NERD I EVER MET IN MY SHORT TIME ON THIS SHITBALL OF A PLANET.
BUT WE JUST DISSOLVED A JUNKIE IN ACID, THERE'S A HEADLESS BODY AT OUR FEET, WE'RE IN THE MIDDLE OF A MINOR DOMESTIC TERRORISM SITUATION, AND FROM THE LOOKS OF IT, AT LEAST FOUR FUCKING PEOPLE DIED MAKING OUR MAN'S FLESH SUIT OVER THERE.
SPIRITUALLY, WE'RE GOOD. BUT LEGALLY, WE MIGHT HAVE A PROBLEM.
CAN WE GET MORE ICE CREAM?
WOO WOO
AW SHIT, IT'S 5-0. SIRENS MAKE MY NUTS LIFT. I TOLD YOU, EDGAR, WE GOTTA GO.
I AGREE, BUT WHERE?
DON'T WORRY, YOU SWEET LITTLE MUFFPIRATE.
I GOT A MOTHERFUCKIN' PLAN.

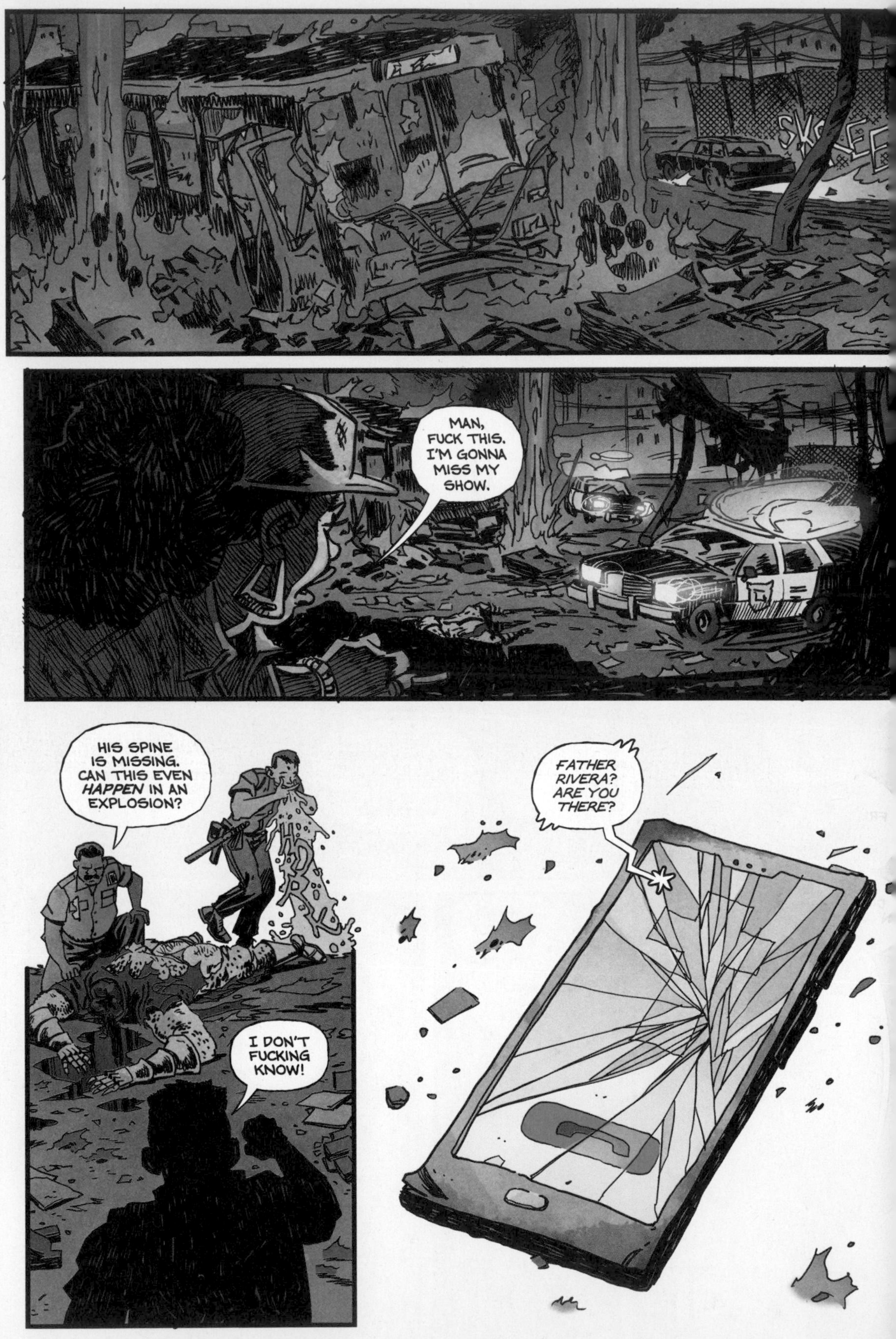
MAN, FUCK THIS. I'M GONNA MISS MY SHOW.
HIS SPINE IS MISSING. CAN THIS EVEN *HAPPEN* IN AN EXPLOSION?
I DON'T FUCKING KNOW!
FATHER RIVERA? ARE YOU THERE?

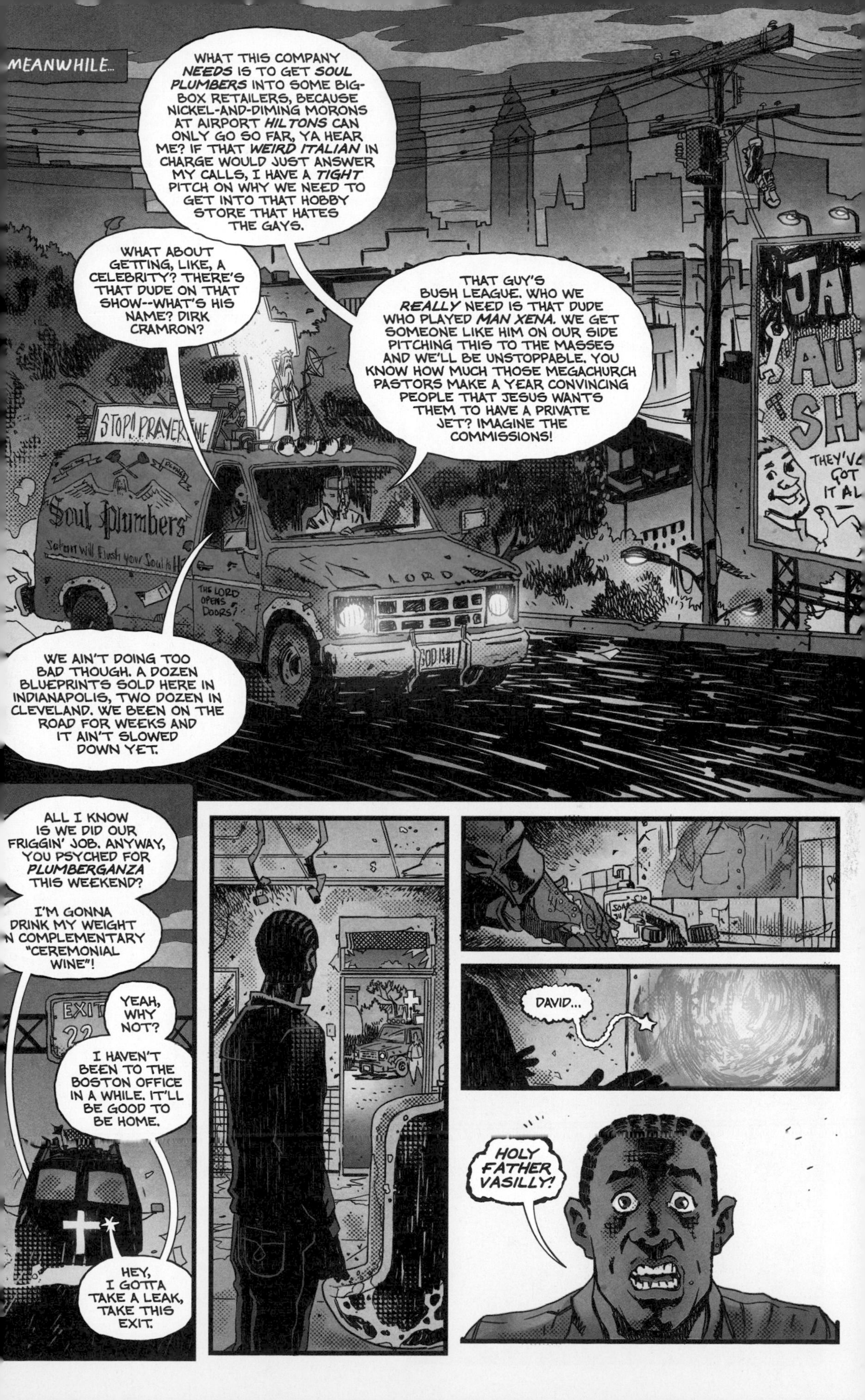
MEANWHILE...
WHAT THIS COMPANY NEEDS IS TO GET SOUL PLUMBERS INTO SOME BIG-BOX RETAILERS, BECAUSE NICKEL-AND-DIMING MORONS AT AIRPORT HILTONS CAN ONLY GO SO FAR, YA HEAR ME? IF THAT WEIRD ITALIAN IN CHARGE WOULD JUST ANSWER MY CALLS, I HAVE A TIGHT PITCH ON WHY WE NEED TO GET INTO THAT HOBBY STORE THAT HATES THE GAYS.
WHAT ABOUT GETTING, LIKE, A CELEBRITY? THERE'S THAT DUDE ON THAT SHOW--WHAT'S HIS NAME? DIRK CRAMRON?
THAT GUY'S BUSH LEAGUE. WHO WE REALLY NEED IS THAT DUDE WHO PLAYED MAN XENA. WE GET SOMEONE LIKE HIM ON OUR SIDE PITCHING THIS TO THE MASSES AND WE'LL BE UNSTOPPABLE. YOU KNOW HOW MUCH THOSE MEGACHURCH PASTORS MAKE A YEAR CONVINCING PEOPLE THAT JESUS WANTS THEM TO HAVE A PRIVATE JET? IMAGINE THE COMMISSIONS!
Soul Plumbers
THE LORD OPENS DOORS!
LORD
GOD IS #1
WE AIN'T DOING TOO BAD THOUGH. A DOZEN BLUEPRINTS SOLD HERE IN INDIANAPOLIS, TWO DOZEN IN CLEVELAND. WE BEEN ON THE ROAD FOR WEEKS AND IT AIN'T SLOWED DOWN YET.
ALL I KNOW IS WE DID OUR FRIGGIN' JOB. ANYWAY, YOU PSYCHED FOR PLUMBERGANZA THIS WEEKEND?
I'M GONNA DRINK MY WEIGHT IN COMPLEMENTARY "CEREMONIAL WINE"!
YEAH, WHY NOT?
I HAVEN'T BEEN TO THE BOSTON OFFICE IN A WHILE. IT'LL BE GOOD TO BE HOME.
HEY, I GOTTA TAKE A LEAK, TAKE THIS EXIT.
DAVID...
HOLY FATHER VASILLY!

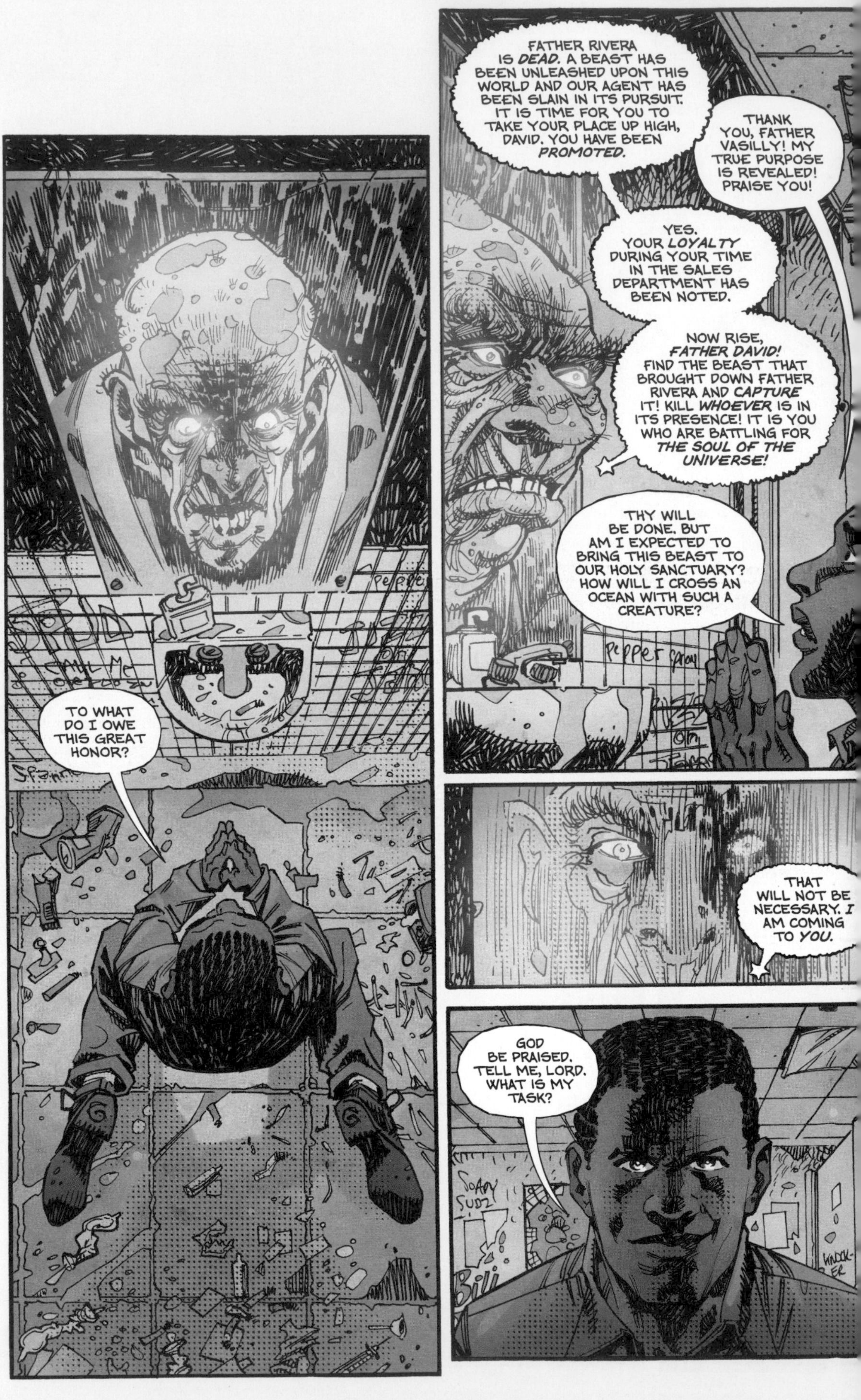
TO WHAT DO I OWE THIS GREAT HONOR?
FATHER RIVERA IS *DEAD*. A BEAST HAS BEEN UNLEASHED UPON THIS WORLD AND OUR AGENT HAS BEEN SLAIN IN ITS PURSUIT. IT IS TIME FOR YOU TO TAKE YOUR PLACE UP HIGH, DAVID. YOU HAVE BEEN *PROMOTED*.
THANK YOU, FATHER VASILLY! MY TRUE PURPOSE IS REVEALED! PRAISE YOU!
YES. YOUR *LOYALTY* DURING YOUR TIME IN THE SALES DEPARTMENT HAS BEEN NOTED.
NOW RISE, *FATHER DAVID!* FIND THE BEAST THAT BROUGHT DOWN FATHER RIVERA AND *CAPTURE* IT! KILL *WHOEVER* IS IN ITS PRESENCE! IT IS YOU WHO ARE BATTLING FOR *THE SOUL OF THE UNIVERSE!*
THY WILL BE DONE. BUT AM I EXPECTED TO BRING THIS BEAST TO OUR HOLY SANCTUARY? HOW WILL I CROSS AN OCEAN WITH SUCH A CREATURE?
THAT WILL NOT BE NECESSARY. *I* AM COMING TO *YOU*.
GOD BE PRAISED. TELL ME, LORD. WHAT IS MY TASK?

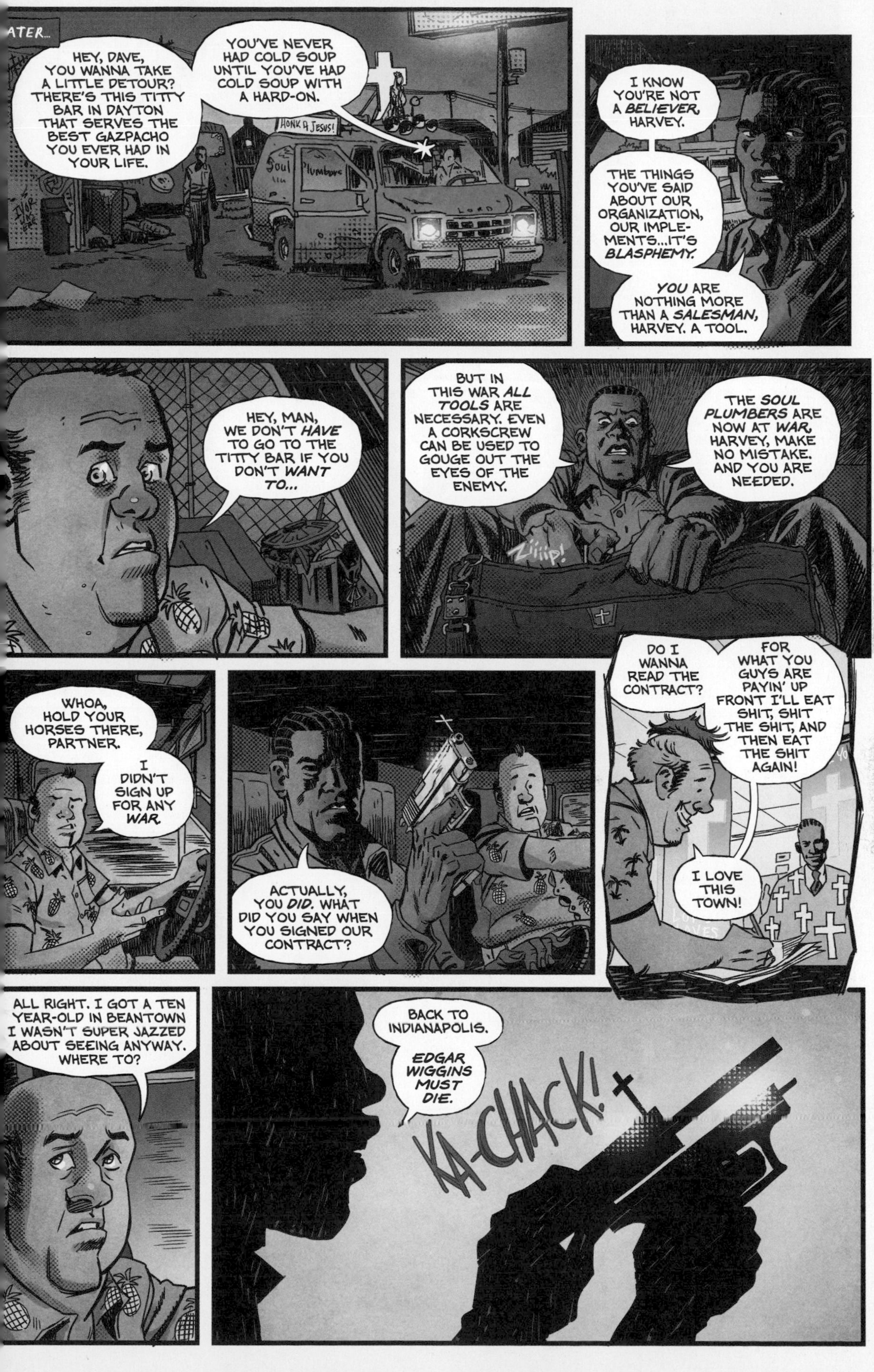
LATER...
HEY, DAVE, YOU WANNA TAKE A LITTLE DETOUR? THERE'S THIS TITTY BAR IN DAYTON THAT SERVES THE BEST GAZPACHO YOU EVER HAD IN YOUR LIFE.
YOU'VE NEVER HAD COLD SOUP UNTIL YOU'VE HAD COLD SOUP WITH A HARD-ON.
HONK 4 JESUS!
Soul Plumbers
I KNOW YOU'RE NOT A BELIEVER, HARVEY.
THE THINGS YOU'VE SAID ABOUT OUR ORGANIZATION, OUR IMPLEMENTS...IT'S BLASPHEMY.
YOU ARE NOTHING MORE THAN A SALESMAN, HARVEY. A TOOL.
HEY, MAN, WE DON'T HAVE TO GO TO THE TITTY BAR IF YOU DON'T WANT TO...
BUT IN THIS WAR ALL TOOLS ARE NECESSARY. EVEN A CORKSCREW CAN BE USED TO GOUGE OUT THE EYES OF THE ENEMY.
THE SOUL PLUMBERS ARE NOW AT WAR, HARVEY, MAKE NO MISTAKE. AND YOU ARE NEEDED.
ZIIIIP!
WHOA, HOLD YOUR HORSES THERE, PARTNER.
I DIDN'T SIGN UP FOR ANY WAR.
ACTUALLY, YOU DID. WHAT DID YOU SAY WHEN YOU SIGNED OUR CONTRACT?
DO I WANNA READ THE CONTRACT?
FOR WHAT YOU GUYS ARE PAYIN' UP FRONT I'LL EAT SHIT, SHIT THE SHIT, AND THEN EAT THE SHIT AGAIN!
I LOVE THIS TOWN!
ALL RIGHT. I GOT A TEN YEAR-OLD IN BEANTOWN I WASN'T SUPER JAZZED ABOUT SEEING ANYWAY. WHERE TO?
BACK TO INDIANAPOLIS.
EDGAR WIGGINS MUST DIE.
KA-CHACK!

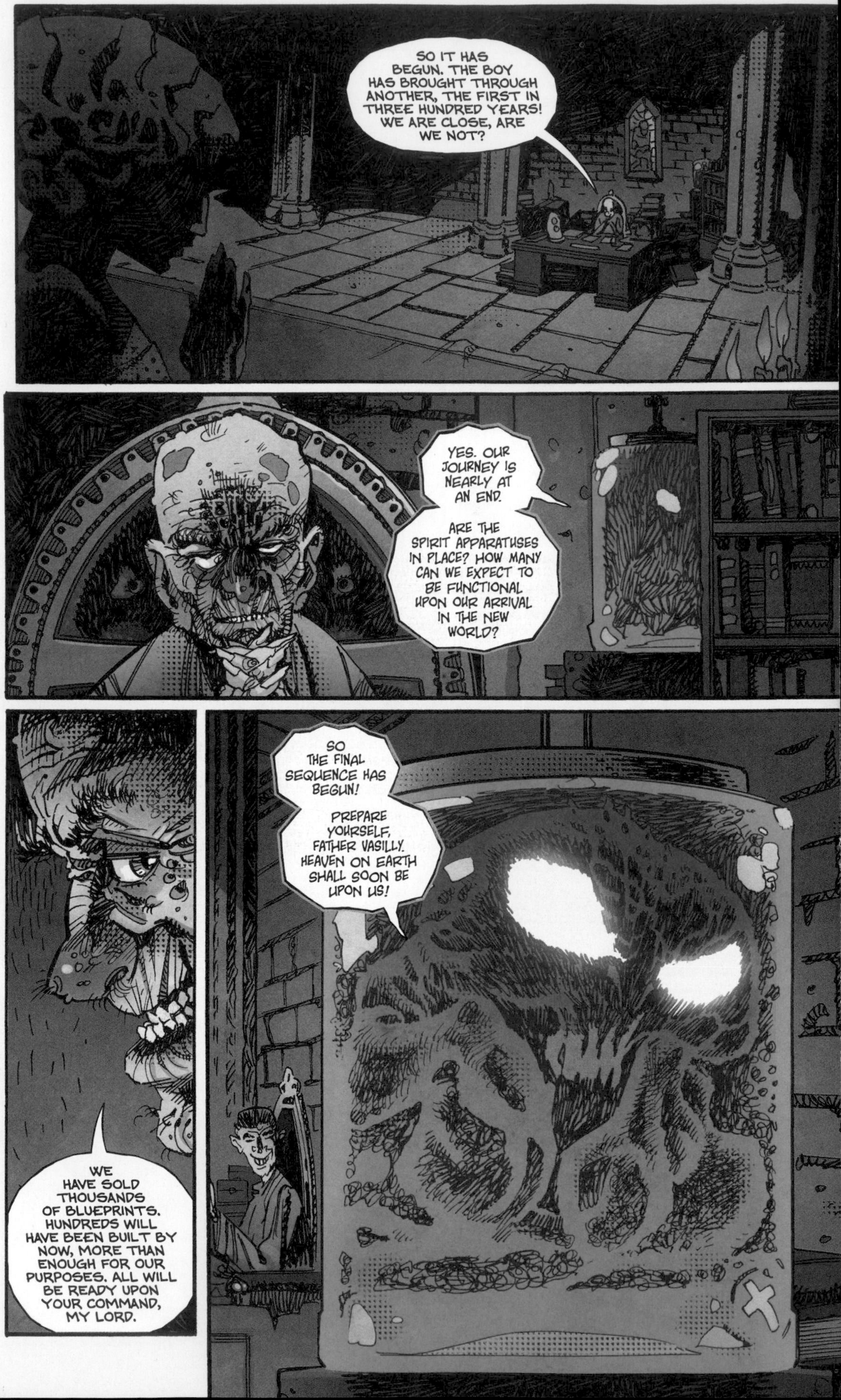
SO IT HAS BEGUN. THE BOY HAS BROUGHT THROUGH ANOTHER, THE FIRST IN THREE HUNDRED YEARS! WE ARE CLOSE, ARE WE NOT?
YES. OUR JOURNEY IS NEARLY AT AN END.
ARE THE SPIRIT APPARATUSES IN PLACE? HOW MANY CAN WE EXPECT TO BE FUNCTIONAL UPON OUR ARRIVAL IN THE NEW WORLD?
WE HAVE SOLD THOUSANDS OF BLUEPRINTS. HUNDREDS WILL HAVE BEEN BUILT BY NOW, MORE THAN ENOUGH FOR OUR PURPOSES. ALL WILL BE READY UPON YOUR COMMAND, MY LORD.
SO THE FINAL SEQUENCE HAS BEGUN!
PREPARE YOURSELF, FATHER VASILLY. HEAVEN ON EARTH SHALL SOON BE UPON US!

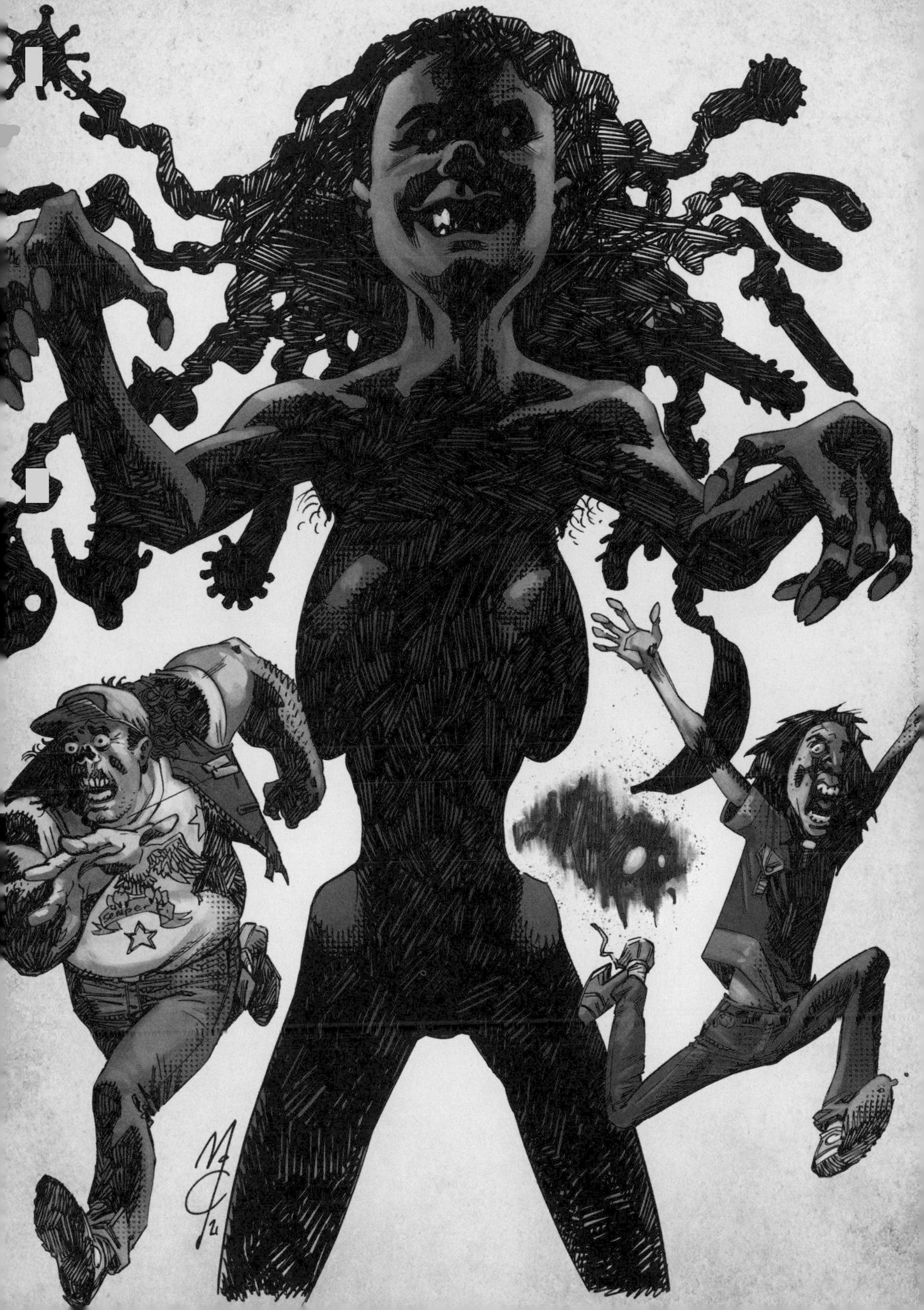

DC Horror Presents: Soul Plumber #4
variant cover by Yanick Paquette
& Nathan Fairbairn

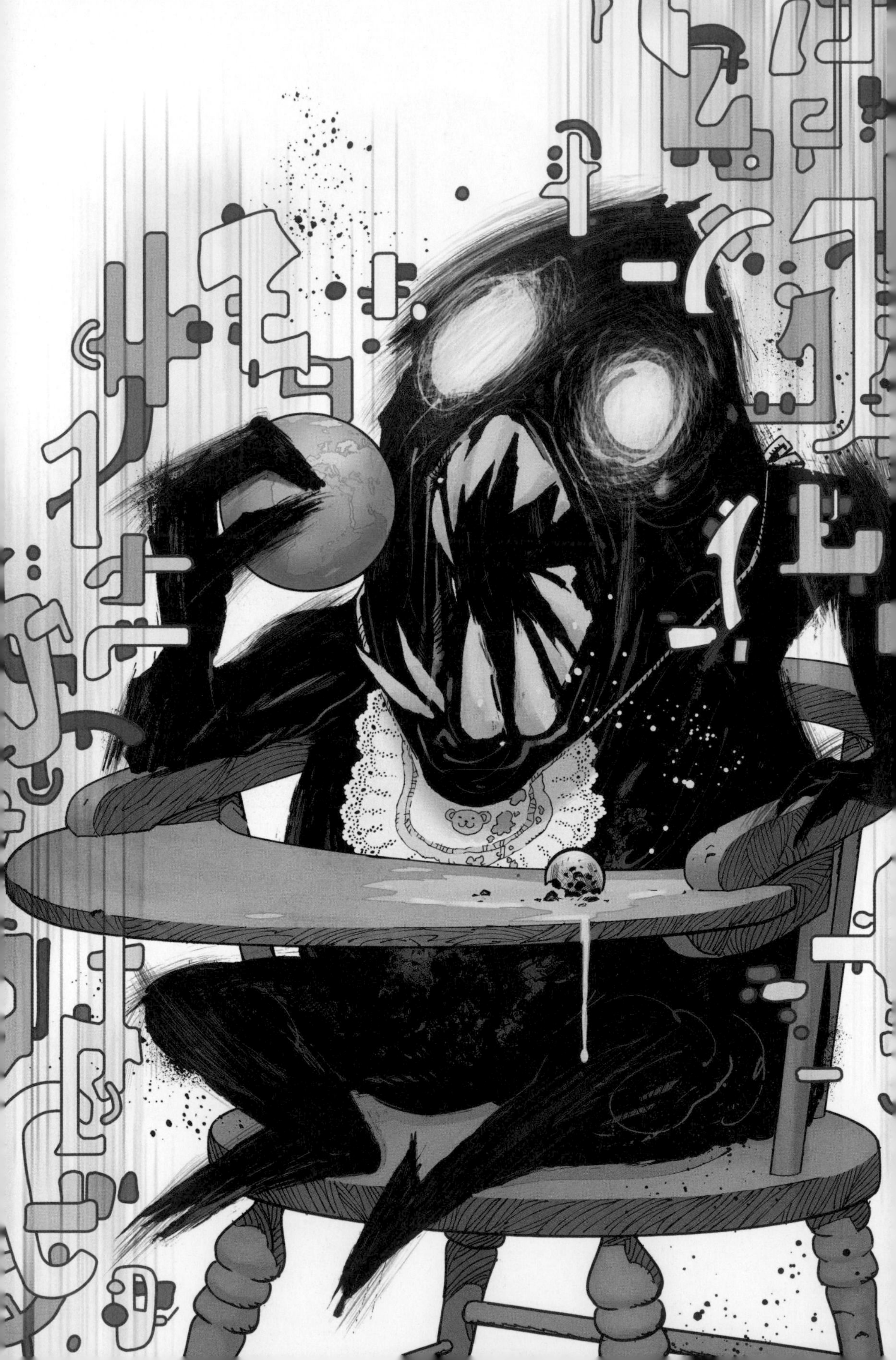

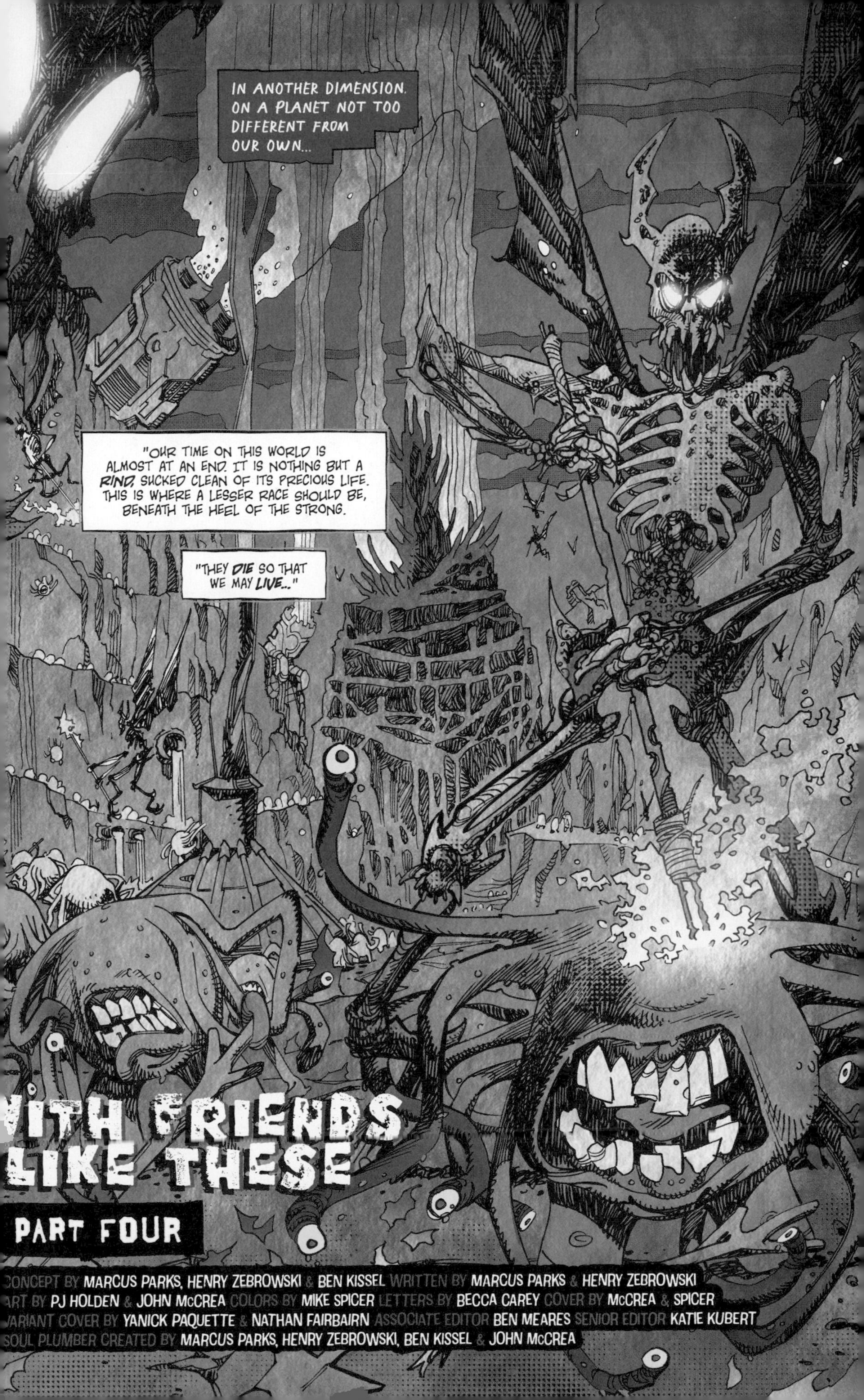
IN ANOTHER DIMENSION. ON A PLANET NOT TOO DIFFERENT FROM OUR OWN...
"OUR TIME ON THIS WORLD IS ALMOST AT AN END. IT IS NOTHING BUT A RIND, SUCKED CLEAN OF ITS PRECIOUS LIFE. THIS IS WHERE A LESSER RACE SHOULD BE, BENEATH THE HEEL OF THE STRONG.
"THEY DIE SO THAT WE MAY LIVE..."
WITH FRIENDS LIKE THESE
PART FOUR
CONCEPT BY MARCUS PARKS, HENRY ZEBROWSKI & BEN KISSEL WRITTEN BY MARCUS PARKS & HENRY ZEBROWSKI
ART BY PJ HOLDEN & JOHN McCREA COLORS BY MIKE SPICER LETTERS BY BECCA CAREY COVER BY McCREA & SPICER
VARIANT COVER BY YANICK PAQUETTE & NATHAN FAIRBAIRN ASSOCIATE EDITOR BEN MEARES SENIOR EDITOR KATIE KUBERT
SOUL PLUMBER CREATED BY MARCUS PARKS, HENRY ZEBROWSKI, BEN KISSEL & JOHN McCREA

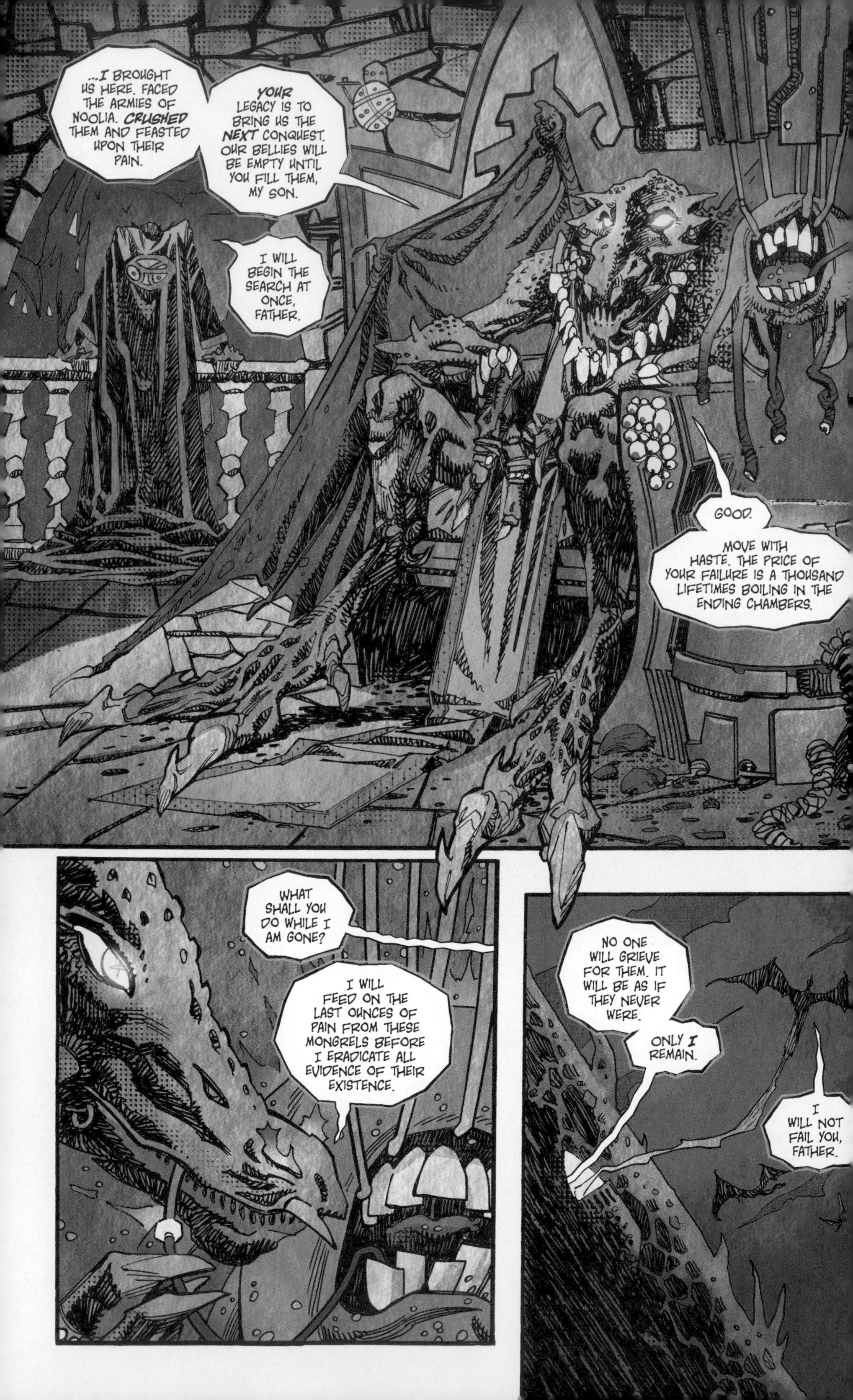
...I BROUGHT US HERE. FACED THE ARMIES OF NOOLIA. CRUSHED THEM AND FEASTED UPON THEIR PAIN.
YOUR LEGACY IS TO BRING US THE NEXT CONQUEST. OUR BELLIES WILL BE EMPTY UNTIL YOU FILL THEM, MY SON.
I WILL BEGIN THE SEARCH AT ONCE, FATHER.
GOOD.
MOVE WITH HASTE. THE PRICE OF YOUR FAILURE IS A THOUSAND LIFETIMES BOILING IN THE ENDING CHAMBERS.
WHAT SHALL YOU DO WHILE I AM GONE?
I WILL FEED ON THE LAST OUNCES OF PAIN FROM THESE MONGRELS BEFORE I ERADICATE ALL EVIDENCE OF THEIR EXISTENCE.
NO ONE WILL GRIEVE FOR THEM. IT WILL BE AS IF THEY NEVER WERE.
ONLY I REMAIN.
I WILL NOT FAIL YOU, FATHER.

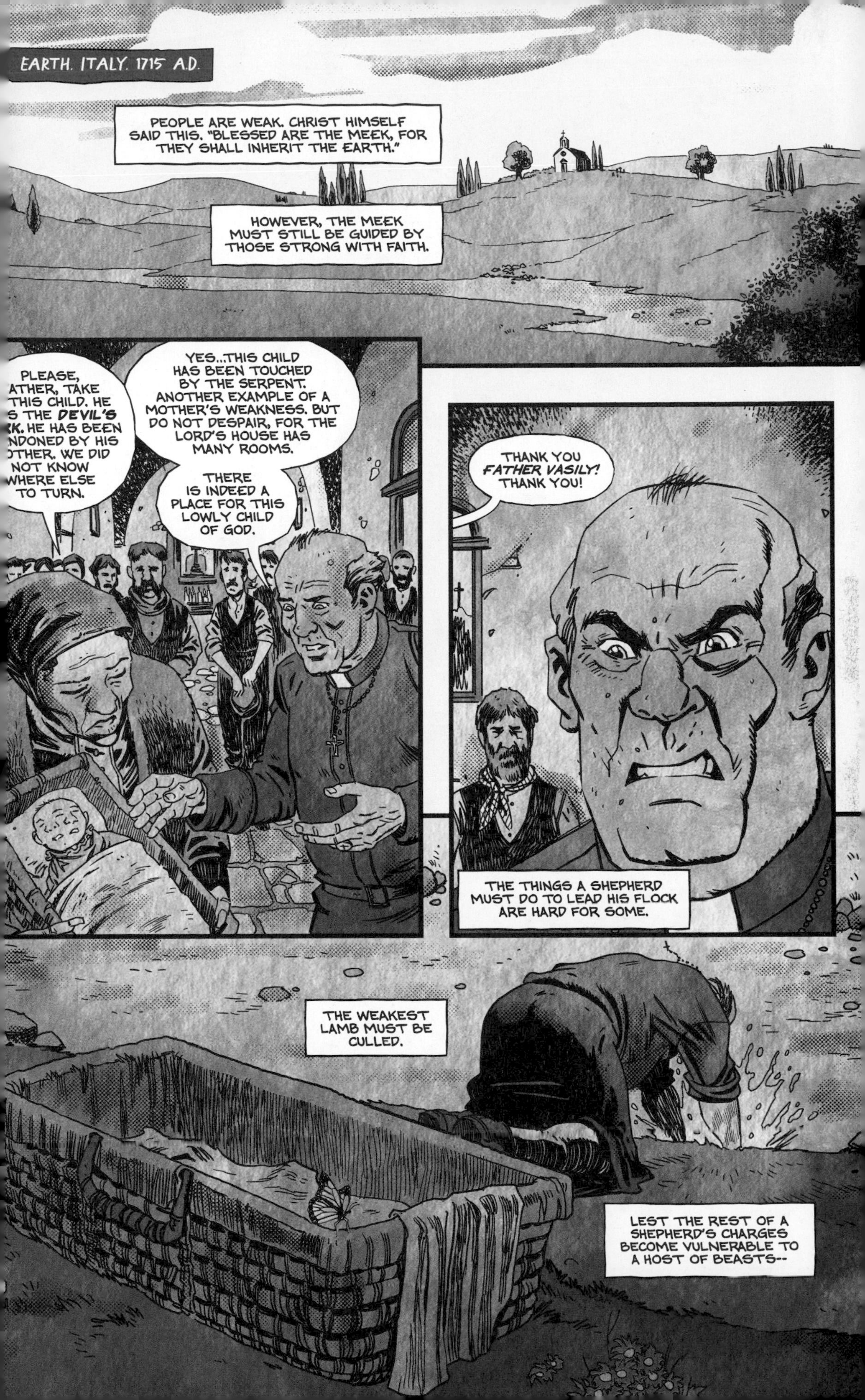
EARTH. ITALY. 1715 A.D.
PEOPLE ARE WEAK. CHRIST HIMSELF SAID THIS. "BLESSED ARE THE MEEK, FOR THEY SHALL INHERIT THE EARTH."
HOWEVER, THE MEEK MUST STILL BE GUIDED BY THOSE STRONG WITH FAITH.
PLEASE, ATHER, TAKE THIS CHILD. HE S THE DEVIL'S K. HE HAS BEEN NDONED BY HIS OTHER. WE DID NOT KNOW WHERE ELSE TO TURN.
YES...THIS CHILD HAS BEEN TOUCHED BY THE SERPENT. ANOTHER EXAMPLE OF A MOTHER'S WEAKNESS. BUT DO NOT DESPAIR, FOR THE LORD'S HOUSE HAS MANY ROOMS.
THERE IS INDEED A PLACE FOR THIS LOWLY CHILD OF GOD.
THANK YOU FATHER VASILY! THANK YOU!
THE THINGS A SHEPHERD MUST DO TO LEAD HIS FLOCK ARE HARD FOR SOME.
THE WEAKEST LAMB MUST BE CULLED.
LEST THE REST OF A SHEPHERD'S CHARGES BECOME VULNERABLE TO A HOST OF BEASTS--

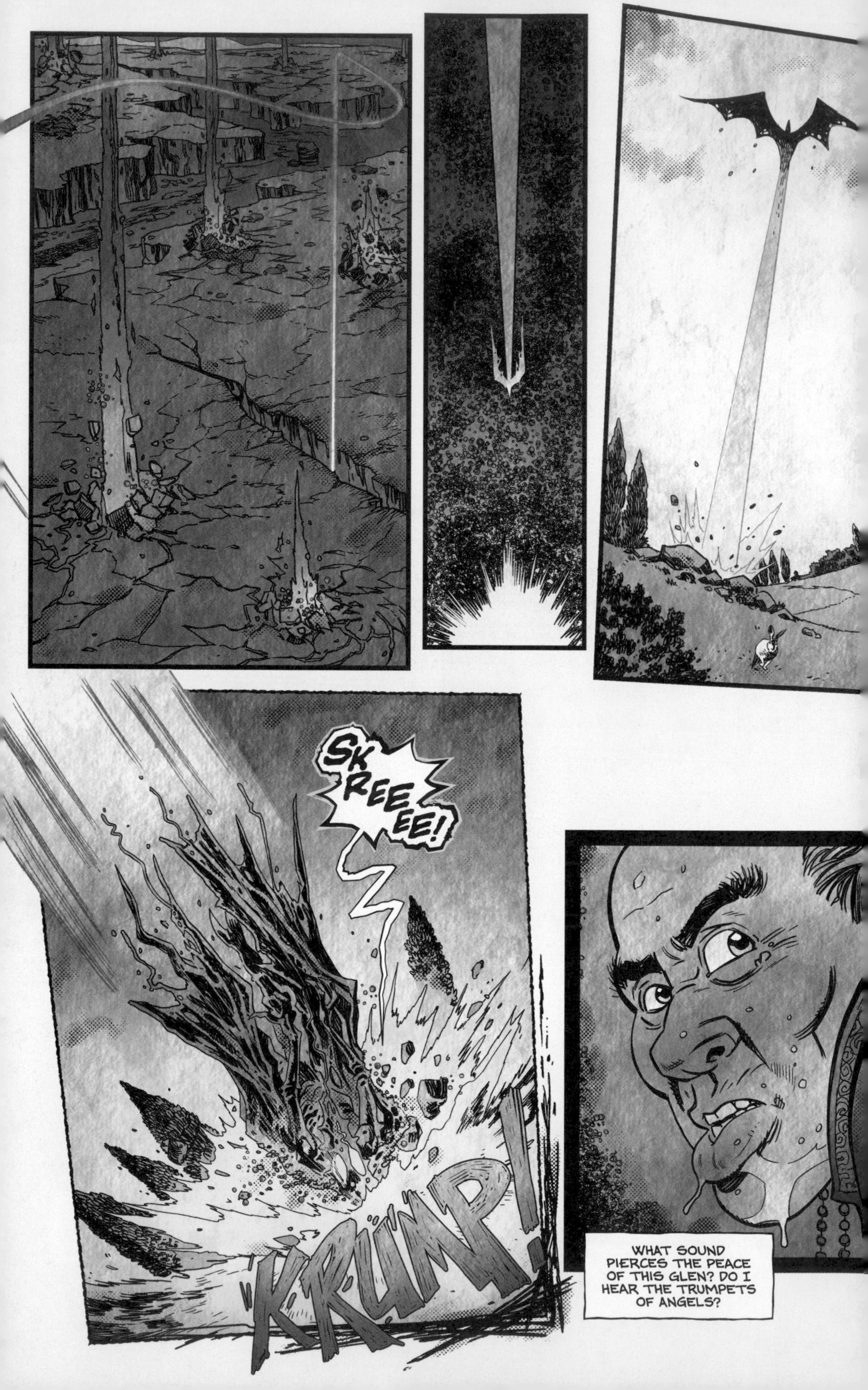
SKREEEEE!
KRUMP!
WHAT SOUND PIERCES THE PEACE OF THIS GLEN? DO I HEAR THE TRUMPETS OF ANGELS?

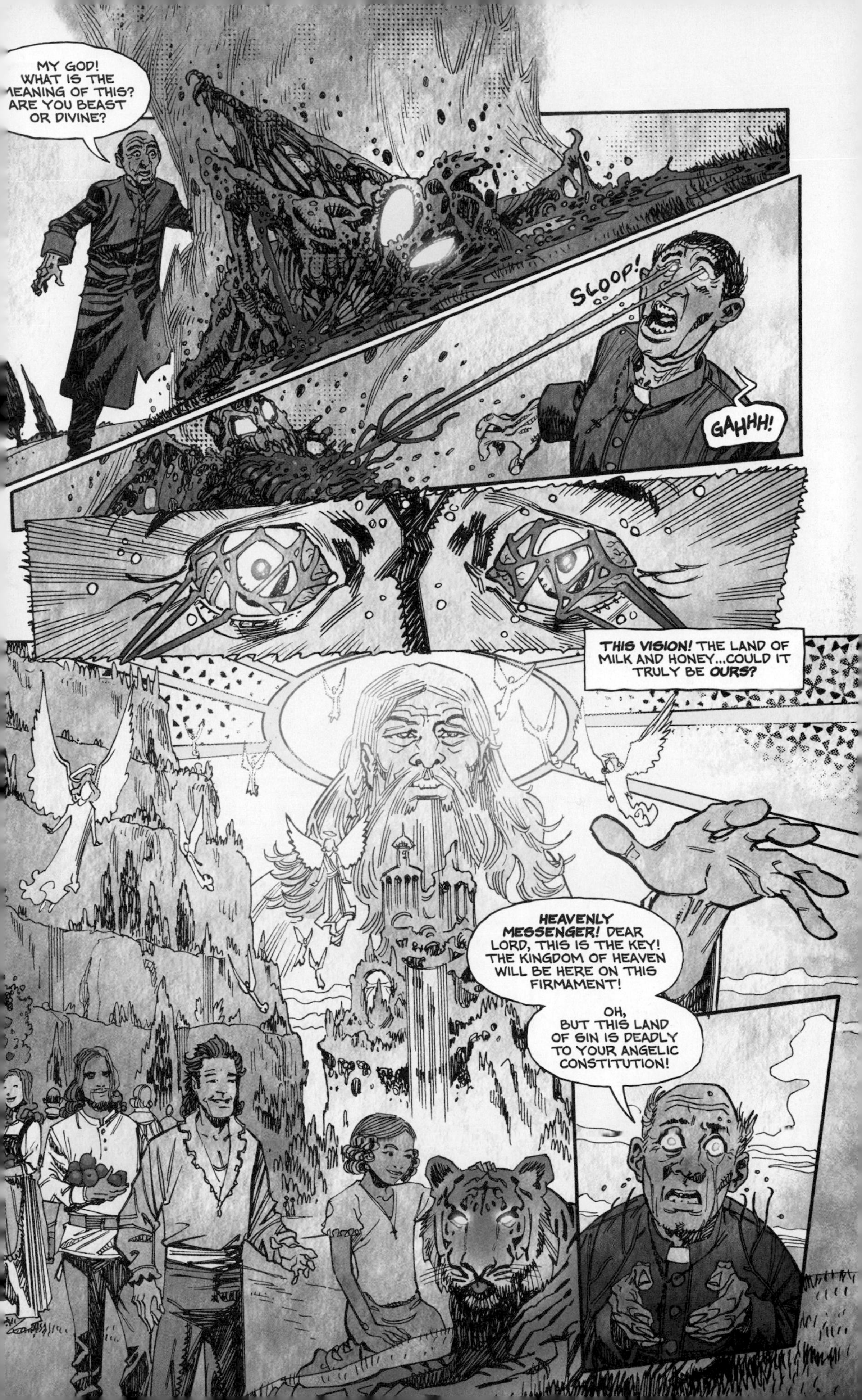
MY GOD! WHAT IS THE MEANING OF THIS? ARE YOU BEAST OR DIVINE?
SLOOP!
GAHHH!
THIS VISION! THE LAND OF MILK AND HONEY...COULD IT TRULY BE OURS?
HEAVENLY MESSENGER! DEAR LORD, THIS IS THE KEY! THE KINGDOM OF HEAVEN WILL BE HERE ON THIS FIRMAMENT!
OH, BUT THIS LAND OF SIN IS DEADLY TO YOUR ANGELIC CONSTITUTION!

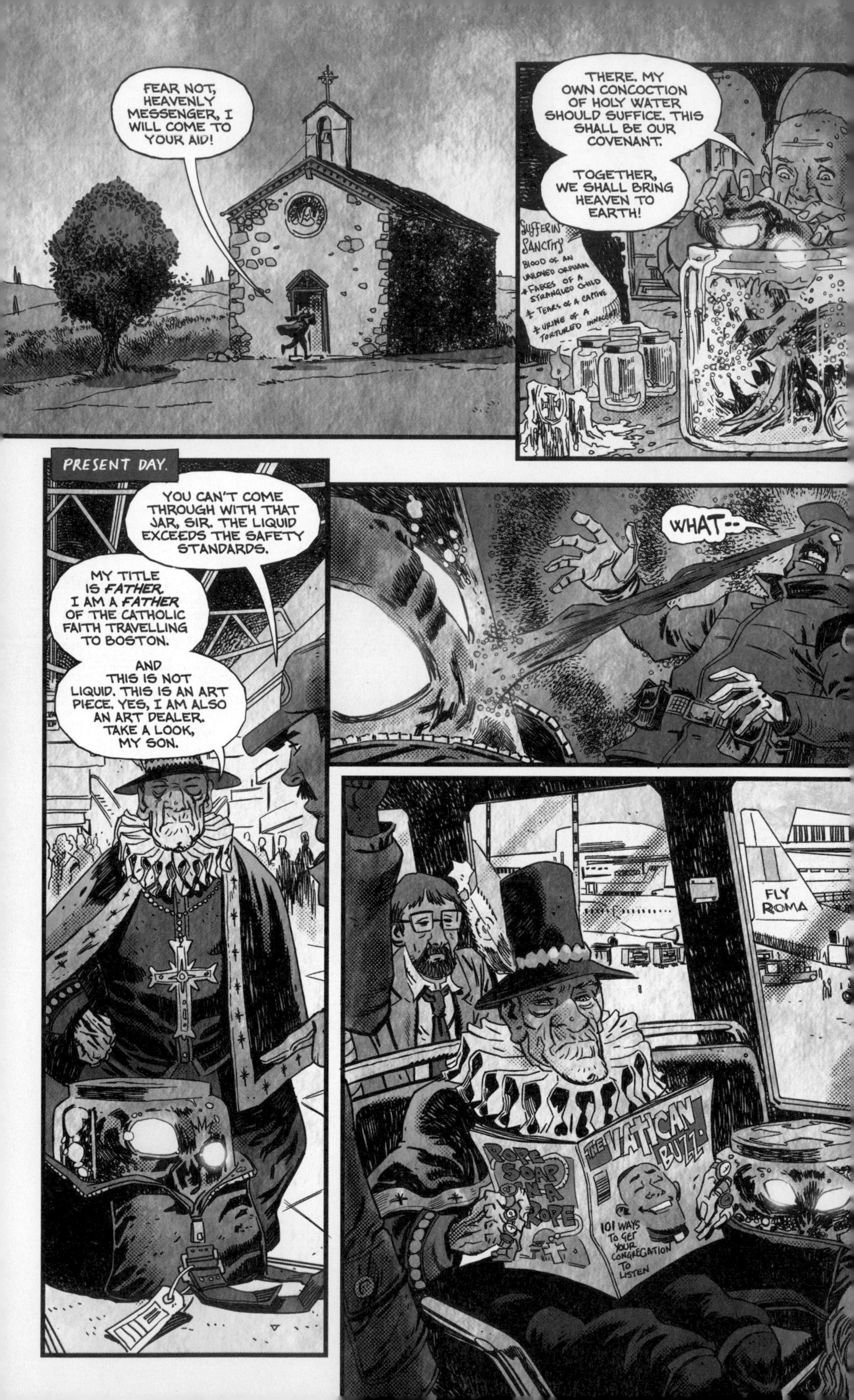
FEAR NOT, HEAVENLY MESSENGER, I WILL COME TO YOUR AID!
THERE. MY OWN CONCOCTION OF HOLY WATER SHOULD SUFFICE. THIS SHALL BE OUR COVENANT.
TOGETHER, WE SHALL BRING HEAVEN TO EARTH!
SUFFERIN SANCTITY
BLOOD OF AN UNLOVED ORPHAN
+ FAECES OF A STRANGLED CHILD
+ TEARS OF A CAPTIVE
+ URINE OF A TORTURED INNOCENT
PRESENT DAY.
YOU CAN'T COME THROUGH WITH THAT JAR, SIR. THE LIQUID EXCEEDS THE SAFETY STANDARDS.
MY TITLE IS *FATHER*. I AM A *FATHER* OF THE CATHOLIC FAITH TRAVELLING TO BOSTON.
AND THIS IS NOT LIQUID. THIS IS AN ART PIECE. YES, I AM ALSO AN ART DEALER. TAKE A LOOK, MY SON.
WHAT--
FLY ROMA
THE VATICAN BUZZ
POPE SOAP ON A ROPE
101 WAYS TO GET YOUR CONGREGATION TO LISTEN

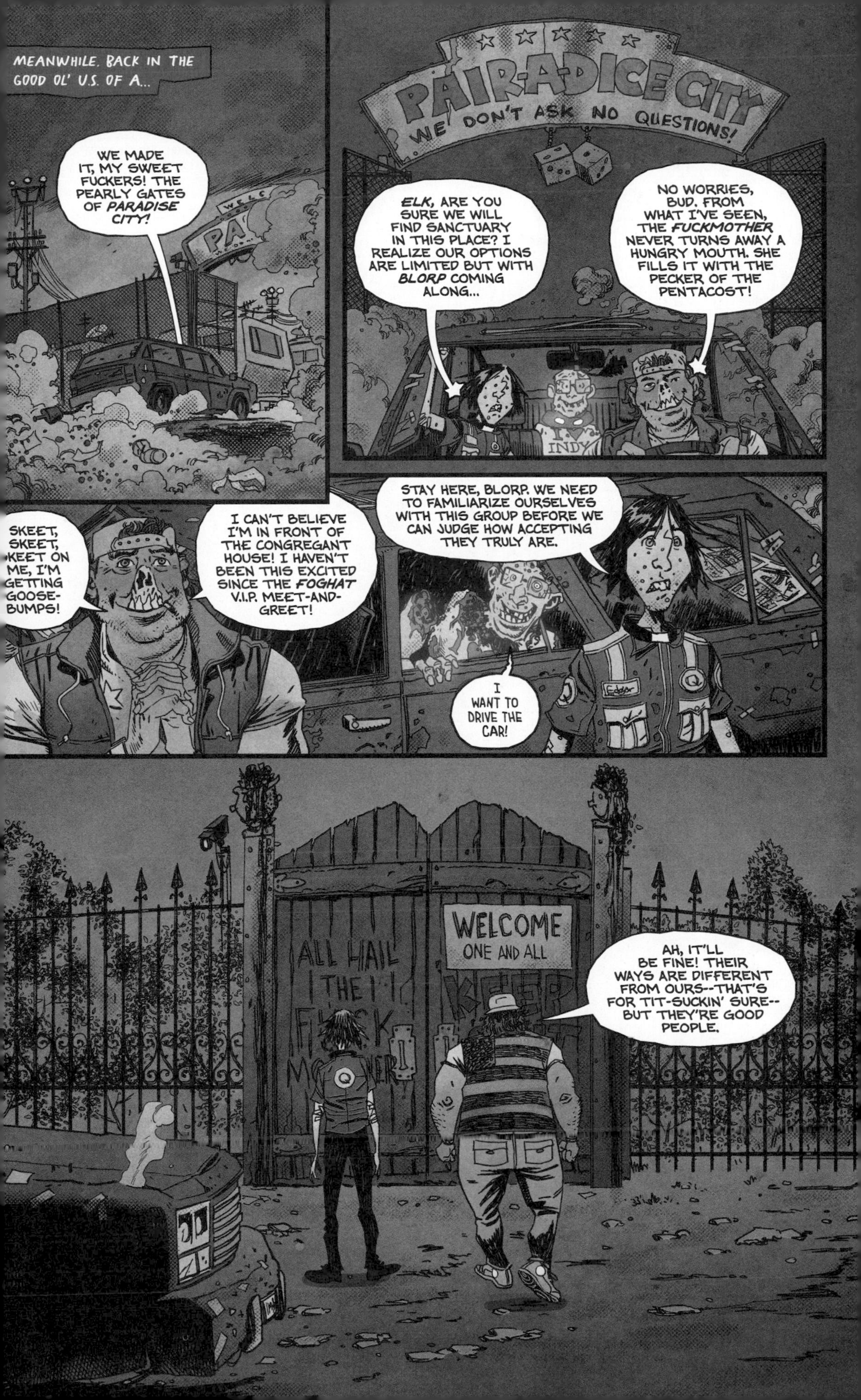

MEANWHILE, BACK IN THE GOOD OL' U.S. OF A...
WE MADE IT, MY SWEET FUCKERS! THE PEARLY GATES OF *PARADISE CITY!*
PAIR-A-DICE CITY
WE DON'T ASK NO QUESTIONS!
ELK, ARE YOU SURE WE WILL FIND SANCTUARY IN THIS PLACE? I REALIZE OUR OPTIONS ARE LIMITED BUT WITH *BLORP* COMING ALONG...
NO WORRIES, BUD. FROM WHAT I'VE SEEN, THE *FUCKMOTHER* NEVER TURNS AWAY A HUNGRY MOUTH. SHE FILLS IT WITH THE PECKER OF THE PENTACOST!
SKEET, SKEET, SKEET ON ME, I'M GETTING GOOSE-BUMPS!
I CAN'T BELIEVE I'M IN FRONT OF THE CONGREGANT HOUSE! I HAVEN'T BEEN THIS EXCITED SINCE THE *FOGHAT* V.I.P. MEET-AND-GREET!
STAY HERE, BLORP. WE NEED TO FAMILIARIZE OURSELVES WITH THIS GROUP BEFORE WE CAN JUDGE HOW ACCEPTING THEY TRULY ARE.
I WANT TO DRIVE THE CAR!
WELCOME ONE AND ALL
ALL HAIL THE FUCK MOTHER
AH, IT'LL BE FINE! THEIR WAYS ARE DIFFERENT FROM OURS--THAT'S FOR TIT-SUCKIN' SURE--BUT THEY'RE GOOD PEOPLE.

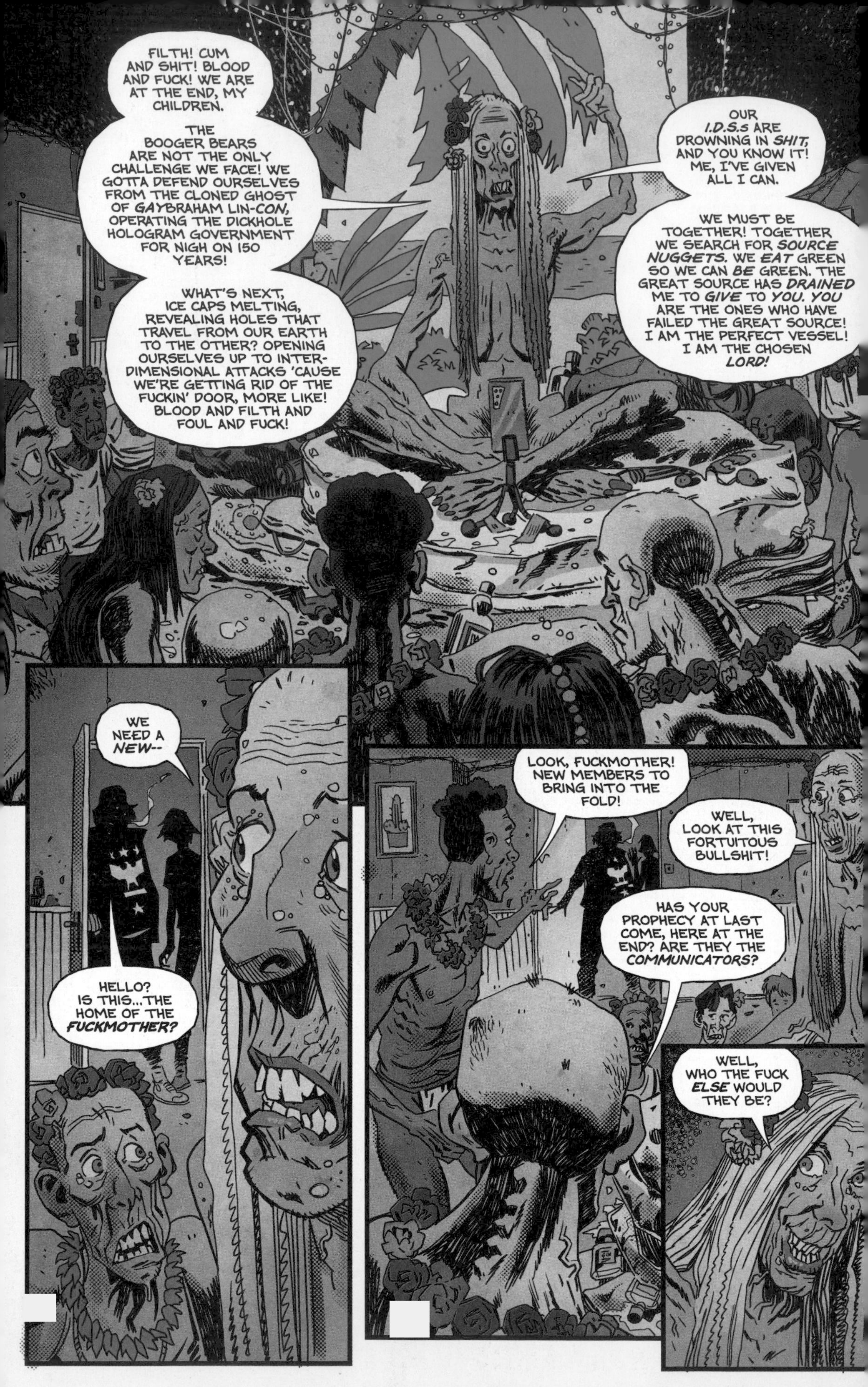
FILTH! CUM AND SHIT! BLOOD AND FUCK! WE ARE AT THE END, MY CHILDREN.
THE BOOGER BEARS ARE NOT THE ONLY CHALLENGE WE FACE! WE GOTTA DEFEND OURSELVES FROM THE CLONED GHOST OF GAYBRAHAM LIN-CON, OPERATING THE DICKHOLE HOLOGRAM GOVERNMENT FOR NIGH ON 150 YEARS!
WHAT'S NEXT, ICE CAPS MELTING, REVEALING HOLES THAT TRAVEL FROM OUR EARTH TO THE OTHER? OPENING OURSELVES UP TO INTER-DIMENSIONAL ATTACKS 'CAUSE WE'RE GETTING RID OF THE FUCKIN' DOOR, MORE LIKE! BLOOD AND FILTH AND FOUL AND FUCK!
OUR I.D.S.s ARE DROWNING IN SHIT, AND YOU KNOW IT! ME, I'VE GIVEN ALL I CAN.
WE MUST BE TOGETHER! TOGETHER WE SEARCH FOR SOURCE NUGGETS. WE EAT GREEN SO WE CAN BE GREEN. THE GREAT SOURCE HAS DRAINED ME TO GIVE TO YOU. YOU ARE THE ONES WHO HAVE FAILED THE GREAT SOURCE! I AM THE PERFECT VESSEL! I AM THE CHOSEN LORD!
WE NEED A NEW--
HELLO? IS THIS...THE HOME OF THE FUCKMOTHER?
LOOK, FUCKMOTHER! NEW MEMBERS TO BRING INTO THE FOLD!
WELL, LOOK AT THIS FORTUITOUS BULLSHIT!
HAS YOUR PROPHECY AT LAST COME, HERE AT THE END? ARE THEY THE COMMUNICATORS?
WELL, WHO THE FUCK ELSE WOULD THEY BE?

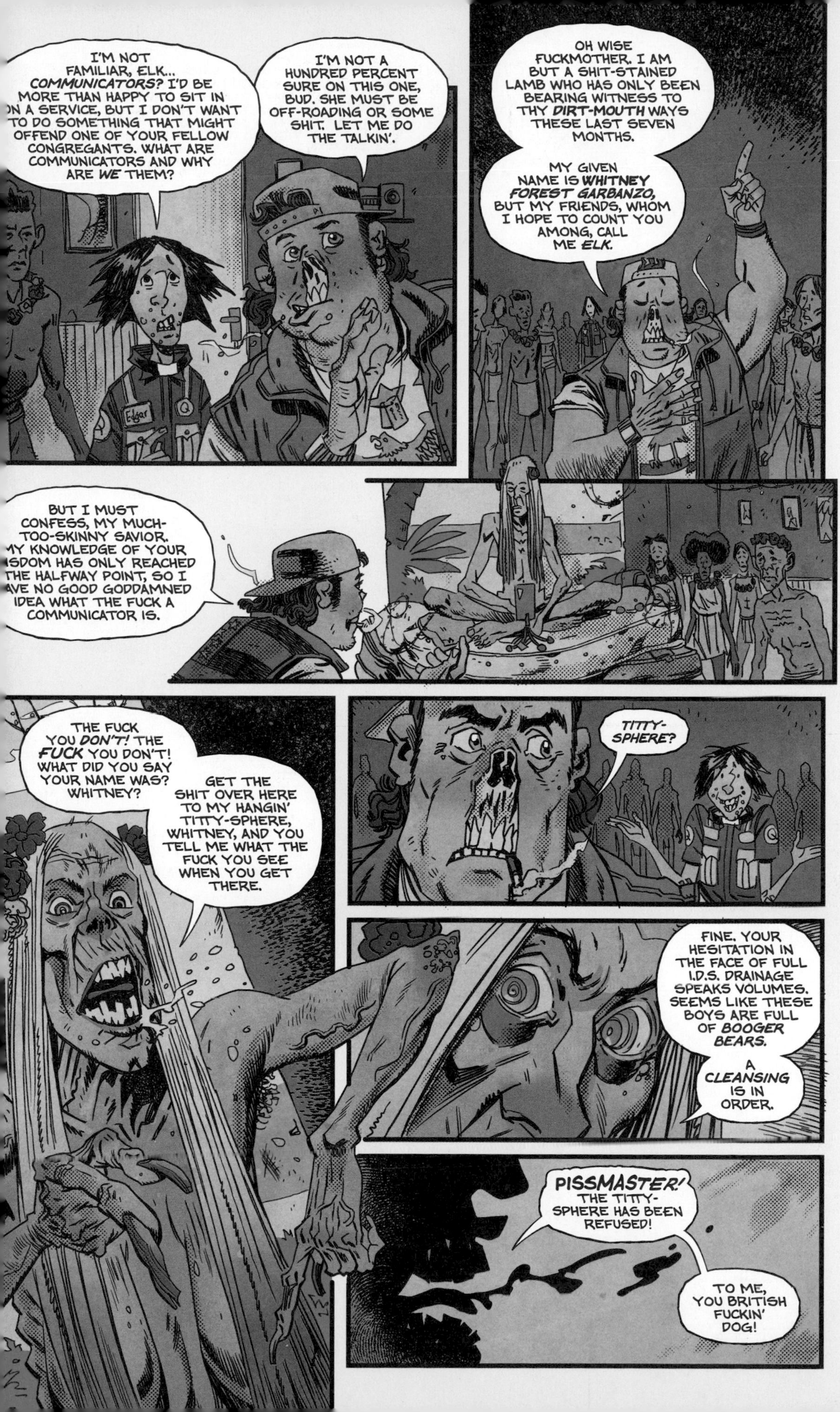

I'M NOT FAMILIAR, ELK... COMMUNICATORS? I'D BE MORE THAN HAPPY TO SIT IN N A SERVICE, BUT I DON'T WANT TO DO SOMETHING THAT MIGHT OFFEND ONE OF YOUR FELLOW CONGREGANTS. WHAT ARE COMMUNICATORS AND WHY ARE WE THEM?
I'M NOT A HUNDRED PERCENT SURE ON THIS ONE, BUD. SHE MUST BE OFF-ROADING OR SOME SHIT. LET ME DO THE TALKIN'.
Edgar
OH WISE FUCKMOTHER. I AM BUT A SHIT-STAINED LAMB WHO HAS ONLY BEEN BEARING WITNESS TO THY DIRT-MOUTH WAYS THESE LAST SEVEN MONTHS.
MY GIVEN NAME IS WHITNEY FOREST GARBANZO, BUT MY FRIENDS, WHOM I HOPE TO COUNT YOU AMONG, CALL ME ELK.
BUT I MUST CONFESS, MY MUCH-TOO-SKINNY SAVIOR. MY KNOWLEDGE OF YOUR ISDOM HAS ONLY REACHED THE HALFWAY POINT, SO I AVE NO GOOD GODDAMNED IDEA WHAT THE FUCK A COMMUNICATOR IS.
THE FUCK YOU DON'T! THE FUCK YOU DON'T! WHAT DID YOU SAY YOUR NAME WAS? WHITNEY?
GET THE SHIT OVER HERE TO MY HANGIN' TITTY-SPHERE, WHITNEY, AND YOU TELL ME WHAT THE FUCK YOU SEE WHEN YOU GET THERE.
TITTY-SPHERE?
FINE. YOUR HESITATION IN THE FACE OF FULL I.D.S. DRAINAGE SPEAKS VOLUMES. SEEMS LIKE THESE BOYS ARE FULL OF BOOGER BEARS.
A CLEANSING IS IN ORDER.
PISSMASTER! THE TITTY-SPHERE HAS BEEN REFUSED!
TO ME, YOU BRITISH FUCKIN' DOG!

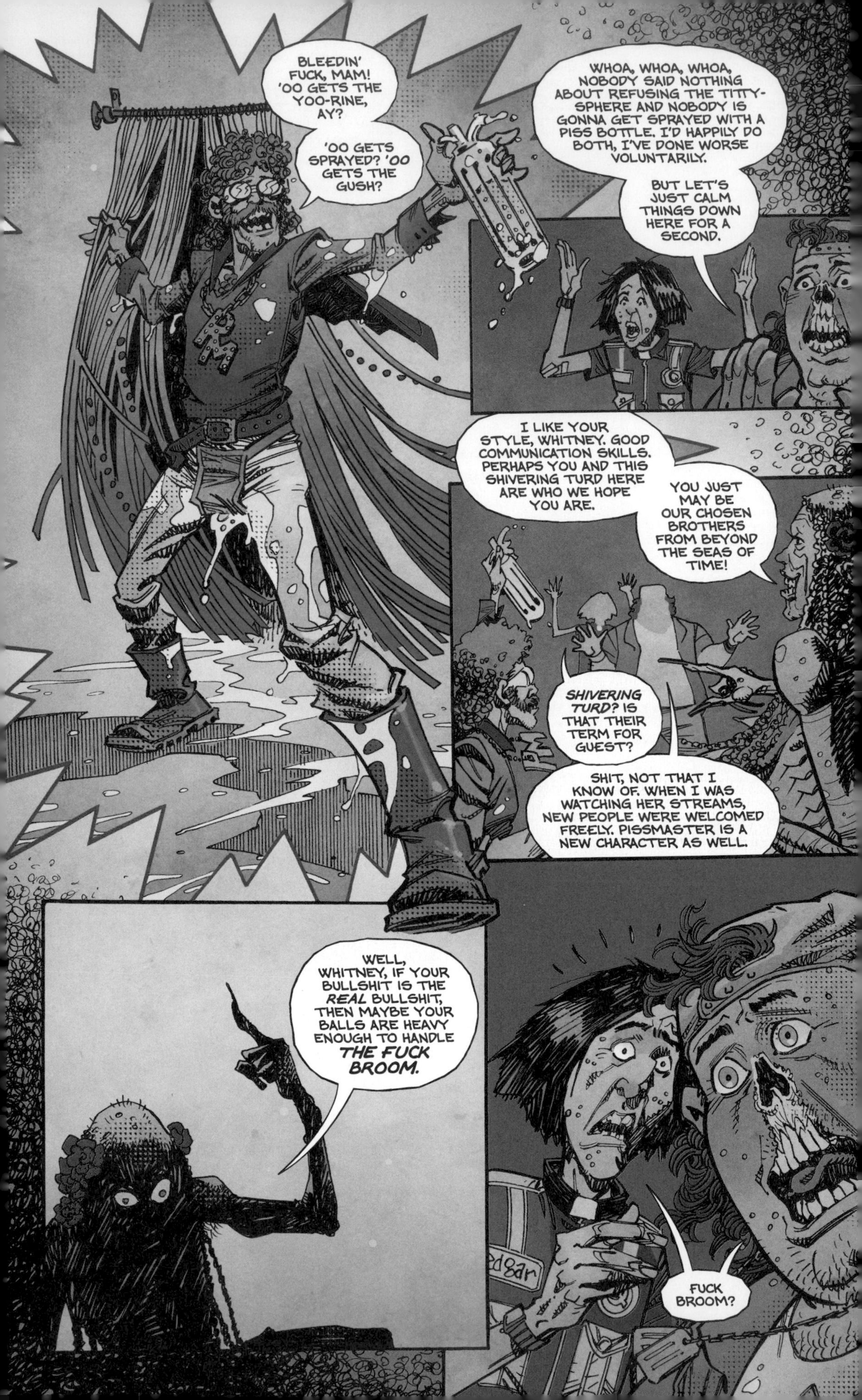
BLEEDIN' FUCK, MAM! 'OO GETS THE YOO-RINE, AY?
'OO GETS SPRAYED? 'OO GETS THE GUSH?
WHOA, WHOA, WHOA, NOBODY SAID NOTHING ABOUT REFUSING THE TITTY-SPHERE AND NOBODY IS GONNA GET SPRAYED WITH A PISS BOTTLE. I'D HAPPILY DO BOTH, I'VE DONE WORSE VOLUNTARILY.
BUT LET'S JUST CALM THINGS DOWN HERE FOR A SECOND.
I LIKE YOUR STYLE, WHITNEY. GOOD COMMUNICATION SKILLS. PERHAPS YOU AND THIS SHIVERING TURD HERE ARE WHO WE HOPE YOU ARE.
YOU JUST MAY BE OUR CHOSEN BROTHERS FROM BEYOND THE SEAS OF TIME!
SHIVERING TURD? IS THAT THEIR TERM FOR GUEST?
SHIT, NOT THAT I KNOW OF. WHEN I WAS WATCHING HER STREAMS, NEW PEOPLE WERE WELCOMED FREELY. PISSMASTER IS A NEW CHARACTER AS WELL.
WELL, WHITNEY, IF YOUR BULLSHIT IS THE *REAL* BULLSHIT, THEN MAYBE YOUR BALLS ARE HEAVY ENOUGH TO HANDLE **THE FUCK BROOM.**
FUCK BROOM?

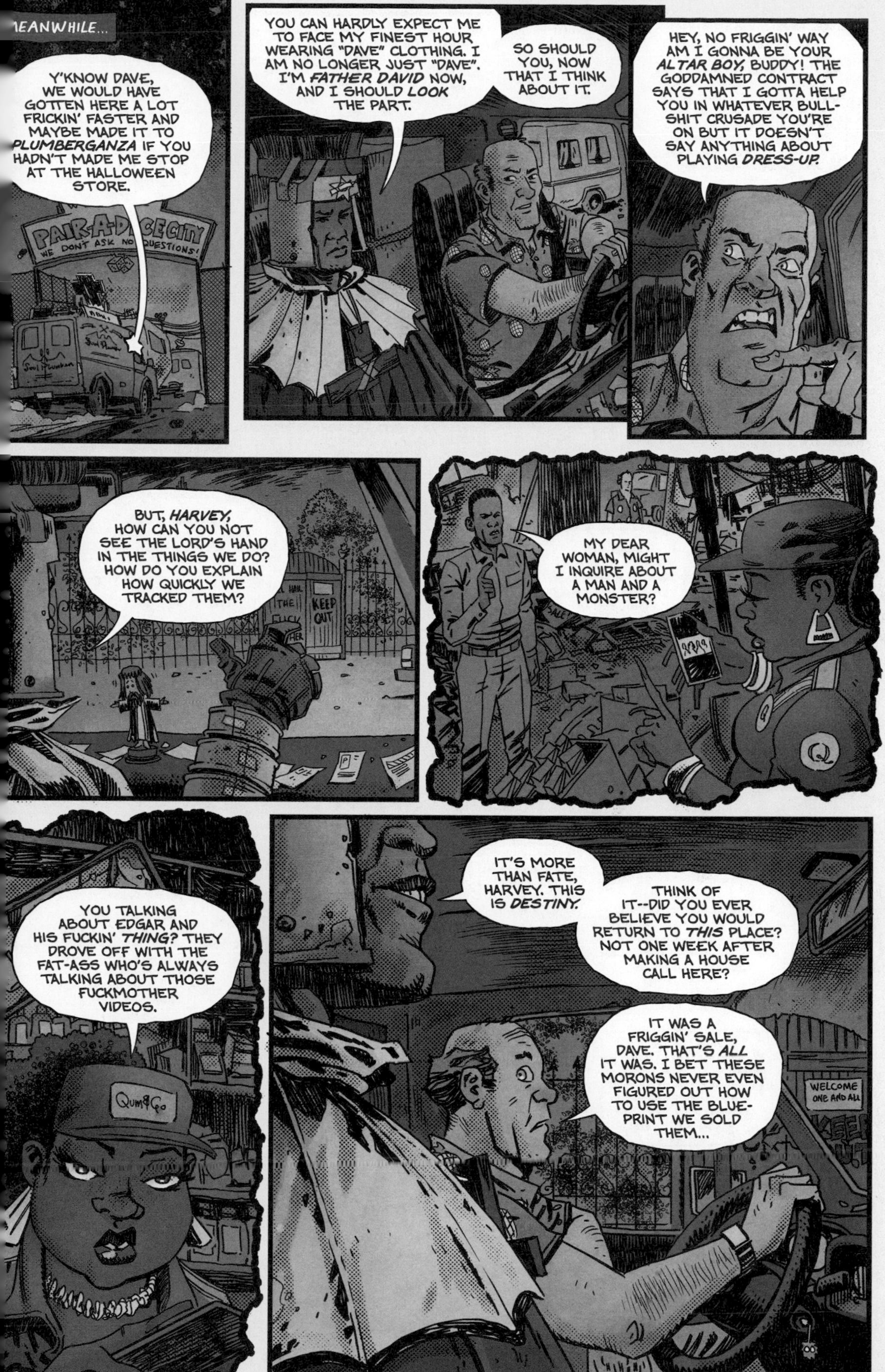
MEANWHILE...
Y'KNOW DAVE, WE WOULD HAVE GOTTEN HERE A LOT FRICKIN' FASTER AND MAYBE MADE IT TO *PLUMBERGANZA* IF YOU HADN'T MADE ME STOP AT THE HALLOWEEN STORE.
PAIR-A-DICE CITY
WE DON'T ASK NO QUESTIONS!
YOU CAN HARDLY EXPECT ME TO FACE MY FINEST HOUR WEARING "DAVE" CLOTHING. I AM NO LONGER JUST "DAVE". I'M *FATHER DAVID* NOW, AND I SHOULD *LOOK* THE PART.
SO SHOULD YOU, NOW THAT I THINK ABOUT IT.
HEY, NO FRIGGIN' WAY AM I GONNA BE YOUR *ALTAR BOY,* BUDDY! THE GODDAMNED CONTRACT SAYS THAT I GOTTA HELP YOU IN WHATEVER BULL-SHIT CRUSADE YOU'RE ON BUT IT DOESN'T SAY ANYTHING ABOUT PLAYING *DRESS-UP.*
BUT, *HARVEY,* HOW CAN YOU NOT SEE THE LORD'S HAND IN THE THINGS WE DO? HOW DO YOU EXPLAIN HOW QUICKLY WE TRACKED THEM?
KEEP OUT
MY DEAR WOMAN, MIGHT I INQUIRE ABOUT A MAN AND A MONSTER?
YOU TALKING ABOUT EDGAR AND HIS FUCKIN' *THING?* THEY DROVE OFF WITH THE FAT-ASS WHO'S ALWAYS TALKING ABOUT THOSE FUCKMOTHER VIDEOS.
Qum&Co
IT'S MORE THAN FATE, HARVEY. THIS IS *DESTINY.*
THINK OF IT--DID YOU EVER BELIEVE YOU WOULD RETURN TO *THIS* PLACE? NOT ONE WEEK AFTER MAKING A HOUSE CALL HERE?
IT WAS A FRIGGIN' SALE, DAVE. THAT'S *ALL* IT WAS. I BET THESE MORONS NEVER EVEN FIGURED OUT HOW TO USE THE BLUE-PRINT WE SOLD THEM...
WELCOME ONE AND ALL

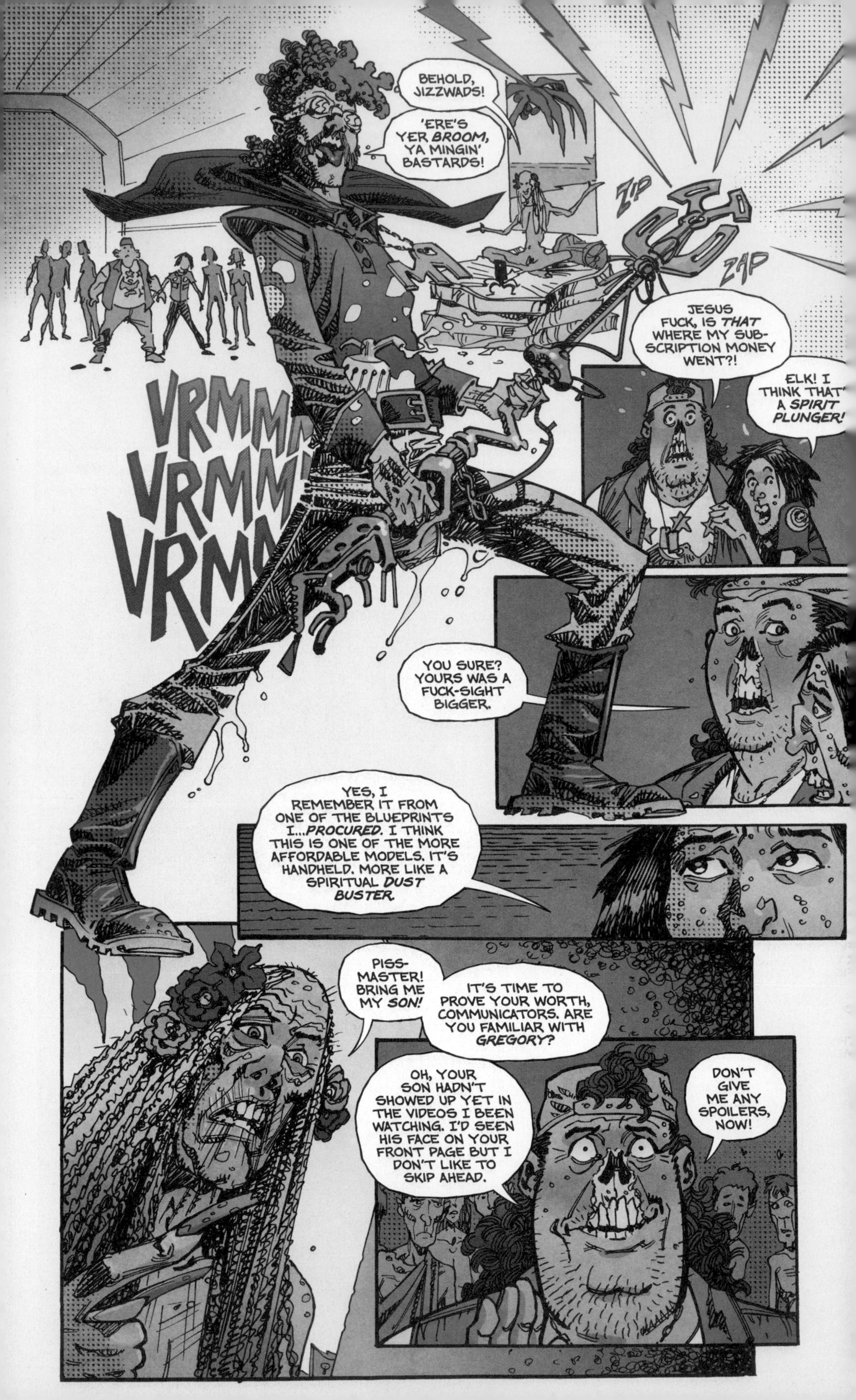
BEHOLD, JIZZWADS!
'ERE'S YER BROOM, YA MINGIN' BASTARDS!
ZIP
ZAP
VRMMM VRMMM VRMM
JESUS FUCK, IS THAT WHERE MY SUB-SCRIPTION MONEY WENT?!
ELK! I THINK THAT A SPIRIT PLUNGER!
YOU SURE? YOURS WAS A FUCK-SIGHT BIGGER.
YES, I REMEMBER IT FROM ONE OF THE BLUEPRINTS I...PROCURED. I THINK THIS IS ONE OF THE MORE AFFORDABLE MODELS. IT'S HANDHELD. MORE LIKE A SPIRITUAL DUST BUSTER.
PISS-MASTER! BRING ME MY SON!
IT'S TIME TO PROVE YOUR WORTH, COMMUNICATORS. ARE YOU FAMILIAR WITH GREGORY?
OH, YOUR SON HADN'T SHOWED UP YET IN THE VIDEOS I BEEN WATCHING. I'D SEEN HIS FACE ON YOUR FRONT PAGE BUT I DON'T LIKE TO SKIP AHEAD.
DON'T GIVE ME ANY SPOILERS, NOW!

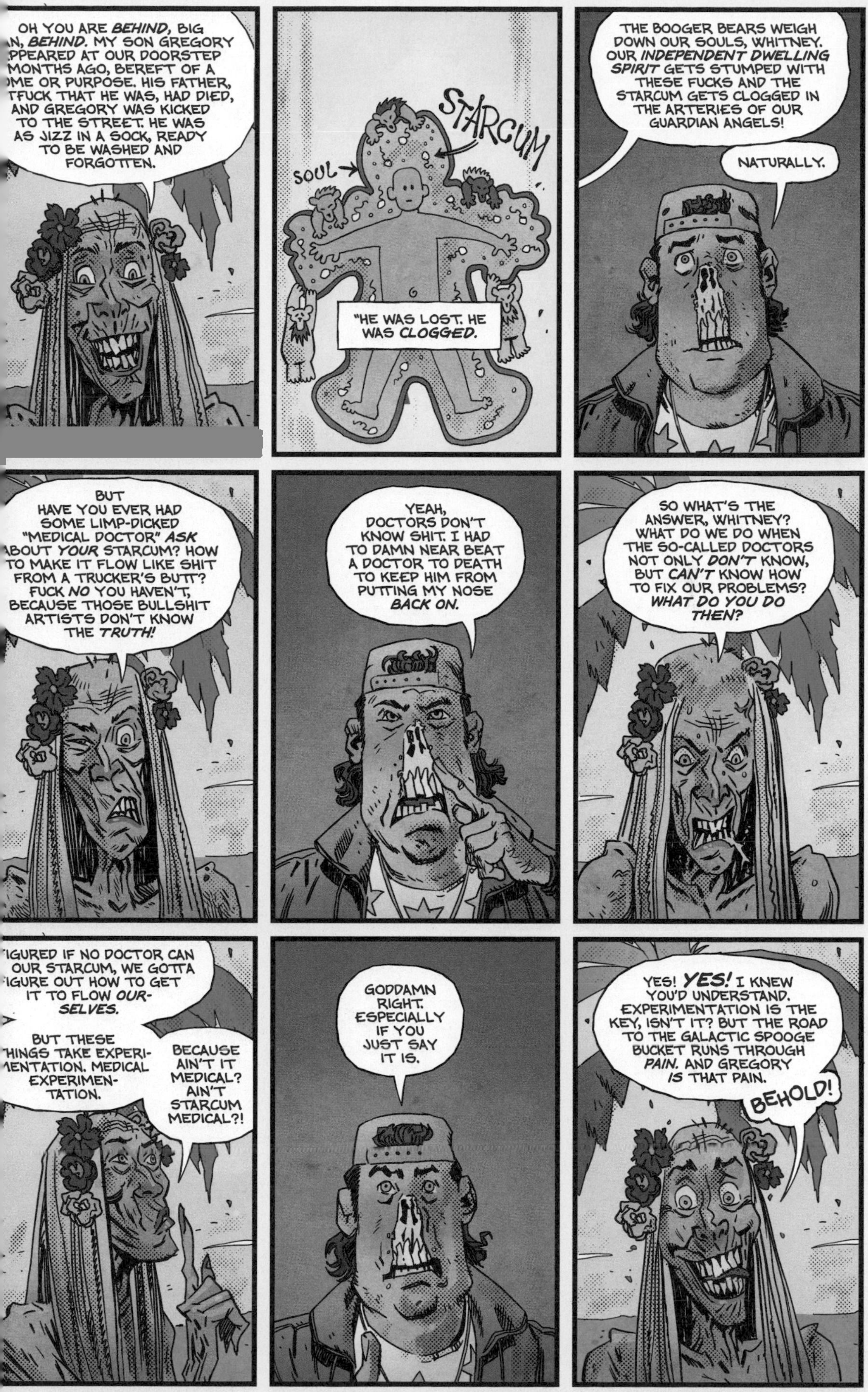
OH YOU ARE BEHIND, BIG N, BEHIND. MY SON GREGORY PPEARED AT OUR DOORSTEP MONTHS AGO, BEREFT OF A OME OR PURPOSE. HIS FATHER, TFUCK THAT HE WAS, HAD DIED, AND GREGORY WAS KICKED TO THE STREET. HE WAS AS JIZZ IN A SOCK, READY TO BE WASHED AND FORGOTTEN.
STARCUM
SOUL
"HE WAS LOST. HE WAS CLOGGED.
THE BOOGER BEARS WEIGH DOWN OUR SOULS, WHITNEY. OUR INDEPENDENT DWELLING SPIRIT GETS STUMPED WITH THESE FUCKS AND THE STARCUM GETS CLOGGED IN THE ARTERIES OF OUR GUARDIAN ANGELS!
NATURALLY.
BUT HAVE YOU EVER HAD SOME LIMP-DICKED "MEDICAL DOCTOR" ASK ABOUT YOUR STARCUM? HOW TO MAKE IT FLOW LIKE SHIT FROM A TRUCKER'S BUTT? FUCK NO YOU HAVEN'T, BECAUSE THOSE BULLSHIT ARTISTS DON'T KNOW THE TRUTH!
YEAH, DOCTORS DON'T KNOW SHIT. I HAD TO DAMN NEAR BEAT A DOCTOR TO DEATH TO KEEP HIM FROM PUTTING MY NOSE BACK ON.
SO WHAT'S THE ANSWER, WHITNEY? WHAT DO WE DO WHEN THE SO-CALLED DOCTORS NOT ONLY DON'T KNOW, BUT CAN'T KNOW HOW TO FIX OUR PROBLEMS? WHAT DO YOU DO THEN?
IGURED IF NO DOCTOR CAN OUR STARCUM, WE GOTTA IGURE OUT HOW TO GET IT TO FLOW OUR-SELVES.
BUT THESE HINGS TAKE EXPERI-MENTATION. MEDICAL EXPERIMEN-TATION.
BECAUSE AIN'T IT MEDICAL? AIN'T STARCUM MEDICAL?!
GODDAMN RIGHT. ESPECIALLY IF YOU JUST SAY IT IS.
YES! YES! I KNEW YOU'D UNDERSTAND. EXPERIMENTATION IS THE KEY, ISN'T IT? BUT THE ROAD TO THE GALACTIC SPOOGE BUCKET RUNS THROUGH PAIN. AND GREGORY IS THAT PAIN.
BEHOLD!

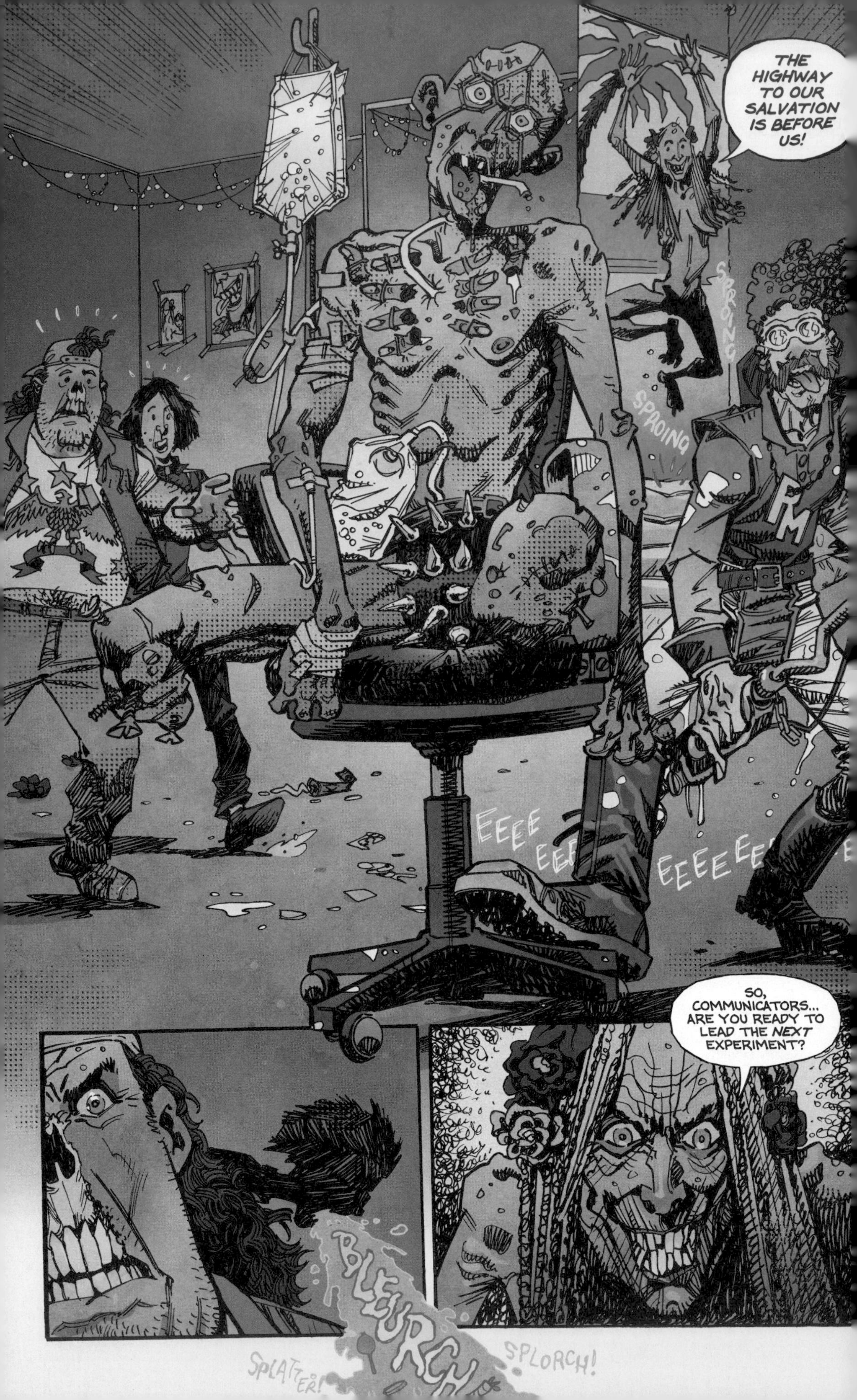
THE HIGHWAY TO OUR SALVATION IS BEFORE US!
SPROING
SPROING
EEEE EEE
EEEEEEE
SO, COMMUNICATORS... ARE YOU READY TO LEAD THE *NEXT* EXPERIMENT?
BLEURCH
SPLATTER!
SPLORCH!

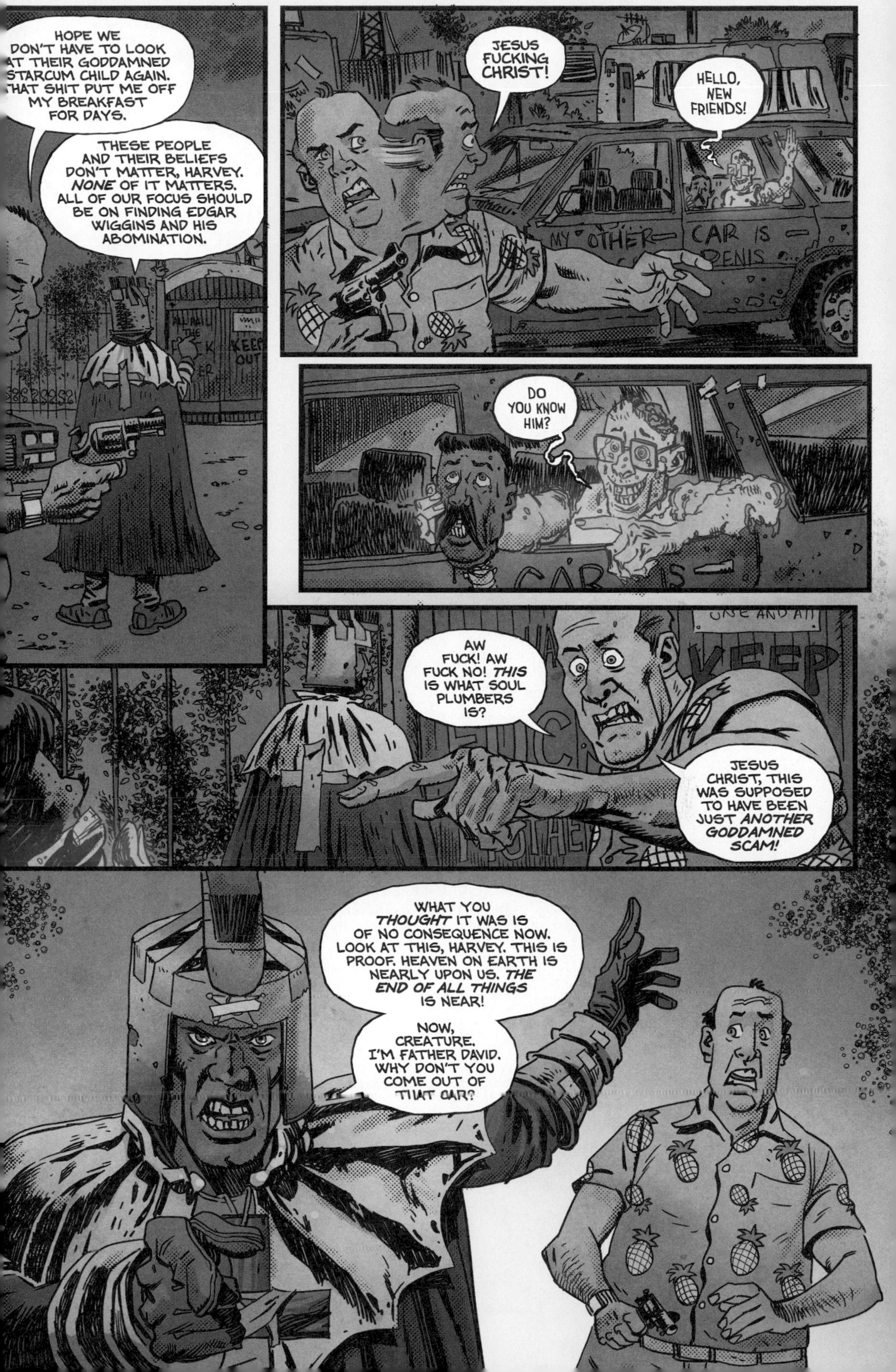
HOPE WE DON'T HAVE TO LOOK AT THEIR GODDAMNED STARCUM CHILD AGAIN. THAT SHIT PUT ME OFF MY BREAKFAST FOR DAYS.
THESE PEOPLE AND THEIR BELIEFS DON'T MATTER, HARVEY. *NONE* OF IT MATTERS. ALL OF OUR FOCUS SHOULD BE ON FINDING EDGAR WIGGINS AND HIS ABOMINATION.
KEEP OUT
JESUS FUCKING CHRIST!
HELLO, NEW FRIENDS!
MY OTHER CAR IS PENIS
DO YOU KNOW HIM?
AW FUCK! AW FUCK NO! *THIS* IS WHAT SOUL PLUMBERS IS?
JESUS CHRIST, THIS WAS SUPPOSED TO HAVE BEEN JUST *ANOTHER GODDAMNED SCAM!*
WHAT YOU *THOUGHT* IT WAS IS OF NO CONSEQUENCE NOW. LOOK AT THIS, HARVEY. THIS IS PROOF. HEAVEN ON EARTH IS NEARLY UPON US. *THE END OF ALL THINGS* IS NEAR!
NOW, CREATURE. I'M FATHER DAVID. WHY DON'T YOU COME OUT OF THAT CAR?

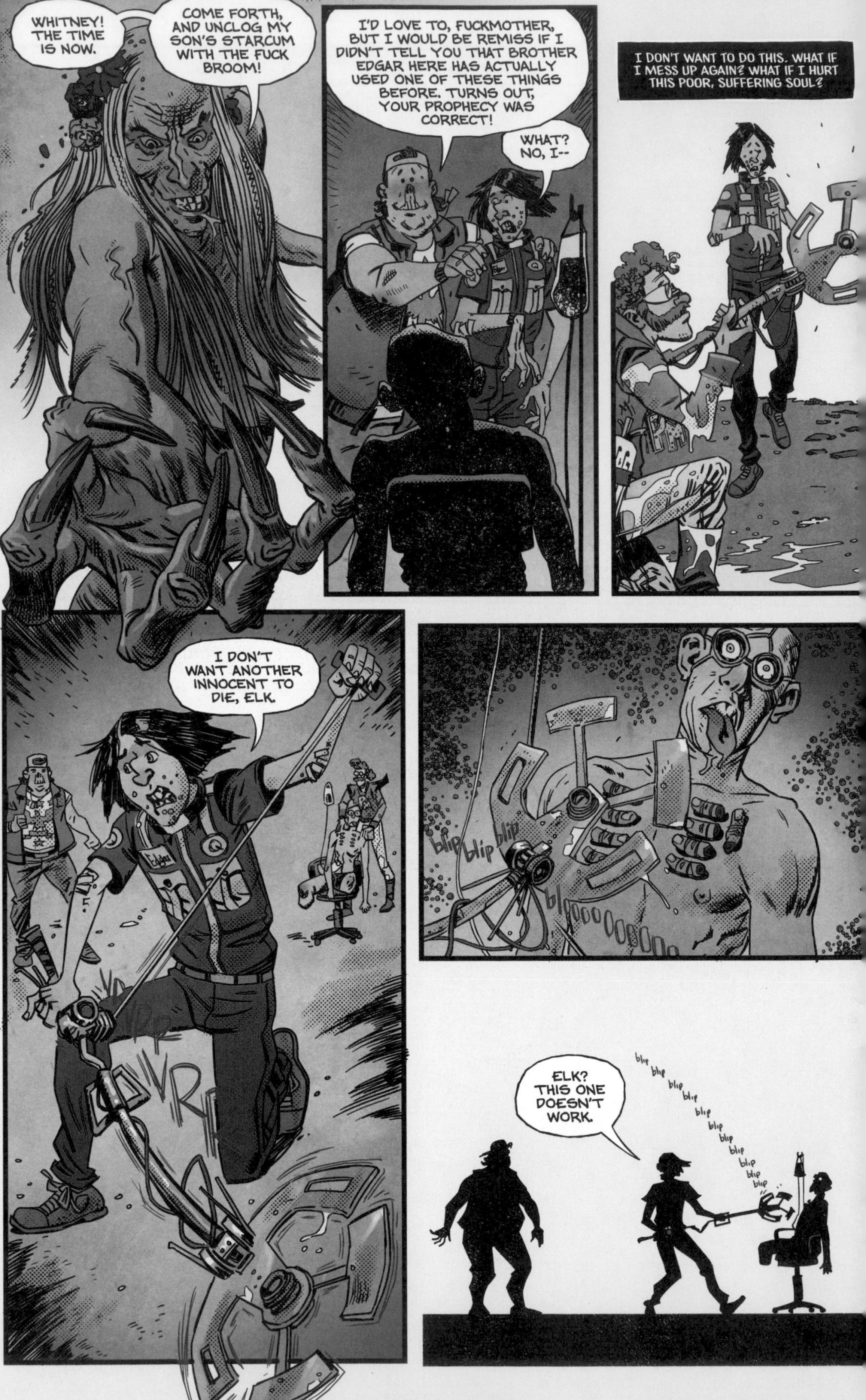
WHITNEY! THE TIME IS NOW.
COME FORTH, AND UNCLOG MY SON'S STARCUM WITH THE FUCK BROOM!
I'D LOVE TO, FUCKMOTHER, BUT I WOULD BE REMISS IF I DIDN'T TELL YOU THAT BROTHER EDGAR HERE HAS ACTUALLY USED ONE OF THESE THINGS BEFORE. TURNS OUT, YOUR PROPHECY WAS CORRECT!
WHAT? NO, I--
I DON'T WANT TO DO THIS. WHAT IF I MESS UP AGAIN? WHAT IF I HURT THIS POOR, SUFFERING SOUL?
I DON'T WANT ANOTHER INNOCENT TO DIE, ELK.
blip blip blip
ELK? THIS ONE DOESN'T WORK.
blip blip blip blip blip blip blip blip blip blip blip

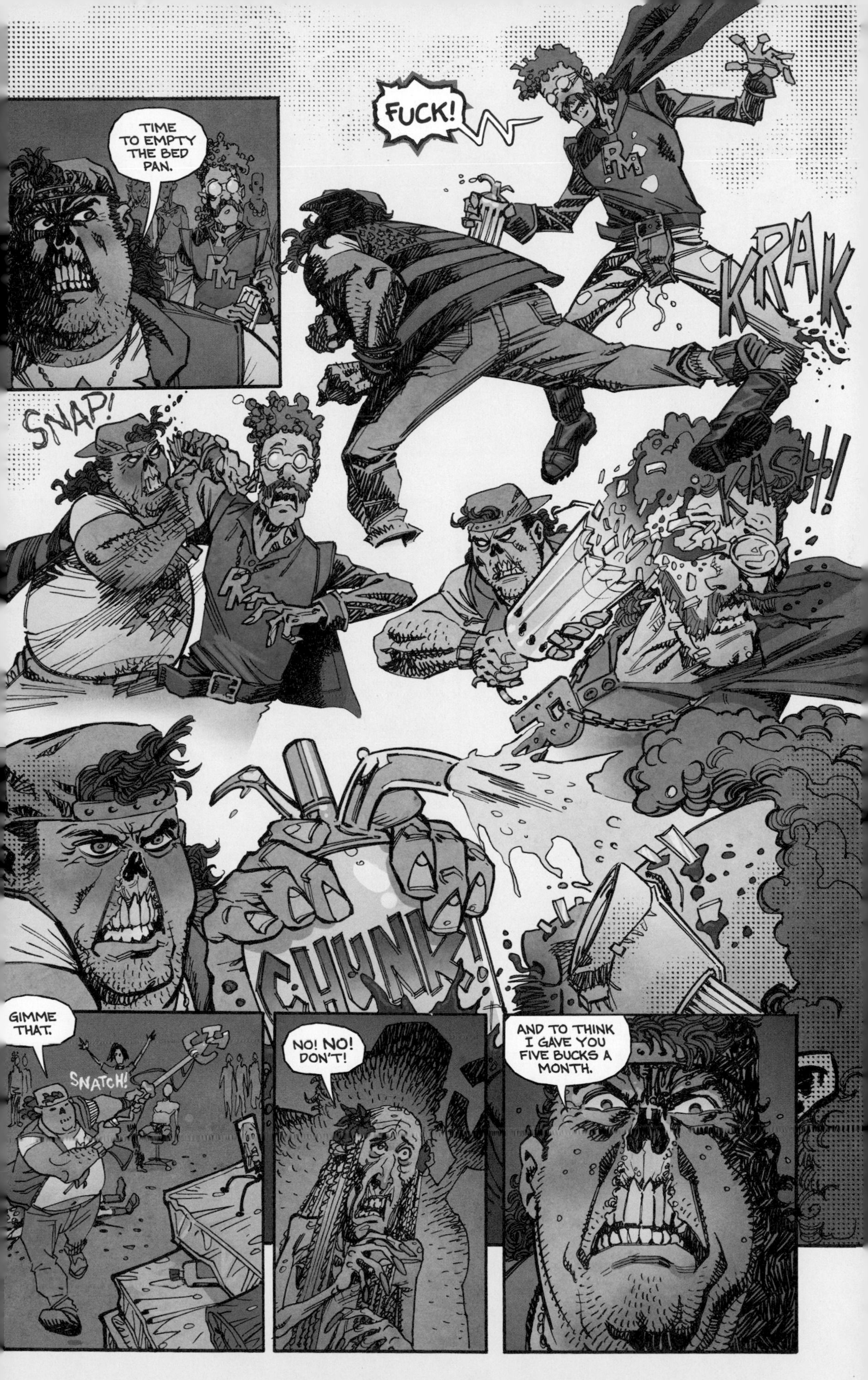
TIME TO EMPTY THE BED PAN.
FUCK!
KRAK
SNAP!
KASH!
CHUNK!
GIMME THAT.
SNATCH!
NO! NO! DON'T!
AND TO THINK I GAVE YOU FIVE BUCKS A MONTH.

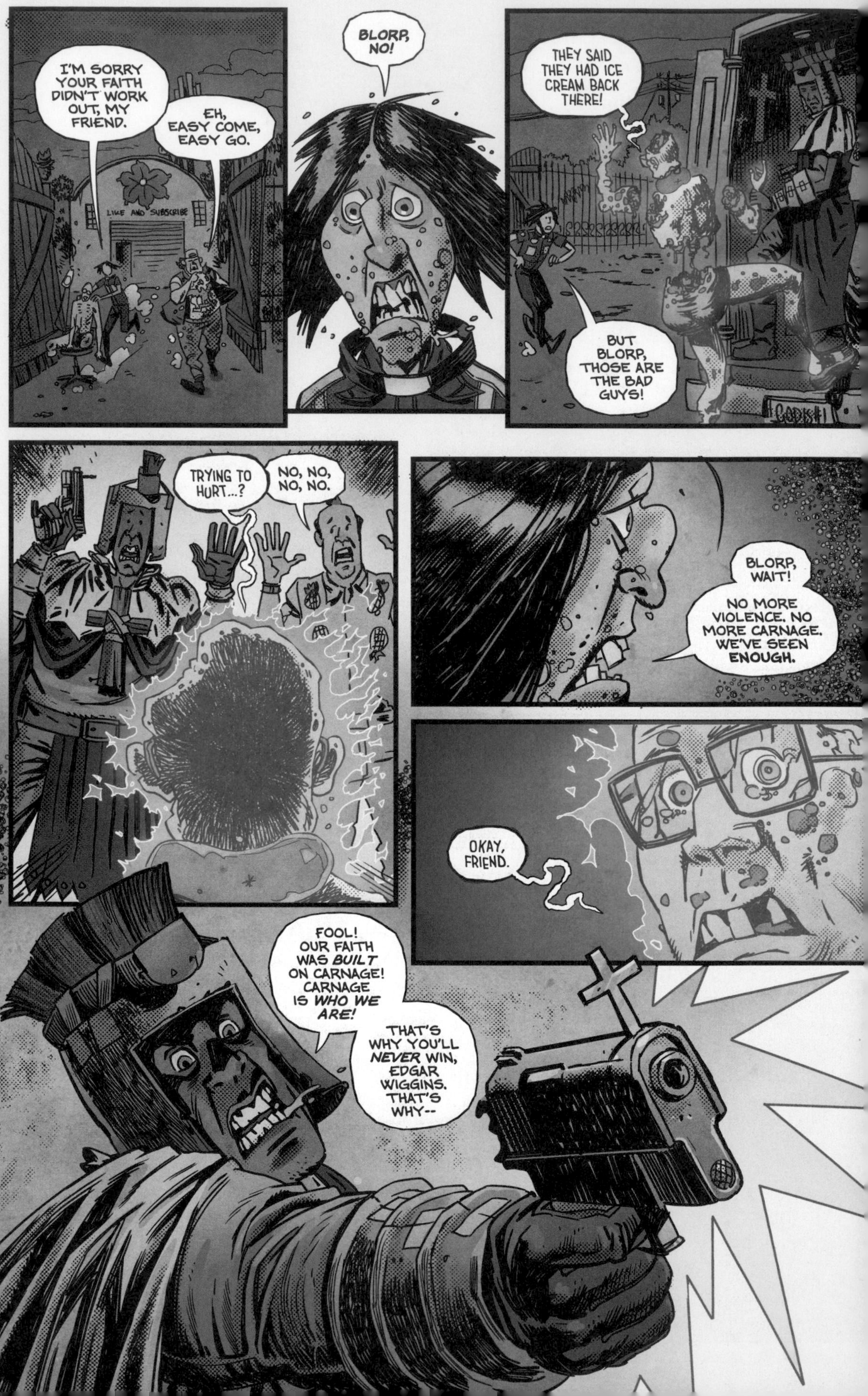
I'M SORRY YOUR FAITH DIDN'T WORK OUT, MY FRIEND.
LIKE AND SUBSCRIBE
EH, EASY COME, EASY GO.
BLORP, NO!
THEY SAID THEY HAD ICE CREAM BACK THERE!
BUT BLORP, THOSE ARE THE BAD GUYS!
TRYING TO HURT...?
NO, NO, NO, NO.
BLORP, WAIT!
NO MORE VIOLENCE. NO MORE CARNAGE. WE'VE SEEN ENOUGH.
OKAY, FRIEND.
FOOL! OUR FAITH WAS BUILT ON CARNAGE! CARNAGE IS WHO WE ARE!
THAT'S WHY YOU'LL NEVER WIN, EDGAR WIGGINS. THAT'S WHY--

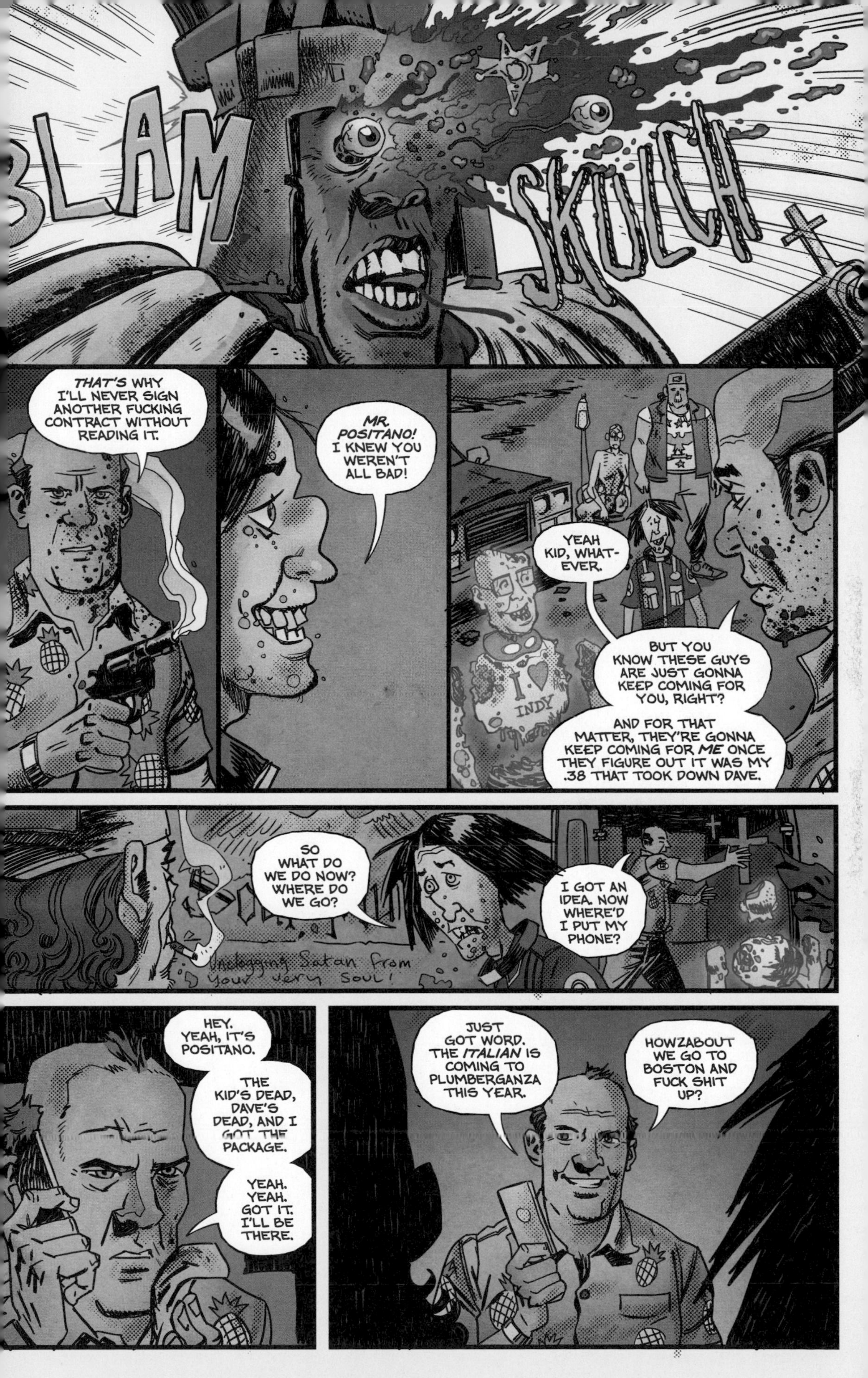
BLAM
SKULCH
THAT'S WHY I'LL NEVER SIGN ANOTHER FUCKING CONTRACT WITHOUT READING IT.
MR. POSITANO! I KNEW YOU WEREN'T ALL BAD!
YEAH KID, WHAT-EVER.
I ♥ INDY
BUT YOU KNOW THESE GUYS ARE JUST GONNA KEEP COMING FOR YOU, RIGHT?
AND FOR THAT MATTER, THEY'RE GONNA KEEP COMING FOR ME ONCE THEY FIGURE OUT IT WAS MY .38 THAT TOOK DOWN DAVE.
SO WHAT DO WE DO NOW? WHERE DO WE GO?
I GOT AN IDEA. NOW WHERE'D I PUT MY PHONE?
Unclogging Satan from your very soul!
HEY. YEAH, IT'S POSITANO.
THE KID'S DEAD, DAVE'S DEAD, AND I GOT THE PACKAGE.
YEAH. YEAH. GOT IT. I'LL BE THERE.
JUST GOT WORD. THE ITALIAN IS COMING TO PLUMBERGANZA THIS YEAR.
HOWZABOUT WE GO TO BOSTON AND FUCK SHIT UP?

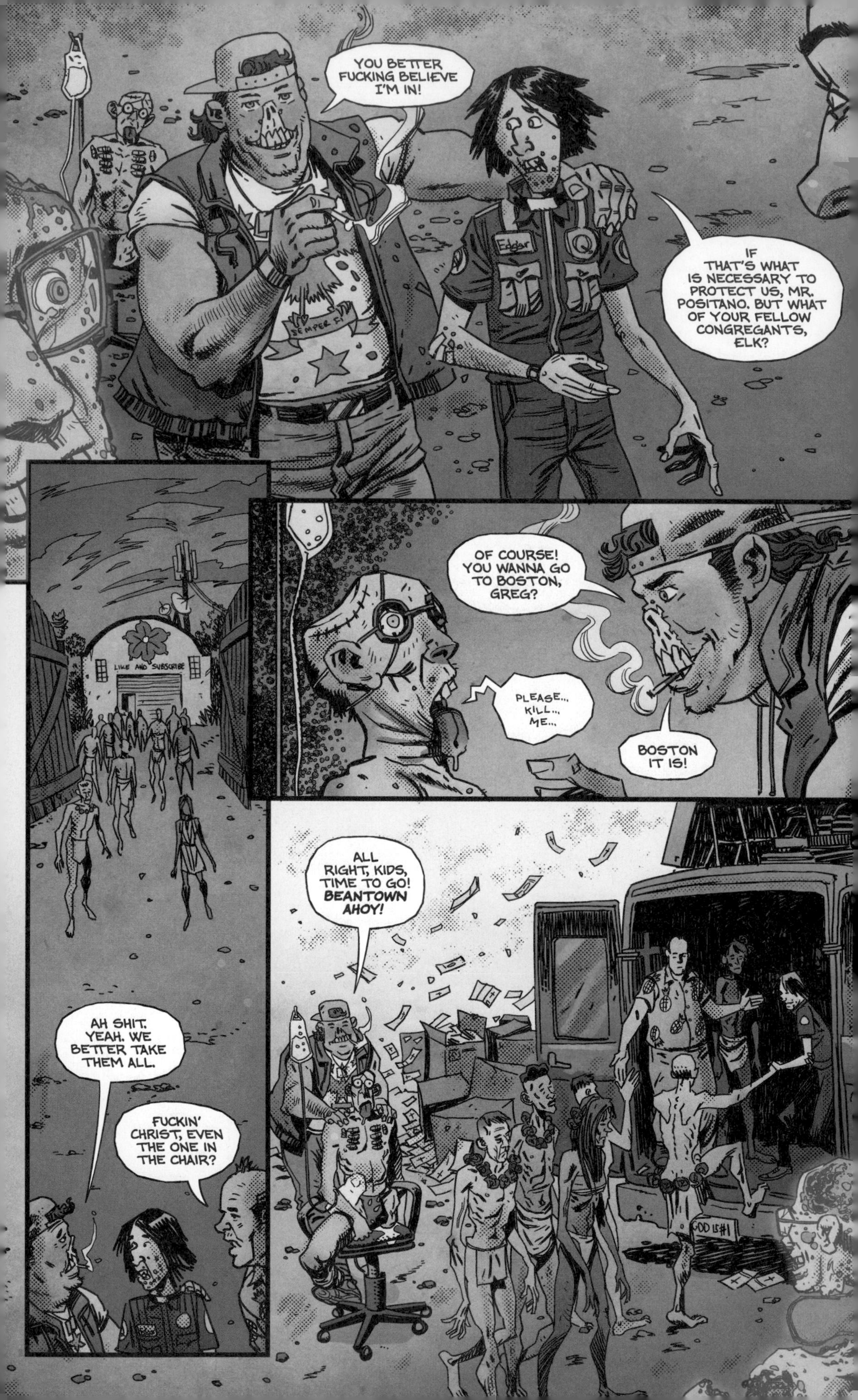
YOU BETTER FUCKING BELIEVE I'M IN!
Edgar
IF THAT'S WHAT IS NECESSARY TO PROTECT US, MR. POSITANO. BUT WHAT OF YOUR FELLOW CONGREGANTS, ELK?
LIKE AND SUBSCRIBE
OF COURSE! YOU WANNA GO TO BOSTON, GREG?
PLEASE... KILL... ME...
BOSTON IT IS!
AH SHIT. YEAH. WE BETTER TAKE THEM ALL.
FUCKIN' CHRIST, EVEN THE ONE IN THE CHAIR?
ALL RIGHT, KIDS, TIME TO GO! BEANTOWN AHOY!

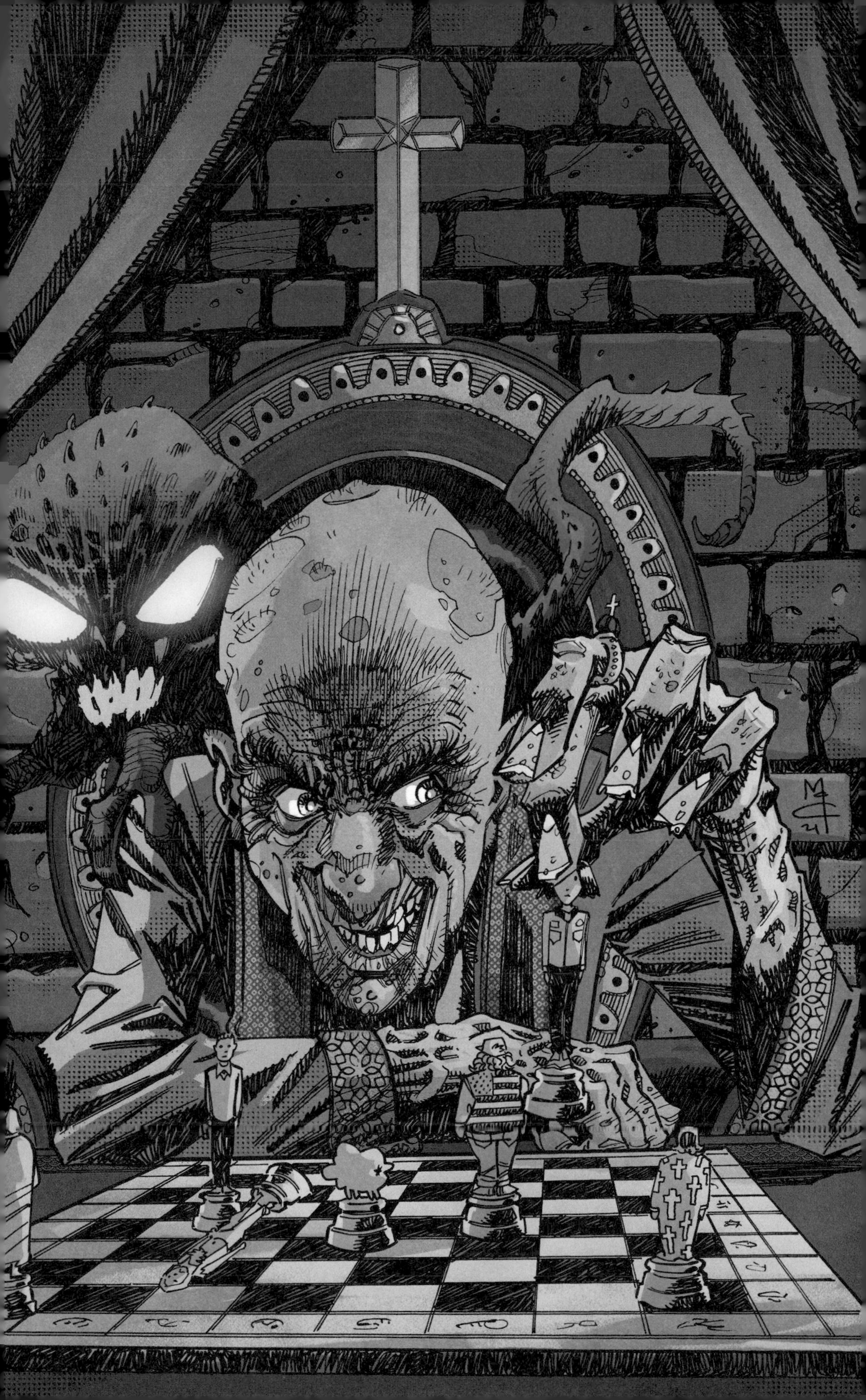

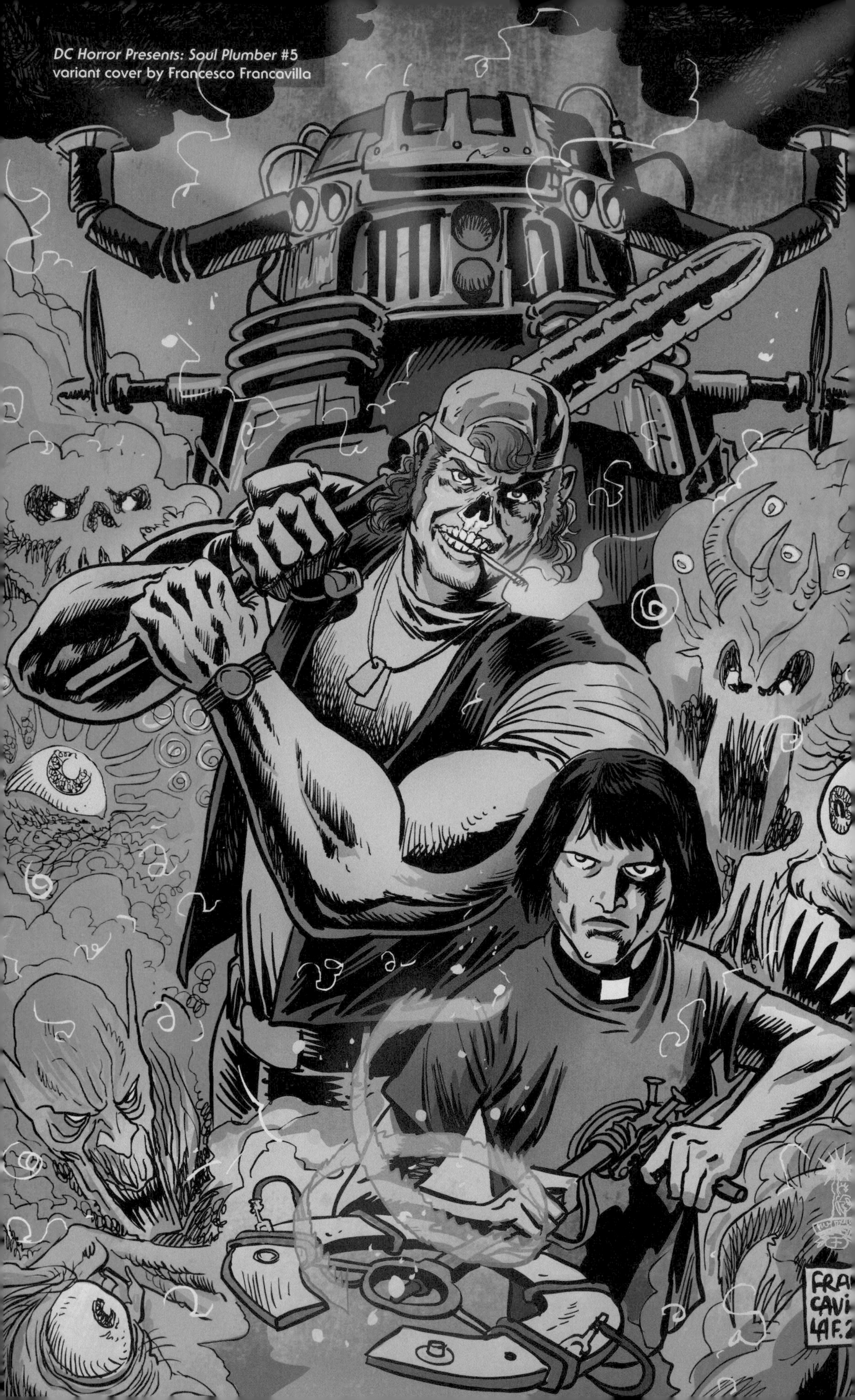

DC Horror Presents: Soul Plumber #5
variant cover by Francesco Francavilla

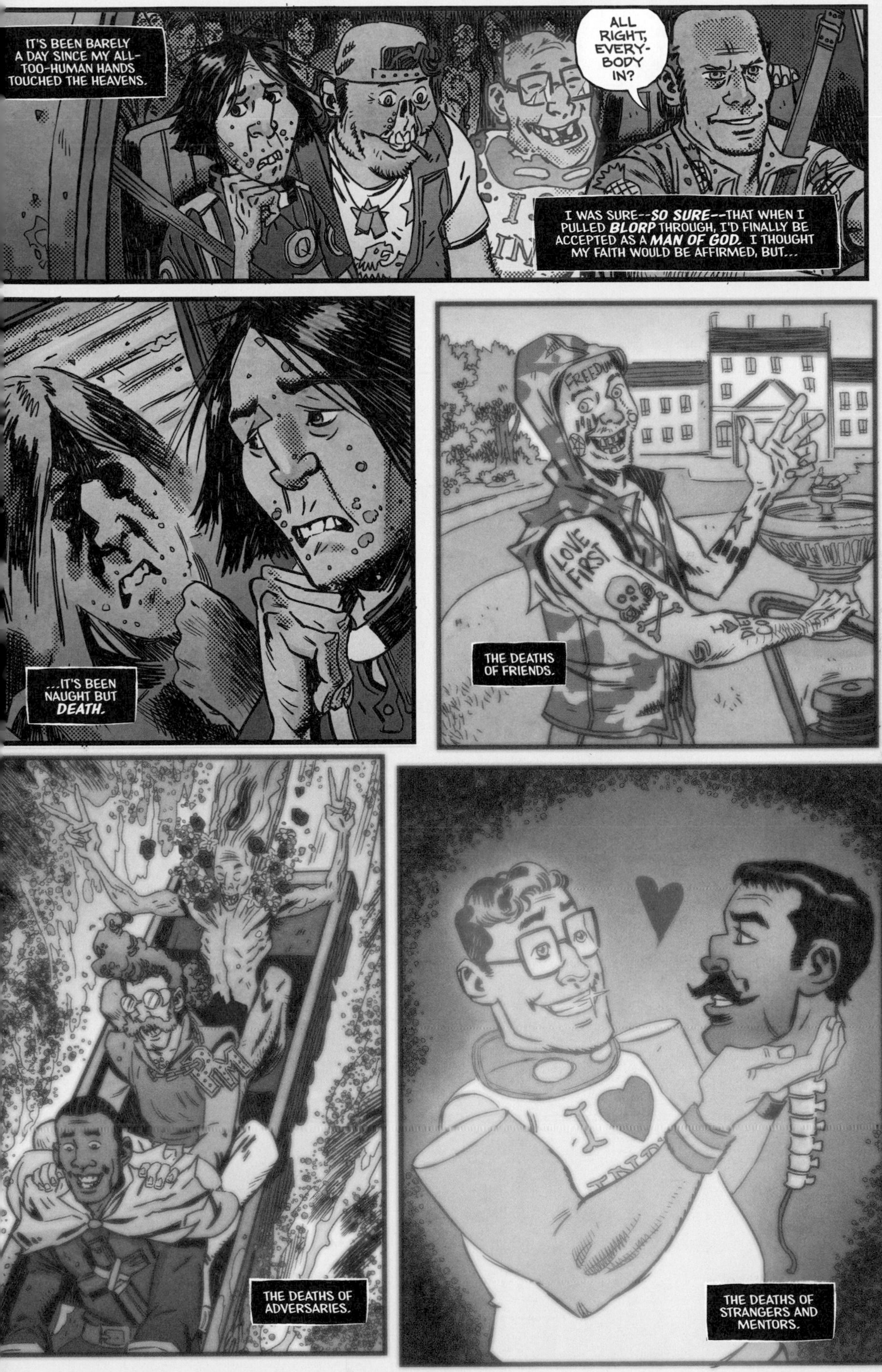
IT'S BEEN BARELY A DAY SINCE MY ALL-TOO-HUMAN HANDS TOUCHED THE HEAVENS.
ALL RIGHT, EVERY-BODY IN?
I WAS SURE--SO SURE--THAT WHEN I PULLED BLORP THROUGH, I'D FINALLY BE ACCEPTED AS A MAN OF GOD. I THOUGHT MY FAITH WOULD BE AFFIRMED, BUT...
...IT'S BEEN NAUGHT BUT DEATH.
FREEDUM
LOVE FIRST
THE DEATHS OF FRIENDS.
THE DEATHS OF ADVERSARIES.
THE DEATHS OF STRANGERS AND MENTORS.

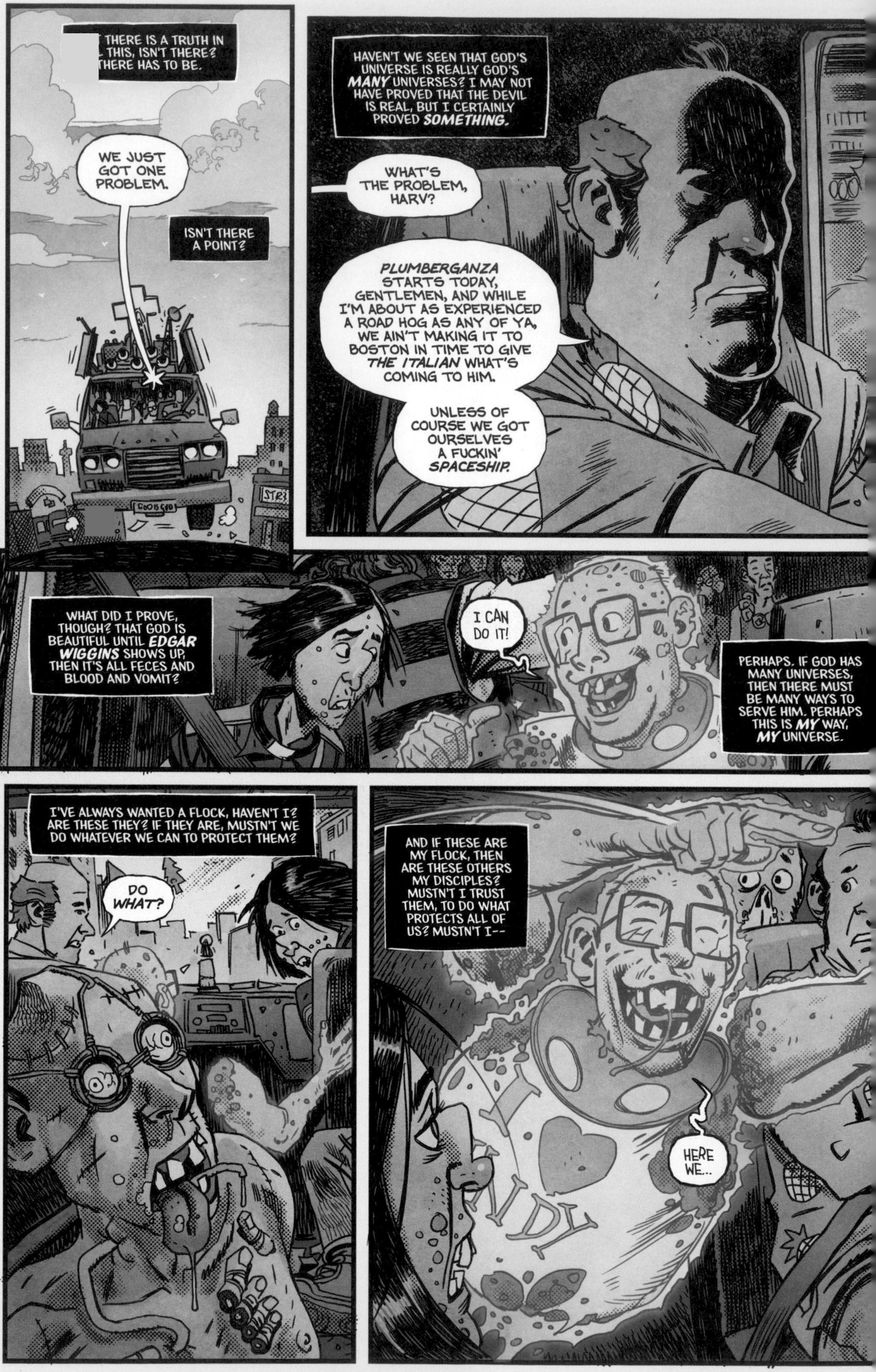
THERE IS A TRUTH IN
L THIS, ISN'T THERE?
THERE HAS TO BE.
WE JUST GOT ONE PROBLEM.
ISN'T THERE A POINT?
HAVEN'T WE SEEN THAT GOD'S UNIVERSE IS REALLY GOD'S MANY UNIVERSES? I MAY NOT HAVE PROVED THAT THE DEVIL IS REAL, BUT I CERTAINLY PROVED SOMETHING.
WHAT'S THE PROBLEM, HARV?
PLUMBERGANZA STARTS TODAY, GENTLEMEN, AND WHILE I'M ABOUT AS EXPERIENCED A ROAD HOG AS ANY OF YA, WE AIN'T MAKING IT TO BOSTON IN TIME TO GIVE THE ITALIAN WHAT'S COMING TO HIM.
UNLESS OF COURSE WE GOT OURSELVES A FUCKIN' SPACESHIP.
WHAT DID I PROVE, THOUGH? THAT GOD IS BEAUTIFUL UNTIL EDGAR WIGGINS SHOWS UP, THEN IT'S ALL FECES AND BLOOD AND VOMIT?
I CAN DO IT!
PERHAPS. IF GOD HAS MANY UNIVERSES, THEN THERE MUST BE MANY WAYS TO SERVE HIM. PERHAPS THIS IS MY WAY, MY UNIVERSE.
I'VE ALWAYS WANTED A FLOCK, HAVEN'T I? ARE THESE THEY? IF THEY ARE, MUSTN'T WE DO WHATEVER WE CAN TO PROTECT THEM?
DO WHAT?
AND IF THESE ARE MY FLOCK, THEN ARE THESE OTHERS MY DISCIPLES? MUSTN'T I TRUST THEM, TO DO WHAT PROTECTS ALL OF US? MUSTN'T I--
HERE WE...

WITH FRIENDS LIKE THESE

PART FIVE

CONCEPT BY MARCUS PARKS, HENRY ZEBROWSKI & BEN KISSEL
WRITTEN BY MARCUS PARKS & HENRY ZEBROWSKI
PENCILS BY PJ HOLDEN
INKS BY PJ HOLDEN & JOHN McCREA
COLORS BY MIKE SPICER
LETTERS BY BECCA CAREY
COVER BY McCREA & SPICER
VARIANT COVER BY FRANCESCO FRANCAVILLA
ASSOCIATE EDITOR BEN MEARES
SENIOR EDITOR KATIE KUBERT
SOUL PLUMBER CREATED BY MARCUS PARKS, HENRY ZEBROWSKI, BEN KISSEL & JOHN McCREA

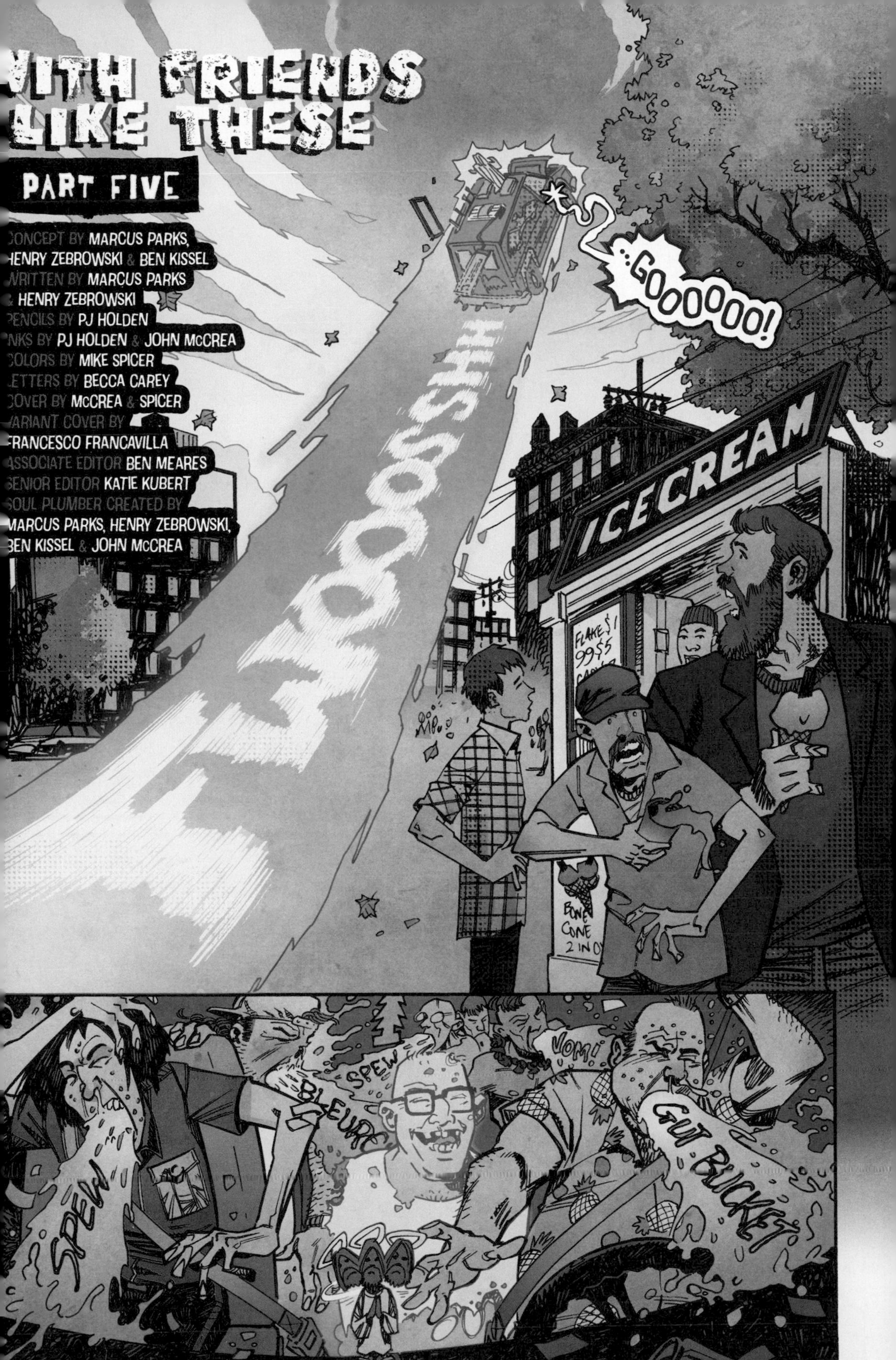

...GOOOOOO!
FWOOOOSSHH
ICECREAM
SPEW
BLEURG
SPEW
VOMI
GUT BUCKET

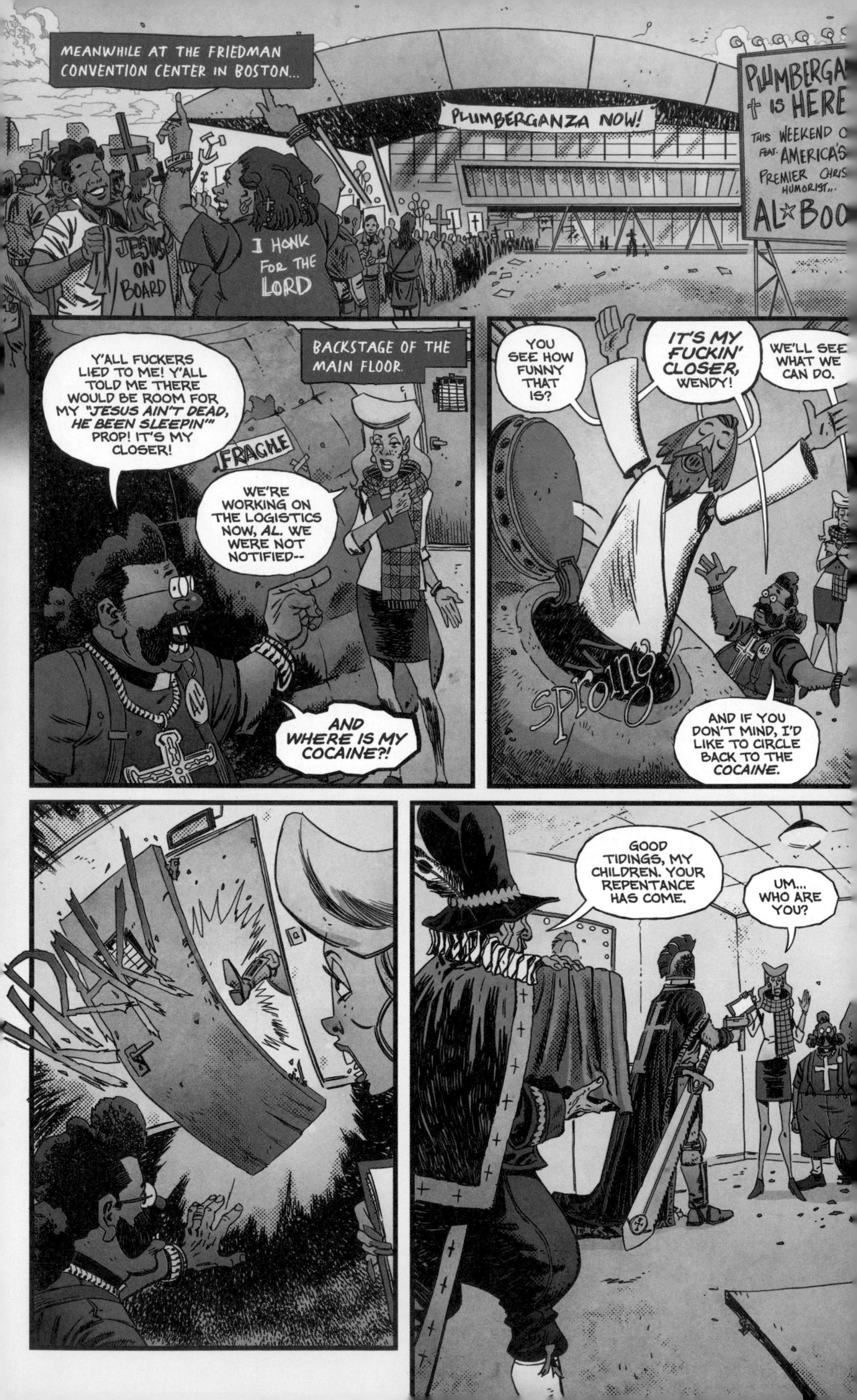
MEANWHILE AT THE FRIEDMAN CONVENTION CENTER IN BOSTON...
PLUMBERGANZA NOW!
PLUMBERGA
IS HERE
THIS WEEKEND O
FEAT. AMERICA'S
PREMIER CHRIS
HUMORIST...
AL☆BOO
JESUS ON BOARD
I HONK FOR THE LORD
BACKSTAGE OF THE MAIN FLOOR.
Y'ALL FUCKERS LIED TO ME! Y'ALL TOLD ME THERE WOULD BE ROOM FOR MY "JESUS AIN'T DEAD, HE BEEN SLEEPIN'" PROP! IT'S MY CLOSER!
FRAGILE
WE'RE WORKING ON THE LOGISTICS NOW, AL. WE WERE NOT NOTIFIED--
AND WHERE IS MY COCAINE?!
YOU SEE HOW FUNNY THAT IS?
IT'S MY FUCKIN' CLOSER, WENDY!
WE'LL SEE WHAT WE CAN DO.
SPROING!
AND IF YOU DON'T MIND, I'D LIKE TO CIRCLE BACK TO THE COCAINE.
GOOD TIDINGS, MY CHILDREN. YOUR REPENTANCE HAS COME.
UM... WHO ARE YOU?

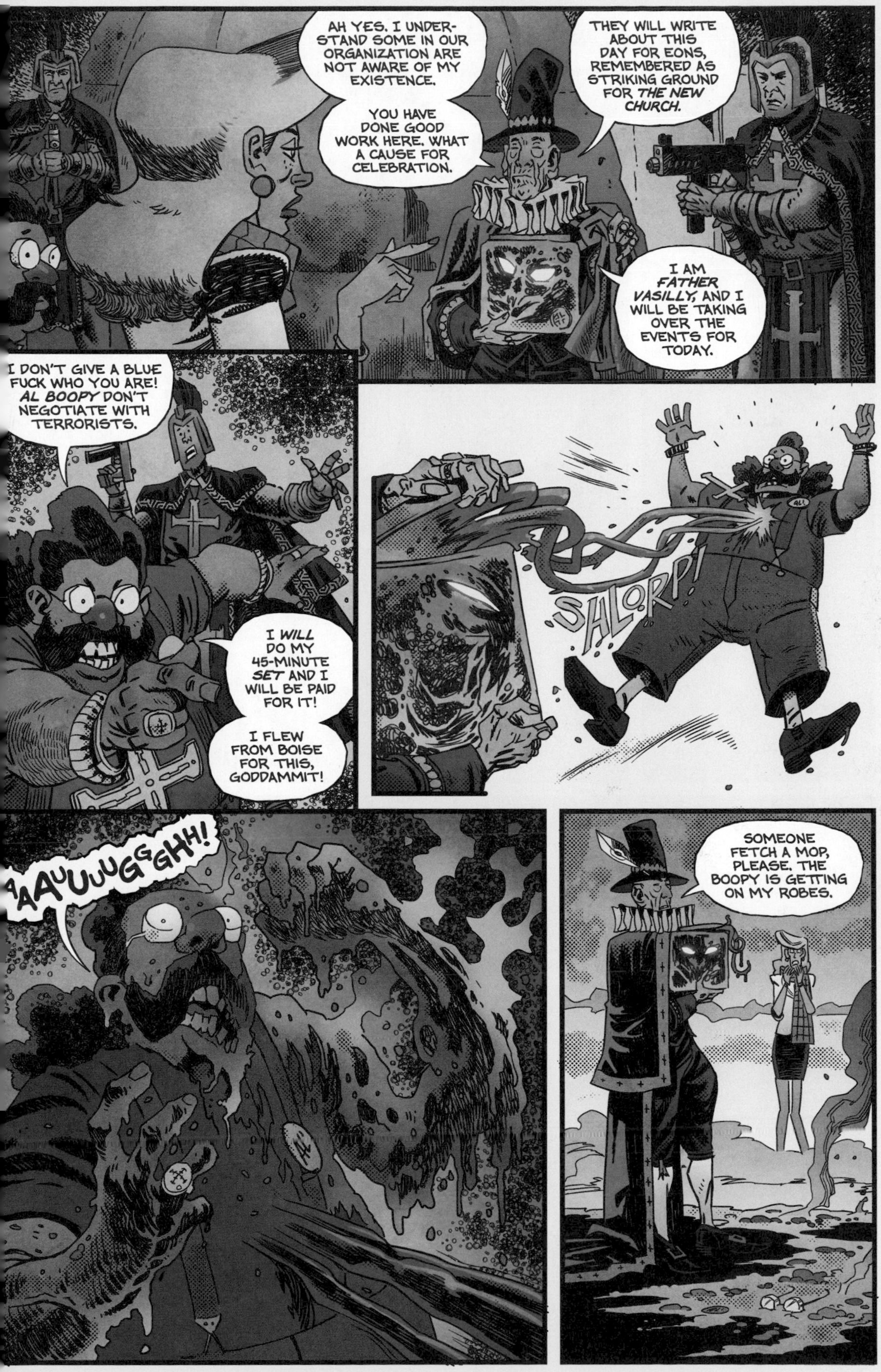
AH YES. I UNDER-STAND SOME IN OUR ORGANIZATION ARE NOT AWARE OF MY EXISTENCE.
YOU HAVE DONE GOOD WORK HERE. WHAT A CAUSE FOR CELEBRATION.
THEY WILL WRITE ABOUT THIS DAY FOR EONS, REMEMBERED AS STRIKING GROUND FOR *THE NEW CHURCH*.
I AM *FATHER VASILLY,* AND I WILL BE TAKING OVER THE EVENTS FOR TODAY.
I DON'T GIVE A BLUE FUCK WHO YOU ARE! *AL BOOPY* DON'T NEGOTIATE WITH TERRORISTS.
I *WILL* DO MY 45-MINUTE *SET* AND I WILL BE PAID FOR IT!
I FLEW FROM BOISE FOR THIS, GODDAMMIT!
SHLORP!
AAUUUGGGHH!
SOMEONE FETCH A MOP, PLEASE. THE BOOPY IS GETTING ON MY ROBES.

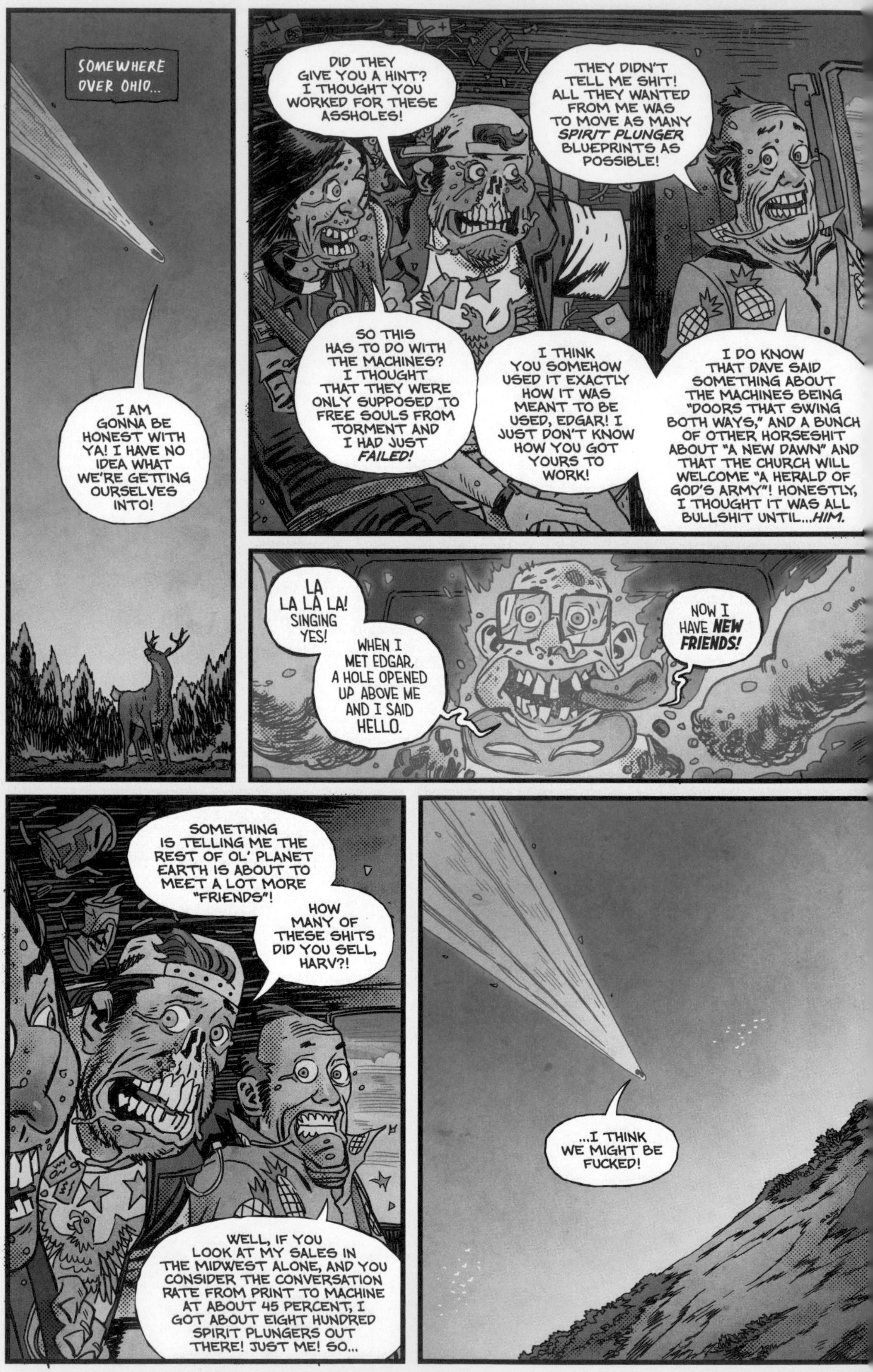
SOMEWHERE OVER OHIO...
I AM GONNA BE HONEST WITH YA! I HAVE NO IDEA WHAT WE'RE GETTING OURSELVES INTO!
DID THEY GIVE YOU A HINT? I THOUGHT YOU WORKED FOR THESE ASSHOLES!
THEY DIDN'T TELL ME SHIT! ALL THEY WANTED FROM ME WAS TO MOVE AS MANY SPIRIT PLUNGER BLUEPRINTS AS POSSIBLE!
SO THIS HAS TO DO WITH THE MACHINES? I THOUGHT THAT THEY WERE ONLY SUPPOSED TO FREE SOULS FROM TORMENT AND I HAD JUST FAILED!
I THINK YOU SOMEHOW USED IT EXACTLY HOW IT WAS MEANT TO BE USED, EDGAR! I JUST DON'T KNOW HOW YOU GOT YOURS TO WORK!
I DO KNOW THAT DAVE SAID SOMETHING ABOUT THE MACHINES BEING "DOORS THAT SWING BOTH WAYS," AND A BUNCH OF OTHER HORSESHIT ABOUT "A NEW DAWN" AND THAT THE CHURCH WILL WELCOME "A HERALD OF GOD'S ARMY"! HONESTLY, I THOUGHT IT WAS ALL BULLSHIT UNTIL...HIM.
LA LA LA LA! SINGING YES!
WHEN I MET EDGAR, A HOLE OPENED UP ABOVE ME AND I SAID HELLO.
NOW I HAVE NEW FRIENDS!
SOMETHING IS TELLING ME THE REST OF OL' PLANET EARTH IS ABOUT TO MEET A LOT MORE "FRIENDS"!
HOW MANY OF THESE SHITS DID YOU SELL, HARV?!
WELL, IF YOU LOOK AT MY SALES IN THE MIDWEST ALONE, AND YOU CONSIDER THE CONVERSATION RATE FROM PRINT TO MACHINE AT ABOUT 45 PERCENT, I GOT ABOUT EIGHT HUNDRED SPIRIT PLUNGERS OUT THERE! JUST ME! SO...
...I THINK WE MIGHT BE FUCKED!

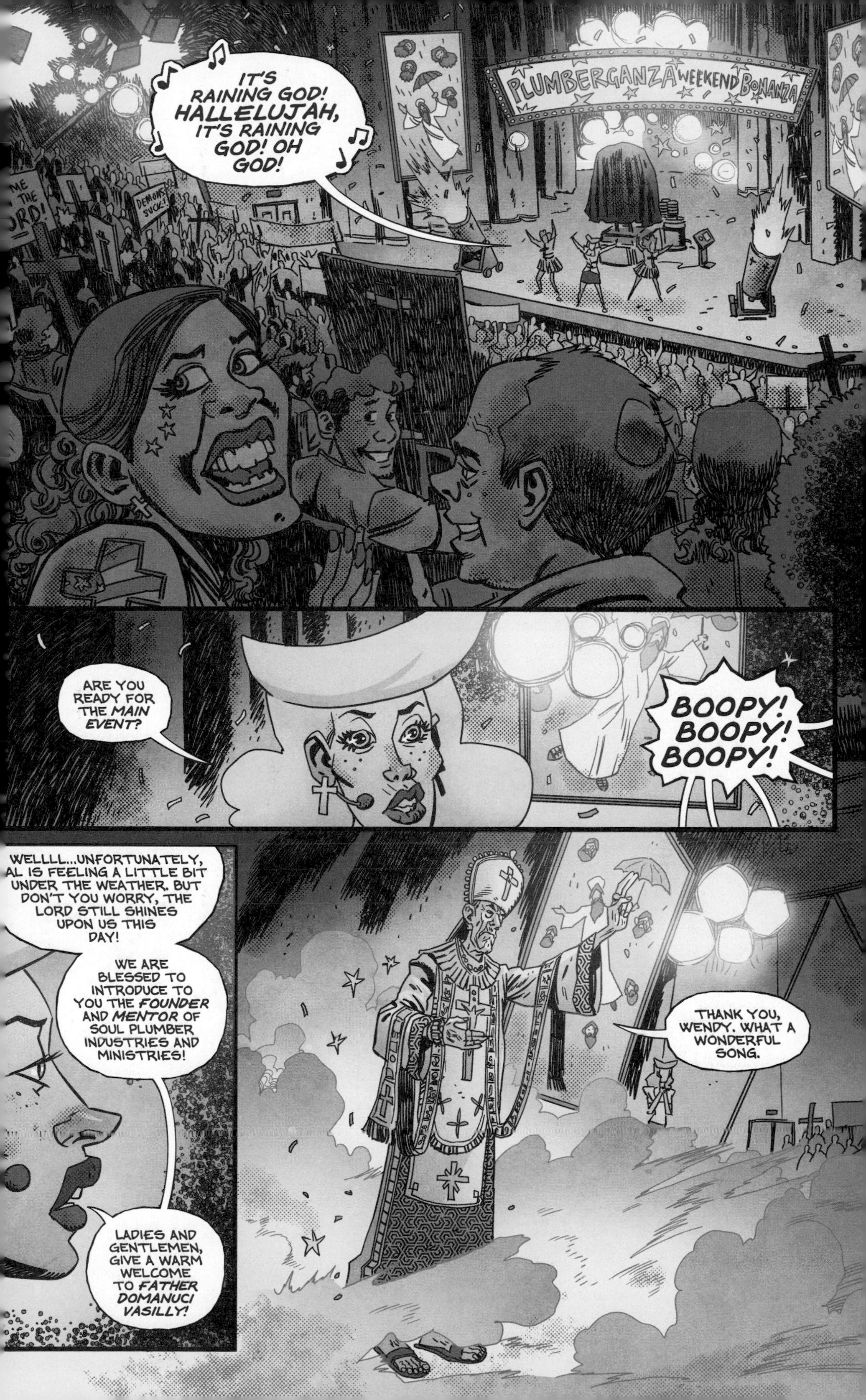
IT'S RAINING GOD! HALLELUJAH, IT'S RAINING GOD! OH GOD!
PLUMBERGANZA WEEKEND BONANZA
DEMONS SUCK!
ARE YOU READY FOR THE *MAIN EVENT*?
BOOPY! BOOPY! BOOPY!
WELLLL...UNFORTUNATELY, AL IS FEELING A LITTLE BIT UNDER THE WEATHER. BUT DON'T YOU WORRY, THE LORD STILL SHINES UPON US THIS DAY!
WE ARE BLESSED TO INTRODUCE TO YOU THE *FOUNDER* AND *MENTOR* OF SOUL PLUMBER INDUSTRIES AND MINISTRIES!
LADIES AND GENTLEMEN, GIVE A WARM WELCOME TO *FATHER DOMANUCI VASILLY!*
THANK YOU, WENDY. WHAT A WONDERFUL SONG.

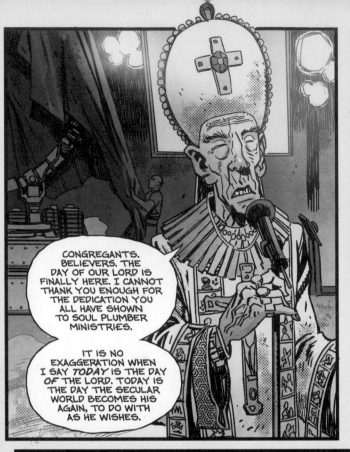

CONGREGANTS. BELIEVERS. THE DAY OF OUR LORD IS FINALLY HERE. I CANNOT THANK YOU ENOUGH FOR THE DEDICATION YOU ALL HAVE SHOWN TO SOUL PLUMBER MINISTRIES.

IT IS NO EXAGGERATION WHEN I SAY *TODAY* IS THE DAY OF THE LORD. TODAY IS THE DAY THE SECULAR WORLD BECOMES HIS AGAIN, TO DO WITH AS HE WISHES.

DO NOT BE FRIGHTENED. THOSE HELPERS YOU SEE ARE ONLY HERE TO MAKE SURE IT IS SAFE FOR OUR LORD.

LONG AGO, I WAS CHOSEN, AS YOU ARE CHOSEN. WE ARE TO WITNESS THE TRUE FORM OF OUR FATHER. HE IS TRULY...

...QUITE REMARKABLE.

SIIIIING TO THE MOUNTAINS... SIIIIING TO THE SEA...

...THIS IS THE DAY THE LORD HAS MADE...

LET ALL THE WORLD... REJOIIIIIICE.

CLUNK

ACTIVA

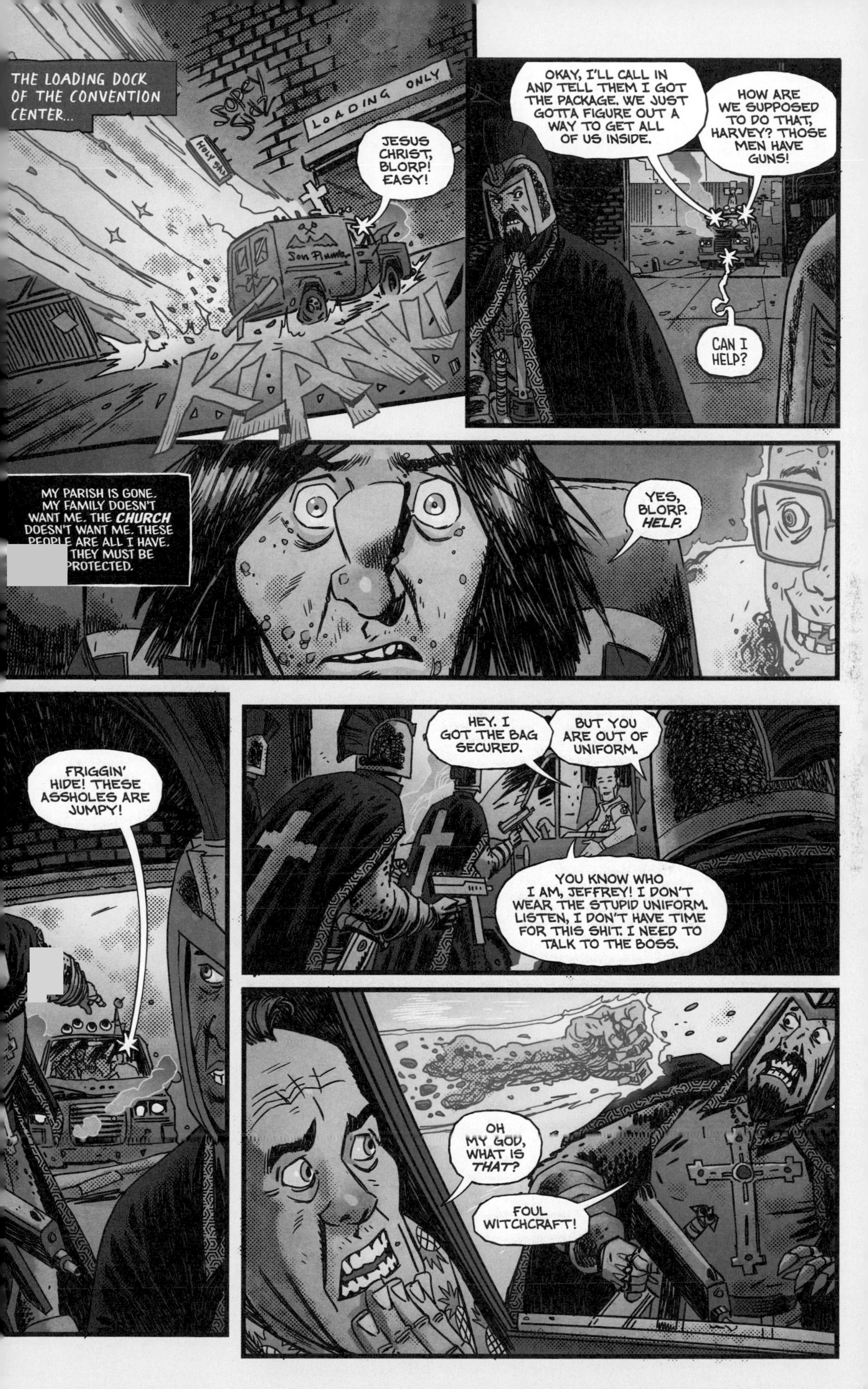

THE LOADING DOCK OF THE CONVENTION CENTER...
LOADING ONLY
JESUS CHRIST, BLORP! EASY!
KLANK
OKAY, I'LL CALL IN AND TELL THEM I GOT THE PACKAGE. WE JUST GOTTA FIGURE OUT A WAY TO GET ALL OF US INSIDE.
HOW ARE WE SUPPOSED TO DO THAT, HARVEY? THOSE MEN HAVE GUNS!
CAN I HELP?
MY PARISH IS GONE. MY FAMILY DOESN'T WANT ME. THE CHURCH DOESN'T WANT ME. THESE PEOPLE ARE ALL I HAVE. THEY MUST BE PROTECTED.
YES, BLORP. HELP.
FRIGGIN' HIDE! THESE ASSHOLES ARE JUMPY!
HEY. I GOT THE BAG SECURED.
BUT YOU ARE OUT OF UNIFORM.
YOU KNOW WHO I AM, JEFFREY! I DON'T WEAR THE STUPID UNIFORM. LISTEN, I DON'T HAVE TIME FOR THIS SHIT. I NEED TO TALK TO THE BOSS.
OH MY GOD, WHAT IS THAT?
FOUL WITCHCRAFT!

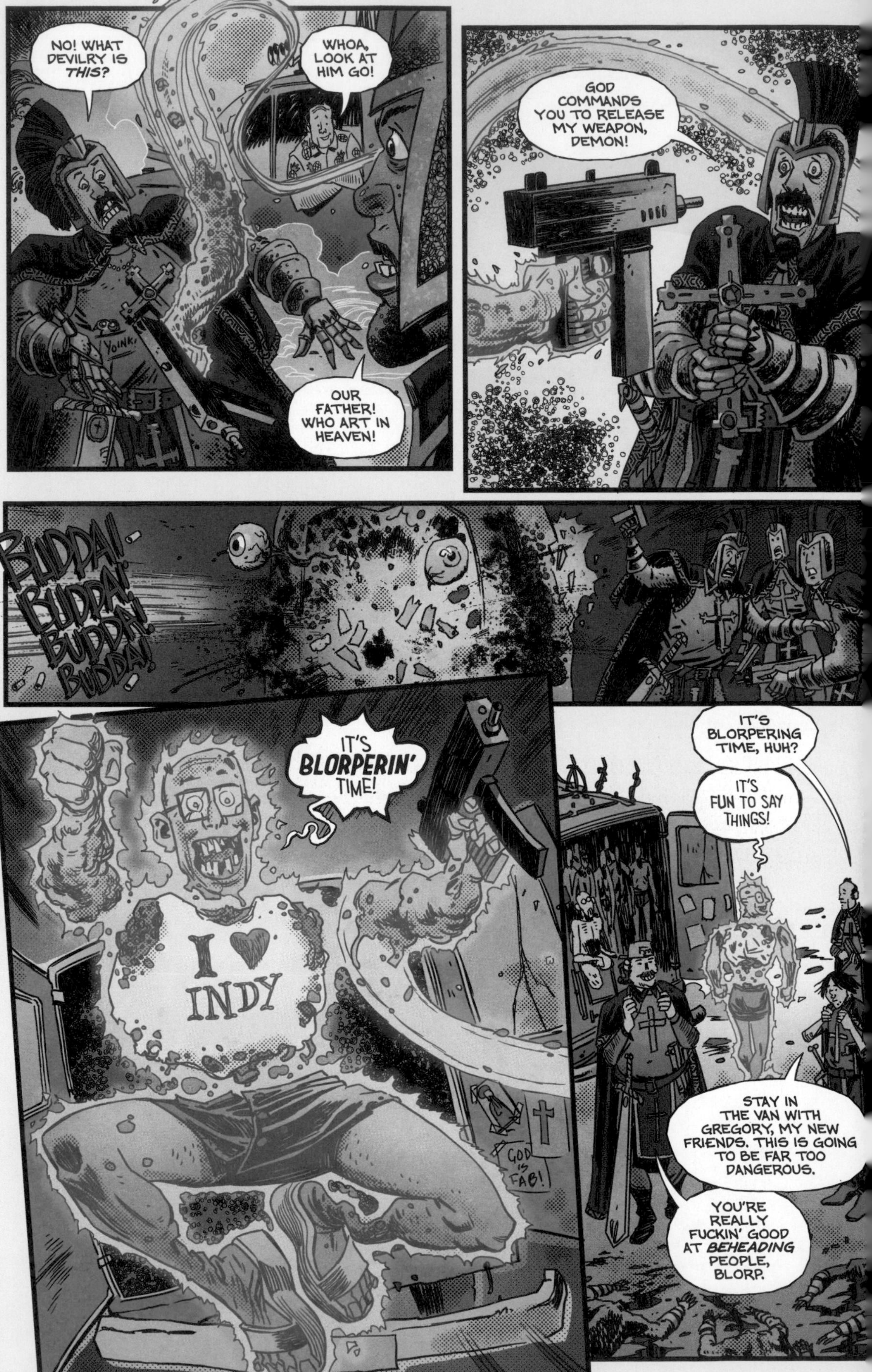

NO! WHAT DEVILRY IS *THIS*?
WHOA, LOOK AT HIM GO!
YOINK!
OUR FATHER! WHO ART IN HEAVEN!
GOD COMMANDS YOU TO RELEASE MY WEAPON, DEMON!
BUDDA! BUDDA! BUDDA! BUDDA!
IT'S **BLORPERIN'** TIME!
I ♥ INDY
GOD IS FAB!
IT'S BLORPERING TIME, HUH?
IT'S FUN TO SAY THINGS!
STAY IN THE VAN WITH GREGORY, MY NEW FRIENDS. THIS IS GOING TO BE FAR TOO DANGEROUS.
YOU'RE REALLY FUCKIN' GOOD AT *BEHEADING* PEOPLE, BLORP.

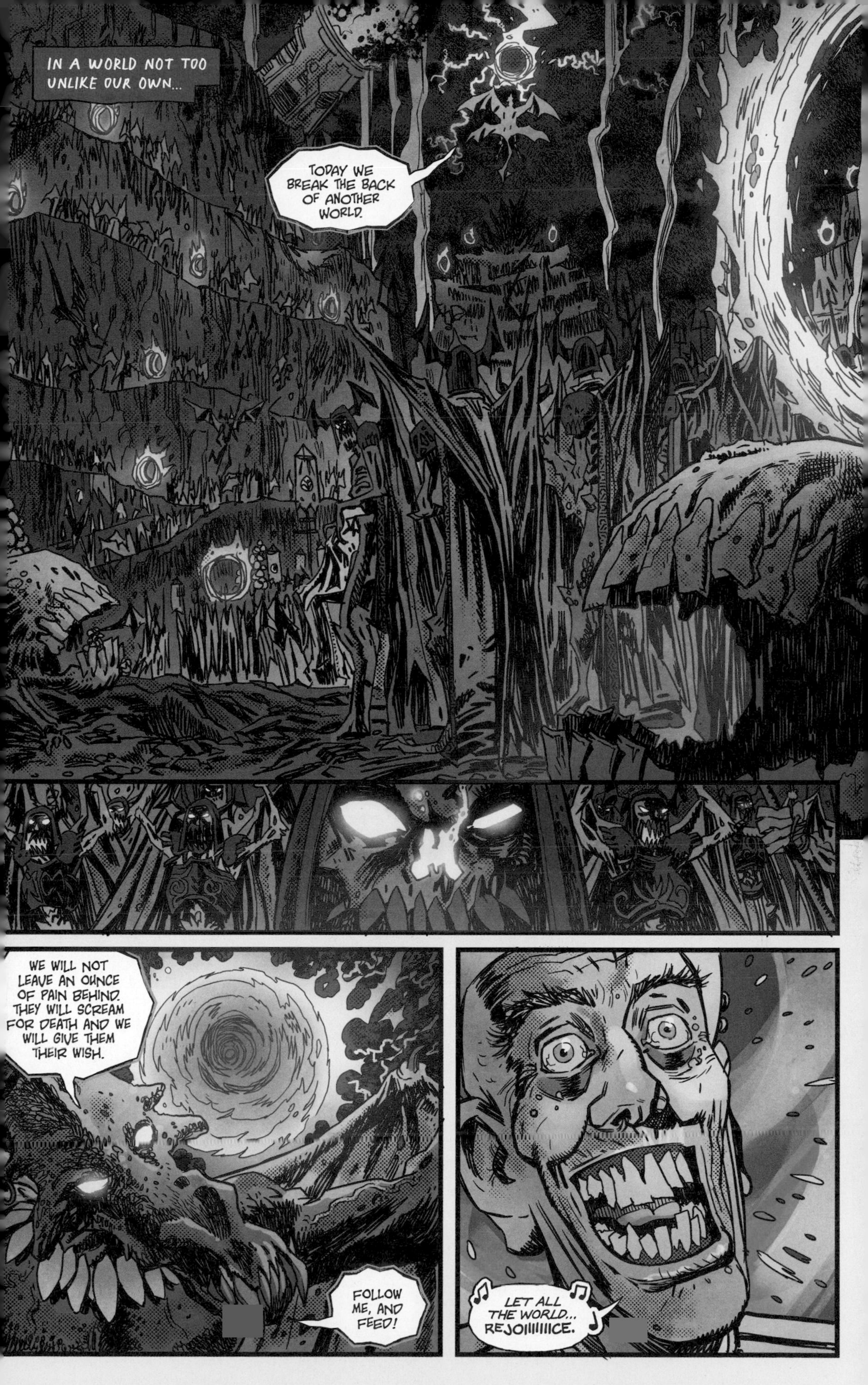
IN A WORLD NOT TOO UNLIKE OUR OWN...
TODAY WE BREAK THE BACK OF ANOTHER WORLD.
WE WILL NOT LEAVE AN OUNCE OF PAIN BEHIND. THEY WILL SCREAM FOR DEATH AND WE WILL GIVE THEM THEIR WISH.
FOLLOW ME, AND FEED!
LET ALL THE WORLD... REJOIIIIIICE.

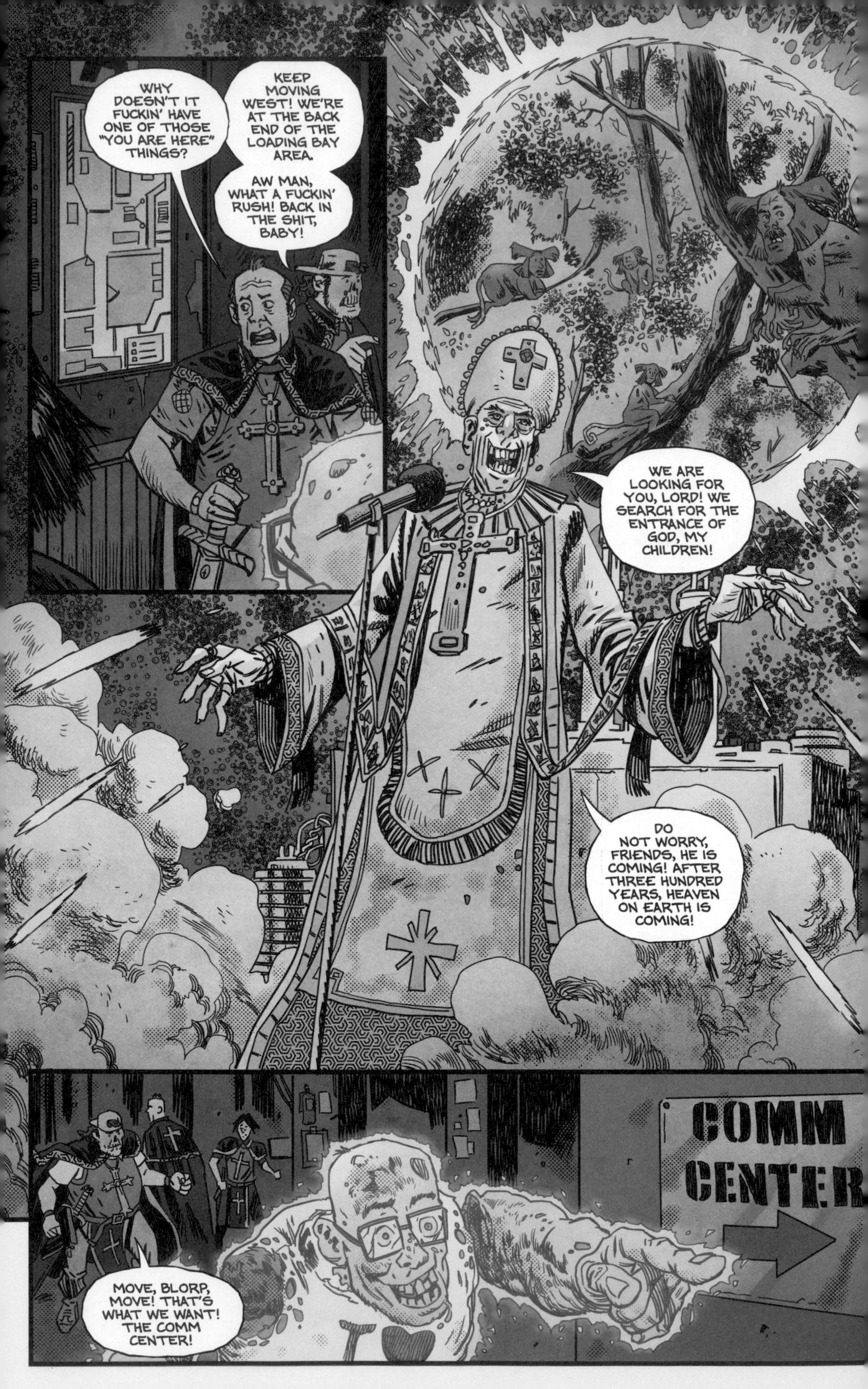
WHY DOESN'T IT FUCKIN' HAVE ONE OF THOSE "YOU ARE HERE" THINGS?
KEEP MOVING WEST! WE'RE AT THE BACK END OF THE LOADING BAY AREA.
AW MAN, WHAT A FUCKIN' RUSH! BACK IN THE SHIT, BABY!
WE ARE LOOKING FOR YOU, LORD! WE SEARCH FOR THE ENTRANCE OF GOD, MY CHILDREN!
DO NOT WORRY, FRIENDS, HE IS COMING! AFTER THREE HUNDRED YEARS, HEAVEN ON EARTH IS COMING!
COMM CENTER
MOVE, BLORP, MOVE! THAT'S WHAT WE WANT! THE COMM CENTER!

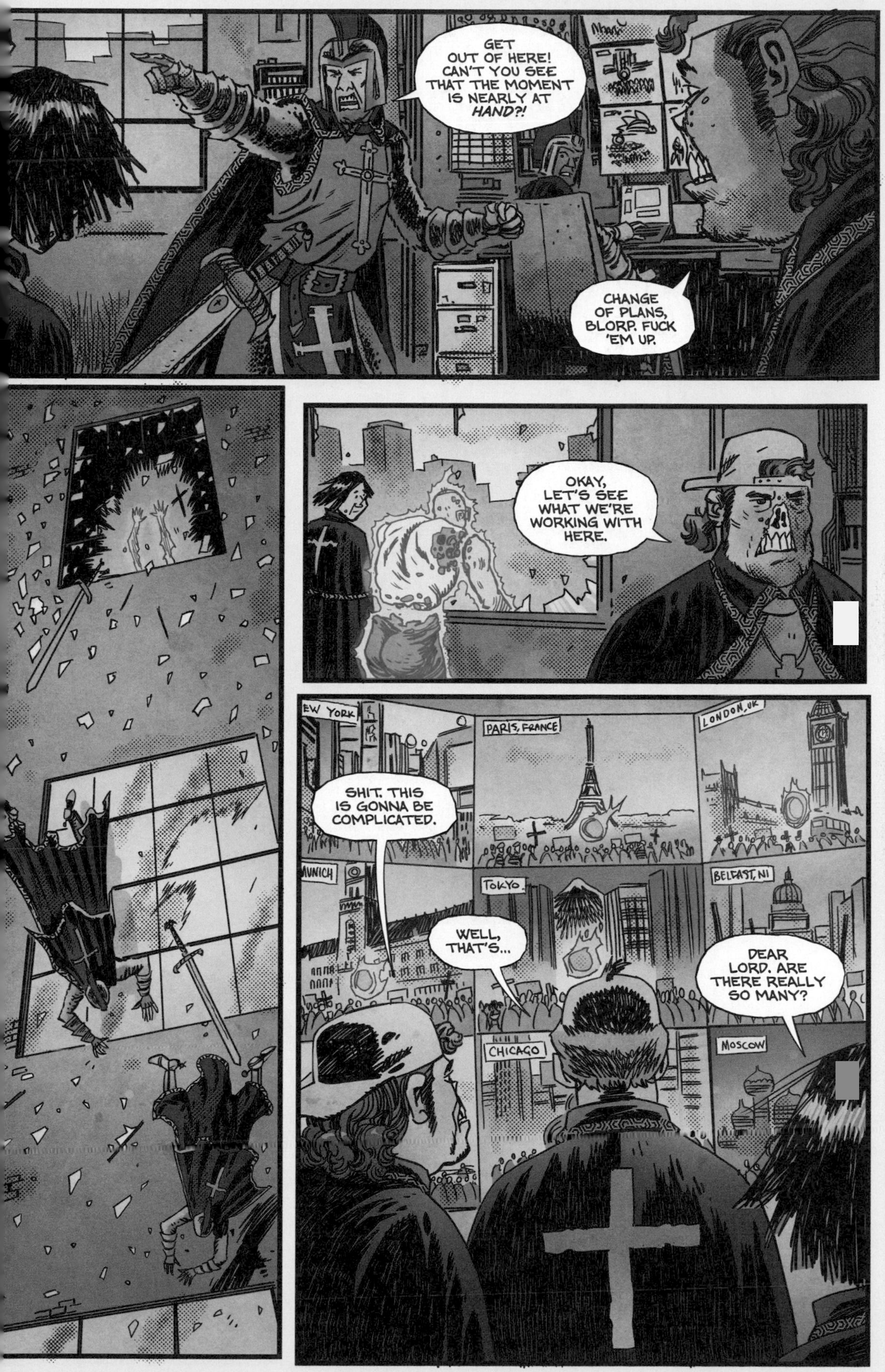
GET OUT OF HERE! CAN'T YOU SEE THAT THE MOMENT IS NEARLY AT HAND?!
CHANGE OF PLANS, BLORP. FUCK 'EM UP.
OKAY, LET'S SEE WHAT WE'RE WORKING WITH HERE.
EW YORK
PARIS, FRANCE
LONDON, UK
MUNICH
TOKYO
BELFAST, NI
CHICAGO
MOSCOW
SHIT. THIS IS GONNA BE COMPLICATED.
WELL, THAT'S...
DEAR LORD. ARE THERE REALLY SO MANY?

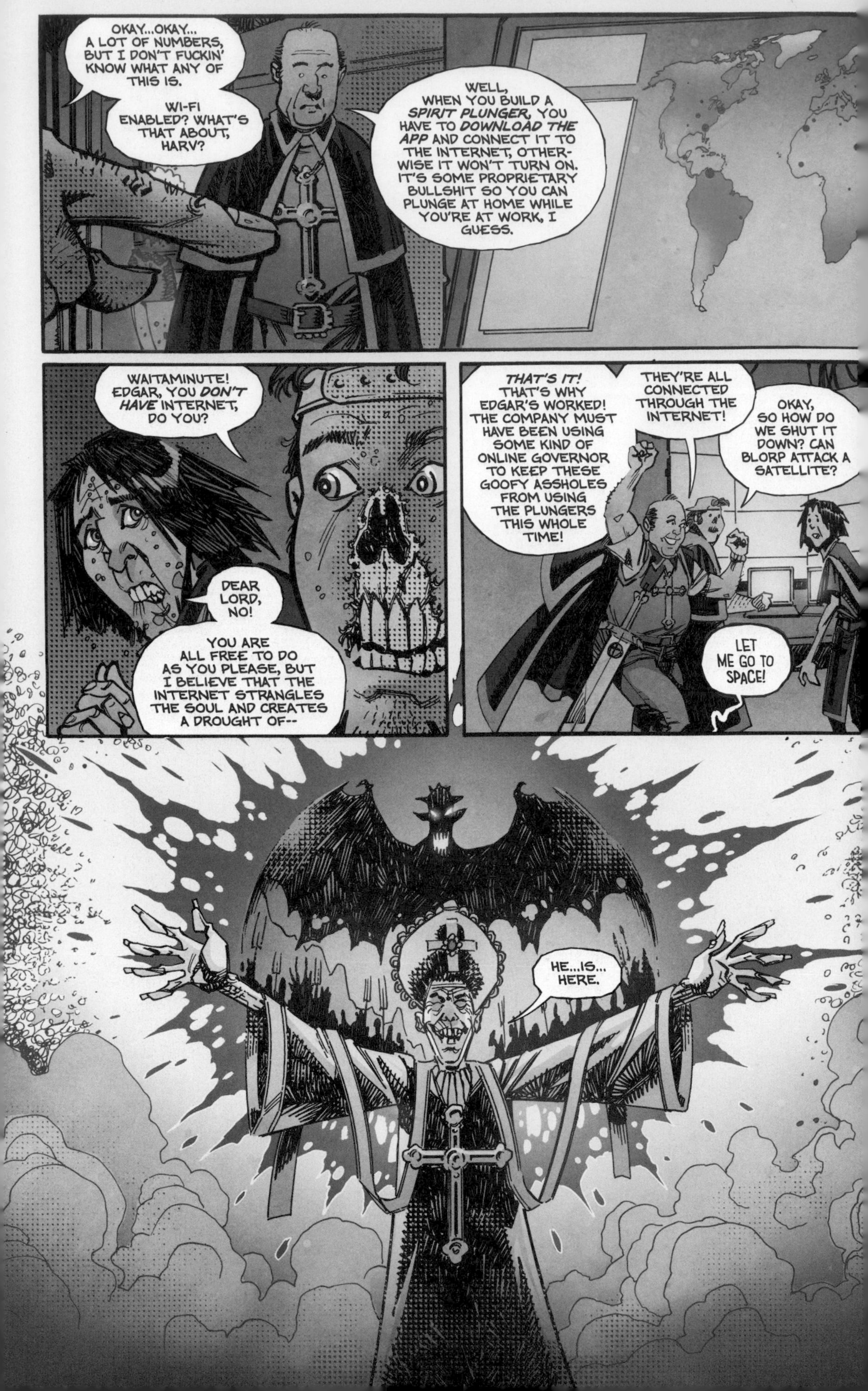
OKAY...OKAY... A LOT OF NUMBERS, BUT I DON'T FUCKIN' KNOW WHAT ANY OF THIS IS.
WI-FI ENABLED? WHAT'S THAT ABOUT, HARV?
WELL, WHEN YOU BUILD A SPIRIT PLUNGER, YOU HAVE TO DOWNLOAD THE APP AND CONNECT IT TO THE INTERNET, OTHERWISE IT WON'T TURN ON. IT'S SOME PROPRIETARY BULLSHIT SO YOU CAN PLUNGE AT HOME WHILE YOU'RE AT WORK, I GUESS.
WAITAMINUTE! EDGAR, YOU DON'T HAVE INTERNET, DO YOU?
DEAR LORD, NO!
YOU ARE ALL FREE TO DO AS YOU PLEASE, BUT I BELIEVE THAT THE INTERNET STRANGLES THE SOUL AND CREATES A DROUGHT OF--
THAT'S IT! THAT'S WHY EDGAR'S WORKED! THE COMPANY MUST HAVE BEEN USING SOME KIND OF ONLINE GOVERNOR TO KEEP THESE GOOFY ASSHOLES FROM USING THE PLUNGERS THIS WHOLE TIME!
THEY'RE ALL CONNECTED THROUGH THE INTERNET!
OKAY, SO HOW DO WE SHUT IT DOWN? CAN BLORP ATTACK A SATELLITE?
LET ME GO TO SPACE!
HE...IS... HERE.

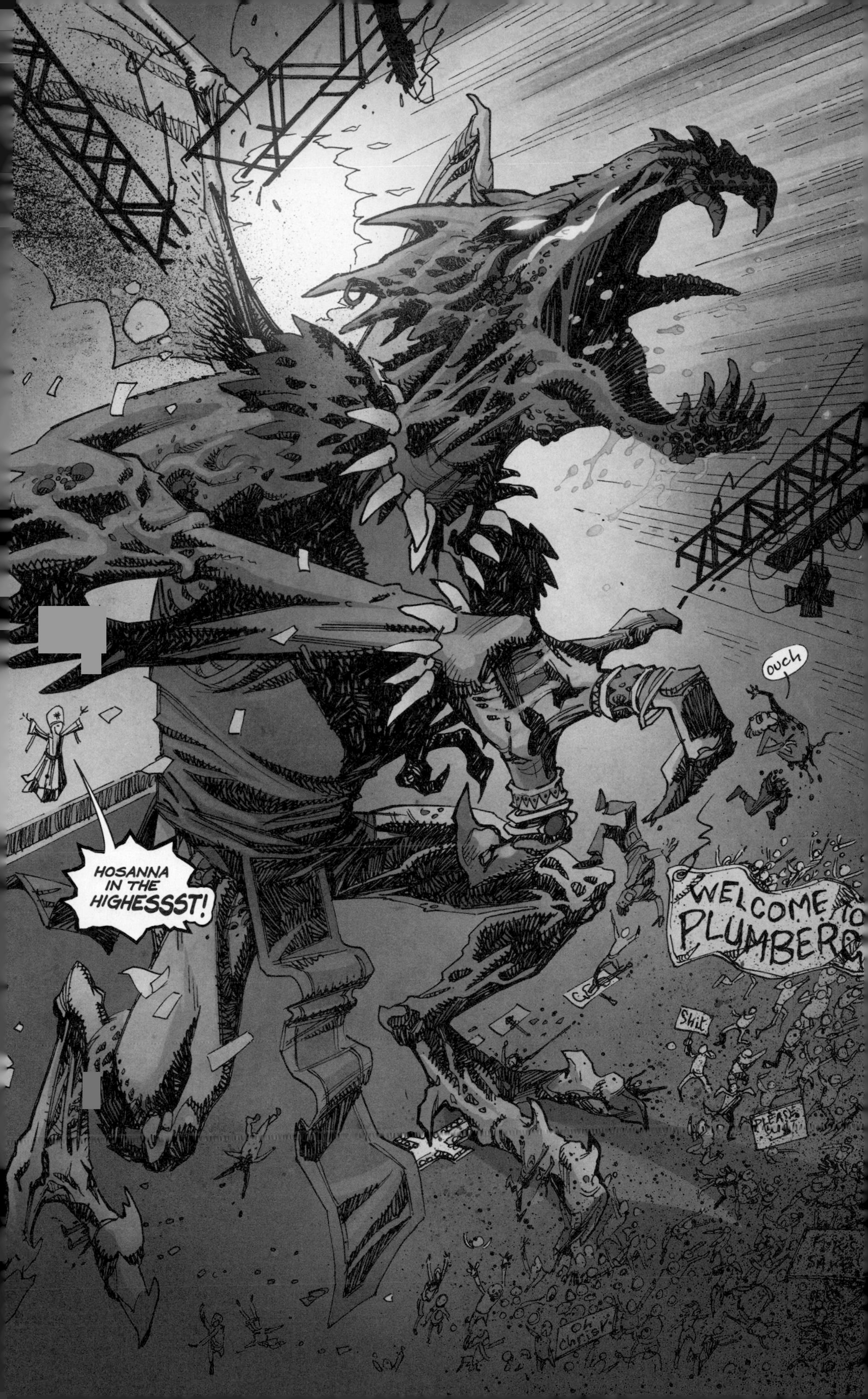
HOSANNA IN THE HIGHESSST!
ouch
WELCOME
PLUMBER
Shit
Oh Christ

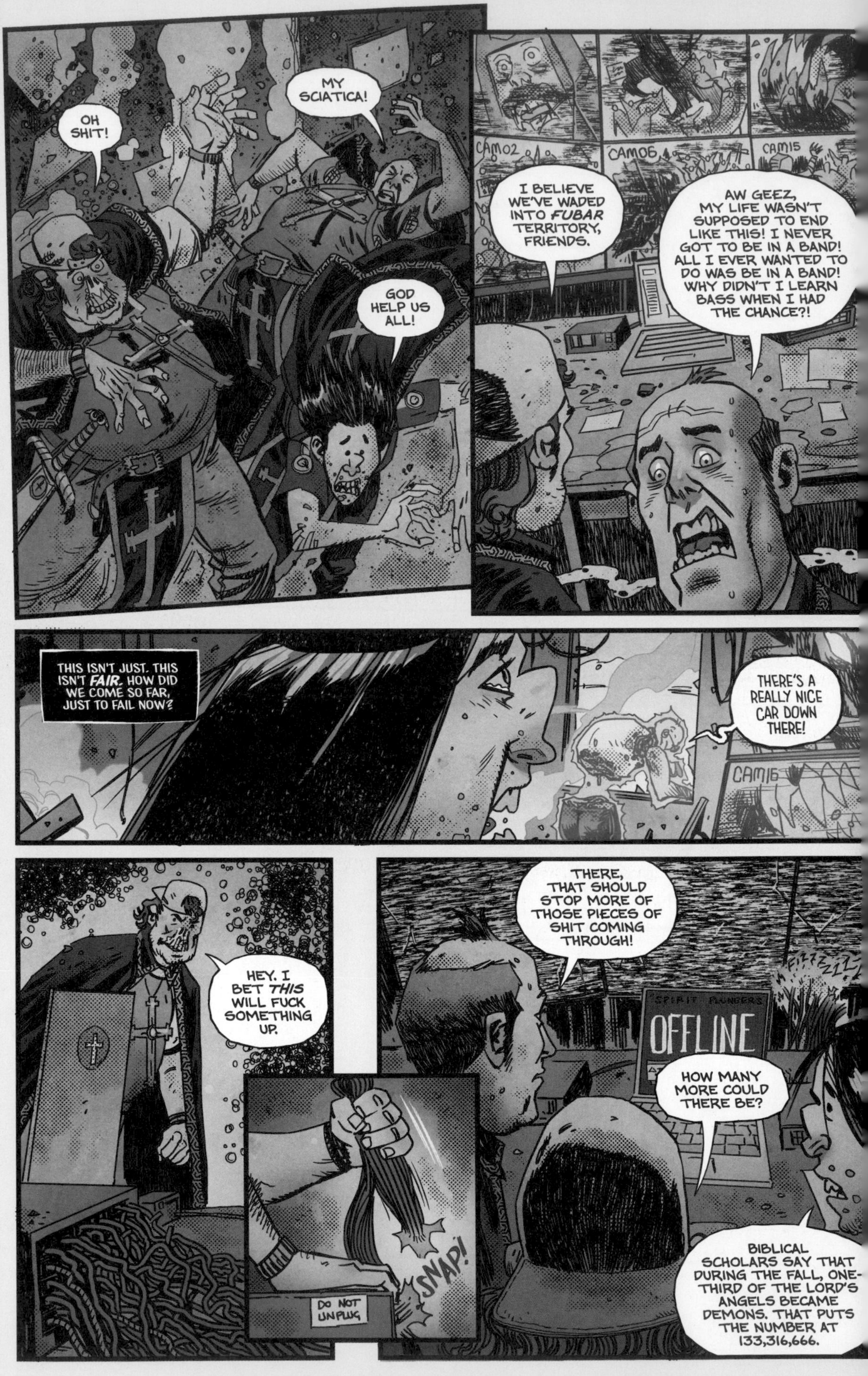
OH SHIT!
MY SCIATICA!
GOD HELP US ALL!
CAM02
CAM06
CAM15
I BELIEVE WE'VE WADED INTO *FUBAR* TERRITORY, FRIENDS.
AW GEEZ, MY LIFE WASN'T SUPPOSED TO END LIKE THIS! I NEVER GOT TO BE IN A BAND! ALL I EVER WANTED TO DO WAS BE IN A BAND! WHY DIDN'T I LEARN BASS WHEN I HAD THE CHANCE?!
THIS ISN'T JUST. THIS ISN'T *FAIR.* HOW DID WE COME SO FAR, JUST TO FAIL NOW?
THERE'S A REALLY NICE CAR DOWN THERE!
CAM16
CAM15
HEY. I BET *THIS* WILL FUCK SOMETHING UP.
DO NOT UNPLUG
SNAP!
THERE, THAT SHOULD STOP MORE OF THOSE PIECES OF SHIT COMING THROUGH!
FIZZZZZ
SPIRIT BANGERS
OFFLINE
HOW MANY MORE COULD THERE BE?
BIBLICAL SCHOLARS SAY THAT DURING THE FALL, ONE-THIRD OF THE LORD'S ANGELS BECAME DEMONS. THAT PUTS THE NUMBER AT 133,316,666.

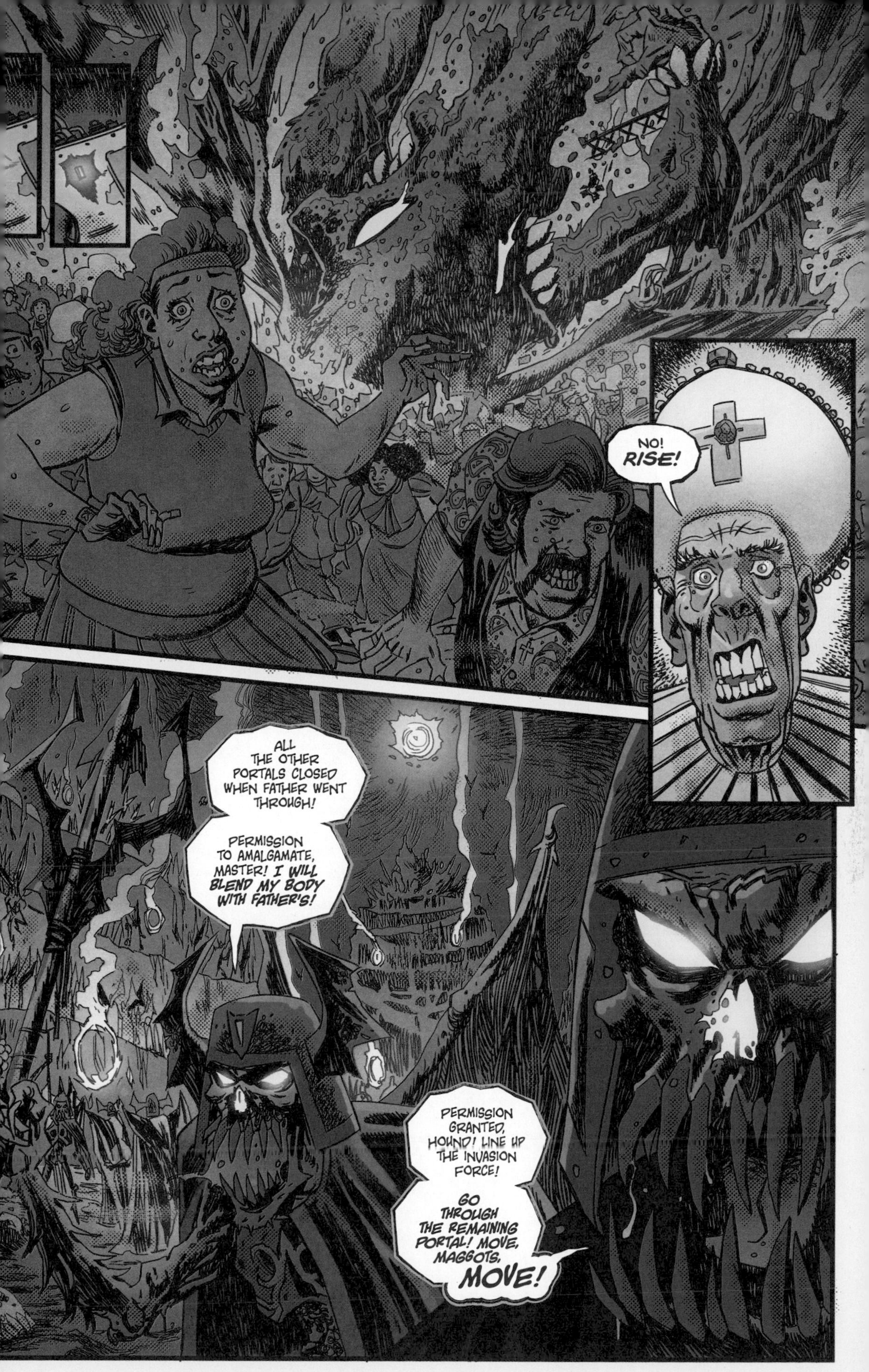
NO! RISE!
ALL THE OTHER PORTALS CLOSED WHEN FATHER WENT THROUGH!
PERMISSION TO AMALGAMATE, MASTER! I WILL BLEND MY BODY WITH FATHER'S!
PERMISSION GRANTED, HOUND! LINE UP THE INVASION FORCE!
GO THROUGH THE REMAINING PORTAL! MOVE, MAGGOTS, MOVE!

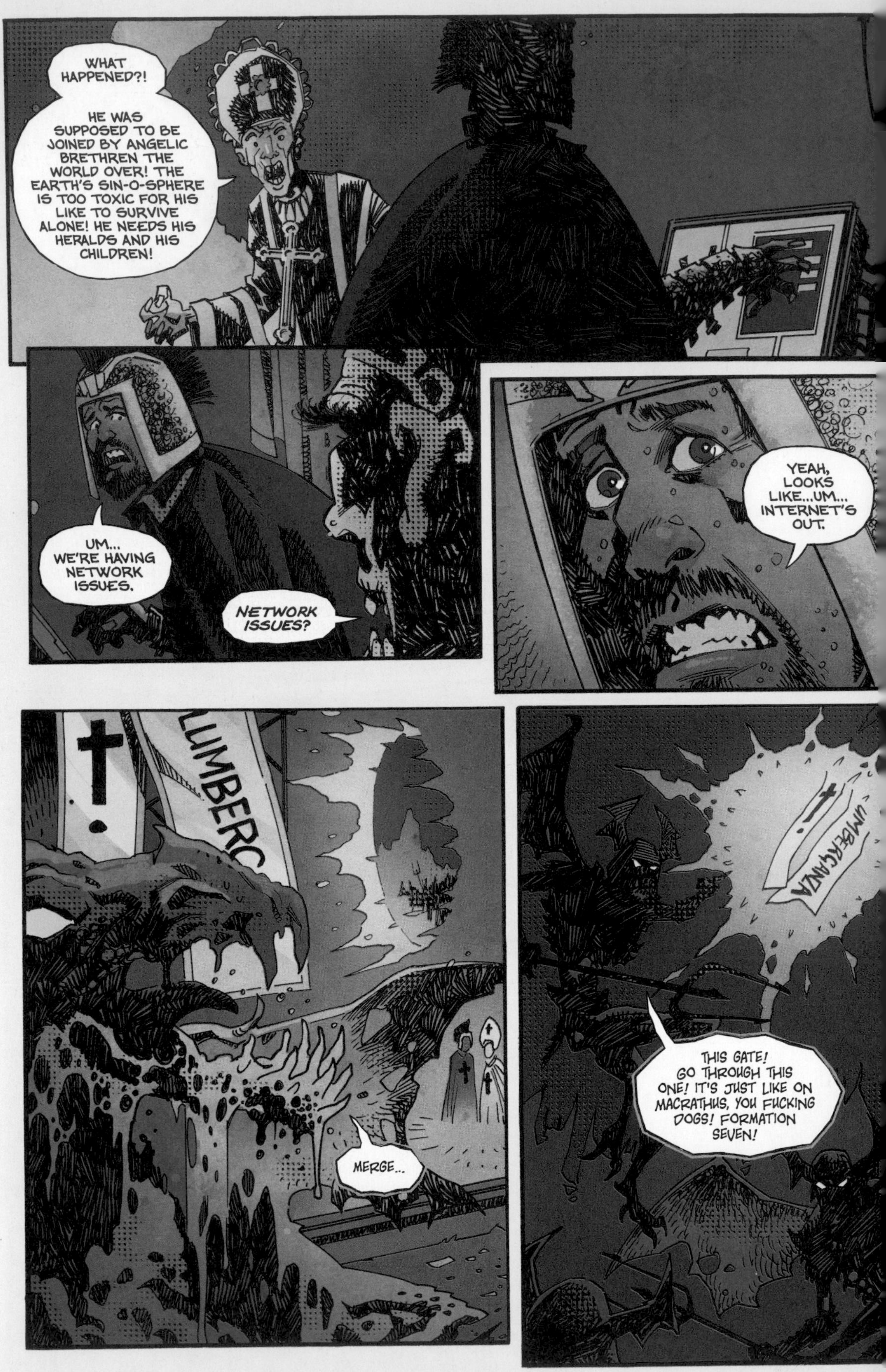
WHAT HAPPENED?!
HE WAS SUPPOSED TO BE JOINED BY ANGELIC BRETHREN THE WORLD OVER! THE EARTH'S SIN-O-SPHERE IS TOO TOXIC FOR HIS LIKE TO SURVIVE ALONE! HE NEEDS HIS HERALDS AND HIS CHILDREN!
UM... WE'RE HAVING NETWORK ISSUES.
NETWORK ISSUES?
YEAH, LOOKS LIKE...UM... INTERNET'S OUT.
LUMBERC
MERGE...
UMBERCANZA
THIS GATE! GO THROUGH THIS ONE! IT'S JUST LIKE ON MACRATHUS, YOU FUCKING DOGS! FORMATION SEVEN!

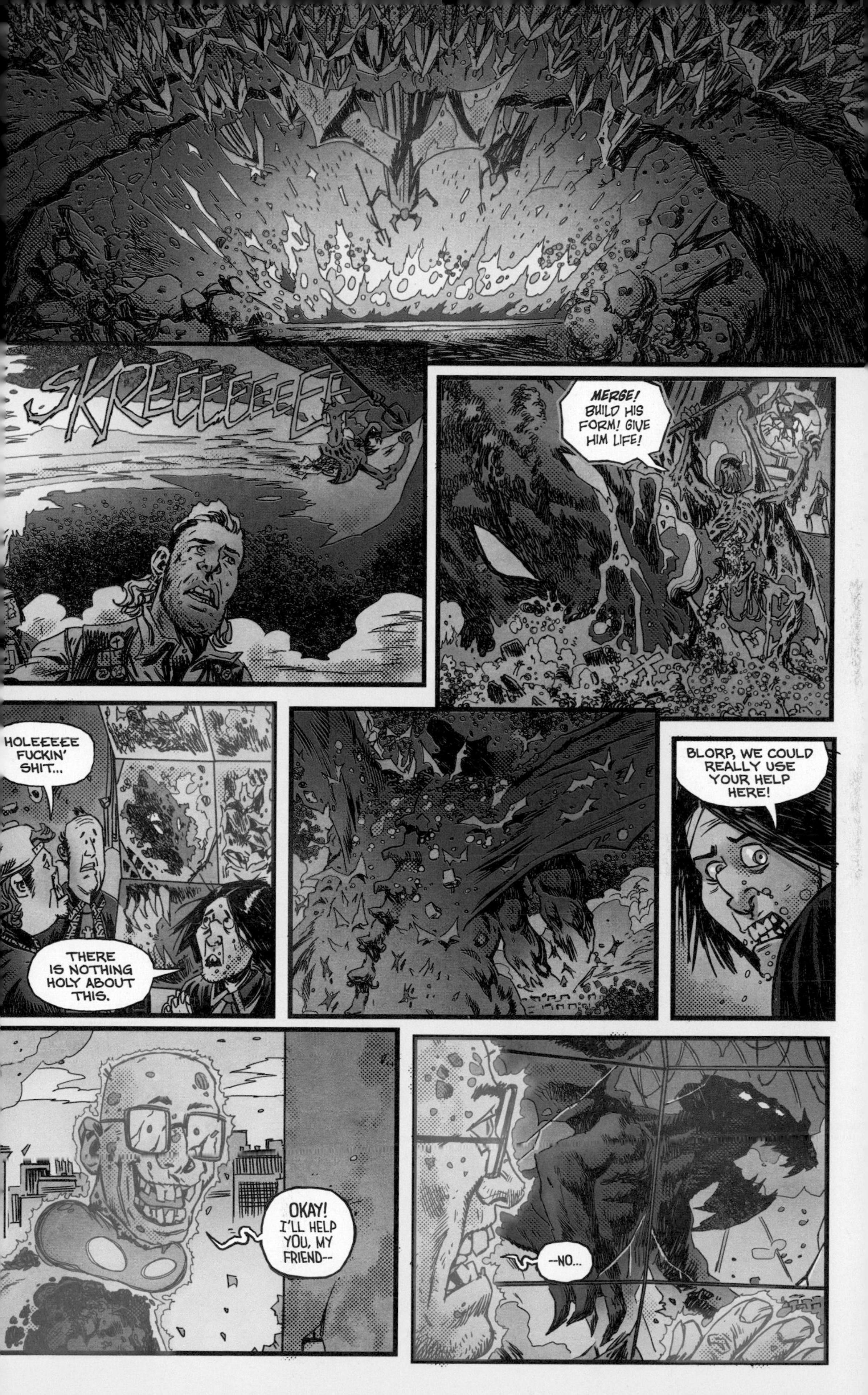
SKREEEEEEEEF
MERGE! BUILD HIS FORM! GIVE HIM LIFE!
HOLEEEEE FUCKIN' SHIT...
THERE IS NOTHING HOLY ABOUT THIS.
BLORP, WE COULD REALLY USE YOUR HELP HERE!
OKAY! I'LL HELP YOU, MY FRIEND--
--NO...

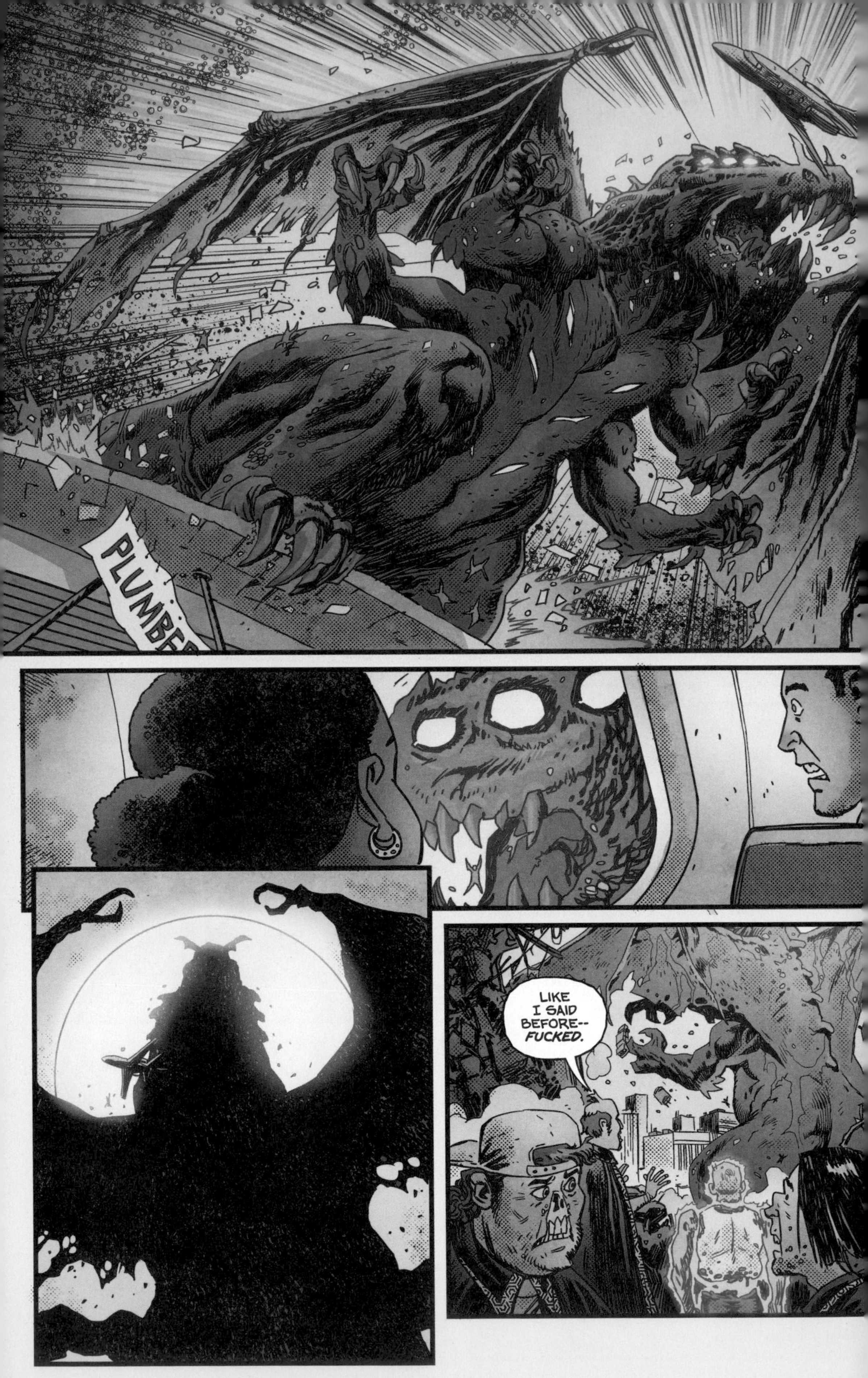
PLUMBER
LIKE I SAID BEFORE--*FUCKED.*

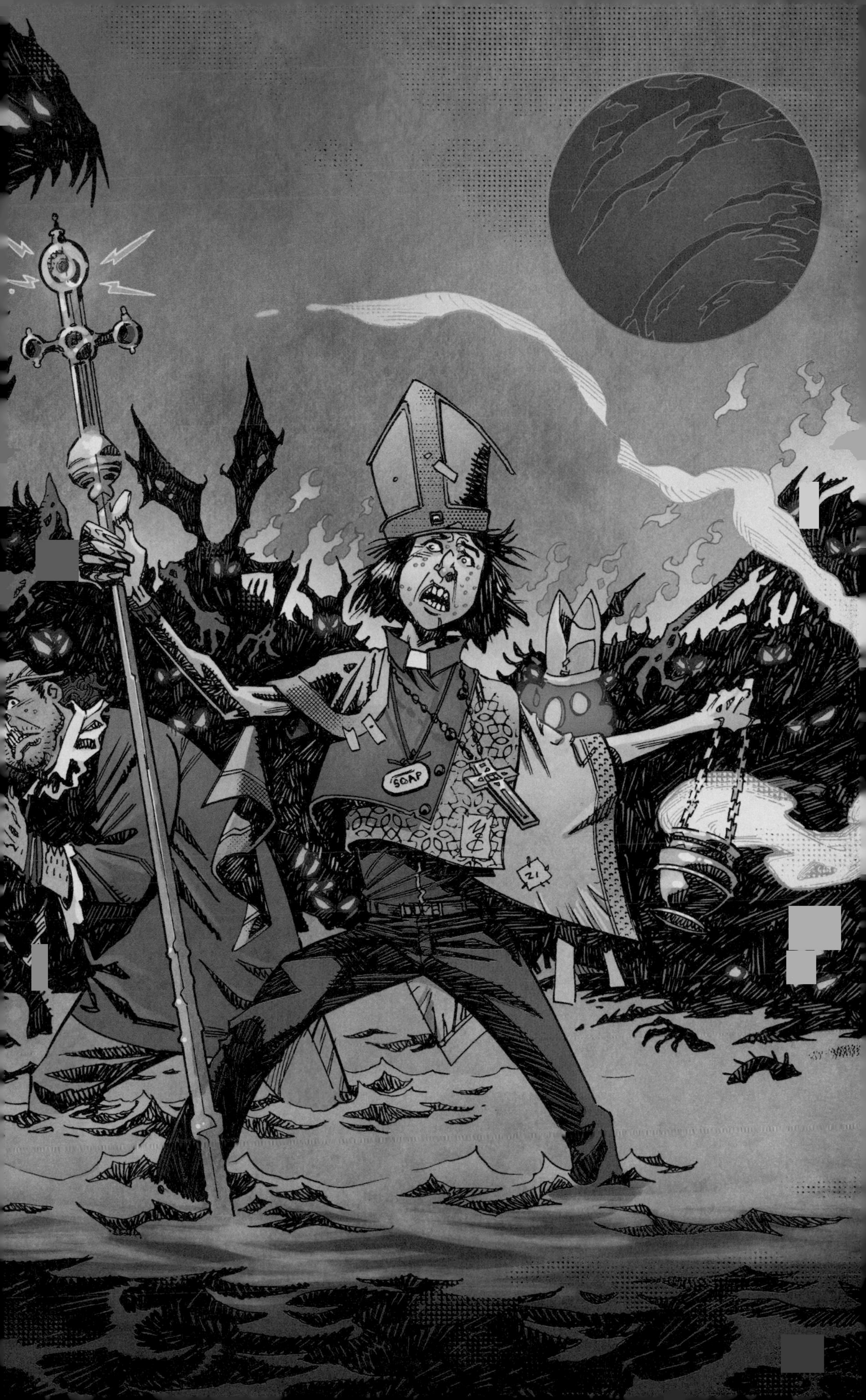
SOAP

DC Horror Presents: Soul Plumber #6
variant cover by Amanda Conner & Alex Sinclair

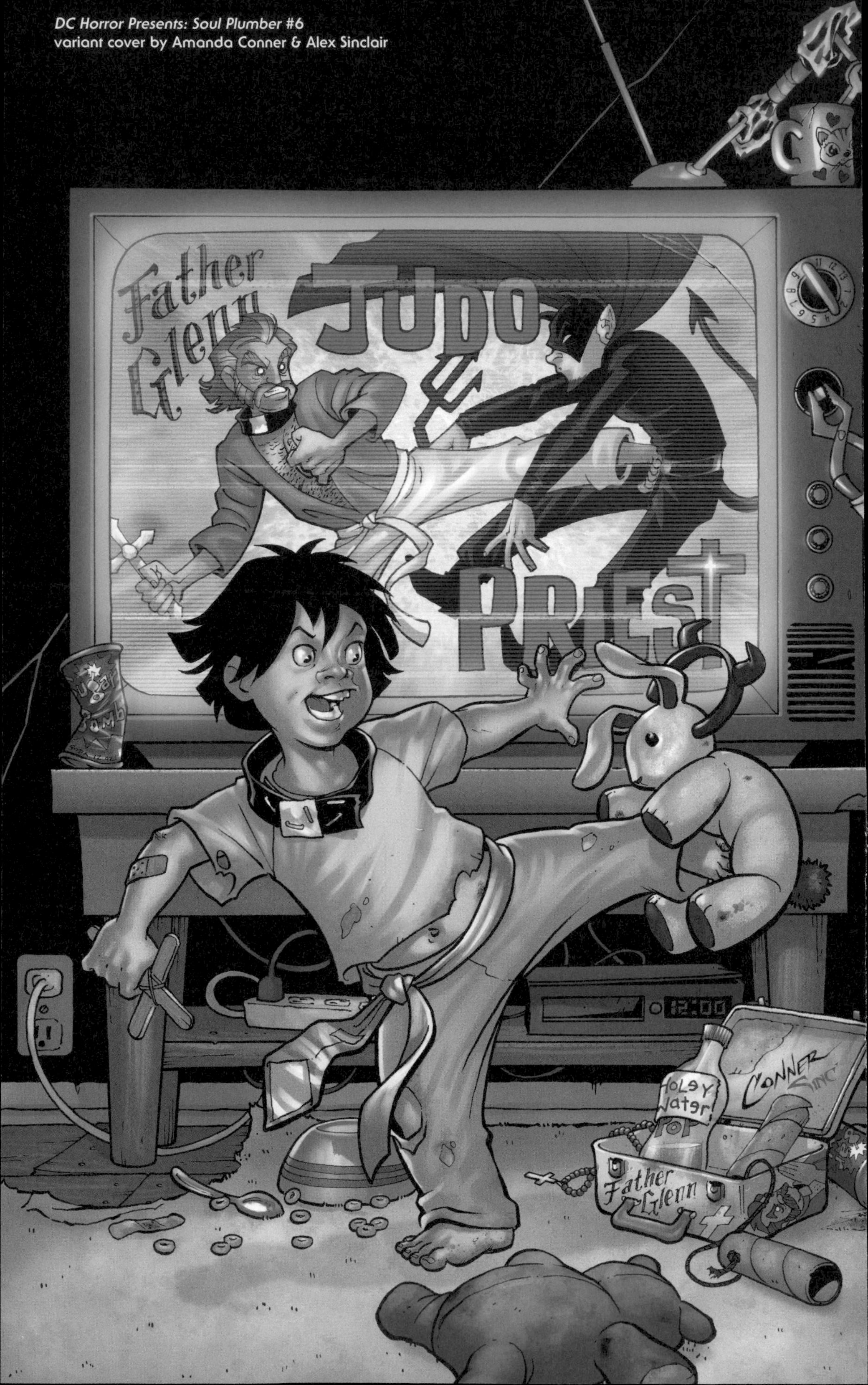
Father Glenn
JUDO PRIEST
Sugar Bomb
Holey Water! Pop
Father Glenn
Conner Sinc
12:00

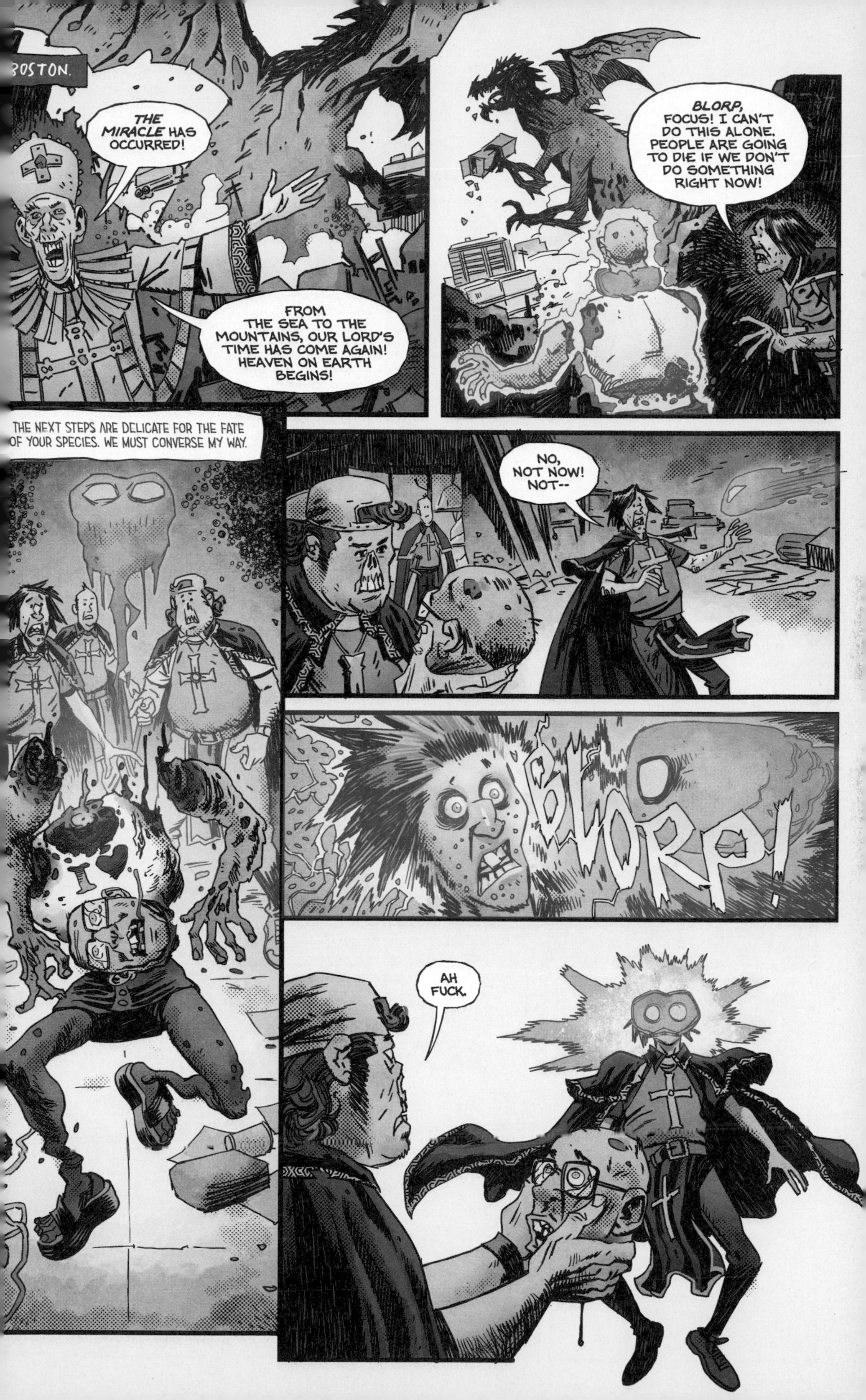
BOSTON.
THE MIRACLE HAS OCCURRED!
FROM THE SEA TO THE MOUNTAINS, OUR LORD'S TIME HAS COME AGAIN! HEAVEN ON EARTH BEGINS!
BLORP, FOCUS! I CAN'T DO THIS ALONE. PEOPLE ARE GOING TO DIE IF WE DON'T DO SOMETHING RIGHT NOW!
THE NEXT STEPS ARE DELICATE FOR THE FATE OF YOUR SPECIES. WE MUST CONVERSE MY WAY.
NO, NOT NOW! NOT--
BLORP!
AH FUCK.

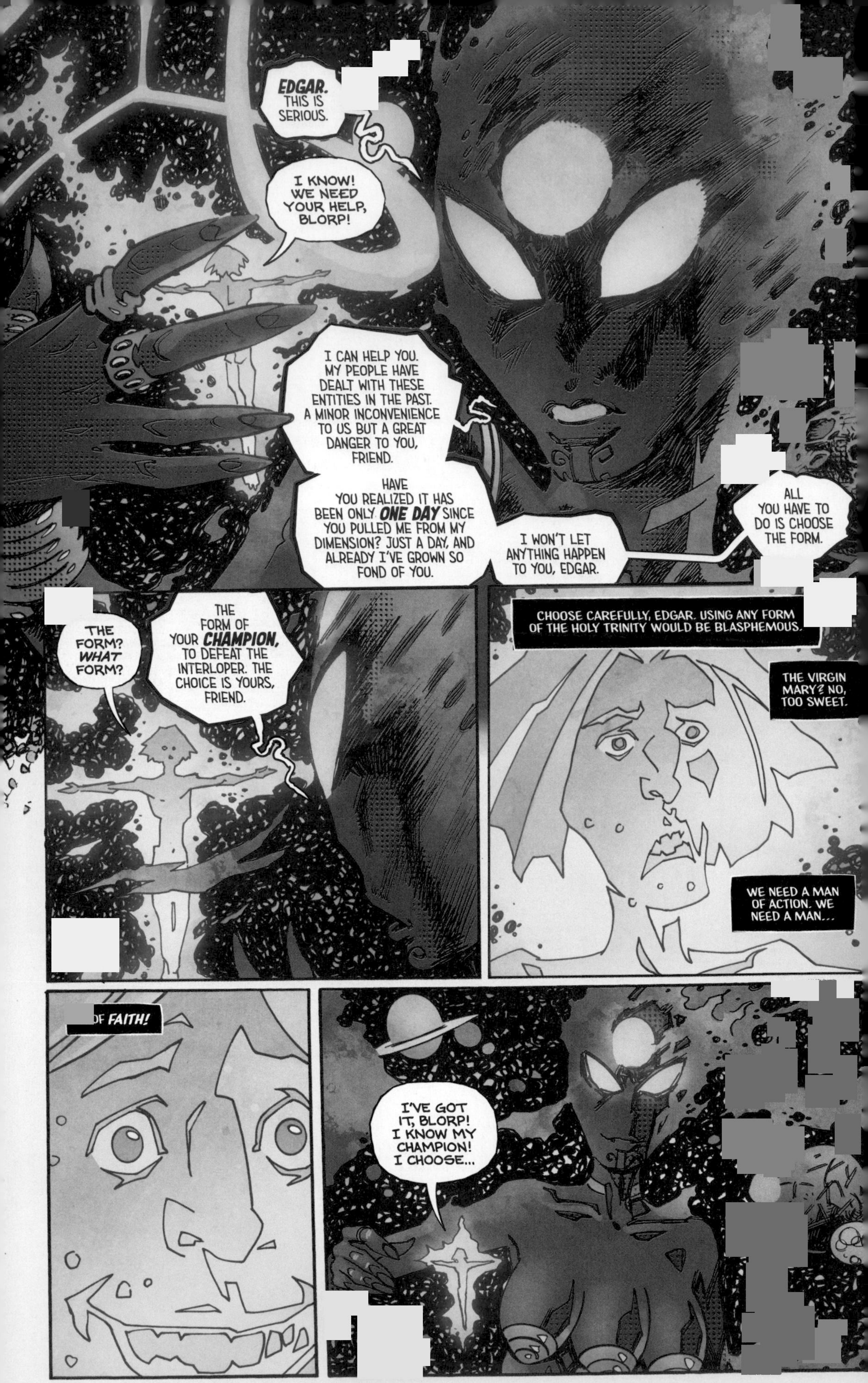

EDGAR. THIS IS SERIOUS.
I KNOW! WE NEED YOUR HELP, BLORP!
I CAN HELP YOU. MY PEOPLE HAVE DEALT WITH THESE ENTITIES IN THE PAST. A MINOR INCONVENIENCE TO US BUT A GREAT DANGER TO YOU, FRIEND.
HAVE YOU REALIZED IT HAS BEEN ONLY ONE DAY SINCE YOU PULLED ME FROM MY DIMENSION? JUST A DAY, AND ALREADY I'VE GROWN SO FOND OF YOU.
I WON'T LET ANYTHING HAPPEN TO YOU, EDGAR.
ALL YOU HAVE TO DO IS CHOOSE THE FORM.
THE FORM? WHAT FORM?
THE FORM OF YOUR CHAMPION, TO DEFEAT THE INTERLOPER. THE CHOICE IS YOURS, FRIEND.
CHOOSE CAREFULLY, EDGAR. USING ANY FORM OF THE HOLY TRINITY WOULD BE BLASPHEMOUS.
THE VIRGIN MARY? NO, TOO SWEET.
WE NEED A MAN OF ACTION. WE NEED A MAN...
OF FAITH!
I'VE GOT IT, BLORP! I KNOW MY CHAMPION! I CHOOSE...

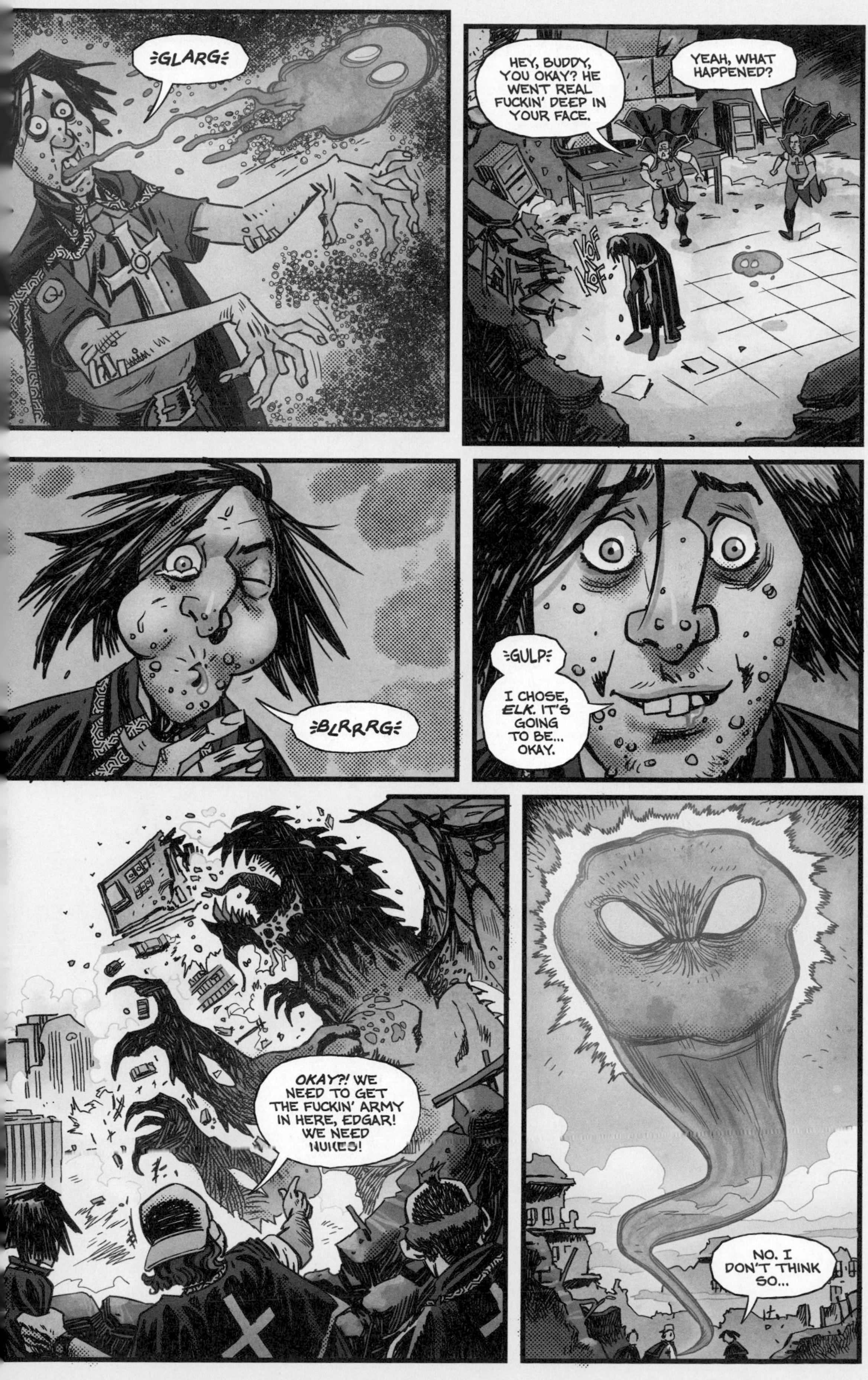
GLARG
HEY, BUDDY, YOU OKAY? HE WENT REAL FUCKIN' DEEP IN YOUR FACE.
YEAH, WHAT HAPPENED?
KOF KOF
BLRRRG
GULP
I CHOSE, *ELK*. IT'S GOING TO BE... OKAY.
OKAY?! WE NEED TO GET THE FUCKIN' ARMY IN HERE, EDGAR! WE NEED NUKES!
NO. I DON'T THINK SO...

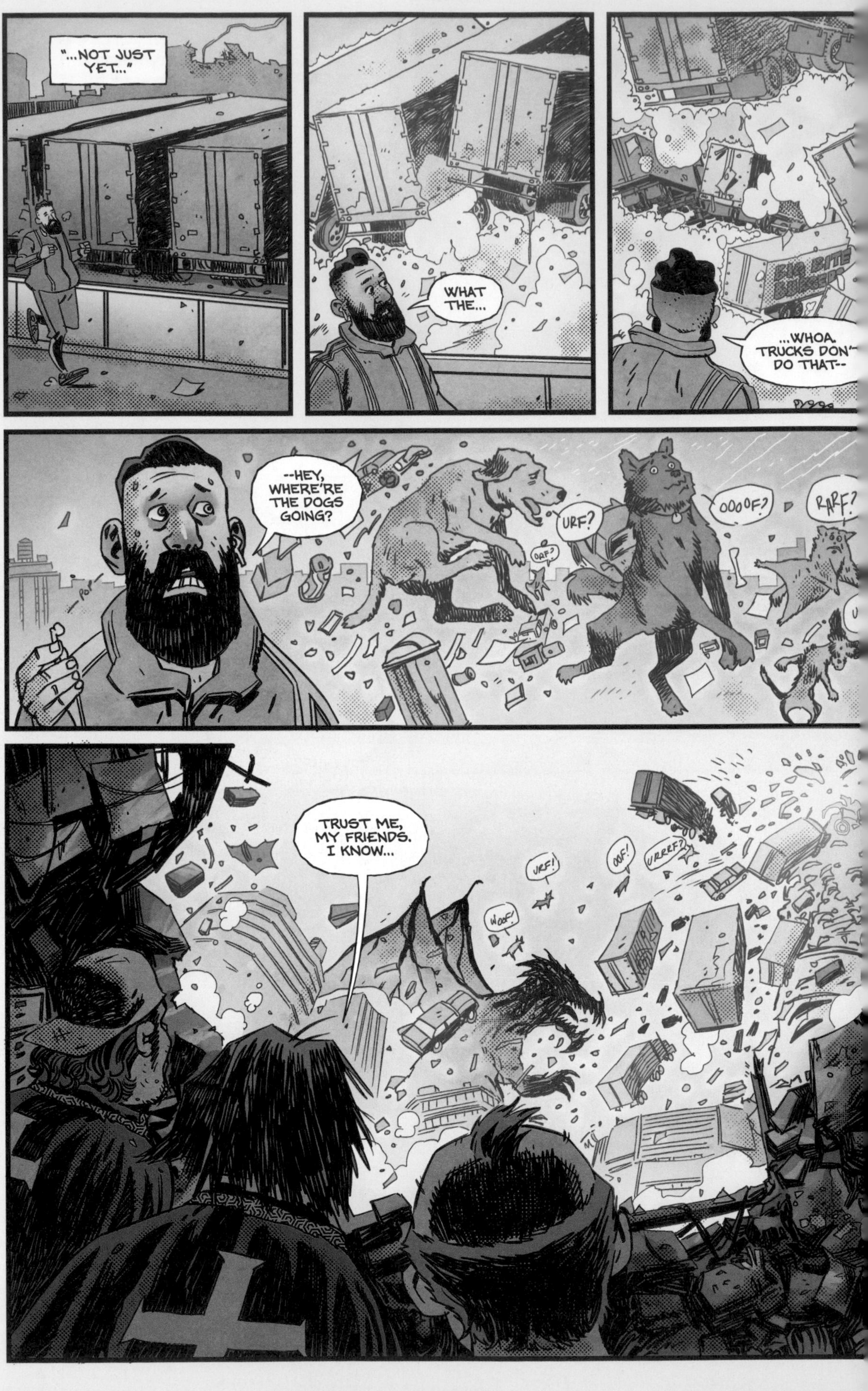
"...NOT JUST YET..."
WHAT THE...
BIG BITE BURGERS
...WHOA. TRUCKS DON'
DO THAT--
--HEY, WHERE'RE THE DOGS GOING?
POP
URF?
OOF?
OOOOF?
RARF?
TRUST ME, MY FRIENDS. I KNOW...
WOOF!
URF!
OOF!
URRRF?

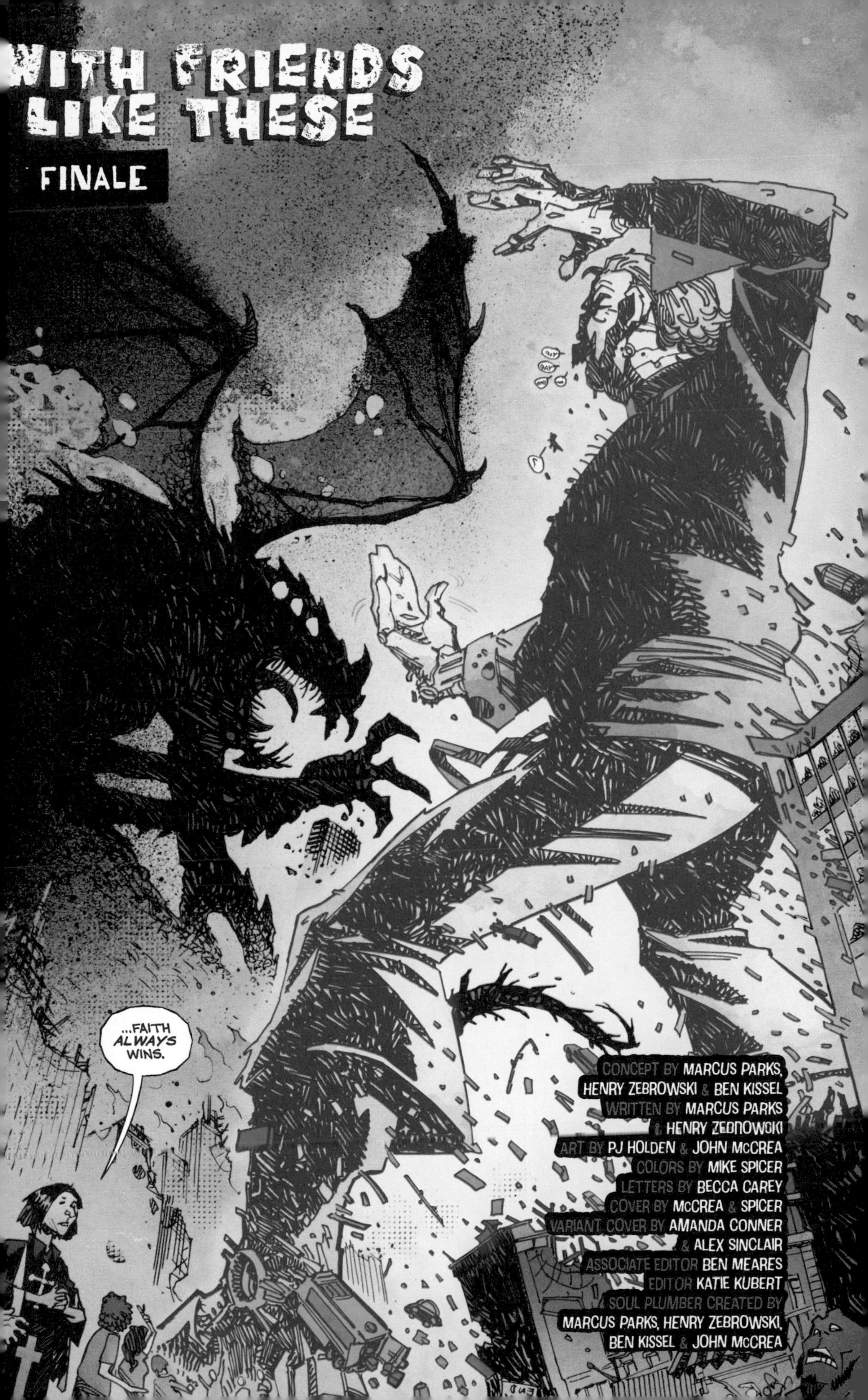

WITH FRIENDS LIKE THESE
FINALE
...FAITH ALWAYS WINS.
CONCEPT BY MARCUS PARKS, HENRY ZEBROWSKI & BEN KISSEL
WRITTEN BY MARCUS PARKS & HENRY ZEBROWSKI
ART BY PJ HOLDEN & JOHN McCREA
COLORS BY MIKE SPICER
LETTERS BY BECCA CAREY
COVER BY McCREA & SPICER
VARIANT COVER BY AMANDA CONNER & ALEX SINCLAIR
ASSOCIATE EDITOR BEN MEARES
EDITOR KATIE KUBERT
SOUL PLUMBER CREATED BY MARCUS PARKS, HENRY ZEBROWSKI, BEN KISSEL & JOHN McCREA

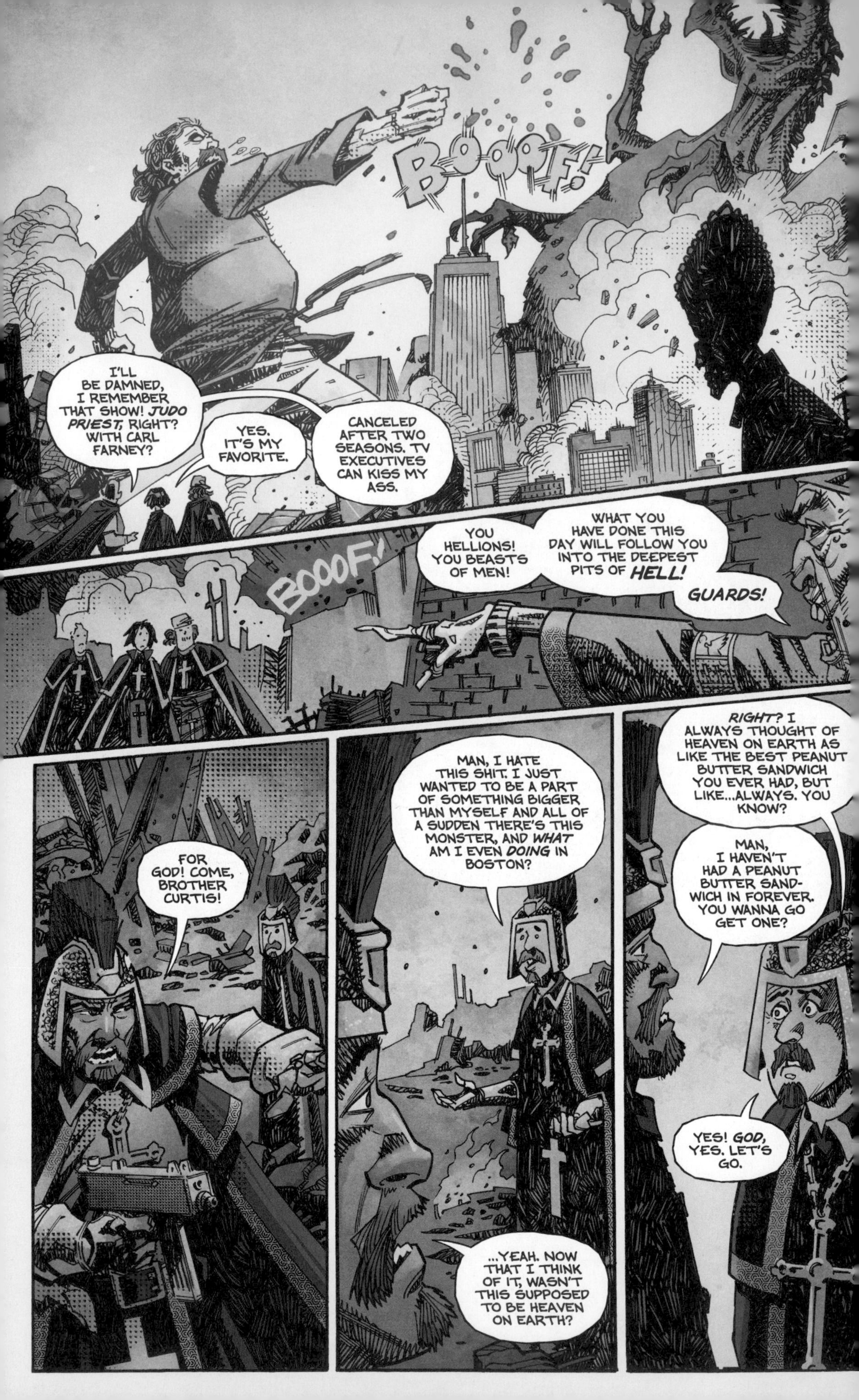
BOOOF!
I'LL BE DAMNED, I REMEMBER THAT SHOW! JUDO PRIEST, RIGHT? WITH CARL FARNEY?
YES. IT'S MY FAVORITE.
CANCELED AFTER TWO SEASONS. TV EXECUTIVES CAN KISS MY ASS.
BOOOF!
YOU HELLIONS! YOU BEASTS OF MEN!
WHAT YOU HAVE DONE THIS DAY WILL FOLLOW YOU INTO THE DEEPEST PITS OF HELL!
GUARDS!
FOR GOD! COME, BROTHER CURTIS!
MAN, I HATE THIS SHIT. I JUST WANTED TO BE A PART OF SOMETHING BIGGER THAN MYSELF AND ALL OF A SUDDEN THERE'S THIS MONSTER, AND WHAT AM I EVEN DOING IN BOSTON?
...YEAH. NOW THAT I THINK OF IT, WASN'T THIS SUPPOSED TO BE HEAVEN ON EARTH?
RIGHT? I ALWAYS THOUGHT OF HEAVEN ON EARTH AS LIKE THE BEST PEANUT BUTTER SANDWICH YOU EVER HAD, BUT LIKE...ALWAYS. YOU KNOW?
MAN, I HAVEN'T HAD A PEANUT BUTTER SANDWICH IN FOREVER. YOU WANNA GO GET ONE?
YES! GOD, YES. LET'S GO.

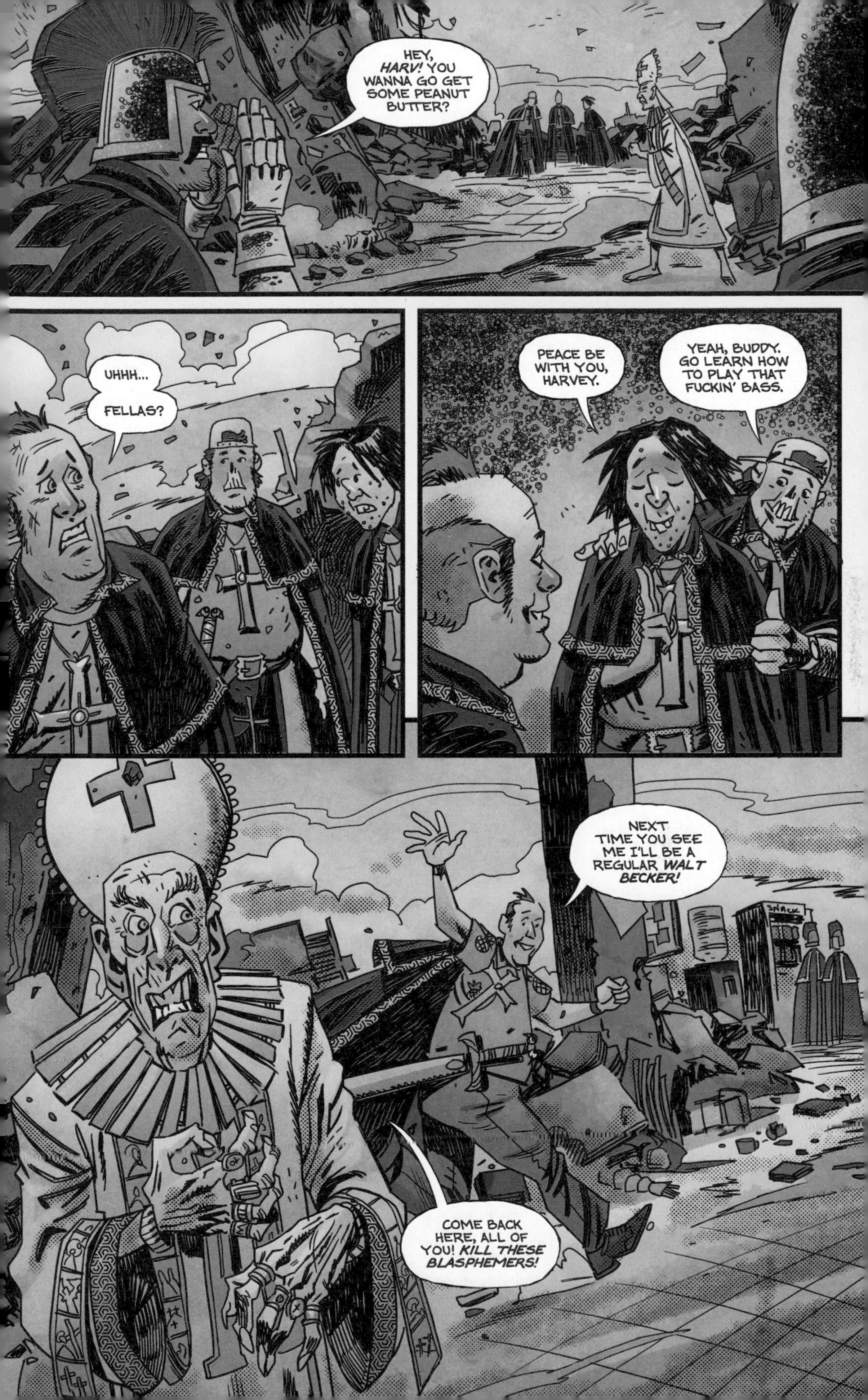
HEY, HARV! YOU WANNA GO GET SOME PEANUT BUTTER?
UHHH...
FELLAS?
PEACE BE WITH YOU, HARVEY.
YEAH, BUDDY. GO LEARN HOW TO PLAY THAT FUCKIN' BASS.
NEXT TIME YOU SEE ME I'LL BE A REGULAR WALT BECKER!
SNACK
COME BACK HERE, ALL OF YOU! KILL THESE BLASPHEMERS!

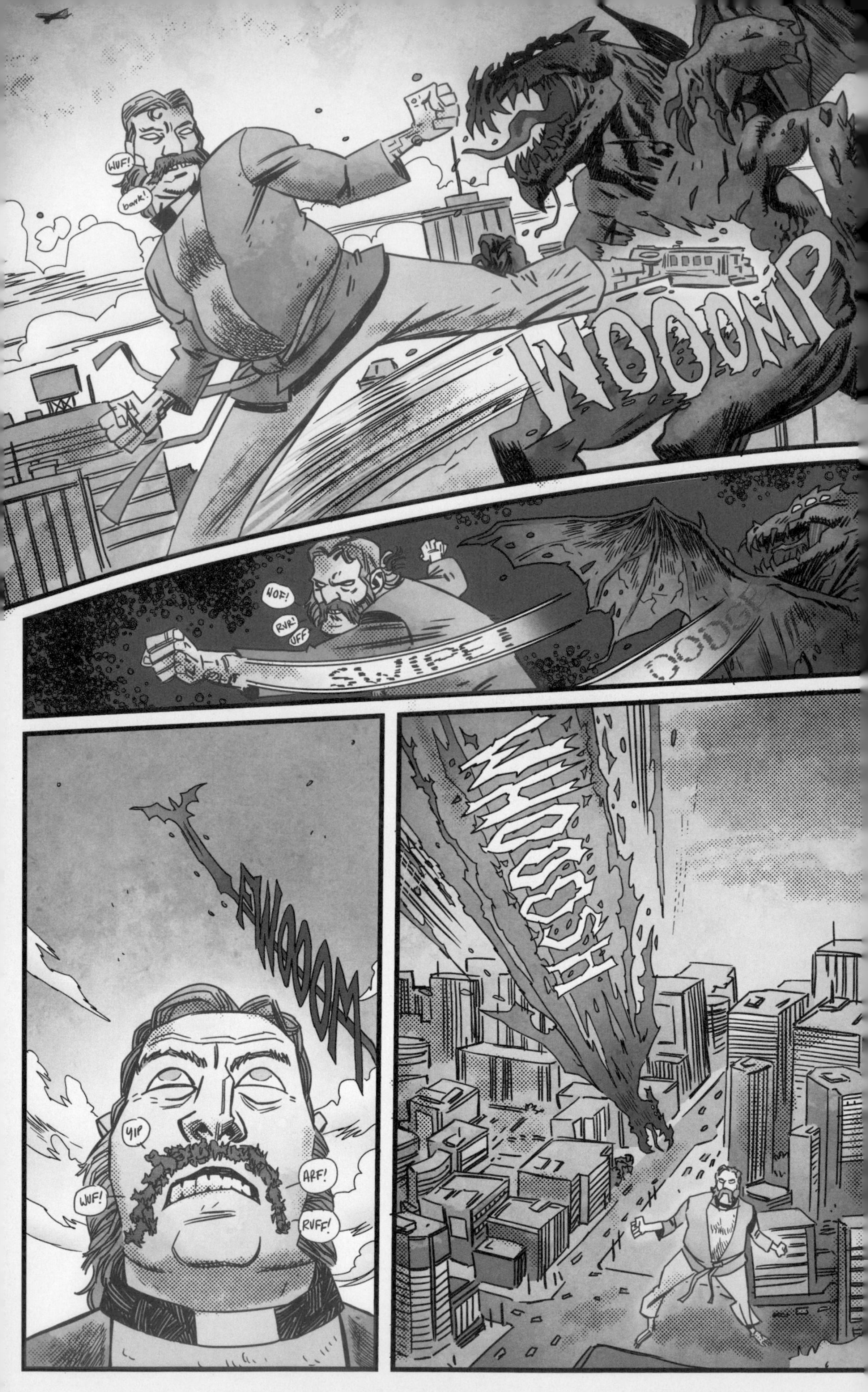
WUF!
bark!
WOOOMP
WOF!
RVR!
UFF
SWIPE
FWOOOM
YIP
WUF!
ARF!
RUFF!
WHOOOSH

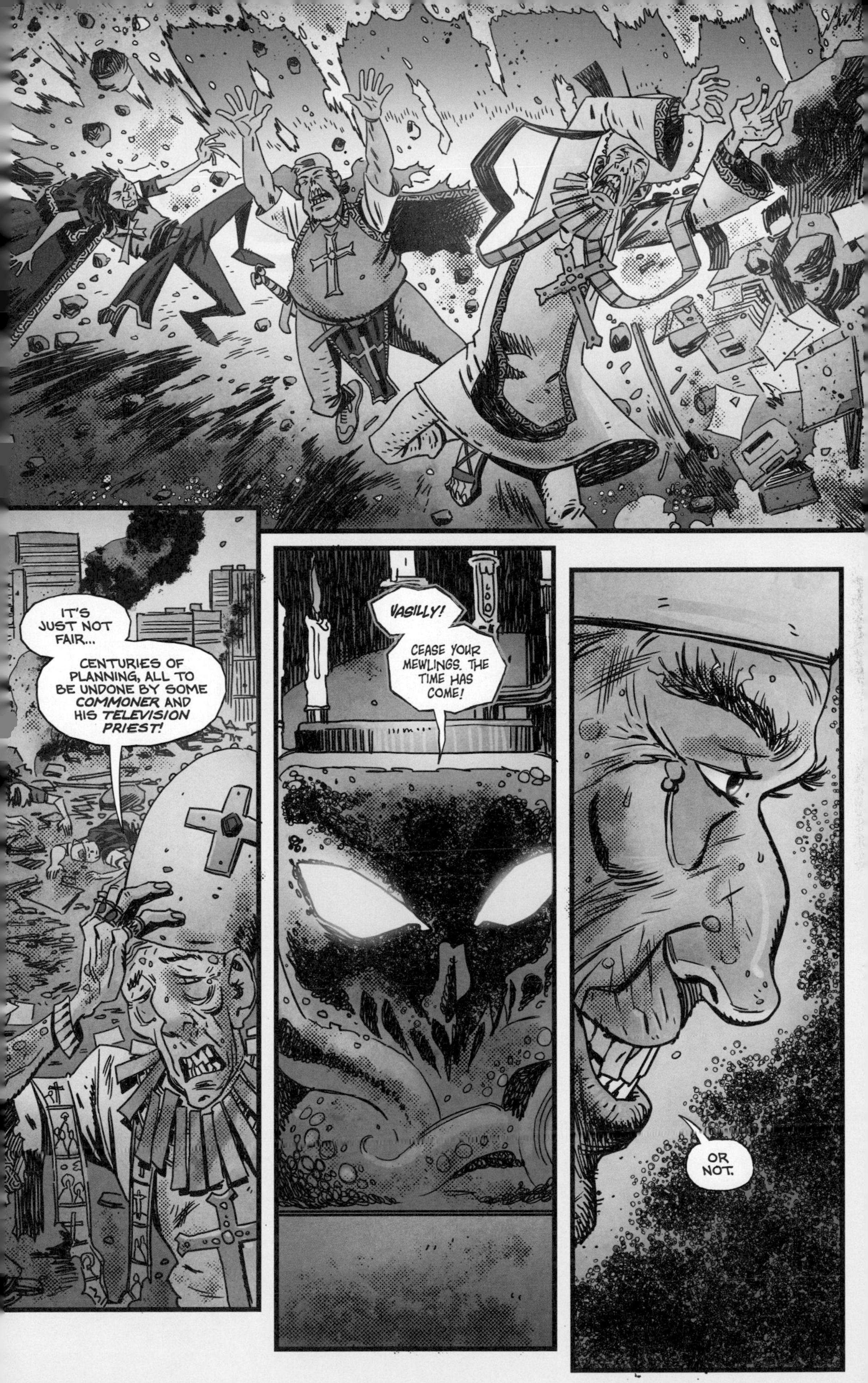
IT'S JUST NOT FAIR...
CENTURIES OF PLANNING, ALL TO BE UNDONE BY SOME *COMMONER* AND HIS *TELEVISION PRIEST!*
VASILLY!
CEASE YOUR MEWLINGS. THE TIME HAS COME!
OR NOT.

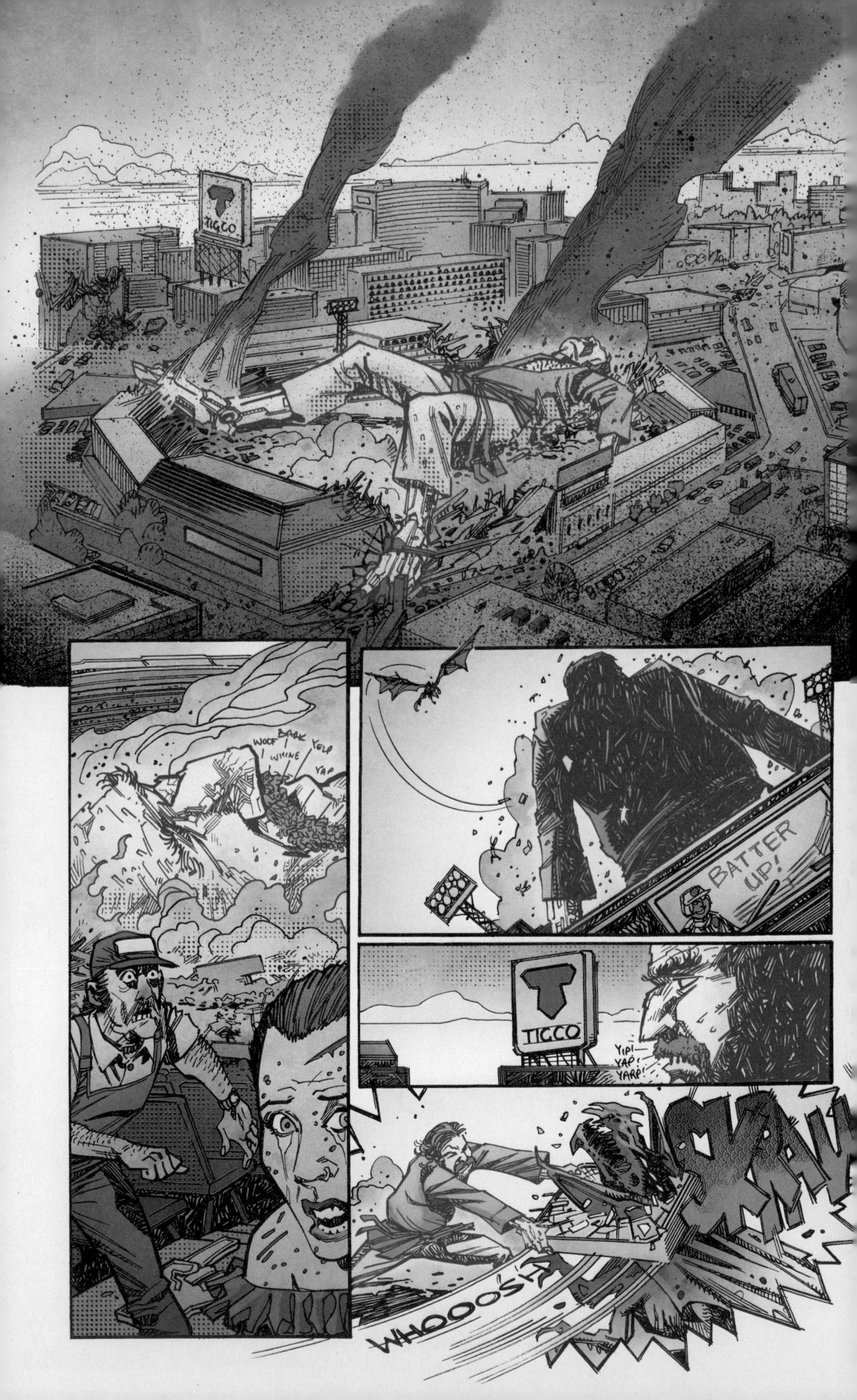
TIGCO
WOOF
BARK
YELA
WHINE
YAP
BATTER UP!
TIGCO
YIP!
YAP!
YARP!
WHOOOSH

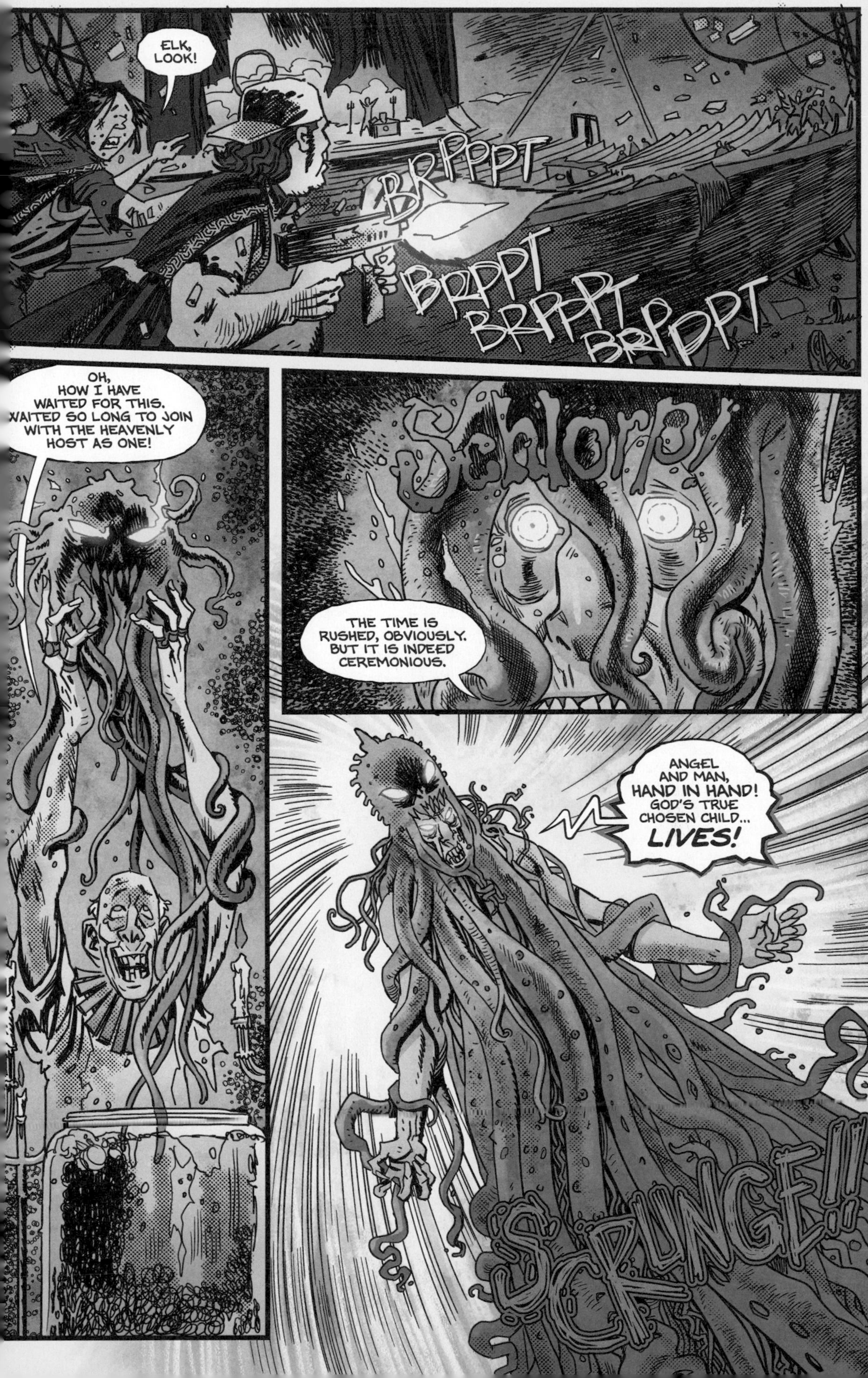
ELK, LOOK!
BRPPPPT
BRPPPT
BRPPPT
BRPPPT
BRPPPT
OH, HOW I HAVE WAITED FOR THIS. WAITED SO LONG TO JOIN WITH THE HEAVENLY HOST AS ONE!
SCHLORP!
THE TIME IS RUSHED, OBVIOUSLY. BUT IT IS INDEED CEREMONIOUS.
ANGEL AND MAN, HAND IN HAND! GOD'S TRUE CHOSEN CHILD... LIVES!
SCRUNGE!!

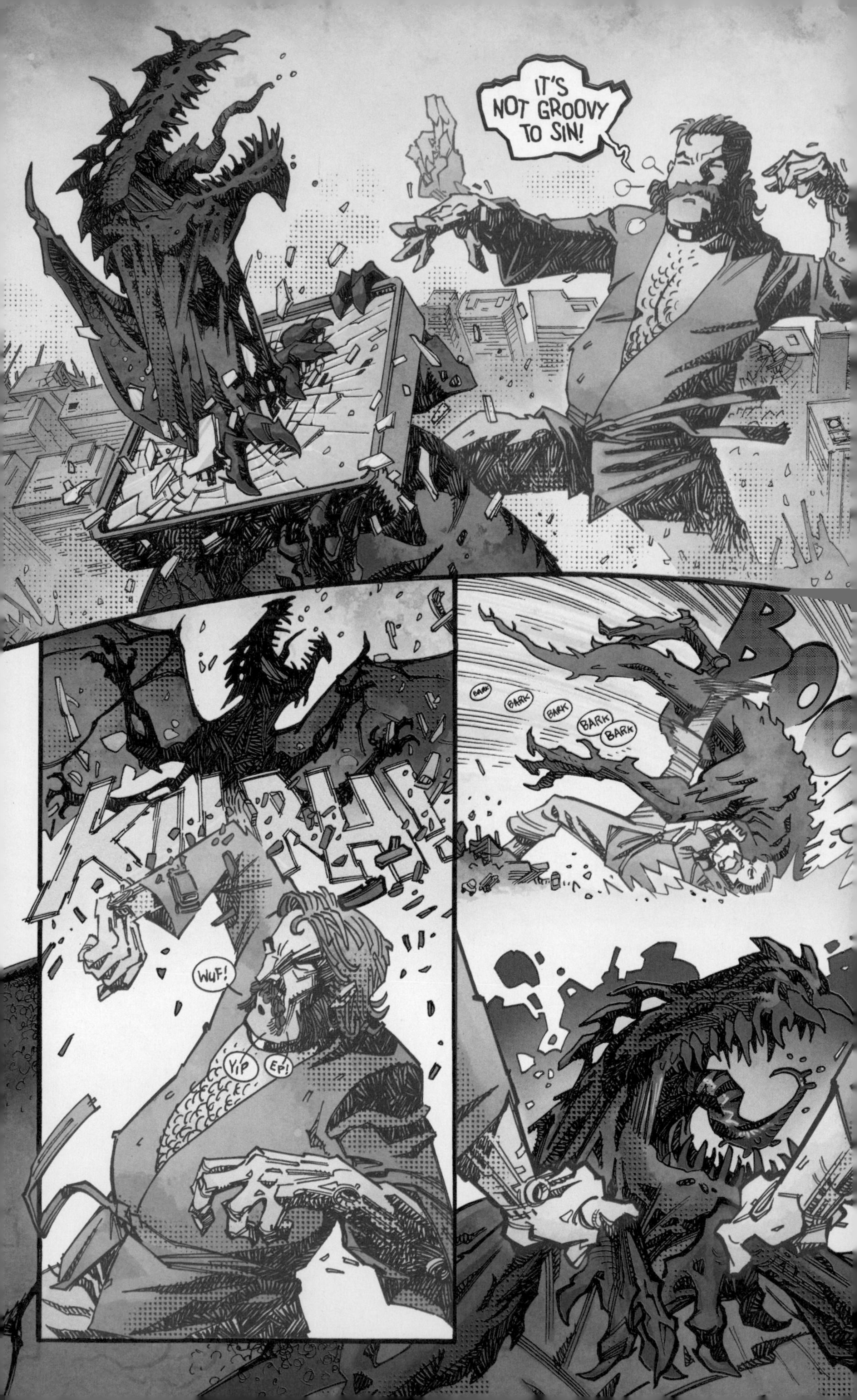
IT'S NOT GROOVY TO SIN!
WUF!
YIP
EP!
BARK
BARK
BARK
BARK
BARK

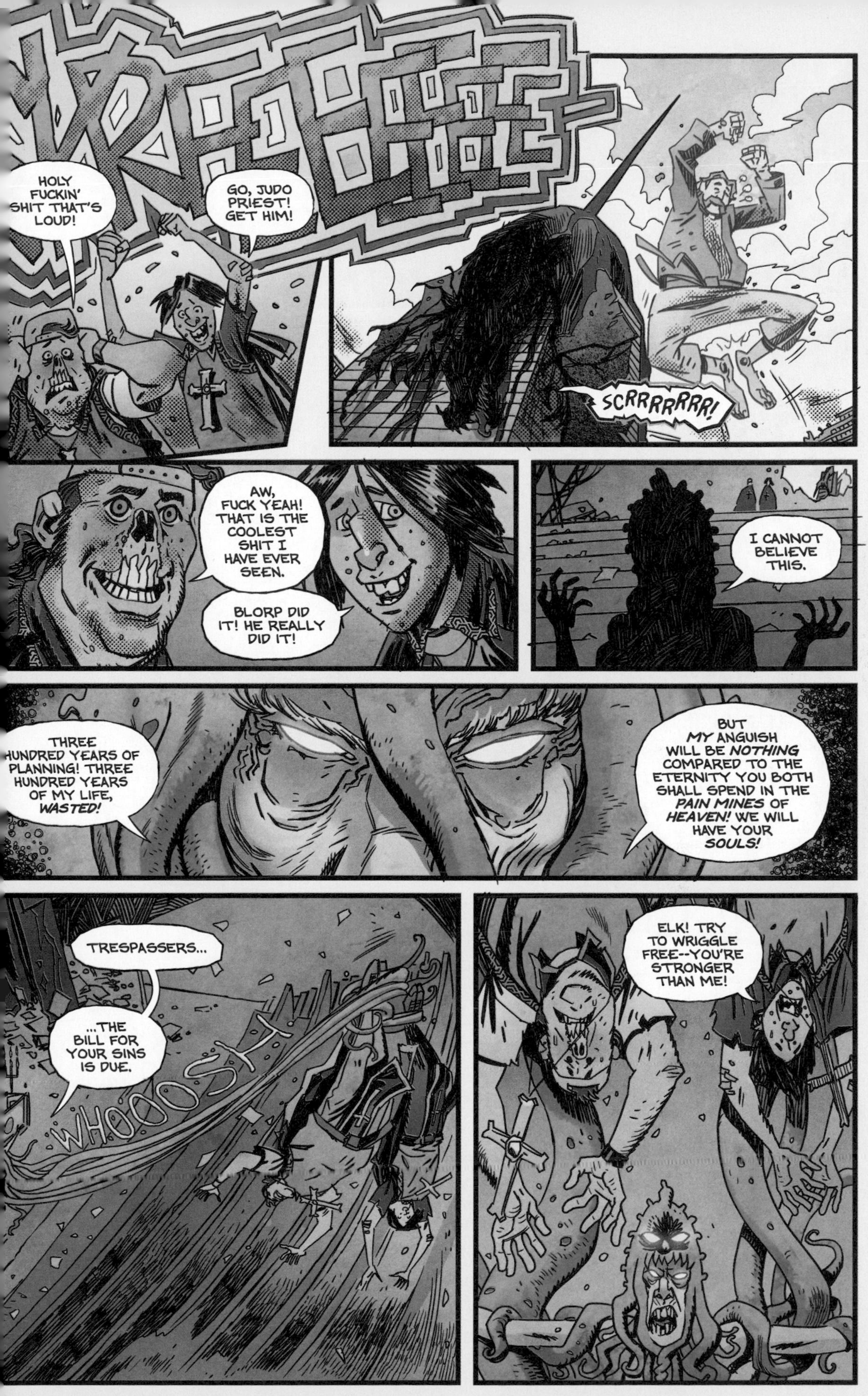
KROOOOOOOOOOOO
HOLY FUCKIN' SHIT THAT'S LOUD!
GO, JUDO PRIEST! GET HIM!
SCRRRRRRR!
AW, FUCK YEAH! THAT IS THE COOLEST SHIT I HAVE EVER SEEN.
BLORP DID IT! HE REALLY DID IT!
I CANNOT BELIEVE THIS.
THREE HUNDRED YEARS OF PLANNING! THREE HUNDRED YEARS OF MY LIFE, WASTED!
BUT MY ANGUISH WILL BE NOTHING COMPARED TO THE ETERNITY YOU BOTH SHALL SPEND IN THE PAIN MINES OF HEAVEN! WE WILL HAVE YOUR SOULS!
TRESPASSERS...
...THE BILL FOR YOUR SINS IS DUE.
WHOOOOSH
ELK! TRY TO WRIGGLE FREE--YOU'RE STRONGER THAN ME!

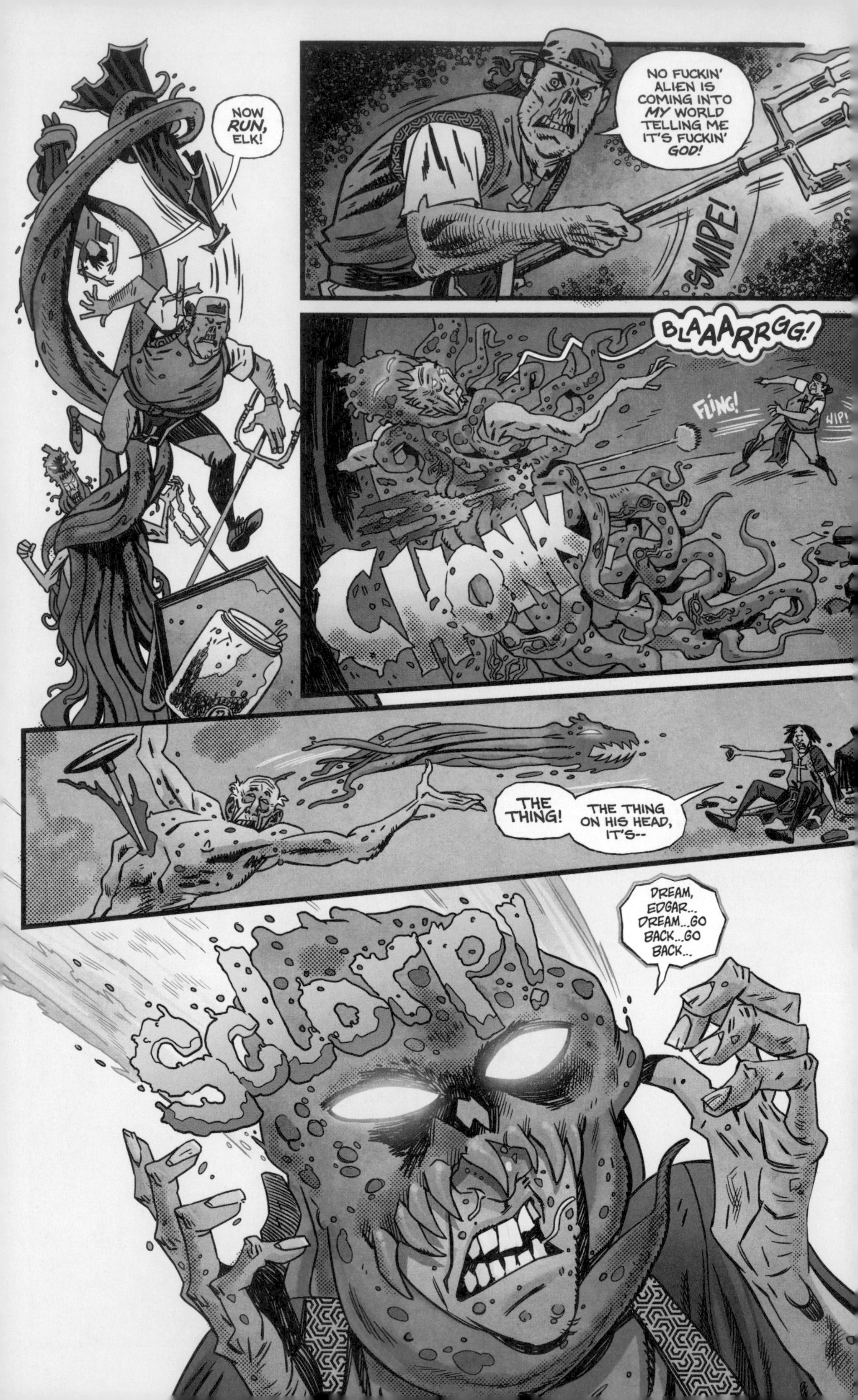
NOW RUN, ELK!
NO FUCKIN' ALIEN IS COMING INTO MY WORLD TELLING ME IT'S FUCKIN' GOD!
SWIPE!
BLAAARRGG!
FLING!
WIP!
CHOMK
THE THING!
THE THING ON HIS HEAD, IT'S--
DREAM, EDGAR... DREAM...GO BACK...GO BACK...
SCLORP!

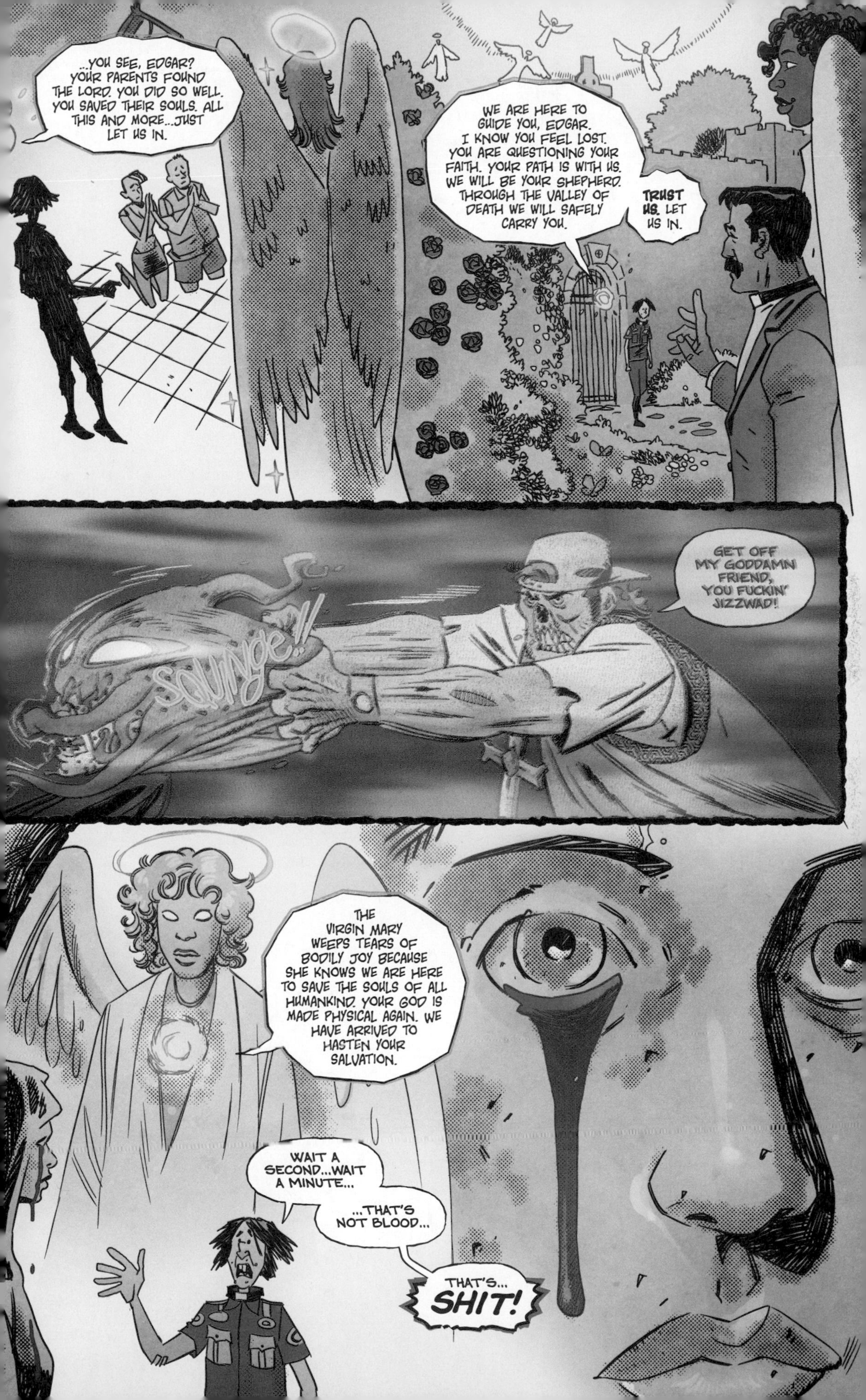
...YOU SEE, EDGAR? YOUR PARENTS FOUND THE LORD. YOU DID SO WELL. YOU SAVED THEIR SOULS. ALL THIS AND MORE...JUST LET US IN.
WE ARE HERE TO GUIDE YOU, EDGAR. I KNOW YOU FEEL LOST. YOU ARE QUESTIONING YOUR FAITH. YOUR PATH IS WITH US. WE WILL BE YOUR SHEPHERD. THROUGH THE VALLEY OF DEATH WE WILL SAFELY CARRY YOU.
TRUST US. LET US IN.
GET OFF MY GODDAMN FRIEND, YOU FUCKIN' JIZZWAD!
SQUNGE!!
THE VIRGIN MARY WEEPS TEARS OF BODILY JOY BECAUSE SHE KNOWS WE ARE HERE TO SAVE THE SOULS OF ALL HUMANKIND. YOUR GOD IS MADE PHYSICAL AGAIN. WE HAVE ARRIVED TO HASTEN YOUR SALVATION.
WAIT A SECOND...WAIT A MINUTE...
...THAT'S NOT BLOOD...
THAT'S... SHIT!

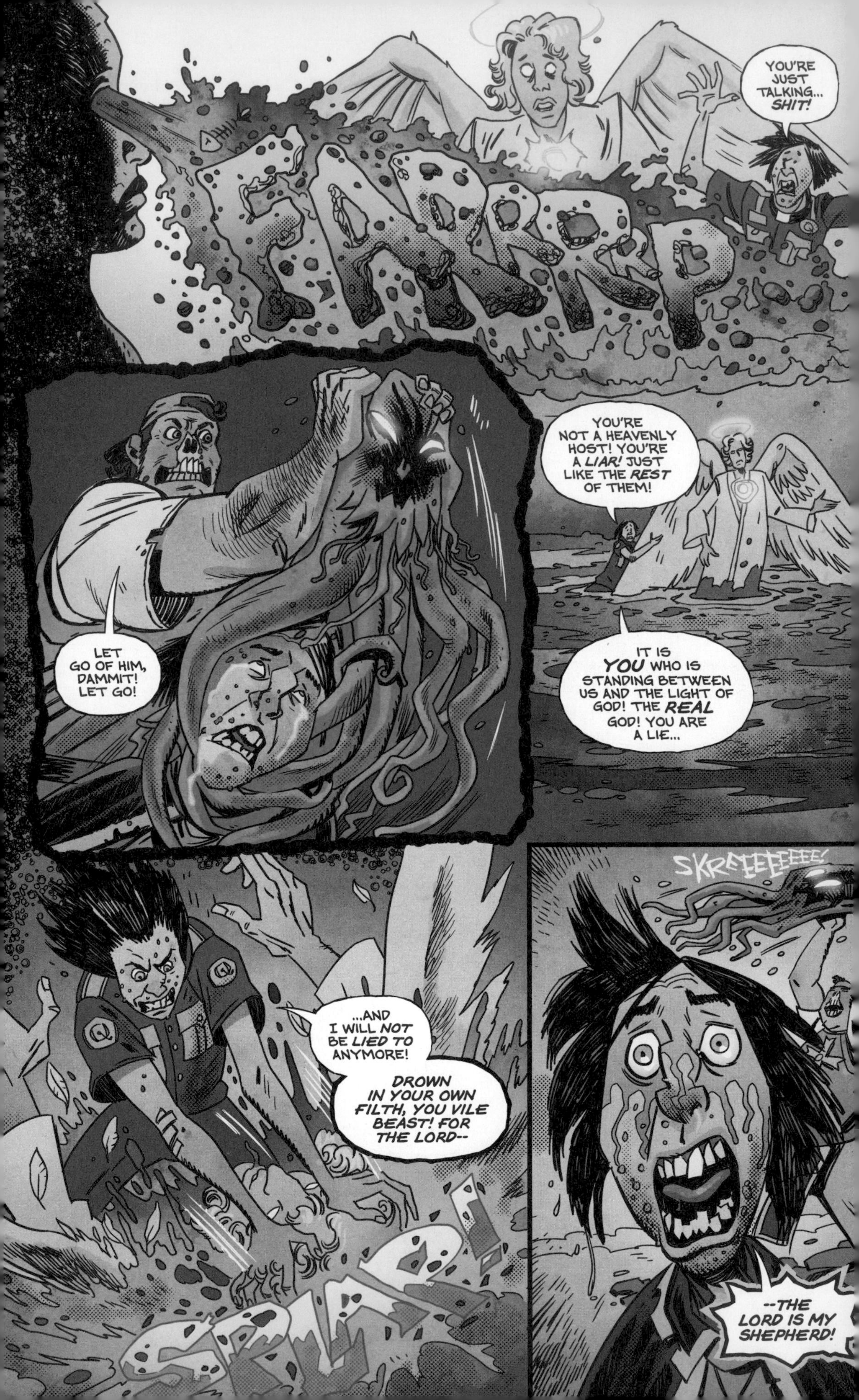

YOU'RE JUST TALKING... SHIT!
LET GO OF HIM, DAMMIT! LET GO!
YOU'RE NOT A HEAVENLY HOST! YOU'RE A LIAR! JUST LIKE THE REST OF THEM!
IT IS YOU WHO IS STANDING BETWEEN US AND THE LIGHT OF GOD! THE REAL GOD! YOU ARE A LIE...
...AND I WILL NOT BE LIED TO ANYMORE!
DROWN IN YOUR OWN FILTH, YOU VILE BEAST! FOR THE LORD--
--THE LORD IS MY SHEPHERD!

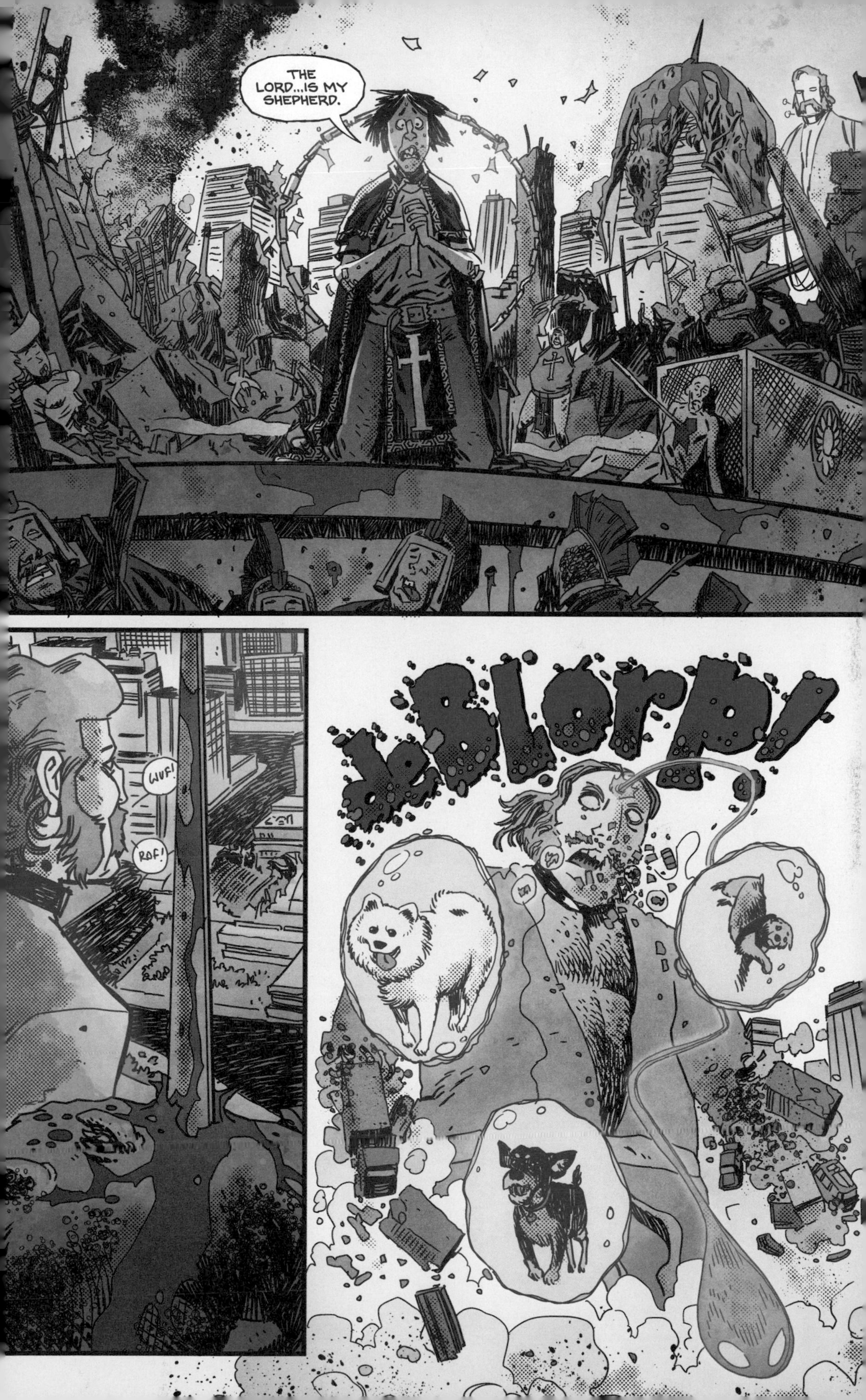
THE LORD...IS MY SHEPHERD.
WUF!
ROF!
BLORP!

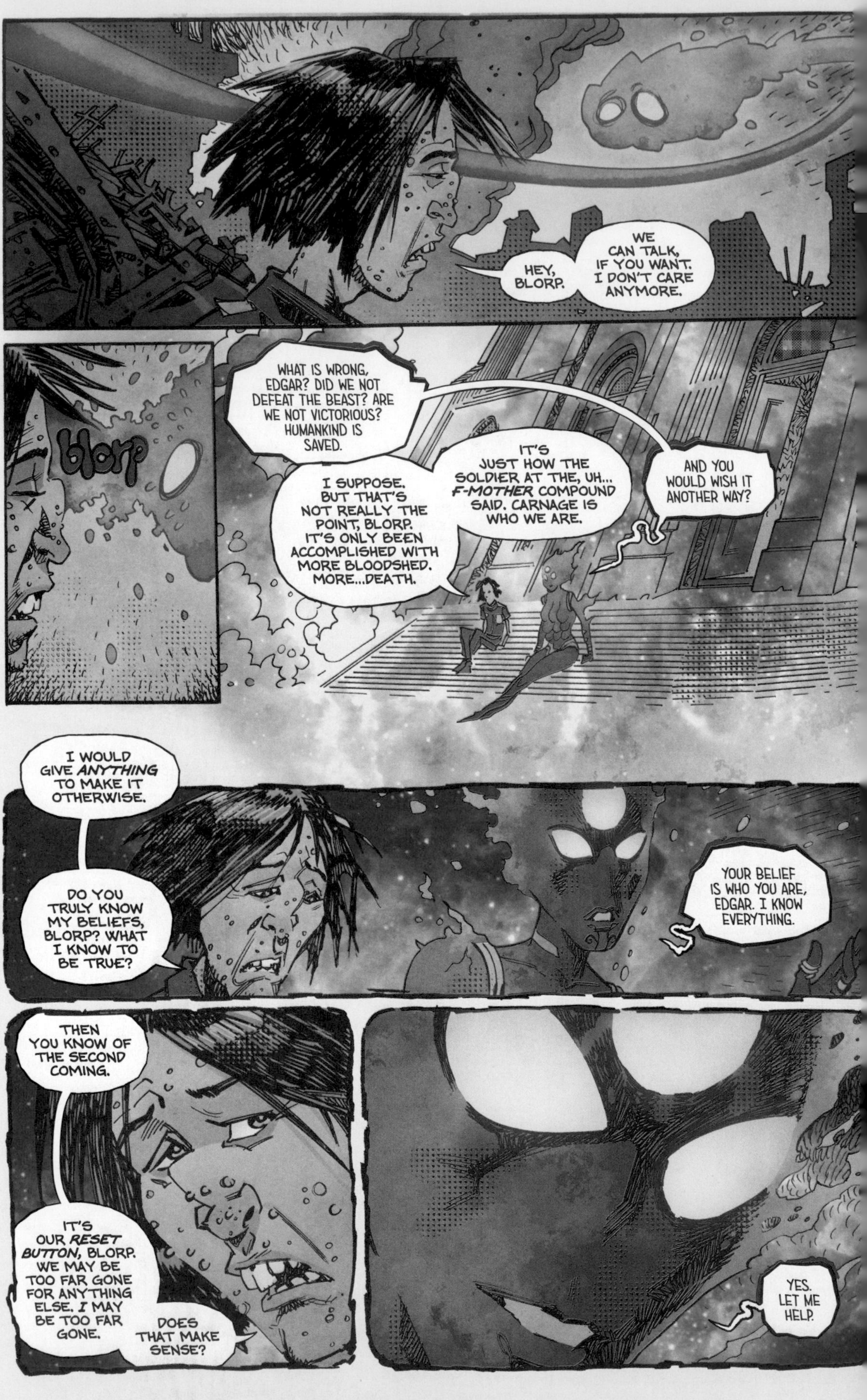

HEY, BLORP.
WE CAN TALK, IF YOU WANT. I DON'T CARE ANYMORE.
blorp
WHAT IS WRONG, EDGAR? DID WE NOT DEFEAT THE BEAST? ARE WE NOT VICTORIOUS? HUMANKIND IS SAVED.
I SUPPOSE. BUT THAT'S NOT REALLY THE POINT, BLORP. IT'S ONLY BEEN ACCOMPLISHED WITH MORE BLOODSHED. MORE...DEATH.
AND YOU WOULD WISH IT ANOTHER WAY?
IT'S JUST HOW THE SOLDIER AT THE, UH... *F-MOTHER* COMPOUND SAID. CARNAGE IS WHO WE ARE.
I WOULD GIVE *ANYTHING* TO MAKE IT OTHERWISE.
DO YOU TRULY KNOW MY BELIEFS, BLORP? WHAT I KNOW TO BE TRUE?
YOUR BELIEF IS WHO YOU ARE, EDGAR. I KNOW EVERYTHING.
THEN YOU KNOW OF THE SECOND COMING.
IT'S OUR *RESET BUTTON,* BLORP. WE MAY BE TOO FAR GONE FOR ANYTHING ELSE. *I* MAY BE TOO FAR GONE.
DOES THAT MAKE SENSE?
YES. LET ME HELP.

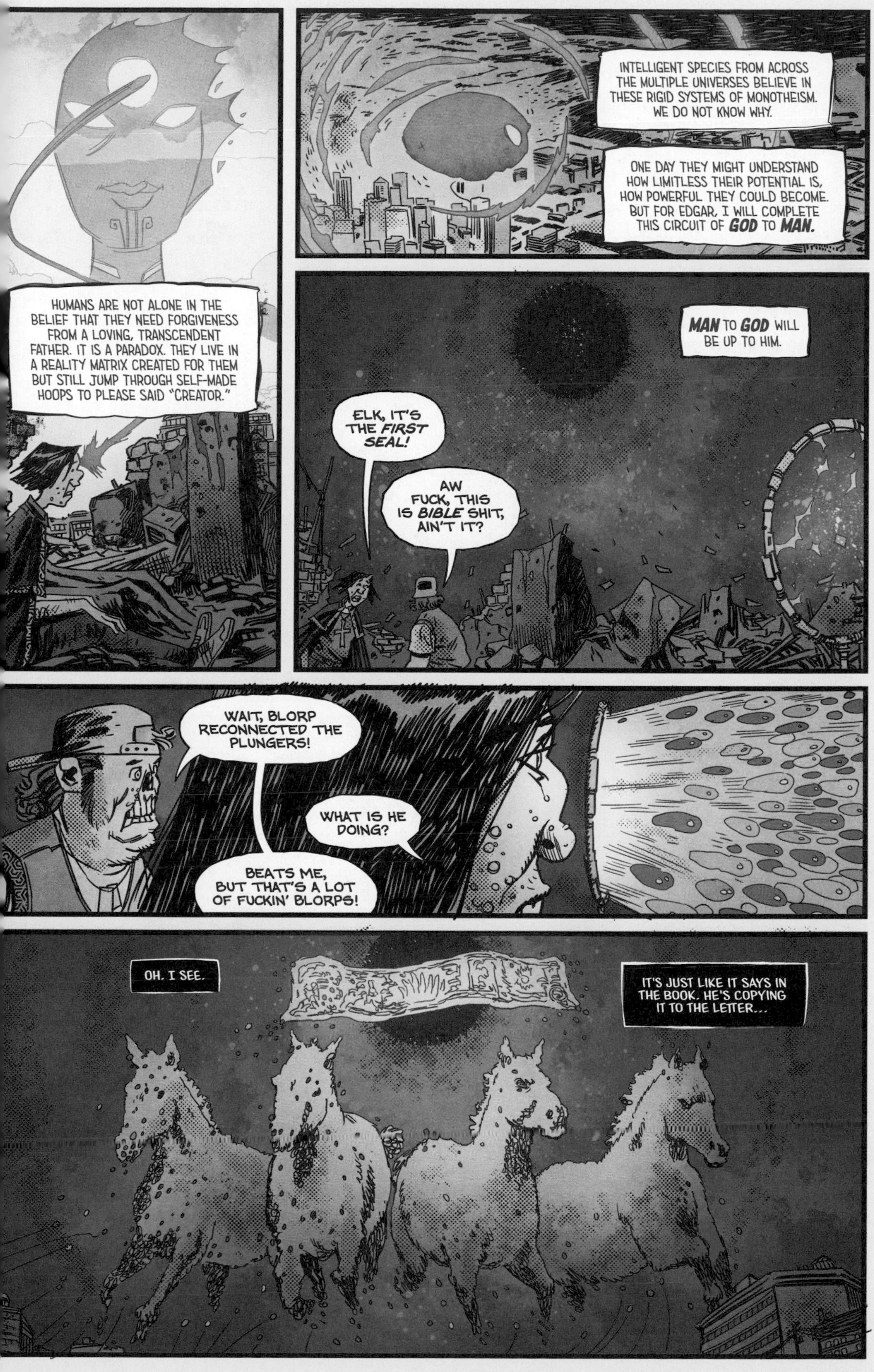
INTELLIGENT SPECIES FROM ACROSS THE MULTIPLE UNIVERSES BELIEVE IN THESE RIGID SYSTEMS OF MONOTHEISM. WE DO NOT KNOW WHY.
ONE DAY THEY MIGHT UNDERSTAND HOW LIMITLESS THEIR POTENTIAL IS, HOW POWERFUL THEY COULD BECOME. BUT FOR EDGAR, I WILL COMPLETE THIS CIRCUIT OF GOD TO MAN.
HUMANS ARE NOT ALONE IN THE BELIEF THAT THEY NEED FORGIVENESS FROM A LOVING, TRANSCENDENT FATHER. IT IS A PARADOX. THEY LIVE IN A REALITY MATRIX CREATED FOR THEM BUT STILL JUMP THROUGH SELF-MADE HOOPS TO PLEASE SAID "CREATOR."
MAN TO GOD WILL BE UP TO HIM.
ELK, IT'S THE FIRST SEAL!
AW FUCK, THIS IS BIBLE SHIT, AIN'T IT?
WAIT, BLORP RECONNECTED THE PLUNGERS!
WHAT IS HE DOING?
BEATS ME, BUT THAT'S A LOT OF FUCKIN' BLORPS!
OH. I SEE.
IT'S JUST LIKE IT SAYS IN THE BOOK. HE'S COPYING IT TO THE LETTER...

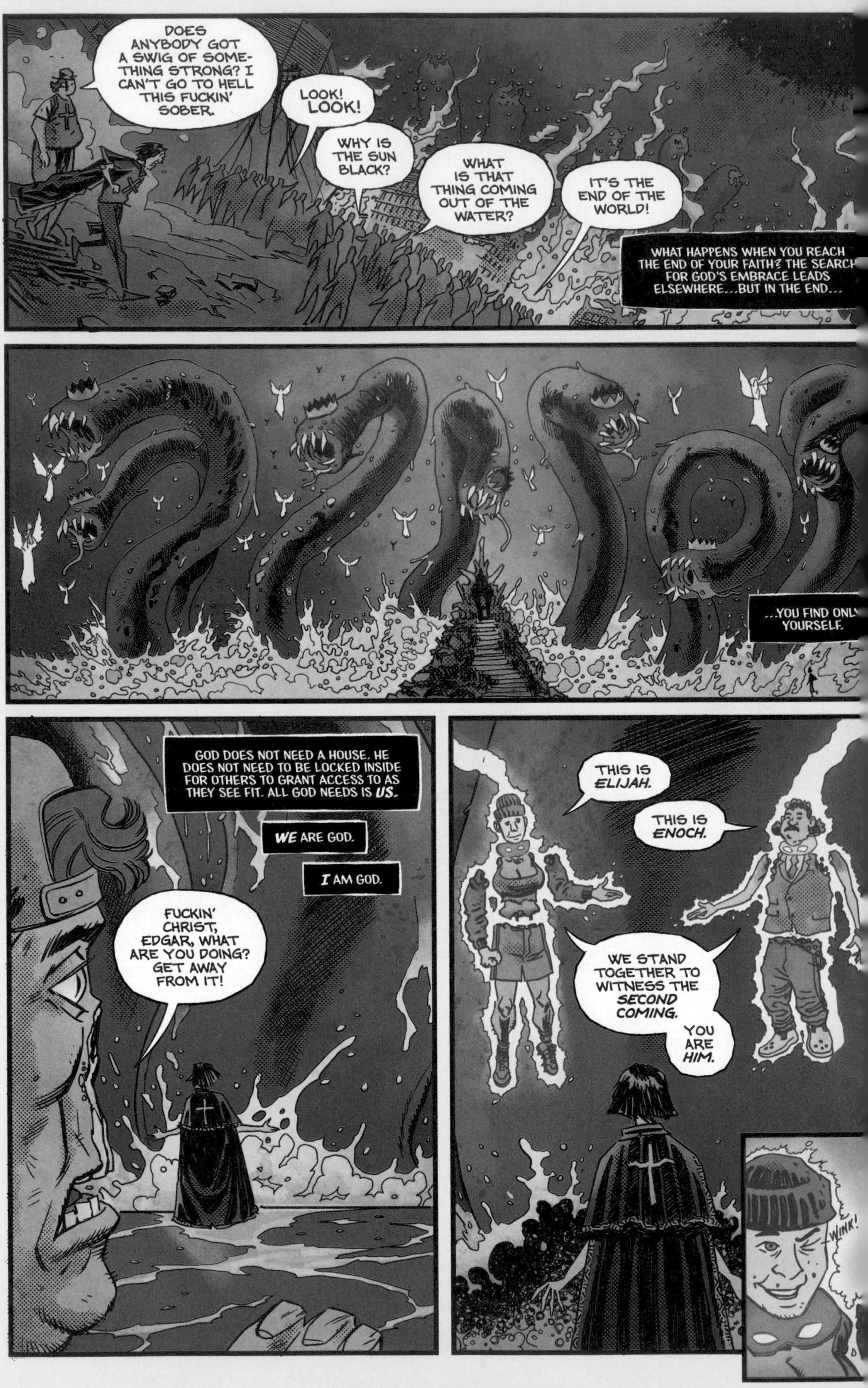
DOES ANYBODY GOT A SWIG OF SOMETHING STRONG? I CAN'T GO TO HELL THIS FUCKIN' SOBER.
LOOK! LOOK!
WHY IS THE SUN BLACK?
WHAT IS THAT THING COMING OUT OF THE WATER?
IT'S THE END OF THE WORLD!
WHAT HAPPENS WHEN YOU REACH THE END OF YOUR FAITH? THE SEARCH FOR GOD'S EMBRACE LEADS ELSEWHERE...BUT IN THE END...
...YOU FIND ONLY YOURSELF.
GOD DOES NOT NEED A HOUSE. HE DOES NOT NEED TO BE LOCKED INSIDE FOR OTHERS TO GRANT ACCESS TO AS THEY SEE FIT. ALL GOD NEEDS IS US.
WE ARE GOD.
I AM GOD.
FUCKIN' CHRIST, EDGAR, WHAT ARE YOU DOING? GET AWAY FROM IT!
THIS IS ELIJAH.
THIS IS ENOCH.
WE STAND TOGETHER TO WITNESS THE SECOND COMING.
YOU ARE HIM.
WINK!

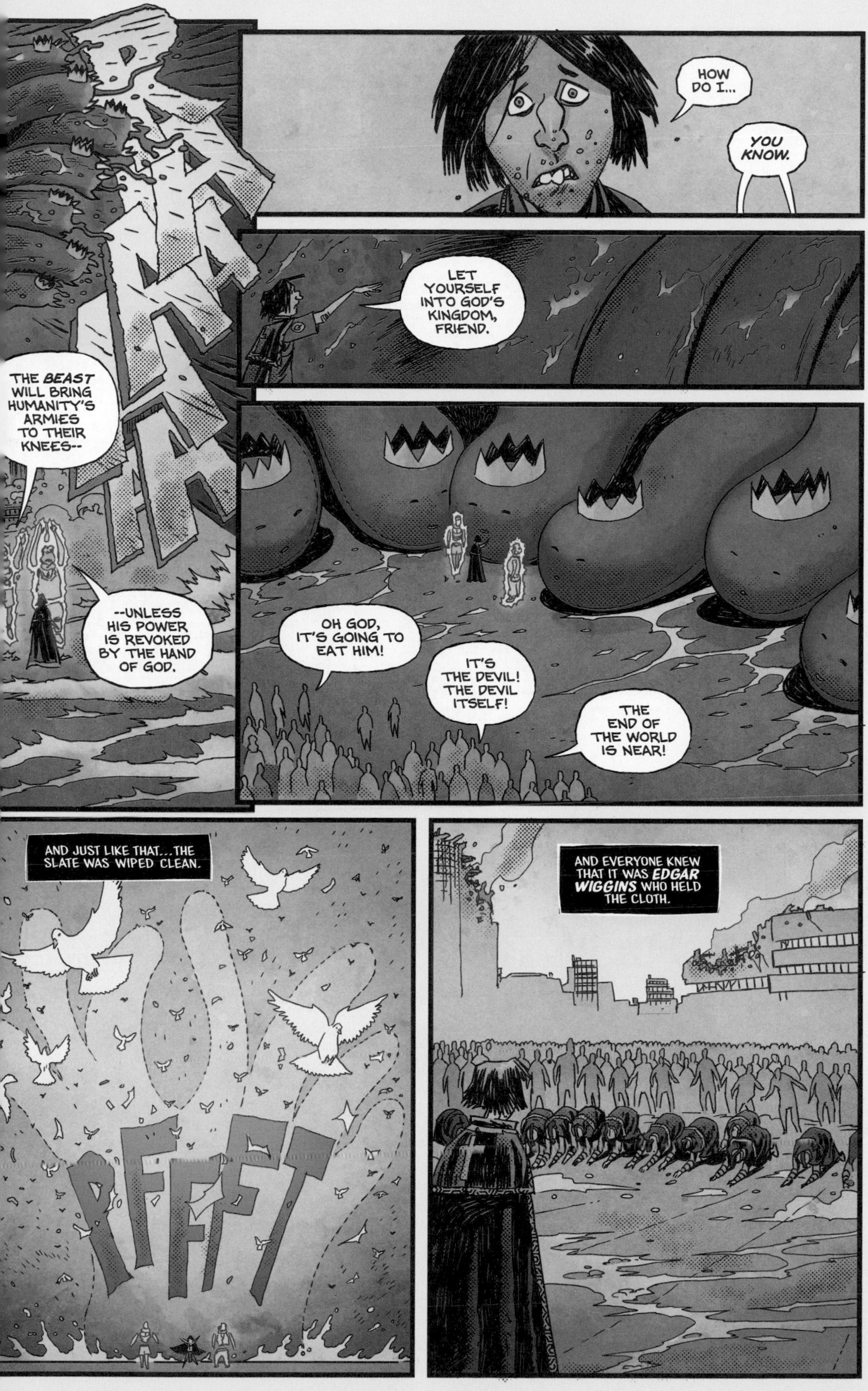
HOW DO I...
YOU KNOW.
LET YOURSELF INTO GOD'S KINGDOM, FRIEND.
THE BEAST WILL BRING HUMANITY'S ARMIES TO THEIR KNEES--
--UNLESS HIS POWER IS REVOKED BY THE HAND OF GOD.
OH GOD, IT'S GOING TO EAT HIM!
IT'S THE DEVIL! THE DEVIL ITSELF!
THE END OF THE WORLD IS NEAR!
AND JUST LIKE THAT... THE SLATE WAS WIPED CLEAN.
PFFFT
AND EVERYONE KNEW THAT IT WAS EDGAR WIGGINS WHO HELD THE CLOTH.

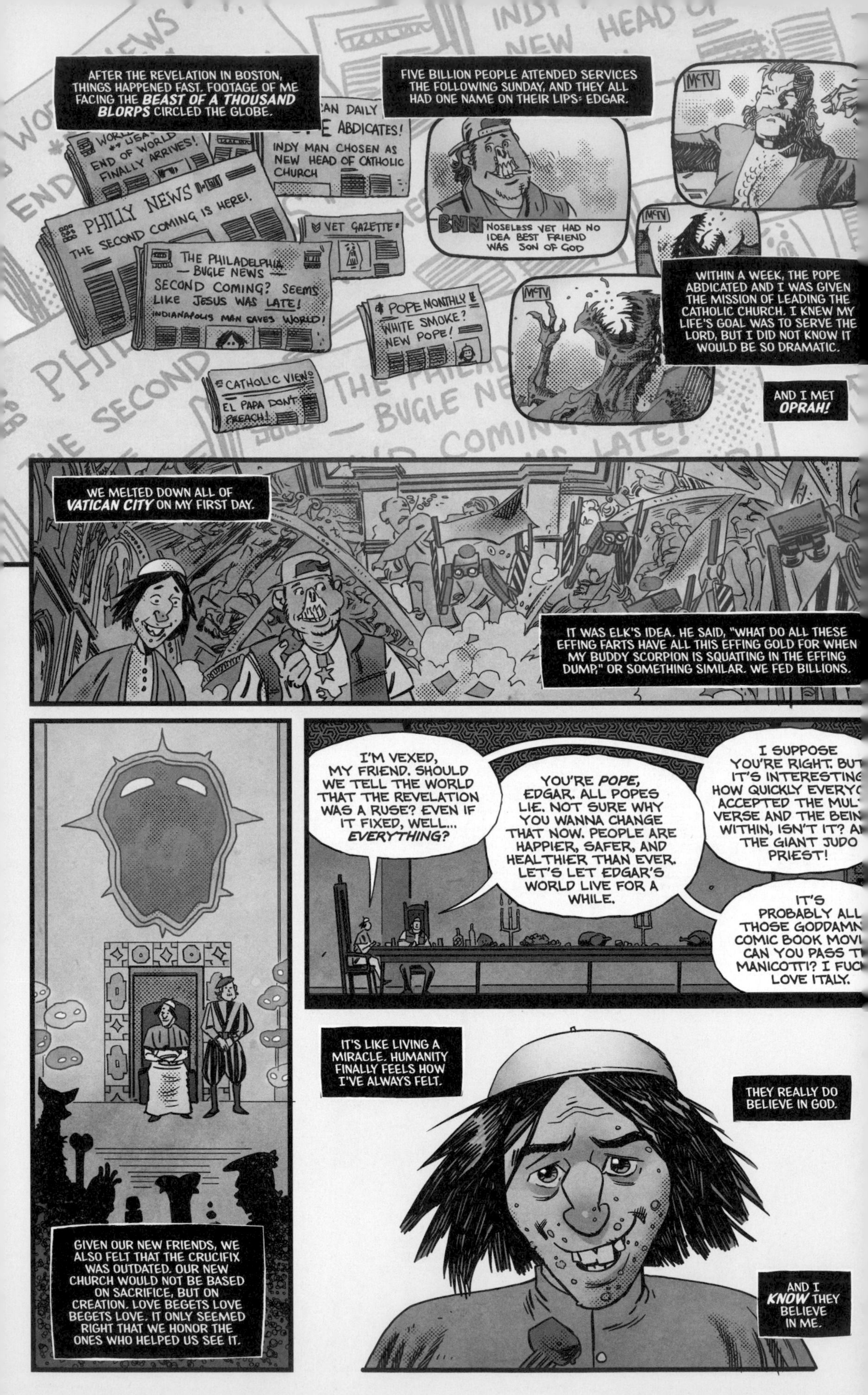

AFTER THE REVELATION IN BOSTON, THINGS HAPPENED FAST. FOOTAGE OF ME FACING THE ***BEAST OF A THOUSAND BLORPS*** CIRCLED THE GLOBE.
END OF WORLD FINALLY ARRIVES!
ABDICATES!
INDY MAN CHOSEN AS NEW HEAD OF CATHOLIC CHURCH
PHILLY NEWS
THE SECOND COMING IS HERE!
VET GAZETTE
THE PHILADELPHIA BUGLE NEWS
SECOND COMING? SEEMS LIKE JESUS WAS LATE!
INDIANAPOLIS MAN SAVES WORLD!
POPE MONTHLY
WHITE SMOKE? NEW POPE!
CATHOLIC VIEW
EL PAPA DON'T PREACH!
FIVE BILLION PEOPLE ATTENDED SERVICES THE FOLLOWING SUNDAY, AND THEY ALL HAD ONE NAME ON THEIR LIPS: EDGAR.
BNN
NOSELESS VET HAD NO IDEA BEST FRIEND WAS SON OF GOD
McTV
McTV
McTV
WITHIN A WEEK, THE POPE ABDICATED AND I WAS GIVEN THE MISSION OF LEADING THE CATHOLIC CHURCH. I KNEW MY LIFE'S GOAL WAS TO SERVE THE LORD, BUT I DID NOT KNOW IT WOULD BE SO DRAMATIC.
AND I MET ***OPRAH!***
WE MELTED DOWN ALL OF ***VATICAN CITY*** ON MY FIRST DAY.
IT WAS ELK'S IDEA. HE SAID, "WHAT DO ALL THESE EFFING FARTS HAVE ALL THIS EFFING GOLD FOR WHEN MY BUDDY SCORPION IS SQUATTING IN THE EFFING DUMP," OR SOMETHING SIMILAR. WE FED BILLIONS.
GIVEN OUR NEW FRIENDS, WE ALSO FELT THAT THE CRUCIFIX WAS OUTDATED. OUR NEW CHURCH WOULD NOT BE BASED ON SACRIFICE, BUT ON CREATION. LOVE BEGETS LOVE BEGETS LOVE. IT ONLY SEEMED RIGHT THAT WE HONOR THE ONES WHO HELPED US SEE IT.
I'M VEXED, MY FRIEND. SHOULD WE TELL THE WORLD THAT THE REVELATION WAS A RUSE? EVEN IF IT FIXED, WELL... *EVERYTHING*?
YOU'RE *POPE*, EDGAR. ALL POPES LIE. NOT SURE WHY YOU WANNA CHANGE THAT NOW. PEOPLE ARE HAPPIER, SAFER, AND HEALTHIER THAN EVER. LET'S LET EDGAR'S WORLD LIVE FOR A WHILE.
I SUPPOSE YOU'RE RIGHT. BUT IT'S INTERESTING HOW QUICKLY EVERYO ACCEPTED THE MUL VERSE AND THE BEIN WITHIN, ISN'T IT? A THE GIANT JUDO PRIEST!
IT'S PROBABLY ALL THOSE GODDAMN COMIC BOOK MOVI CAN YOU PASS T MANICOTTI? I FUC LOVE ITALY.
IT'S LIKE LIVING A MIRACLE. HUMANITY FINALLY FEELS HOW I'VE ALWAYS FELT.
THEY REALLY DO BELIEVE IN GOD.
AND I ***KNOW*** THEY BELIEVE IN ME.

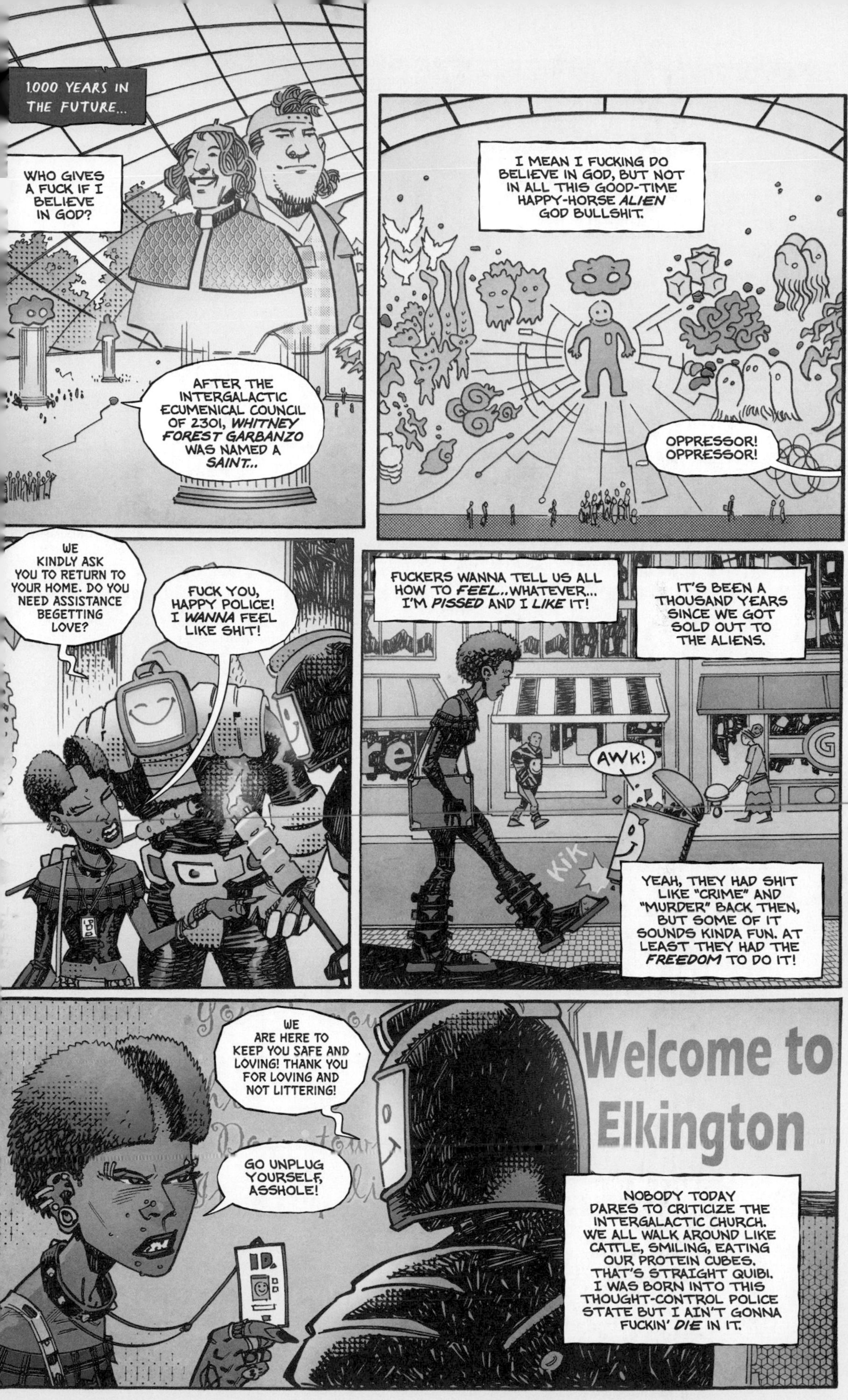
1,000 YEARS IN THE FUTURE...
WHO GIVES A FUCK IF I BELIEVE IN GOD?
AFTER THE INTERGALACTIC ECUMENICAL COUNCIL OF 2301, WHITNEY FOREST GARBANZO WAS NAMED A SAINT...
I MEAN I FUCKING DO BELIEVE IN GOD, BUT NOT IN ALL THIS GOOD-TIME HAPPY-HORSE ALIEN GOD BULLSHIT.
OPPRESSOR! OPPRESSOR!
WE KINDLY ASK YOU TO RETURN TO YOUR HOME. DO YOU NEED ASSISTANCE BEGETTING LOVE?
FUCK YOU, HAPPY POLICE! I WANNA FEEL LIKE SHIT!
FUCKERS WANNA TELL US ALL HOW TO FEEL...WHATEVER... I'M PISSED AND I LIKE IT!
IT'S BEEN A THOUSAND YEARS SINCE WE GOT SOLD OUT TO THE ALIENS.
AWK!
KIK
YEAH, THEY HAD SHIT LIKE "CRIME" AND "MURDER" BACK THEN, BUT SOME OF IT SOUNDS KINDA FUN. AT LEAST THEY HAD THE FREEDOM TO DO IT!
WE ARE HERE TO KEEP YOU SAFE AND LOVING! THANK YOU FOR LOVING AND NOT LITTERING!
Welcome to Elkington
GO UNPLUG YOURSELF, ASSHOLE!
ID.
NOBODY TODAY DARES TO CRITICIZE THE INTERGALACTIC CHURCH. WE ALL WALK AROUND LIKE CATTLE, SMILING, EATING OUR PROTEIN CUBES. THAT'S STRAIGHT QUIBI. I WAS BORN INTO THIS THOUGHT-CONTROL POLICE STATE BUT I AIN'T GONNA FUCKIN' DIE IN IT.

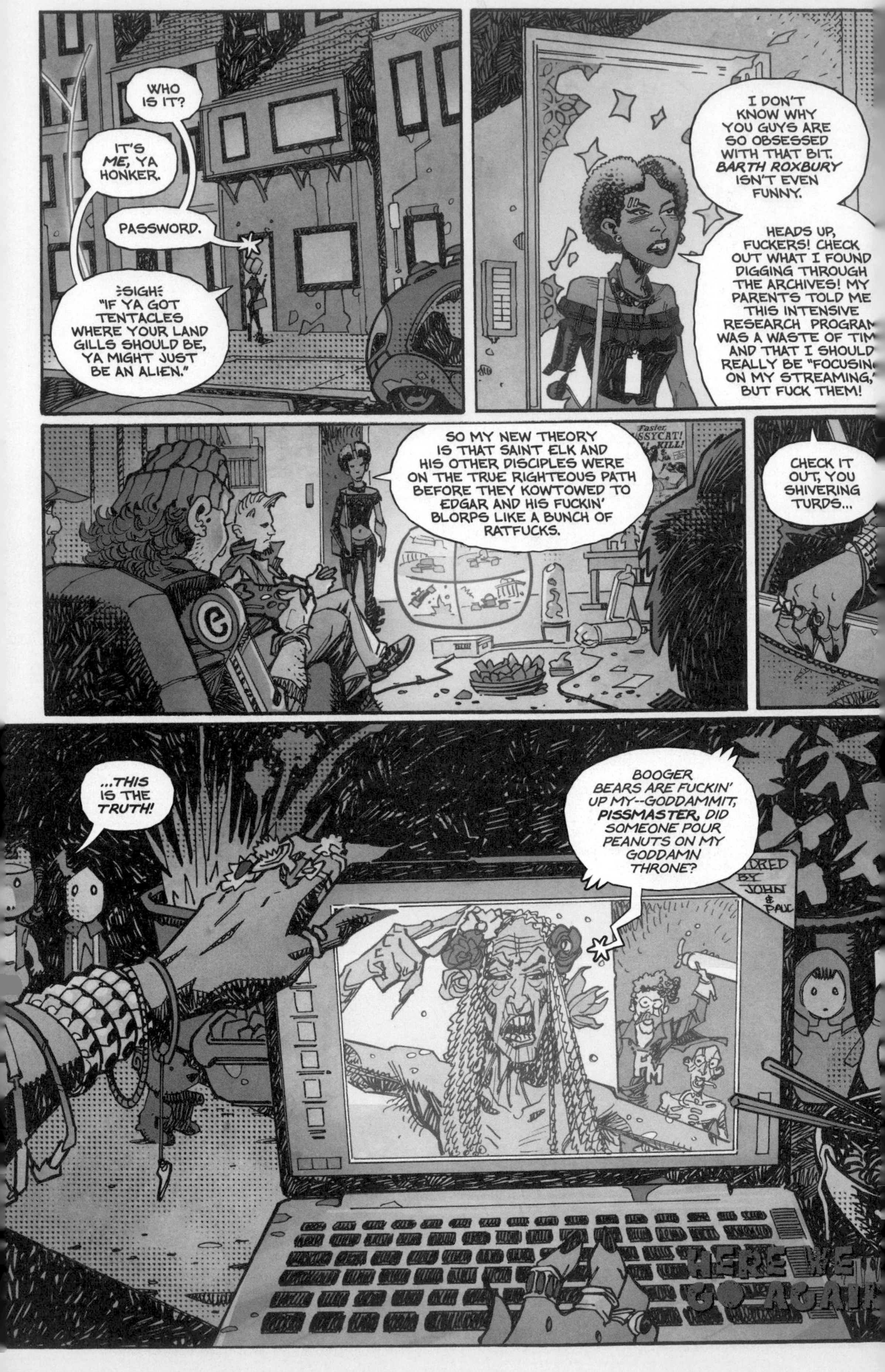
WHO IS IT?
IT'S ME, YA HONKER.
PASSWORD.
⁝SIGH⁝ "IF YA GOT TENTACLES WHERE YOUR LAND GILLS SHOULD BE, YA MIGHT JUST BE AN ALIEN."
I DON'T KNOW WHY YOU GUYS ARE SO OBSESSED WITH THAT BIT. BARTH ROXBURY ISN'T EVEN FUNNY.
HEADS UP, FUCKERS! CHECK OUT WHAT I FOUND DIGGING THROUGH THE ARCHIVES! MY PARENTS TOLD ME THIS INTENSIVE RESEARCH PROGRAM WAS A WASTE OF TIM AND THAT I SHOULD REALLY BE "FOCUSIN ON MY STREAMING," BUT FUCK THEM!
SO MY NEW THEORY IS THAT SAINT ELK AND HIS OTHER DISCIPLES WERE ON THE TRUE RIGHTEOUS PATH BEFORE THEY KOWTOWED TO EDGAR AND HIS FUCKIN' BLORPS LIKE A BUNCH OF RATFUCKS.
CHECK IT OUT, YOU SHIVERING TURDS...
...THIS IS THE TRUTH!
BOOGER BEARS ARE FUCKIN' UP MY--GODDAMMIT, PISSMASTER, DID SOMEONE POUR PEANUTS ON MY GODDAMN THRONE?

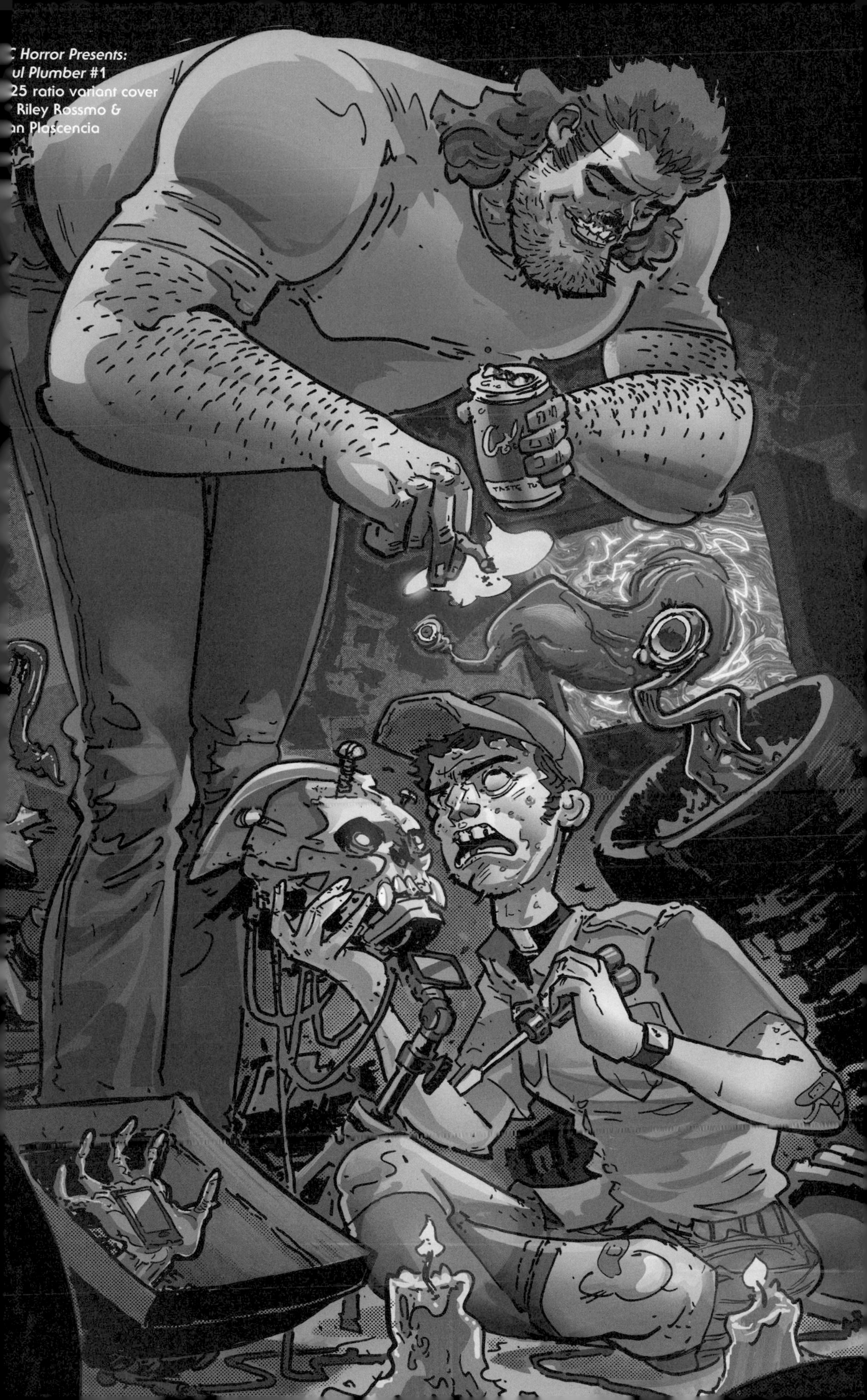

C Horror Presents:
ul Plumber #1
25 ratio variant cover
Riley Rossmo &
an Plascencia

SKETCHES BY JOHN McCREA

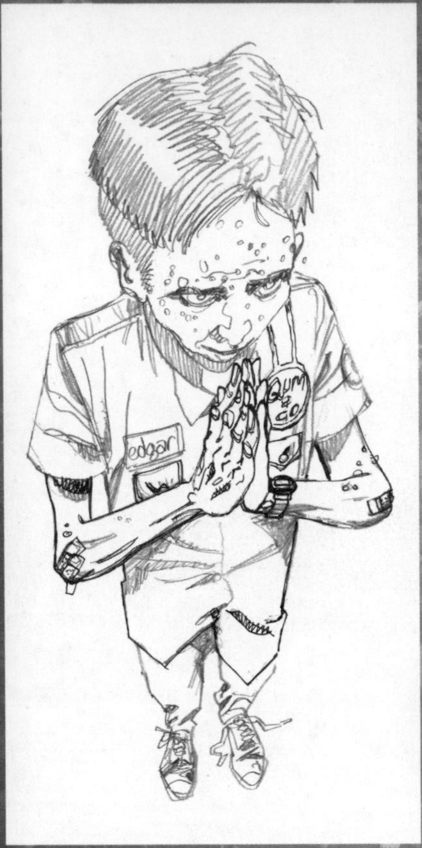
edgar

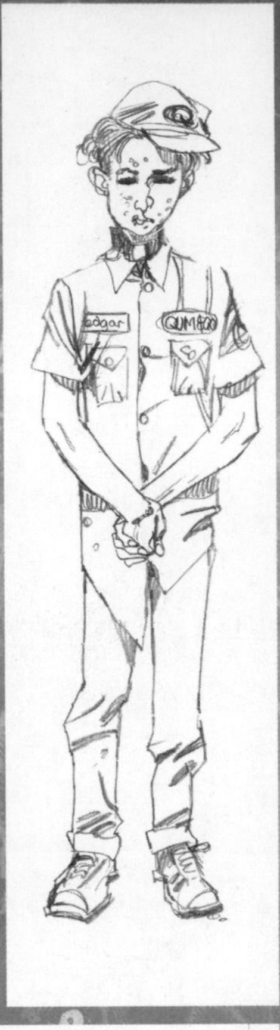
edgar

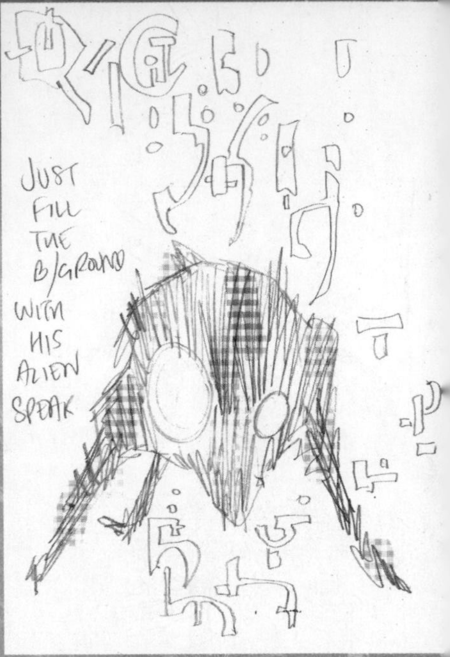
JUST FILL THE B/GROUND WITH HIS ALIEN SPEAK

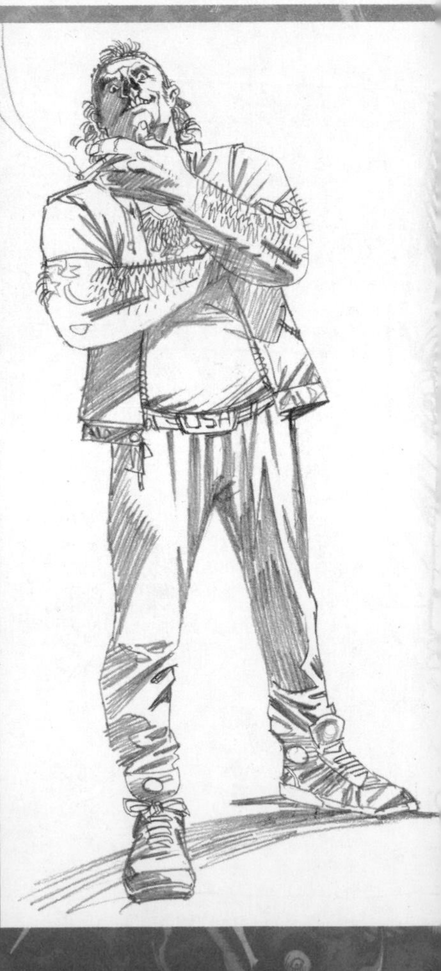
USA

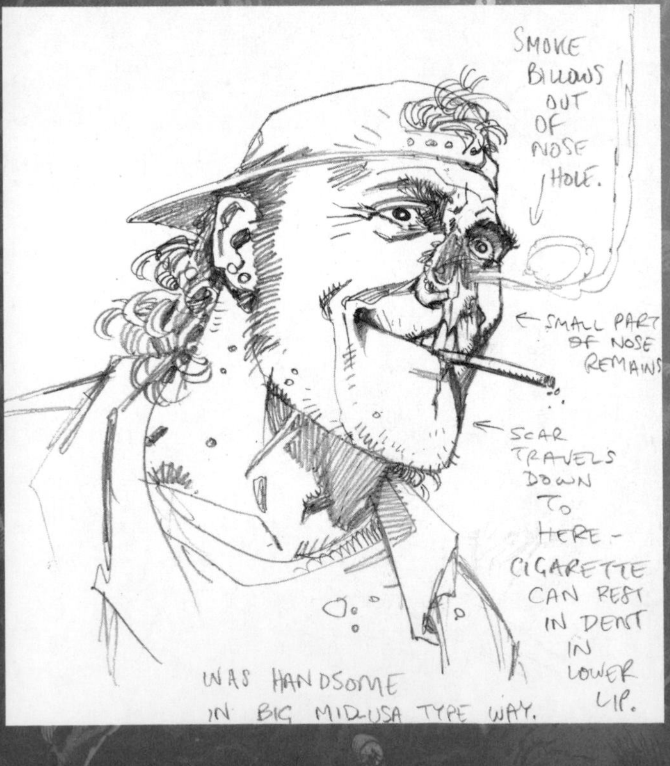
SMOKE BILLOWS OUT OF NOSE HOLE.
SMALL PART OF NOSE REMAINS
SCAR TRAVELS DOWN TO HERE - CIGARETTE CAN REST IN DENT IN LOWER LIP.
WAS HANDSOME IN BIG MID-USA TYPE WAY.

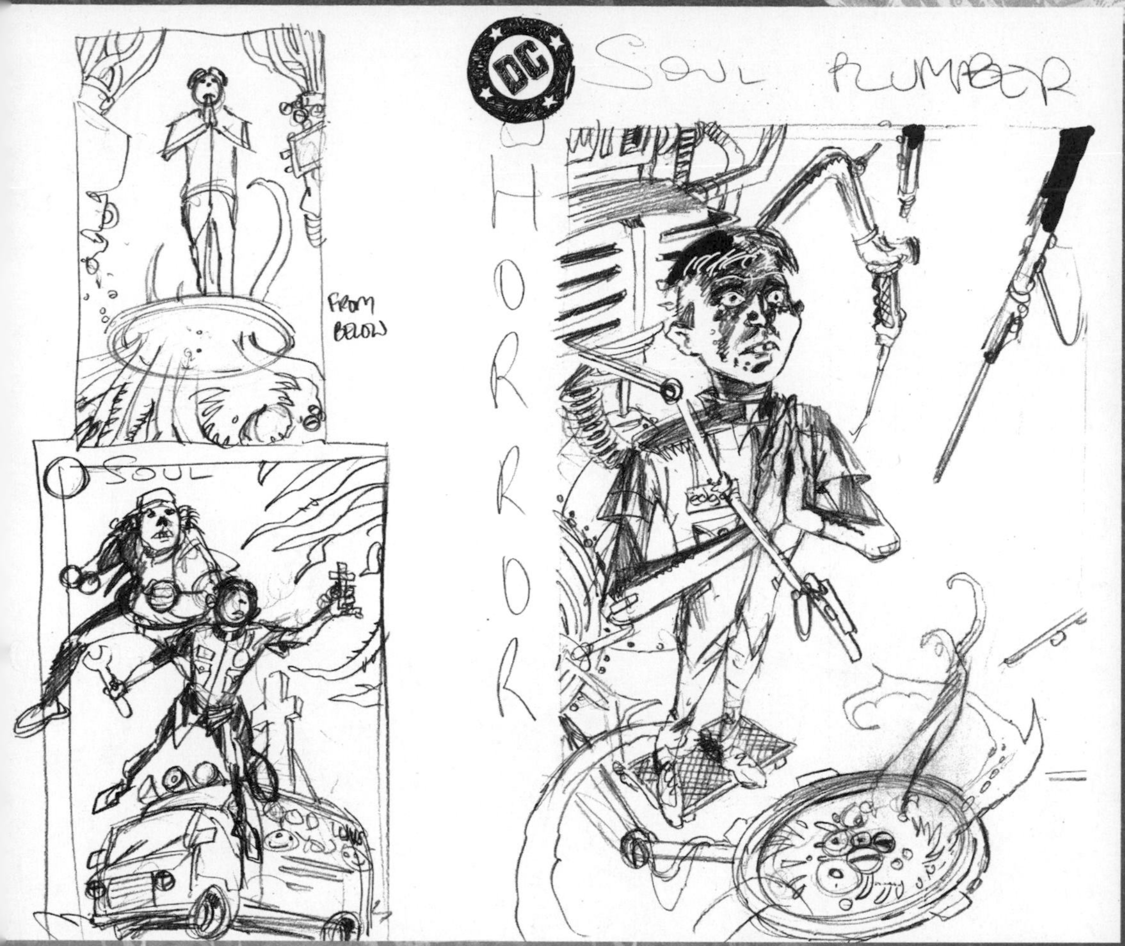
FROM BELOW
SOUL
SOUL PLUMBER
HORROR

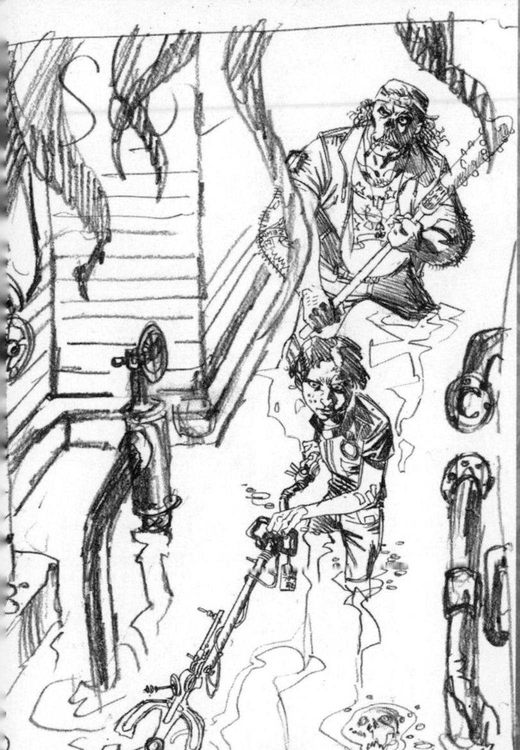

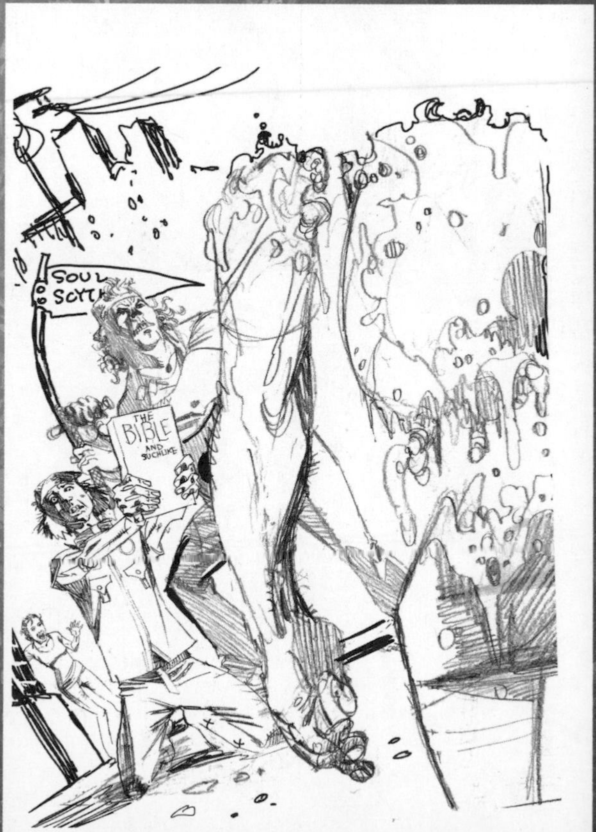
THE BIBLE AND SUCHLIKE

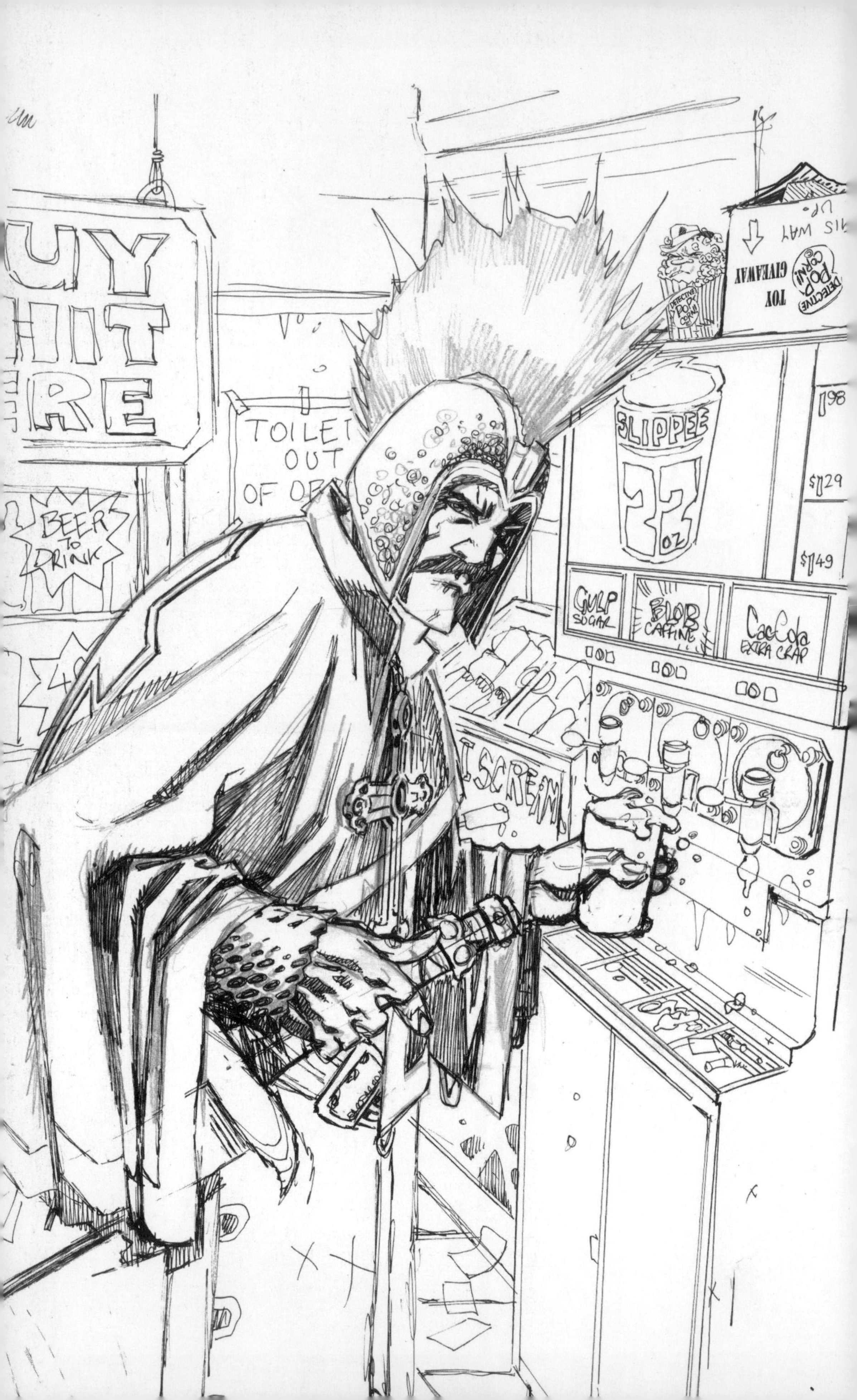
UY
HIT
RE
TOILET
OUT
OF OR
BEER TO DRINK
SLIPPEE
33 OZ
GULP SUGAR
BLOB CAFFINE
CacCola EXTRA CRAP
I SCREAM
DETECTIVE POP CORN!
TOY GIVEAWAY